MARQUEE SERIES

Using
COMPUTERS
in the
Medical
Office

MICROSOFT **Word**
Excel
PowerPoint 2007
with **Windows XP** and
Internet Explorer 7.0

Nita Rutkosky

Denise Seguin

Audrey Rutkosky Roggenkamp

Paradigm
PUBLISHING

Senior Developmental Editor: Christine Hurney
Developmental Editor: Brenda Palo
Production Editor: Amy McGuire
Testers: Susan Capecchi, Lindsay Ryan

Production Specialists: Jack Ross, Petrina Nyhan, Ryan Hamner
Cover Designer: Jaana Bykonich
Cover and Internal Images: Gettyimages, Corbis

Care has been taken to verify the accuracy of information presented in this book. However, the authors, editors, and publisher cannot accept responsibility for Web, e-mail, newsgroup, or chat room subject matter or content, or for consequences from application of the information in this book, and make no warranty, expressed or implied, with respect to its content.

Some of the product names and company names included in this book have been used for identification purposes only and may be trademarks or registered trade names of their respective manufacturers and sellers. The authors, editors, and publisher disclaim any affiliation, association, or connection with, or sponsorship or endorsement by, such owners.

We have made every effort to trace the ownership of all copyrighted material and to secure permission from copyright holders. In the event of any question arising as to the use of any material, we will be pleased to make the necessary corrections in future printings.
ISBN 978-0-76383-725-9 (Text 978-0-76383-724-2 plus Student CD)

© 2010 by Paradigm Publishing, Inc.
875 Montreal Way
St. Paul, MN 55102
E-mail: educate@emcp.com
Web site: www.emcp.com

Brief Contents

Contents

Preface

Using Computers in the Medical Office: Microsoft Word, Excel, and PowerPoint 2007 prepares students to work with Microsoft Office 2007 in medical office settings. Medical offices are fast-paced environments that require proficiency with a variety of duties specific to the healthcare environment. Many of these duties require skill in using the Microsoft Office suite of programs. Throughout *Using Computers in the Medical Office,* authentic medical documents provide the context for learning essential computer tasks performed in the medical office.

Throughout the book, students are asked to prepare documents, reports, and presentations for two medical clinics and a hospital. Cascade View Pediatrics is a full-service pediatric clinic that provides comprehensive primary pediatric care to infants, children, and adolescents. North Shore Medical Clinic is an internal medicine clinic, and the healthcare providers in this clinic specialize in a number of fields including internal medicine, family practice, cardiology, and dermatology. Columbia River General Hospital is an independent, not-for-profit hospital providing high-quality, comprehensive care. All of the computer skills are taught in the context of preparing materials to support the services provided by these three healthcare settings.

The text directs students to create a series of projects for Cascade View Pediatrics, North Shore Medical Clinic, and Columbia River General Hospital. In Word, students are asked to:

- produce an x-ray report
- create and maintain medical records and chart notes
- edit and format informative documents for patients about appointment scheduling, disease prevention, and education opportunities
- prepare envelopes, mailing labels, and documents for mailings to patient lists
- create patient questionnaires and forms for gathering patient information

In Excel, some of the projects students are asked to complete include preparing:

- a report calculating the average standard cost for cardiac surgery patient stays
- purchase orders and statistic calculations for costs of exam room supplies
- invoices for medical services
- inventory reports
- a lab requisitions billing report
- a radiology requisition form
- a bypass surgery report
- a dermatology patient tracking worksheet
- cardiac nurse call lists
- revenue summary reports

Students are also asked to create PowerPoint presentations to inform patients about clinic and hospital services, cholesterol, fibromyalgia, sickle cell anemia, and chicken pox. Through these engaging projects, students learn Microsoft Office skills in the context of caring for patients through working as a valuable part of the healthcare team.

Using Computers in the Medical Office is divided into five units. In Unit 1, students are introduced to Windows XP and the basics of using this operating system to display and manage information. In Unit 2, students are introduced to the Internet through Internet Explorer 7.0. Skills taught in this section include using URLs and hyperlinks, searching, and downloading resources. In Unit 3, Word is used as a full-featured word processing program. Basic skills as well as more advanced functions such as using layout and design features and creating and editing forms are taught in the context of the medical office. Unit 4 focuses on using Excel to present and analyze types of data used in the medical office. In Unit 5, students are shown how to create colorful and effective presentations using PowerPoint.

Within each section, activities present computer program features in a highly visual, project-based manner. Each activity introduces a topic, presents a short paragraph or two about the topic, and then guides the student through a hands-on computer project. The book offers several additional elements to enhance student learning, including:

- In Addition—Sidebars offer extra information on key features and subfeatures.
- In Brief—Bare-bones summaries of major commands and features provide instant review and a quick reference of the steps required to accomplish a task.
- Features Summary—Commands taught in the section are listed with button, ribbon tab, Quick Access toolbar, and keyboard actions.
- Knowledge Check—Objective completion exercises allow students to assess their comprehension and recall of program features, terminology, and functions.
- Skills Review—Additional hands-on computer exercises to reinforce learning. These review activities include some guidance, but less than the section activities.
- Skills Assessment—Framed in a workplace project perspective, these less-guided assessments evaluate students' abilities to apply section skills and concepts in solving realistic problems. They require demonstrating program skills as well as decision-making skills and include Help and Internet-based activities.
- Marquee Challenge—Culminating assessments test students' problem-solving abilities and mastery of program features.

An Integrating Programs section follows both Unit 4 and Unit 5. These sections include projects demonstrating how to share data between programs within the Microsoft Office suite. Projects include copying, exporting, linking, and embedding data. These sections emphasize the ability to integrate data from one program seamlessly into another program and thus allow the students to learn how to best use these tools to manage data efficiently in the medical office.

System Requirements

This interactive text is designed for the student to complete section work on a computer running a standard installation of Microsoft Office 2007, Professional Edition, and the Microsoft Windows XP operating system with Service Pack 2 or later. To effectively run this suite and operating system, your computer should be outfitted with the following:

- 500 megahertz (MHz) processor or higher; 256 megabytes (MB) of RAM
- DVD or CD-ROM drive
- 2 gigabytes (GB) of available hard-disk space
- 1024 by 768 monitor resolution *Note: Screen captures in this book were created using 1024 by 768 resolution; screens with higher resolution may look different.*
- Computer mouse or compatible pointing device

Resources for the Student

The Student Resources CD that accompanies this textbook contains pretyped documents and files required for completing section activities and end-of-section exercises. A CD icon and folder name displayed on the opening page of a section indicates that the student needs to copy a folder of files from the CD to a storage medium before beginning the section activities. (See the inside back cover for instructions on copying a folder.) The Student Resources CD also contains model answers in PDF format for guided section activities so students can check their work. Model answers are not provided for the Knowledge Check, Skills Review, Skills Assessment, or Marquee Challenge.

The Internet Resource Center for this book at www.emcp.net/medicaloffice07 provides additional material for students preparing to work in the medical office. Here students will find the same PDF files of intra-section model answers as are on the Student Resources CD along with study tools, Web links, and other resources specifically useful in the medical office.

Resources for the Instructor

Instructor resources are available at the password-protected section of the Internet Resource Center for this title at www.emcp.net/medicaloffice07. Besides providing access to the materials on the Student Resources CD, the Instructor Resources section offers PDF and live files for all section activities and end-of-section exercises.

Other Medical Office Resources

In addition to *Using Computers in the Medical Office: Microsoft Word, Excel, and PowerPoint 2007*, Paradigm Publishing also offers several resources to support job-training for the medical office. Titles include:
- *Applied Anatomy and Physiology: A Case Study Approach*
- *Medical Assisting: A Commitment to Service—Administrative and Clinical Competencies*
- *Medical Terminology, Second Edition*
- *Medical Transcription, Third Edition*
- *Keyboarding in the Medical Office: Sessions 1–60*
- *What Language Does Your Patient Hurt In? A Practical Guide to Culturally Competent Patient Care, Second Edition*
- *The Language of Medicine CD*
- *Essential Healthcare Terminology for English Language Learners*
- *Emergency Preparedness for Health Professionals*
- *Health-Care CareerVision Book and DVD: View What You'd Do*

For a complete listing of these and other titles, visit www.emcp.com.

About the Authors

Nita Rutkosky began teaching business education courses at Pierce College in Puyallup, Washington, in 1978. Since then she has taught a variety of software applications to students in postsecondary Information Technology certificate and degree programs. In addition to *Using Computers in the Medical Office: Microsoft Word, Excel, and PowerPoint 2007* and *2003*, she has authored textbooks for Paradigm Publishing on keyboarding; WordPerfect; desktop publishing; voice recogniton; and the many releases of Microsoft Office, including Marquee, Benchmark, and Signature series titles on Word, PowerPoint, Excel, Access, and the combined Office suite.

Denise Seguin has been teaching at Fanshawe College in London, Ontario, since 1986. She has taught a variety of software applications to learners in postsecondary Information Technology diploma programs and in Continuing Education courses. In addition to *Using Computers in the Medical Office: Microsoft Word, Excel, and PowerPoint 2007* and *2003*, she has authored *Macromedia Flash MX: Design and Application; Microsoft Outlook 2007* (and prior versions); and has co-authored the Benchmark and Marquee series on Microsoft Office and its individual programs for Paradigm Publishing, Inc.

Audrey Rutkosky Roggenkamp has been teaching courses in the Business Information Technology department at Pierce College in Puyallup including keyboarding, skill building, and Microsoft Office programs. In addition to co-authoring *Using Computers in the Medical Office: Microsoft Word, Excel, and PowerPoint 2007* and *2003*, she has co-authored the Benchmark and Marquee series on Office 2007.

Acknowledgements

The authors would like to thank the editorial team at Paradigm Publishing, Inc. as well as the following list of reviewers and contributors for their expert advice and opinion on how to make this an effective and realistic learning tool.

Jerri Adler, CMA, CMT
Eugene, Oregon

Tracie Fuqua, BS, CMA
Wallace State Community College
Hanceville, Alabama

Debbie Gamracy, BEd
Fanshawe College
London, Ontario
Canada

Connie Lieseke
Olympic College
Bremerton, Washington

Linda Maatta
Davis College
Toledo, Ohio

Tanya Mercer, BS, RN, MA
Fayetteville, Georgia

Donna Reynolds
Cascade Eye & Skin Centers
Puyallup, Washington

Using
Windows
XP

Windows XP
Exploring the Operating System

Skills

- Display the Windows XP desktop
- Perform the following actions using the mouse: point, click, double-click, and drag
- Start and close a program
- Open and close a window
- Shut down Windows XP
- Move a window
- Minimize, maximize, and restore a window
- Cascade and tile windows
- Display the Date and Time Properties dialog box
- Use components of a dialog box
- Display the Volume slider
- Display the Taskbar and Start Menu Properties dialog box

Projects Overview

North Shore Medical Clinic has received new computers with the Windows XP operating system. You will explore the Windows XP desktop; open, close, and manipulate windows; open a program using the Start button; use options in the notification area of the Taskbar; and customize the Taskbar.

Activity
1.1

Exploring the Windows XP Desktop

The main portion of the screen that displays when Windows XP is loaded is called the *desktop*. This desktop can be compared to the top of a desk in an office. A business person places necessary tools—such as pencils, pens, paper, files, calculator—on his or her desktop to perform functions. Like those tools, the tools on the Windows XP desktop help a person to operate the computer. These tools are logically grouped and placed in dialog boxes or windows that can be accessed using the icons located on the Windows XP desktop.

Project

You work for North Shore Medical Clinic, and the clinic has just received new computers with the Windows XP operating system. You want to explore the Windows XP desktop to familiarize yourself with this new operating system.

1 Complete the steps needed to display the Windows XP desktop.

Check with your instructor to determine the specific steps required to display Windows XP on your computer. This may be as simple as turning on the computer or may involve additional steps for logging on to the computer system. When Windows XP is loaded, you will see a desktop similar to the one shown in Figure WIN1.1. Your desktop may contain additional icons or have a different background than the desktop shown in Figure WIN1.1.

2 Move the mouse on the desk and notice how the corresponding pointer moves on the Windows desktop.

The *mouse* is a device that controls the pointer that identifies your location on the screen. Move the mouse on the desk (preferably on a mouse pad) and the pointer moves on the screen. For information on mouse terms, refer to Table WIN1.1 and for information on mouse icons, refer to Table WIN1.2.

FIGURE WIN1.1 Windows XP Desktop

TABLE WIN1.1 Mouse Terms

Term	Action
point	Position the mouse pointer on the desired item.
click	Quickly tap a button on the mouse once.
double-click	Tap the left mouse button twice in quick succession.
drag	Press and hold down the left mouse button, move the mouse pointer to a specific location, and then release the mouse button.

TABLE WIN1.2 Mouse Icons

Icon	Description
I	The mouse appears as an I-beam pointer in a program screen where you enter text (such as in Microsoft Word) and also in text boxes. You can use the I-beam pointer to move the insertion point or select text.
↖	The mouse pointer appears as an arrow pointing up and to the left (called the *arrow pointer*) on the Windows desktop and also in other program Title bars, Menu bars, and toolbars. Less frequently, the arrow points up and to the right when positioned in certain locations in a file, such as the left margin in a Word document.
↘↗ ↔↕	The mouse pointer becomes a double-headed arrow (either pointing left and right, up and down, or diagonally) when performing certain functions, such as changing the size of a window.
✛↖	Select an object such as a picture or image in a program, and the mouse pointer becomes a four-headed arrow with the mouse pointer attached. Use this four-headed arrow pointer to move the object left, right, up, or down.
⧖	When a request is being processed or a program is being loaded, the mouse pointer may display with an hourglass beside it. The hourglass means "please wait." When the process is completed, the hourglass image is removed.
👆	When you position the mouse pointer on certain icons or hyperlinks, it turns into a hand with a pointing index finger. This image indicates that clicking the icon or hyperlink will display additional information.

③ Move the mouse pointer to the current time that displays at the far right side of the Taskbar and after approximately one second, the current day and date will display in a yellow pop-up box.

To identify the location of the Taskbar, refer to Figure WIN1.1.

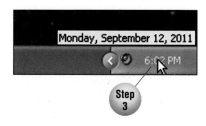

continues

4 Position the mouse pointer on the Start button ![start] on the Taskbar and then click the left mouse button.

> Clicking the Start button causes the Start menu to display. The Start menu contains a list of software programs, documents, and other options available on your computer. The menu is divided into two columns. Links to the most recently used programs display in the left column and links to folders, the Control Panel, online help, and the search feature display in the right column. The bottom of the Start menu contains options for logging off or turning off the computer.

5 At the Start menu, point to *All Programs* and then point to *Microsoft Office*.

> To point to a menu option, simply position the mouse pointer on the option. Do not click a mouse button. Pointing to *All Programs* causes a side menu to display with a list of programs. A right-pointing triangle displays at the right of some options on the Start menu. This triangle indicates that a side menu will display when you point to the option.

6 Move the mouse pointer to *Microsoft Office Word 2007* in the side menu and then click the left mouse button.

> Clicking *Microsoft Office Word 2007* causes the Word program to open and display on the screen.

7 Close Microsoft Word by clicking the Close button ![X] that displays in the upper right corner of the program.

Step 7

8 On the Windows XP desktop, position the mouse pointer on the *Recycle Bin* icon and then double-click the left mouse button.

> Icons provide an easy method for opening programs or documents. Double-clicking the *Recycle Bin* icon displays the Recycle Bin window. When you open a program, a defined work area, referred to as a *window*, appears on the screen.

Step 8

9 Close the Recycle Bin window by clicking the Close button (contains a white X on a red background) that displays in the upper right corner of the window.

10 Shut down Windows XP by clicking the Start button and then, depending on your computer system, click either *Turn off computer* or *Shut Down* at the Start menu. If you are using a standalone computer (not part of a domain, which is a group of computers that are part of a network and share a common directory), you will have the *Turn off computer* option. If your computer is part of a domain, the *Shut Down* option displays.

> Before shutting down a computer in a school setting, check with your instructor.

11 If you are using a standalone computer, a Turn off computer window (shown below at the left) will display. If you are using a networked computer, a Shut Down Windows dialog box (shown below at the right) will display. To shut down a standalone computer, click the Turn Off option. To shut down a computer that is part of a domain, click the down-pointing arrow at the right side of the *What do you want the computer to do?* option box and then click *Shut down* at the drop-down list.

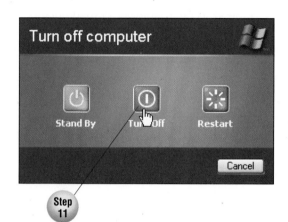

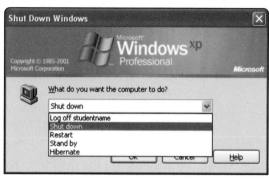

Step 11

In Brief

Start Program
1. Click Start button.
2. Point to *All Programs*.
3. Click desired program.

Shut Down Windows

For Standalone Computer
1. Click Start button.
2. Click *Turn Off Computer*.
3. At Turn off computer window, click Turn Off.

For Networked Computer
1. Click Start button.
2. Click *Shut Down*.
3. At Shut Down Windows dialog box, click down-pointing arrow.
4. Click *Shut Down*.

In Addition

Putting the Computer on Stand By or Hibernate

When you shut down Windows, you can choose to shut down the computer completely, shut down and then restart, put the computer on stand by, or tell the computer to hibernate. Click the Stand By option at the Turn off computer window or the *Stand by* option at the Shut Down Windows dialog box and the computer switches to a low power state, causing some devices such as the monitor and hard disks to turn off. With these devices off, the computer uses less power. Stand by is particularly useful for saving battery power for portable computers. Tell the computer to "hibernate" by clicking the *Hibernate* option at the Shut Down Windows dialog box or by holding down the Shift key while clicking the Stand By option at the Turn off computer window. In hibernate mode, the computer saves everything in memory on disk, turns off the monitor and hard disk, and then turns off the computer. When you restart the computer, the desktop is restored exactly as you left it. You can generally restore your desktop from either stand by or hibernate by pressing once on the computer's power button. Bringing a computer out of hibernation takes a little longer than bringing a computer out of stand by.

Activity 1.2

Opening and Manipulating Windows

When you open a program, a defined work area, referred to as a *window*, appears on the screen. You can move a window on the desktop and change the size of a window. The top of a window is called the Title bar and generally contains but- tons at the right side for closing the window and minimizing, maximizing, or restoring the size of the window. More than one window can be open at a time and open windows can be cascaded or tiled.

Project

You will continue your exploration of the Windows XP desktop by opening and manipulating windows.

1. On the Windows XP desktop, double-click the *Recycle Bin* icon.

   This opens the Recycle Bin window on the desktop. If the Recycle Bin window fills the entire desktop, click the Restore Down button, which is the second button from the right (immediately left of the Close button) located in the upper right corner of the window.

   Step 1

2. Move the window on the desktop. To do this, position the mouse pointer on the window Title bar (the bar along the top of the window), hold down the left mouse button, drag the window to a different location on the desktop, and then release the mouse button.

3. Click the Start button on the Taskbar and then click *My Computer* at the Start menu.

   The *My Computer* option is located in the right column of the Start menu. If the My Computer window fills the entire desktop, click the Restore Down button (immediately left of the Close button). You now have two windows open on the desktop—My Computer and Recycle Bin.

   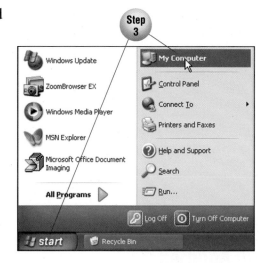

   Step 3

4. Make sure the Title bar of the Recycle Bin window is visible (if not, move the My Computer window) and then click the Recycle Bin Title bar.

   Clicking the Recycle Bin Title bar makes the Recycle Bin window active, moving it in front of the My Computer window.

5. Minimize the Recycle Bin window to a task button on the Taskbar by clicking the Minimize button (contains an underscore symbol) located toward the right side of the Recycle Bin Title bar.

   Step 5

6. Minimize the My Computer window to a task button on the Taskbar by clicking the Minimize button located at the right side of the Title bar.

7 Redisplay the Recycle Bin window by clicking the Recycle Bin task button on the Taskbar.

Step 7

In Brief

Move Window
1. Position mouse pointer on window Title bar.
2. Hold down left mouse button.
3. Drag window to desired position.
4. Release mouse button.

Tile Windows Horizontally
1. Right-click an empty section of Taskbar.
2. Click *Tile Windows Horizontally* at shortcut menu.

Cascade Windows
1. Right-click an empty section of Taskbar.
2. Click *Cascade Windows* at shortcut menu.

8 Redisplay the My Computer window by clicking the My Computer task button on the Taskbar.

9 Click the Maximize button located at the right side of the My Computer window.

Clicking the Maximize button causes the window to expand to fill the entire desktop.

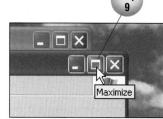

Step 9

Maximize

10 Click the Restore Down button located at the right side of the My Computer window.

Clicking the Restore Down button restores the window to the size it was before it was maximized.

Step 10

Restore Down

11 Right-click on an empty section of the Taskbar and then click *Tile Windows Horizontally*.

Tiled windows fill the desktop with the Title bar and a portion of each window visible.

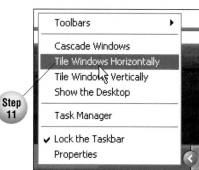

Step 11

Toolbars
Cascade Windows
Tile Windows Horizontally
Tile Windows Vertically
Show the Desktop
Task Manager
✓ Lock the Taskbar
Properties

12 Right-click on an empty section of the Taskbar and then click *Cascade Windows* at the shortcut menu.

Cascaded windows display in the upper left corner of the desktop with the Title bar of each open window visible.

13 Close the My Computer window by clicking the Close button (contains a white X on a red background) located at the right side of the Title bar.

14 Close the Recycle Bin window by clicking the Close button.

In Addition

Sizing a Window

Using the mouse, you can increase or decrease the size of a window. To increase the size horizontally, position the mouse pointer on the border at the right or left side of the window until it turns into a left- and right-pointing arrow. Hold down the left mouse button, drag the border to the right or left, and then release the mouse button. Complete similar steps to increase or decrease the size of the window vertically, using the bottom border of the window. To change the size of the window both horizontally and vertically at the same time, position the mouse pointer at the left or right corner of the window until the pointer turns into a diagonally pointing double-headed arrow and then drag to change the size.

Activity 1.3

Exploring the Taskbar

The bar that displays at the bottom of the desktop is called the *Taskbar* and it is divided into three sections: the Start button, the task buttons area, and the notification area. Click the Start button to start a program, use the Help and Support feature, change settings, open files, or shut down the computer. Open programs display as task buttons in the task buttons area of the Taskbar. You can right-click an empty portion of the Taskbar to display a shortcut menu with options for customizing the Taskbar. The notification area displays at the right side of the Taskbar and contains a digital clock and specialized programs that run in the background.

Project

As you continue exploring Windows XP, you want to learn more about the features available on the Taskbar.

(1) On the Windows XP desktop, double-click the current time that displays at the far right side of the Taskbar.

> Figure WIN1.2 identifies the components of the Taskbar. Double-clicking the time causes the Date and Time Properties dialog box to display. Please refer to Table WIN1.3 for information on dialog box components.

(2) Check to make sure the correct date and time display in the Date and Time Properties dialog box.

> If the date is incorrect, click the down-pointing arrow at the right side of the month list box in the *Date* section and then click the correct month at the drop-down list. Click the up- or down-pointing arrows in the year text box to increase or decrease the year. Click the correct day in the updated calendar. To change the time, double-click either the hour, minute, or seconds and use the up- and down-pointing arrows to adjust the time.

(3) Click the Time Zone tab located toward the top of the Date and Time Properties dialog box.

> Check to make sure the correct time zone displays. If it is not correct, click the down-pointing arrow at the right side of the list box and then click the desired time zone at the drop-down list. If the computer you are using is part of a domain (a group of computers that are part of a network and share a common directory), the Date and Time Properties dialog box will not contain the Internet Time tab.

(4) Click OK to close the Date and Time Properties dialog box.

FIGURE WIN1.2 Taskbar

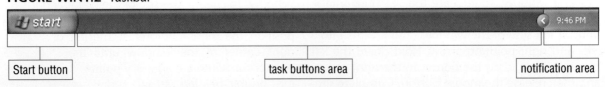

TABLE WIN1.3 Dialog Box Components

Name	Image	Function
tabs	Date & Time / Time Zone / Internet Time	Click a dialog box tab and the dialog box options change.
text box	A word or phrase in the file: / Indentation / Left: 0"	Type or edit text in a text box. A text box may contain up- and down-pointing arrows to allow you to choose a number or an option instead of typing it in.
drop-down list box	Theme: / Windows XP / My Current Theme / Windows XP / Windows Classic / More themes online... / Browse...	Click the down-pointing arrow at the right side of a drop-down list box and a list of choices displays.
list box	Font style: / Regular / Regular / Italic / Bold / Bold Italic	A list box displays a list of options.
check boxes	Effects / ☑ Strikethrough / ☐ Double strikethrough / ☑ Superscript / ☐ Subscript	If a check box contains a check mark, the option is active; if the check box is empty, the option is inactive. Any number of check boxes can be active.
option buttons	Zoom to / ○ 200% / ◉ 100% / ○ 75%	Only one option button in a dialog box section can be selected at any time. An active option button contains a dark or colored circle.
command buttons	OK / Cancel / Apply	Click a command button to execute or cancel a command. If a command button name is followed by an ellipsis (. . .), clicking the button will open another dialog box.
slider	Screen resolution / Less — More / 800 by 600 pixels	Using the mouse, drag a slider to increase or decrease the number, speed, or percentage of the option.
scroll bar	Size: / 12 / 8 / 9 / 10 / 11 / 12	A scroll bar displays when the amount of information in a window is larger than can fit comfortably in a single window.

continues

5 Position the mouse pointer on the Volume button located toward the right side of the Taskbar and then click the left mouse button.

Clicking the Volume button causes a slider bar to display. Use this slider to increase or decrease the volume. Insert a check mark in the *Mute* check box if you want to turn off the sound. If the Volume button is not visible, click the left-pointing arrow located at the left side of the notification area. This expands the area to show all buttons. If you do not see a left-pointing arrow, or, if the volume button is still not visible, click the Start button, point to *All Programs*, point to *Accessories*, point to *Entertainment*, and then click *Volume Control*. A Volume Control dialog box opens, wherein you can increase or decrease the volume.

Step 5

6 After viewing the Volume slider, click on any empty location on the desktop to remove the slider. If you had to open the Volume Control dialog box, click the Close button.

7 Right-click on any empty location on the Taskbar and then click *Properties* at the shortcut menu that displays.

This displays the Taskbar and Start Menu Properties dialog box with the Taskbar tab selected. Notice that the dialog box contains check boxes. A check mark in a check box indicates that the option is active. By default, the *Group similar taskbar buttons* option is active. With this option active, if the Taskbar becomes crowded with task buttons, task buttons for the same program are collapsed into a single button. Click a button representing collapsed files for the same program and a list of the files displays above the button.

8 Click the *Auto-hide the taskbar* option to insert a check mark in the check box.

9 Click the Apply command button located toward the bottom of the dialog box.

(10) Click the OK button to close the Taskbar and Start Menu Properties dialog box.

Notice that the Taskbar is no longer visible.

In Brief

Display Date and Time Properties Dialog Box
Double-click current time at right side of Taskbar.

Display Volume Slider
Click Volume button on Taskbar.

Display Taskbar and Start Menu Properties Dialog Box
1. Right-click an empty location on Taskbar.
2. Click *Properties* at shortcut menu.

(11) Display the Taskbar by moving the mouse pointer to the bottom of the desktop.

(12) Right-click on any empty location on the Taskbar and then click *Properties* at the shortcut menu.

(13) Click the *Auto-hide the taskbar* option to remove the check mark.

(14) Click the Apply command button.

(15) Click the OK button to close the Taskbar and Start Menu Properties dialog box.

In Addition

Using Natural Keyboard Shortcuts

If you are using a Microsoft Natural Keyboard or a compatible keyboard, you can use the Windows logo key and the Application key to access the following features.

Press	To do this
	display the Start menu
+ M	minimize all windows
+ E	open My Computer
+ F	search for a file or folder
+ F1	display Help and Support Center window
+ R	open the Run dialog box
	display the shortcut menu for selected item

Features Summary

Feature	Button	Action
close window	✕	Click Close button on Title bar.
Date and Time Properties dialog box		Double-click time on Taskbar.
maximize window	☐	Click Maximize button on Title bar.
minimize window	_	Click Minimize button on Title bar.
move window on desktop		Drag window Title bar.
My Computer window		Click Start button, click *My Computer*.
restore window	⧉	Click Restore Down button on Title bar.
shut down computer		Click Start button, click *Turn Off Computer*, click Turn Off at Turn off computer window.
Start menu	*start*	Click Start button on Taskbar.
Taskbar and Start Menu Properties dialog box		Right-click empty location on Taskbar, click *Properties* at shortcut menu.
Taskbar shortcut menu		Right-click empty location on Taskbar.
volume slider	🔊	Click Volume button on Taskbar.

Knowledge Check

Completion: In the space provided at the right, write in the correct term, command, or option.

1. This mouse term refers to positioning the mouse pointer on the desired item.
2. This mouse term refers to tapping the left mouse button twice in quick succession.
3. This symbol is attached to the mouse pointer when a request is being processed and means "please wait."
4. Click this button on a window Title bar to reduce the window to a task button on the Taskbar.
5. Click this button on a window Title bar to expand the window so it fills the entire screen.
6. Double-click the time located at the right side of the Taskbar and this dialog box displays.
7. This component of a dialog box generally displays when the amount of information is larger than can fit comfortably in the dialog box.
8. Drag this component in a dialog box to increase or decrease the number, speed, or percentage of an option.

Skills Review

Review 1 Opening and Manipulating Windows

1. On the Windows XP desktop, click the Start button on the Taskbar and then click *My Documents*. (If the My Documents window fills the desktop, click the Restore Down button located in the upper right corner of the window.)
2. Click the Start button on the Taskbar and then click *My Computer*. (If the My Computer window fills the desktop, click the Restore Down button.)
3. Position the mouse pointer on the My Computer Title bar, hold down the left mouse button, and then drag the My Computer window so the My Documents Title bar is visible.
4. Click the My Documents Title bar to make it the active window.
5. Right-click on an empty location on the Taskbar and then click *Cascade Windows* at the shortcut menu.
6. Click the Minimize button (located toward the right side of the Title bar) on the My Documents window Title bar to reduce the window to a task button on the Taskbar.
7. Click the Minimize button on the My Computer window to reduce the window to a task button on the Taskbar.
8. Click the My Computer task button to restore the My Computer window on the desktop.
9. Click the My Documents task button to restore the My Documents window on the desktop.
10. Click the Maximize button on the My Documents Title bar to expand the window to fill the screen.
11. Click the Restore Down button on the My Documents Title bar to reduce the size of the My Documents window.
12. Close the My Documents window.
13. Close the My Computer window.

Review 2 Exploring the Taskbar

1. On the Windows XP desktop, double-click the time that displays in the notification area at the right side of the Taskbar.
2. At the Date and Time Properties dialog box, click the down-pointing arrow at the right side of the month list box and then click the next month (from the current month) at the drop-down list.
3. Click the OK button.
4. Display the Date and Time Properties dialog box again, change the month back to the current month, and then click OK to close the dialog box.
5. Click the Start button, point to *All Programs*, point to *Microsoft Office*, and then click *Microsoft Office Excel 2007*.
6. Close Excel by clicking the Close button located at the right side of the Microsoft Office Excel Title bar.

Skills Assessment

Assessment 1 Manipulating Windows

1. Click the Start button and then click *My Pictures*. (If the My Pictures window fills the entire desktop, click the Restore Down button.)
2. Click the Start button and then click *My Music*. (If the My Music window fills the entire desktop, click the Restore Down button.)
3. Cascade the two windows.
4. Make the My Pictures window the active window and then reduce it to a task button on the Taskbar.
5. Reduce the My Music window to a task button on the Taskbar.
6. Restore the My Pictures window.
7. Restore the My Music window.
8. Close the My Music window and then close the My Pictures window.

Assessment 2 Exploring the Taskbar

1. On the Windows XP desktop, display the Date and Time Properties dialog box.
2. Change the current hour one hour ahead and then close the dialog box.
3. Open the Date and Time Properties dialog box, change the hour back to the current hour, and then close the dialog box.
4. Display the Volume slider bar, drag the slider to increase the volume, and then click the desktop outside the slider to close it.
5. Display the Volume slider bar and then drag the slider to the original position.
6. Display the Taskbar and Start Menu Properties dialog box, remove the check mark from the *Show the clock* option, and then close the dialog box. (Notice that the time no longer displays on the Taskbar.)
7. Display the Taskbar and Start Menu Properties dialog box, insert a check mark in the *Show the clock* option, and then close the dialog box.

UNIT
2

Using
Internet
Explorer
7.0

Internet Explorer

Accessing Internet Resources

- Visit specific sites by using the site URL
- Click hyperlinks to navigate to specific sites and/or Web pages
- Search for sites containing specific information
- Narrow a search using advanced search options
- Use the Research pane to look up specific information and translate text
- Download a Web page to a separate file
- Download an image to a separate file

Projects Overview

Visit Web sites for the Department of Health and Human Services and the Centers for Disease Control and Prevention. Search for Web sites that sell office forms, equipment, and supplies. Use advanced search options to locate information on the symptoms and treatments of Hodgkin's disease. Search for information on Portland State University and translate some English words into French. Locate a Web site for Crater Lake National Park, save the Web page as a file, and save an image as a file.

Visit the Web site for Oregon State University. Search for Web sites about mountain climbing and specifically in British Columbia. Translate a word from English to Spanish. Locate a Web site on parasailing, save the Web page as a file, and save an image as a file. Print the Web site home pages for the *New York Times* and *USA Today* online newspapers. Print Web site pages for degree programs at Oregon Health & Science University School of Medicine and the MD program at the University of Washington School of Medicine. Locate a Web site on a snow skiing resort in Utah, save the Web page as a file, and save an image as a file.

Activity 1.1

Using the Internet, people can access a phenomenal amount of information for private or public use. To use the Internet, three things are generally required—an Internet Service Provider (ISP), a program to browse the Web (called a *Web browser*), and a *search engine*. In this section, you will use the Microsoft Internet Explorer Web browser to locate information on the Internet. *Uniform Resource Locators*, referred to as URLs, are the method used to identify locations on the Internet. The steps for browsing the Internet vary but generally include: opening Internet Explorer, typing the URL for the desired site, navigating the various pages of the site, printing Web pages, and then closing Internet Explorer.

Project

Dr. St. Claire is preparing a presentation on current health issues and has asked you to display and print the Web pages of the Department of Health and Human Services and the Centers for Disease Control and Prevention.

1. Make sure you are connected to the Internet through an Internet Service Provider and that the Windows desktop displays.

   Check with your instructor to determine if you need to complete steps for accessing the Internet.

2. Launch Microsoft Internet Explorer by double-clicking the *Internet Explorer* icon located on the Windows desktop.

   Depending on your system configuration, the steps you complete to open Internet Explorer may vary. Figure IE1.1 identifies the elements of the Internet Explorer, version 7, window. The Web page that displays in your Internet Explorer window may vary from what you see in Figure IE1.1.

FIGURE IE1.1 Internet Explorer Window

③ At the Internet Explorer window, click in the Address bar (refer to Figure IE1.1), type **www.hhs.gov**, and then press Enter.

> For information on URL names, please refer to the *In Addition* section at the bottom of the page.

④ Scroll down the home page for the United States Department of Health and Human Services by clicking the down-pointing arrow on the vertical scroll bar located at the right side of the Internet Explorer window.

⑤ Print the home page by clicking the Print button located on the Internet Explorer command bar.

> Refer to Figure IE1.2 for the names of the buttons located on the Internet Explorer command bar.

⑥ Display the home page for Center for Disease Control and Prevention by clicking in the Address bar, typing **www.cdc.gov**, and then pressing Enter.

⑦ Print the home page by clicking the Print button located on the Internet Explorer command bar.

⑧ Close Internet Explorer by clicking the Close button (contains an X) located in the upper right corner of the Internet Explorer window.

In Brief

Display Specific Web Site
1. On Windows desktop, double-click *Internet Explorer* icon.
2. Click in Address bar, type Web site URL, press Enter.

FIGURE IE1.2 Internet Explorer Tools

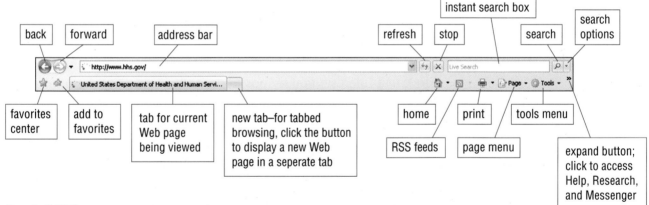

In Addition

Understanding URLs

URLs (Uniform Resource Locators) are the method used to identify locations on the Internet. The format of a URL is *http://server-name.domain*. The first part of the URL, *http*, stands for HyperText Transfer Protocol, which is the protocol or language used to transfer data within the World Wide Web (www). The colon and slashes separate the protocol from the server name. The server name is the second component of the URL. For example, in the URL http://www.microsoft.com, the server name is *microsoft*. The last part of the URL specifies the domain to which the server belongs. For example, *.com* refers to "commercial" and establishes that the URL is a commercial company. Other examples of domains include *.edu* for "educational," *.gov* for "government," and *.mil* for "military."

Activity 1.2

Navigating Using Hyperlinks; Searching for Specific Sites

Most Web pages contain *hyperlinks* that you click to connect to another page within the Web site or to another site on the Internet. Hyperlinks may display in a Web page as underlined text in a specific color or as images or icons. To use a hyperlink, position the mouse pointer on the desired hyperlink until the mouse pointer turns into a hand and then click the left mouse button. If you do not know the URL for a specific site or you want to find information on the Internet but do not know what site to visit, complete a search with a search engine. A variety of search engines is available on the Internet, each offering the opportunity to search for specific information. One method for searching for information is to click in the Instant Search box, type a keyword or phrase related to your search, and then click the Search button or press Enter. Another method for completing a search is to visit the home page for a search engine and use options at the site.

Project

North Shore Medical Clinic

You work at North Shore Medical Clinic and Lee Elliott, the office manager, has asked you to locate sites on the Internet that sell medical office forms, equipment, and supplies. The clinic will be purchasing new equipment, forms, and supplies in the near future.

1. Make sure you are connected to the Internet and then double-click the *Internet Explorer* icon on the Windows desktop.

2. At the Internet Explorer window, click in the Instant Search box.

3. Type **medical office forms** and then click the Search button (or press Enter).

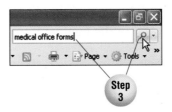

Step 3

4. When a list of sites displays in the Search results tab, scroll down the list and then click a hyperlink that interests you by positioning the mouse pointer on the hyperlink until the pointer turns into a hand and then clicking the left mouse button.

   By default, Internet Explorer uses Live Search. You can change the search provider default or add search providers using the Search Options button.

5. When the Web site displays, click the Print button.

6. Use the Yahoo! Web site to find sites that sell medical office equipment by clicking in the Address bar, typing **www.yahoo.com**, and then pressing Enter.

   You can also click the Search Options button and click *Yahoo! Search* at the drop-down list if Yahoo! has been added to the search providers list. Internet Explorer automatically repeats the search request using the text in the Instant Search box at Yahoo!'s Web page. Click *Find More Providers* at the search options drop-down list to add your favorite search engines to the search providers list.

7 At the Yahoo! Web site, type **medical office equipment** in the search text box and then press Enter.

In Brief
Search for Web Site
1. At Internet Explorer window, type text in Instant Search box related to desired Web site.
2. Click Search button.

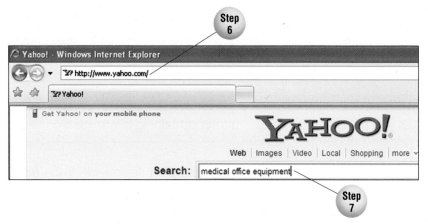

8 Click a hyperlink to a site that interests you.

9 When the site displays, click the Print button on the Internet Explorer command bar.

10 Use the Google search engine to find sites on medical office supplies by clicking in the Address bar, typing **www.google.com**, and then pressing Enter.

11 When the Google home page displays, type **medical office supplies** in the search text box and then press Enter.

12 Click a hyperlink to a site that interests you.

13 When the Web site displays, click the Print button on the Internet Explorer command bar.

14 Close Internet Explorer.

In Addition

Adding Favorites to the Favorites Center

If you find a site you want to visit on a regular basis, add the site to the Favorites Center. To do this, click the Add to Favorites button located at the left of the browser tabs and then click *Add to Favorites* at the drop-down list. At the Add a Favorite dialog box that displays, make sure the information in the *Name* text box is the title by which you want to refer to the Web site (if not, select the text and then type your own title for the page) and then click the Add button. The new Web site is added to the Favorites Center drop-down list. Jump quickly to the site by clicking the Favorites Center button and then clicking the site name at the drop-down list.

Activity 1.3

Completing Advanced Searches for Specific Sites

The Internet contains an extraordinary amount of information. Depending on what you are searching for on the Internet and the search engine you use, some searches can result in several thousand "hits" (sites). Wading through a large number of sites can be very time-consuming and counterproductive. Narrowing a search to very specific criteria can greatly reduce the number of hits for a search. To narrow a search, use the advanced search options offered by the search engine.

Project

Lee Elliott has asked you to locate sites on the Internet containing information on the symptoms and treatments of Hodgkin's disease.

1. Make sure you are connected to the Internet and then double-click the *Internet Explorer* icon on the Windows desktop.

2. Click in the Address bar, type **www.yahoo.com**, and then press Enter.

3. At the Yahoo! home page, click the Web Search button [Web Search] next to the Search text box.

4. Click the *Options* hyperlink and then click *Advanced Search* at the drop-down list.

    The *Options* hyperlink will probably display at the right side of the search text box. The location and name may vary.

5. At the Advanced Web Search page, click in the *the exact phrase* text box (the name of this option may vary) and then type **symptoms of Hodgkin's disease**.

    This limits the search to Web sites with the exact phrase "symptoms of Hodgkin's disease."

6. Click the *Only .com domains* option. (The name of this option may vary.)

    Clicking this option tells Yahoo! to display only Web sites with a .com domain and to ignore any other domain.

7. Click the Yahoo! Search button.

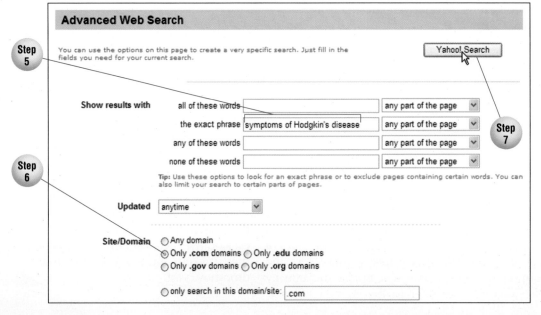

⑧ When the list of Web sites displays, click a hyperlink that interests you.

⑨ Click the Print button on the Internet Explorer command bar to print the Web page.

⑩ Click the Back button (located left of the address bar) on the Internet Explorer command bar until the Yahoo! Advanced Web Search page displays.

⑪ Select and then delete the text *symptoms of Hodgkin's disease* located in the *the exact phrase* text box.

⑫ Click in the *all of these words* text box and then type **treatment Hodgkin's disease lymphoma**.

> You want to focus on Web sites that offer information on the treatment of Hodgkin's lymphoma disease.

⑬ Click the *Any domain* option.

⑭ Click the Yahoo! Search button.

In Brief

Complete Advanced Search Using Yahoo!
1. At Internet Explorer window, click in Address bar, type **www.yahoo.com**, then press Enter.
2. Click Web Search button, click *Options* hyperlink, click *Advanced Search*.
3. Click in search text box, type specific text related to desired Web sites.
4. Select search method and search area.
5. Click Yahoo! Search button.

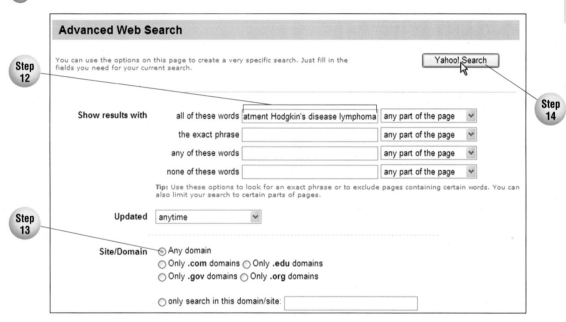

⑮ When the list of Web sites displays, click a hyperlink that interests you and then print the Web page.

⑯ Close Internet Explorer.

In Addition

Displaying a List of Sites Visited

As you view various Web pages, Internet Explorer keeps track of the Web sites visited. Display the History pane by clicking the Tools button on the Internet Explorer command bar, pointing to *Toolbars* and then clicking *History* at the drop-down list. Click the timeframe for which the Web page would have been viewed to expand the list and display the sites visited. For example, click *Last Week* to expand the list and view the pages that you visited within the past week. Click the desired hyperlink to revisit the page. At the top of the History pane, click the View History down-pointing arrow to change the order in which the history list is displayed. You can display Web sites in the History pane *By Date, By Site, By Most Visited,* or *By Order Visited Today.* Click *Search History* at the View History drop-down list to search the Web sites in the history pane by keyword or phrase.

Researching and Requesting Information

Click the expand button located at the right side of the Internet Explorer command bar (at the right of Tools) and then click *Research* at the drop-down list to open the Research pane at the left side of the window. Use options in this pane to search for and request specific information from online sources and to translate words to and from a variety of languages. The online resources available to you depend on the locale to which your system is set, authorization information indicating that you are allowed to download the information, and your Internet service provider. Determine the resources available by clicking the down-pointing arrow at the right of the resources list box. The drop-down list contains lists of reference books, research sites, business and financial sites, and other services. If you want to use a specific reference in your search, click the desired reference at the drop-down list, type the desired word or topic in the *Search for* text box, and then press Enter. Items matching your word or topic display in the pane list box. Depending on the item, the list box may contain hyperlinks you can click to access additional information on the Internet.

Project

Dr. Cárdenas has asked you for assistance on locating information on Portland State University. She wants you to use the Research feature of Internet Explorer to search for information on the university as well as use the translation tool to translate some English words to French.

1. Open Internet Explorer.

2. Click the expand button located at the right end of the Internet Explorer command bar and then click *Research* at the drop-down list.

3. Type **Portland State University** in the *Search for* text box in the Research pane.

4. Click the down-pointing arrow at the right of the resources list box (the down-pointing arrow immediately below the Start searching button—a white arrow pointing to the right on a green background) and then click *Encarta Encyclopedia: English (North America)* at the drop-down list.

   If this reference is not available, click any encyclopedia that is available.

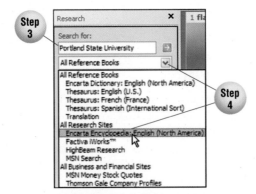

5. Look at the information that displays in the Research pane and then click a hyperlink about the university that interests you.

6 Use the translation feature to translate *treatment* from English to French. To begin, select the text in the *Search for* text box and then type **treatment**.

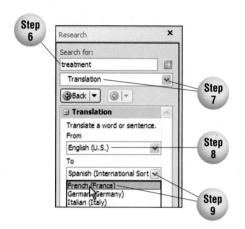

Step 6
Step 7
Step 8
Step 9

7 Click the down-pointing arrow at the right of the resources list box and then click *Translation* at the drop-down list.

8 Make sure that *English (U.S.)* displays in the *From* option box.

> If it does not, click the down-pointing arrow at the right of the *From* option box and then click *English (U.S.)* at the drop-down list.

9 Click the down-pointing arrow at the right of the *To* option box and then click *French (France)* at the drop-down list.

10 Make a note of the translation of *treatment* into French.

11 Select *treatment* in the *Search for* text box, type **prescription**, and then press Enter.

12 When the translation of *prescription* displays in the Research pane, make a note of the translation.

13 Click the Close button located at the top right of the Research pane, or click the expand button located at the right end of the Internet Explorer command bar and then click *Research* at the drop-down list to close the pane.

14 Close Internet Explorer.

In Brief

Use Research Pane
1. At Internet Explorer window, click expand button.
2. Click *Research*.
3. Click in *Search for* text box, then type specific text.
4. Click down-pointing arrow at right of resources list box, then click desired resource.

In Addition

Choosing Research Options

Determine the resources available by clicking the down-pointing arrow at the right of the resources list box (the list box located below the *Search for* text box). The drop-down list contains lists of reference books, research sites, business and financial sites, and other services. You can control the available research options by clicking the *Research options* hyperlink located at the bottom of the Research pane. This displays the Research Options dialog box shown at the right. (The options in your dialog box may vary.) At this dialog box, insert a check mark before those items you want available and remove the check mark from those items you do not want available.

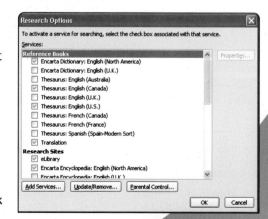

Activity 1.5

Downloading Images, Text, and Web Pages from the Internet

You can save as a separate file the image(s) and/or text that displays when you open a Web page. This separate file can be viewed, printed, or inserted in another file. The information you want to save in a separate file is downloaded from the Internet by Internet Explorer and saved in a folder of your choosing with the name you specify. Copyright laws protect much of the information on the Internet. Before using information downloaded from the Internet, check the site for restrictions. If you do use information, make sure you properly cite the source.

Project

Dr. St. Claire has asked you to locate a site on the Internet for Crater Lake National Park. She wants you to save the Web page as a file and save a picture of the park in another file.

1. Make sure you are connected to the Internet and then double-click the *Internet Explorer* icon on the Windows desktop.

2. Search for sites on the Internet for Crater Lake National Park.

3. From the list of sites that displays, explore several until you find a site you like that contains information about Crater Lake National Park and at least one image of the park.

4. Save the chosen Web page as a separate file by clicking the Page button on the Internet Explorer command bar and then clicking *Save As* at the drop-down list.

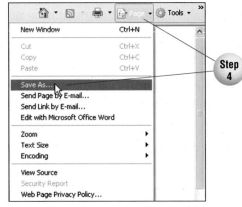

5. At the Save Webpage dialog box, click the down-pointing arrow at the right side of the *Save in* option box and then click the drive you are using as your storage medium at the drop-down list.

6. Select the text in the *File name* text box, type **CraterLakeWebPage**, and then click Save or press Enter.

7. Save an image as a separate file by right-clicking an image of the park on the Web page.

   The image that displays may vary from what you see on the next page.

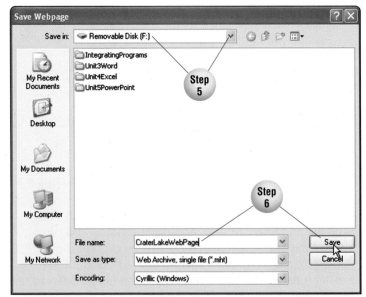

8 At the shortcut menu that displays, click *Save Picture As*.

9 At the Save Picture dialog box, change the *Save in* location to your storage medium.

10 Select the text in the *File name* text box, type **CraterLakeImage**, and then click Save or press Enter.

11 Close Internet Explorer.

Optional Steps

12 Open Microsoft Word by clicking the Start button on the Taskbar, pointing to *All Programs*, pointing to *Microsoft Office*, and then clicking *Microsoft Office Word 2007*.

13 With Microsoft Word open, click the Insert tab and then click the Picture button in the Illustrations group.

14 At the Insert Picture dialog box, change the *Look in* option to the location where you saved the Crater Lake image and then double-click *CraterLakeImage.jpg*.

15 When the image displays in the Word document, print the document by clicking the Quick Print button on the Quick Access toolbar. (If the Quick Print button is not available on the Quick Access toolbar, click the Office button, point to *Print*, and then click the Quick Print button.)

16 Close the document by clicking the Office button and then clicking *Close* at the drop-down list. At the message asking if you want to save the changes, click No.

17 Open the **CraterLakeWebPage.mht** file by clicking the Office button and then clicking *Open* at the drop-down list.

18 At the Open dialog box, change the *Look in* option to the location where you saved the Crater Lake Web page and then double-click *CraterLakeWebPage.mht*. Click No if a message appears asking if you want to make Word your default Web page editor.

19 Print the Web page by clicking the Quick Print button on the Quick Access toolbar.

20 Close the **CraterLakeWebPage.mht** file by clicking the Office button and then clicking *Close*.

21 Close Word by clicking the Close button that displays in the upper right corner of the screen.

Features Summary

Feature	Button	Keyboard Shortcut
close Internet Explorer		Alt + F4
go back to previous Web page		Alt + Left Arrow
go forward to next Web page		Alt + Right Arrow
History pane		Ctrl + Shift + H
launch Internet Explorer		
print current Web page		Ctrl + P
Research pane		
save a Web page as separate file		
save image as separate file		
select Address bar		Alt + D
select Instant Search box		Ctrl + E

Knowledge Check

Completion: In the space provided at the right, write in the correct term, command, or option.

1. Type a URL in this bar at the Internet Explorer window. _____

2. The letters *URL* stand for this. _____

3. Click this button on the Internet Explorer command bar to display the previous Web page. _____

4. Click in this box to locate Web pages using a keyword or phrase. _____

5. Use options in this pane to request specific information from online sources and to translate words to and from a variety of languages. _____

6. Save a Web page as a separate file by clicking the Page button on the Internet Explorer command bar and then clicking this option at the drop-down list. _____

7. Save an image as a separate file by right-clicking the image and then clicking this option at the shortcut menu. _____

Skills Review

Review 1 Browsing the Internet and Navigating with Hyperlinks

1. Launch Internet Explorer.
2. Click in the Address bar, type **www.oregonstate.edu**, and then press Enter. (This is the home page for Oregon State University.)
3. Using hyperlinks, navigate to a page that interests you on the Oregon State University site and then print the Web page.
4. Click the Back button until the Oregon State University home page displays.

Review 2 Searching for Specific Sites

1. At the Internet Explorer window, use the Instant Search box to look for Web sites on mountain climbing.
2. Visit a site that interests you and then print the Web page.
3. Display the Yahoo! Web site and then use advanced options to search for Web sites on mountain climbing in British Columbia, Canada.
4. Visit a site that interests you and then print the Web page.

Review 3 Requesting Information and Translating Words

1. At the Internet Explorer window, click the expand button at the right side of the Internet Explorer command bar, and then click the Research button to display the Research pane.
2. Use options in the Research pane to find information on the history of medicine in an encyclopedia.
3. Click a hyperlink that interests you and then print the Web page.
4. Use options in the Research pane to translate the English word *history* into Spanish.
5. Make a note of the Spanish word and then close the Research pane.

Review 4 Downloading a Web Page

1. Using a search engine of your choosing, search for Web sites on parasailing in Hawaii. Find a site that contains a parasailing image.
2. When the Web page displays, save it as a separate file by clicking the Page button and then *Save As*.
3. At the Save Webpage dialog box, change the location to your storage medium, type **ParasailWebPage** in the *File name* text box, and then press Enter.
4. Save an image by right-clicking an image on the Web page and then clicking *Save Picture As* at the shortcut menu.
5. At the Save Picture dialog box, change the location to your storage medium, type **ParasailImage** in the *File name* text box, and then press Enter.
6. Close Internet Explorer.

Skills Assessment

Assessment 1 Visiting and Printing Web Pages

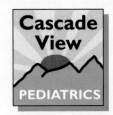

1. Joseph Yarborough, a doctor at Cascade View Pediatrics, likes to keep up-to-date with current events by reading the daily headlines for various newspapers. He has asked you to print the home pages for two online newspapers—the *New York Times* and *USA Today*. To begin, launch Internet Explorer.
2. Visit the Web site of the *New York Times* at www.nytimes.com and then print the home page.
3. Visit the Web site of *USA Today* at www.usatoday.com and then print the home page.

Assessment 2 Navigating Web Sites

1. You work at Cascade View Pediatrics and Dr. Severin has asked you to print the Web pages for the school of medicine at two universities. Visit the home page for the Oregon Health & Science University School of Medicine at www.ohsu.edu/som.
2. Using hyperlinks, navigate to the Web page containing information on degree programs and then print the Web page.
3. Visit the home page for the University of Washington School of Medicine at www.uwmedicine.washington.edu.
4. Using hyperlinks, navigate to the Web page containing information on the MD program and then print the Web page.

Assessment 3 Researching Information

1. Dr. Severin is thinking about taking a snow skiing vacation in Utah and has asked you to locate information on vacation packages. Using Internet Explorer, search for information on snow skiing resorts in Utah.
2. Visit a Web site that interests you and contains an image of the resort or mountains.
3. Save the Web page as a separate file and name it **UtahSkiResortWebPage**.
4. Save an image as a separate file and name it **UtahResortImage**.
5. Close Internet Explorer.

Optional Steps

6. Open Microsoft Word.
7. Insert the image into a Word document and then print the document.
8. Close the document without saving it.
9. Open the file containing the Web page and then print it.
10. Close the document and then close Word.

Using Word *in the* Medical Office

Introducing
Word 2007

Microsoft Word 2007 is a word processing program used to create documents such as memos, letters, medical reports, medical research papers, brochures, announcements, newsletters, envelopes, labels, and much more. Word is a full-featured word processing program that provides a wide variety of editing and formatting features as well as sophisticated visual elements.

This unit on Microsoft Word 2007 in the medical office contains four sections that guide you in learning and applying the features of Word 2007. In Section 1, you will create and edit medical documents including inserting, replacing, and deleting text; checking the spelling and grammar in documents; using the AutoCorrect feature and Thesaurus; highlighting text, changing document views; creating documents using a template; and managing documents. Section 2 focuses on formatting characters and paragraphs and includes applying fonts, aligning text in paragraphs, indenting text, changing line and paragraph spacing, inserting bullets and numbers, inserting symbols, setting tabs, adding borders and shading, and applying styles and Quick Styles sets. In Section 3, you will learn how to format and enhance documents. In that section, you will find and replace text; cut, copy, and paste text; use the Clipboard task pane; insert page breaks and page numbers; change margins and page orientation; insert headers and footers, images, WordArt, and shapes in a document; and prepare envelopes and labels. In Section 4, you will learn how to merge main documents with data sources, sort and filter records, create and modify tables, and prepare and edit forms.

In each of the four Word sections, you will prepare medical documents for two clinics and a hospital as described below.

Cascade View Pediatrics is a full-service pediatric clinic that provides comprehensive primary pediatric care to infants, children, and adolescents.

North Shore Medical Clinic is an internal medicine clinic dedicated to providing exceptional care to all patients. The physicians in the clinic specialize in a number of fields including internal medicine, family practice, cardiology, and dermatology.

Columbia River General Hospital is an independent, not-for-profit hospital with the mission of providing high-quality, comprehensive care to patients and improving the health of members of the community.

Word SECTION 1

Creating and Editing a Document

Skills

- Complete the word processing cycle
- Move the insertion point
- Insert and delete text
- Scroll and navigate in a document
- Select and delete text
- Use Undo and Redo
- Check the spelling and grammar in a document
- Use AutoCorrect
- Use Thesaurus
- Use the Help feature
- Highlight text
- Change document views
- Preview a document
- Print a document
- Insert the date and time in a document
- Insert Quick Parts in a document
- Close a document
- Create a document using a template
- Create and rename a folder
- Save a document in a different format

Student Resources

Before beginning this section:
1. Copy to your storage medium the WordMedS1 subfolder from the Unit3Word folder on the Student Resources CD.
2. Make WordMedS1 the active folder.

In addition to containing the data files needed to complete section work, the Student Resources CD contains model answers in PDF format for each of the projects in this section; model answers for end-of-section exercises are not provided.

Projects Overview

Prepare an x-ray report document, edit and format a history and physical examination document, manage files, and edit and format a consultation report document.

Prepare a letter requesting interpreting services, edit and format a notice to employees regarding a diabetes presentation, prepare a letter to a doctor, and prepare a chart note.

Prepare a memo regarding well-child checkup appointments and edit and format a document containing information on scheduling well-child checkup appointments.

Activity 1.1

Completing the Word Processing Cycle

The process of creating a document in Microsoft Word generally follows a word processing cycle. The steps in the cycle vary but typically include: opening Word; creating and editing the document; saving, printing, and closing the document; and then exiting Word.

Project

As the medical office assistant for North Shore Medical Clinic, you are responsible for preparing medical records. You need to type the results of a portable chest x-ray for a patient at the clinic.

1 On the Windows desktop, click the Start button **start** on the Taskbar, point to *All Programs* at the pop-up menu, point to *Microsoft Office*, and then click *Microsoft Office Word 2007*.

Depending on your system configuration, these steps may vary.

2 At the Word document screen, identify the various features by comparing your screen with the one shown in Figure W1.1.

Refer to Table W1.1 for a description of the screen features.

3 Type **Name: Joseph Ingram** as shown in Figure W1.2 and then hold down the Shift key, press the Enter key, and then release the Shift key.

Shift + Enter is the New Line command. Use this command to keep lines of text within the same paragraph, which creates less space between one line and the next.

4 Type **Procedure: Portable chest x-ray** and then press Shift + Enter.

5 Type **Date of Procedure: 05/18/2011** and then press Enter.

Pressing the Enter key begins a new paragraph in the document.

6 Type the remainder of the text shown in Figure W1.2.

Type the text as shown. When you type *adn* and then press the spacebar, the AutoCorrect feature will automatically correct it to *and*. When you type *teh* and then press the spacebar, AutoCorrect corrects it to *the*. Do not press the Enter key to end a line of text. Word will automatically wrap text to the next line.

FIGURE W1.1 Word Document Screen

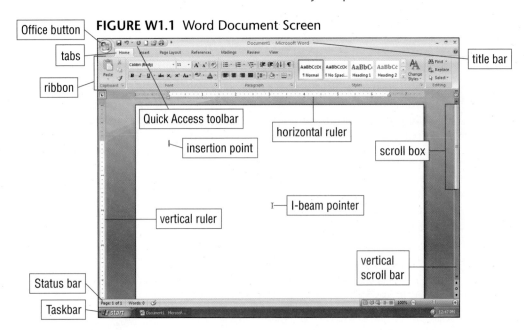

FIGURE W1.2 Steps 3–6

Name: Joseph Ingram
Procedure: Portable chest x-ray
Date of Procedure: 05/18/2011

Comparison: A single portable view of teh chest is provided and comparison is made with earlier study of the same date.

Findings: Endotracheal tube adn right chest tubes are in place. Heart appears to be generous in size and right border is somewhat indistinct of perihilar vascular structure. No sign of pneumothorax was observed.

Opinion: Satisfactory post median sternotomy chest.

---

⑦ Save the document by clicking the Save button 💾 on the Quick Access toolbar.

⑧ At the Save As dialog box, make sure the WordMedS1 folder on your storage medium is the active folder, type **WordMedS1-01** in the *File name* text box, and then press Enter (or click the Save button).

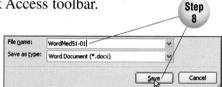
Step 8

Word automatically adds the file extension *.docx* to the end of a document name. The *Save in* option at the Save As dialog box displays the active folder. If you need to make the WordMedS1 folder on your storage medium the active folder, click the down-pointing arrow at the right side of the *Save in* option and then click the location of your storage medium. Double-click *WordMedS1* in the list box.

⑨ Print the document by clicking the Quick Print button 🖨 on the Quick Access toolbar.

If the Quick Print button does not display on the Quick Access toolbar, click the Customize Quick Access Toolbar button that displays at the right side of the toolbar and then click *Quick Print* at the drop-down list.

TABLE W1.1 Screen Features and Descriptions

Feature	Description
Office button	displays as a Microsoft Office logo and, when clicked, displays a list of options and most recently opened documents
Quick Access toolbar	contains buttons for commonly used commands
Title bar	displays document name followed by program name
tabs	contains commands and features organized into groups
ribbon	area containing the tabs and commands divided into groups
horizontal ruler	used to set margins, indents, and tabs
vertical ruler	used to set top and bottom margins
I-beam pointer	used to move the insertion point or to select text
insertion point	indicates location of next character entered at the keyboard
vertical scroll bar	used to view various parts of the document
Status bar	displays number of pages and words, View buttons, and Zoom slider bar

⑩ Close the document by clicking the Office button ⊙ and then clicking *Close* at the drop-down list.

The Office button displays as the Microsoft Office logo and is located in the upper left corner of the screen.

In Addition

Default Document Formatting

A Word document is based on a template that applies default formatting. Some of the default formats include 11-point Calibri as the font, line spacing of 1.15, and 10 points of spacing after each paragraph (a press of the Enter key). You will learn more about fonts and paragraph spacing in Section 2.

Correcting Errors

Word contains a spelling feature that inserts a wavy red line below words that are not contained in the Spelling dictionary. You can edit the word or leave it as written. The wavy red line does not print.

Activity 1.2

Moving the Insertion Point; Inserting and Deleting Text

Many documents you create will need to have changes made to them. These changes may include adding text, called *inserting*, or removing text, called *deleting*. To insert or delete text, move the insertion point to certain locations without erasing the text through which it passes. To insert text, position the insertion point in the desired location and then type the text. Delete text in a document by pressing the Backspace key or Delete key.

Project

As a medical office assistant for Columbia River General Hospital, you are responsible for typing history and physical examination documents for patients admitted to the hospital.

1. At the Word document screen, click the Open button on the Quick Access toolbar.

   If the Open button does not display on the Quick Access toolbar, click the Customize Quick Access Toolbar button that displays at the right side of the toolbar and then click *Open* at the drop-down list.

2. At the Open dialog box, make sure the WordMedS1 folder on your storage medium is the active folder and then double-click **CRGHh&p.docx** in the list box.

   Step 2

   Open

Look in:	WordMedS1
Trusted Templates	CRGHConsultation.docx
	CRGHh&p.docx
My Recent Documents	CVPApptSchedule.docx
	CVPMemoForm.docx
Desktop	NSMCDiabetesNotice.docx
	NSMCLtrhd.docx
My Documents	WordMedS1-01.docx

   ❓ PROBLEM

   If the **CRGHh&p.docx** document does not display in the Open dialog box, check with your instructor.

3. Click the Office button and then click *Save As*.

4. At the Save As dialog box, type **WordMedS1-02** in the *File name* text box and then press Enter.

   If you open an existing document, make changes to it, and then want to save it with the same name, click the Save button on the Quick Access toolbar. If you want to keep the original document and save the document with the changes with a new name, click the Office button and then click *Save As*.

   Step 4

File name:	WordMedS1-02
Save as type:	Word Document (*.docx)

5. Position the mouse pointer at the beginning of the HISTORY OF PRESENT ILLNESS paragraph and then click the left mouse button.

   This moves the insertion point to the location of the mouse pointer.

6. Press the Up, Down, Left, and Right arrow keys located at the right of the regular keys on the keyboard.

   Use the information shown in Table W1.2 to practice moving the insertion point in the document.

TABLE W1.2 Insertion Point Keyboard Control

Press	To move insertion point
End key	to end of line
Home key	to beginning of line
Pg Up key	up one screen
Pg Down key	down one screen
Ctrl + Home	to beginning of document
Ctrl + End	to end of document

(7) Move the insertion point to the beginning of the name *Shawn Lipinski, MD* located toward the beginning of the document and then type **Physician:**. Press the spacebar once after typing the colon.

> By default, text you type in a document is inserted in the document and existing text is moved to the right.

(8) Click immediately right of the last number in the ID number *10572* and then press the Backspace key until all of the numbers are deleted.

> Press the Backspace key to delete any character immediately left of the insertion point.

(9) Type **11345**.

(10) Click on any character in the last sentence in the HISTORY OF PRESENT ILLNESS paragraph (the sentence that begins *He notes that he usually runs a rapid pulse…*).

In Brief

Open Document
1. Click Open button on Quick Access toolbar.
2. Double-click document name.

Save Document
1. Click Save button.
2. Type document name.
3. Click Save or press Enter.

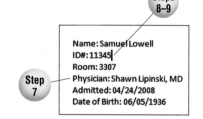

Steps 8–9

Step 7

Name: Samuel Lowell
ID#: 11345
Room: 3307
Physician: Shawn Lipinski, MD
Admitted: 04/24/2008
Date of Birth: 06/05/1936

(11) Press the Backspace key until the insertion point is positioned immediately right of the period that ends the previous sentence and then press the Delete key until you have deleted the remainder of the sentence.

> Press the Delete key to delete any character immediately right of the insertion point.

(12) Click the Save button 🖫 on the Quick Access toolbar.

> Clicking the Save button saves the document with the same name (**WordMedS1-02.docx**).

In Addition

Using Overtype Mode

By default, text you type in a document is inserted in the document and existing text is moved to the right. If you want to type over something, you need to turn on the Overtype mode. With the Overtype mode on, anything you type will replace existing text. To turn on the Overtype mode, click the Office button and then click the Word Options button located toward the bottom of the drop-down list. At the Word Options dialog box, click *Advanced* in the left pane. In the *Editing options* section, insert a check mark in the *Use overtype mode* check box if you want the Overtype mode always on in the document. Or, insert a check mark in the *Use the Insert key to control overtype mode* check box if you want to use the Insert key to turn Overtype mode on and off. After making your selection, click the OK button located in the lower right corner of the dialog box.

Activity 1.3

Scrolling and Navigating in a Document

In addition to moving the insertion point to a specific location, you can use the mouse to move the display of text in the document screen. Use the mouse along with the vertical scroll bar to scroll through text in a document. The vertical scroll bar displays toward the right side of the screen. Scrolling in a document changes the text displayed but does not move the insertion point. The Select Browse Object button located at the bottom of the vertical scroll bar contains options for browsing through a document. Scrolling in a document changes the text displayed, while browsing in a document moves the insertion point.

Project

After viewing and editing the History and Physical Examination document for Samuel Lowell, you need to review it and make additional edits.

1. With **WordMedS1-02.docx** open, press Ctrl + Home to move the insertion point to the beginning of the document.

2. Position the mouse pointer on the down scroll arrow on the vertical scroll bar and then click the left mouse button several times.

   This scrolls down the lines of text in the document. Scrolling changes the display of text but does not move the insertion point.

Step 2

3. Position the mouse pointer on the vertical scroll bar below the scroll box and then click the left mouse button a couple of times.

   The scroll box on the vertical scroll bar indicates the location of the text in the document screen in relation to the remainder of the document. Clicking on the vertical scroll bar below the scroll box scrolls down one screen of text at a time.

4. Position the mouse pointer on the scroll box on the vertical scroll bar, hold down the left mouse button, drag the scroll box to the top of the vertical scroll bar, and then release the mouse button.

   Dragging the scroll box to the top of the vertical scroll bar displays text at the beginning of the document.

Step 4

5. Click the Select Browse Object button 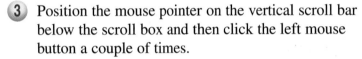 located in the lower right corner of the screen and then click the *Go To* option.

   The location of the *Go To* option may vary. It may be the first option from the left in the top row. Position the arrow pointer on the option and the name of the option displays at the top of the palette. Use other options at the palette to browse to document features such as a field, endnote, footnote, comment, section, heading, and graphic.

Step 5

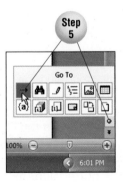

6 At the Find and Replace dialog box with the Go To tab selected, type **2** in the *Enter page number* text box, press the Enter key, and then click the Close button to close the dialog box.

With options available at the Find and Replace dialog box with the Go To tab selected, you can move the insertion point to various locations in a document such as a specific page, section, line, bookmark, and so on.

In Brief
Display Find and Replace Dialog Box
1. Click Select Browse Object button.
2. Click *Go To* option.

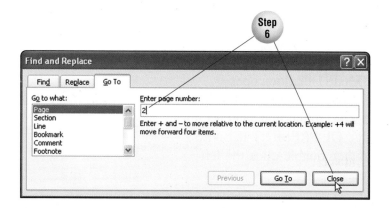

Step 6

7 Click the Previous Page button located above the Select Browse Object button.

Clicking the Previous Page button moves the insertion point to the beginning of the previous page. Depending on the last navigation you completed in the document, the full name of the Previous (Page) button and of the Next (Page) button, as well as the tasks the buttons complete, may vary.

Step 7

Step 8

8 Click the Next Page button located below the Select Browse Object button.

9 Press Ctrl + Home to move the insertion point to the beginning of the document.

10 Save the document by clicking the Save button on the Quick Access toolbar.

In Addition

Option Buttons

As you insert and edit text in a document, you may notice an option button popping up in your text. The name and appearance of this option button varies depending on the action. If a word you type is corrected by AutoCorrect, if you create an automatic list, or if autoformatting is applied to text, the AutoCorrect Options button appears near the text. Click this button to undo the specific automatic action. If you paste text in a document, the Paste Options button appears near the text. Click this button to display options for controlling the formatting of pasted text.

Activity 1.4

Selecting and Deleting Text; Using Undo and Redo

Previously, you learned to delete text by pressing the Backspace key or Delete key. You can also select text and then delete it, replace it with other text, or apply formatting to selected text. If you make a change to text, such as deleting selected text, and then change your mind, use the Undo and/or Redo buttons on the Quick Access toolbar.

Project To minimize the need for additional editing, you have decided to review carefully the History and Physical Examination document on screen.

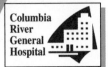

Columbia River General Hospital

1. With **WordMedS1-02.docx** open, position the mouse pointer on the word *leg* (the last word in the first sentence in the HISTORY OF PRESENT ILLNESS section) and then double-click the left mouse button.

HISTORY OF PRESENT ILLNESS
Mr. Lowell is a 40-year-old male admitted to thrombophlebitis in his left lower leg. He wa healthy, never been hospitalized, and has ha

Step 1

Selected text displays with a blue background. You can also drag through text with the mouse to select the text. When you select text, a dimmed Mini toolbar displays. You will learn more about the Mini toolbar in Activity 2.1.

 PROBLEM

If you select the wrong text and want to deselect it, click in the document outside the selected text.

2. Type **extremity**.

When you type *extremity*, it takes the place of *leg*.

3. Move the insertion point immediately left of the comma after the word *healthy* (located in the third sentence in the HISTORY OF PRESENT ILLNESS section) and then press the F8 function key on the keyboard. Press the Right Arrow key until the words , *never been hospitalized* and the comma that follows *hospitalized* are selected.

HISTORY OF PRESENT ILLNESS
Mr. Lowell is a 40-year-old male admitted to thrombophlebitis in his left lower extremity. been healthy, never been hospitalized, and h ago, when he developed a superficial thromb

Step 3

Pressing the F8 function key turns on the Extend mode. Use the insertion point movement keys to select text in Extend mode.

4. Press the Delete key.

Pressing the Delete key deletes the selected text. If you want to cancel a selection, press the Esc key and then press any arrow key.

5. Position the mouse pointer on any character in the second sentence in the HISTORY OF PRESENT ILLNESS section (the sentence that begins *He was brought to the hospital . . .*), hold down the Ctrl key, click the mouse button, and then release the Ctrl key.

Holding down the Ctrl key while clicking the mouse button selects the entire sentence.

6. Press the Delete key to delete the selected sentence.

(7) Click the Undo button 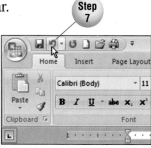 on the Quick Access toolbar.

Step 7

When you click the Undo button, the deleted sentence reappears. Clicking the Undo button reverses the last command or deletes the last entry you typed. Click the down-pointing arrow at the right side of the Undo button and a drop-down list displays containing changes made to the document since it was opened. Click an action and the action, along with any actions listed above it in the drop-down list, is undone.

(8) Click the Redo button 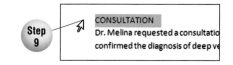 on the Quick Access toolbar.

Clicking the Redo button deletes the selected sentence. If you click the Undo button and then decide you do not want to reverse the original action, click the Redo button.

(9) Position the mouse pointer between the left edge of the page and the heading *CONSULTATION* until the pointer turns into an arrow pointing up and to the right (instead of the left) and then click the left mouse button.

The space between the left edge of the page and the text is referred to as the selection bar. Use the selection bar to select specific amounts of text. Refer to Table W1.3 for more information on selecting text.

Step 9

CONSULTATION
Dr. Melina requested a consultatio
confirmed the diagnosis of deep ve

(10) Deselect the text by clicking in the document outside the selected area.

(11) Save the document by clicking the Save button 🖫 on the Quick Access toolbar.

TABLE W1.3 Selecting with the Mouse

To select	Complete these steps using the mouse
a word	Double-click the word.
a line of text	Click in the selection bar at the left of the line.
multiple lines of text	Drag in the selection bar at the left of the lines.
a sentence	Hold down the Ctrl key and then click anywhere in the sentence.
a paragraph	Double-click in the selection bar next to the paragraph or triple-click anywhere in the paragraph.
multiple paragraphs	Drag in the selection bar.
an entire document	Triple-click in the selection bar.

In Addition

Undoing Multiple Actions

Word maintains actions in temporary memory. If you want to undo an action performed earlier, click the Undo button arrow. This causes a drop-down list to display. To make a selection from this drop-down list, click the desired action. Any actions listed above the selection in the drop-down list are also undone. Multiple actions must be undone in sequence.

Activity 1.5

Checking the Spelling and Grammar in a Document

Use Word's spelling checker to find and correct misspelled words and find duplicated words (such as *and and*). The spelling checker compares words in your document with words in its dictionary. If a match is found, the word is passed over. If no match is found for the word, the spelling checker stops, selects the word, and offers replacements. The grammar checker will search a document for errors in grammar, style, punctuation, and word usage. The spelling checker and the grammar checker can help you create a well-written document but do not replace the need for proofreading.

Project

Continuing with the editing process, you are ready to check the spelling and grammar in the History and Physical Examination document.

1. With **WordMedS1-02.docx** open, press Ctrl + Home to move the insertion point to the beginning of the document, click the Review tab, and then click the Spelling & Grammar button [ABC] in the Proofing group.

2. When the word *traetment* is selected, make sure *treatment* is selected in the *Suggestions* list box and then click the Change button in the Spelling and Grammar dialog box.

   Refer to Table W1.4 for an explanation of the buttons in the Spelling and Grammar dialog box.

3. When the word *thrombophlebitis* is selected, click the Ignore All button.

   This medical term is spelled correctly.

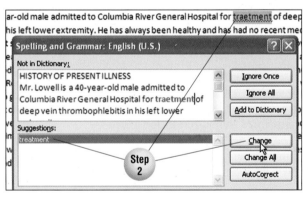 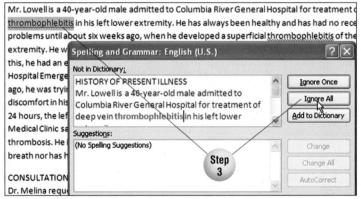

4. When the word *pyelogram* is selected, click the Ignore All button.

   This medical term is spelled correctly.

5. When the word *swolen* is selected, make sure *swollen* is selected in the *Suggestions* list box and then click the Change button.

6. When the sentence that begins *He has not have an undue shortness …* is selected, click the Change button.

7. When the word *juandice* is selected, make sure *jaundice* is selected in the *Suggestions* list box and then click the Change button.

? PROBLEM

If you accidentally click outside the Spelling and Grammar dialog box, resume the checking by clicking the Resume button.

TABLE W1.4 Spelling and Grammar Dialog Box Buttons

Button	Function
Ignore Once	during spell checking, skips that occurrence of the word; in grammar checking, leaves currently selected text as written
Ignore All	during spell checking, skips that occurrence and all other occurrences of the word in the document
Ignore Rule	during grammar checking, leaves currently selected text as written and ignores the current rule for remainder of the grammar check
Add to Dictionary	adds selected word to the main spelling check dictionary
Delete	deletes the currently selected word(s)
Change	replaces selected word in sentence with selected word in *Suggestions* list box
Change All	replaces selected word in sentence with selected word in *Suggestions* list box and all other occurrences of the word
Explain	during grammar checking, displays information about the grammar rule
AutoCorrect	inserts selected word and correct spelling of word in AutoCorrect dialog box
Undo	reverses most recent spelling and grammar action
Next Sentence	accepts manual changes made to sentence and then continues grammar checking
Options	displays a dialog box with options for customizing a spelling and grammar check

In Brief

Check Spelling and Grammar
1. Click Review tab.
2. Click Spelling & Grammar button in Proofing group.
3. Ignore or change as needed.
4. Click OK.

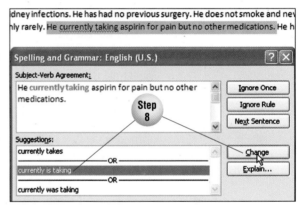

8 When the sentence that begins *He currently taking aspirin for pain ...* is selected, click *currently is taking* in the *Suggestions* list box and then click the Change button.

9 When the word *thyromegaly* is selected, click the Ignore All button.

   This medical term is spelled correctly.

10 When the word *hepatosplenomegaly* is selected, click the Ignore All button.

   This medical term is spelled correctly.

11 When the text *SL:SN* is selected, click the Ignore Rule button.

12 At the message telling you that spell check is complete, click the OK button.

   If the Readability Statistics dialog box displays, read the information and then click the OK button.

13 Click the Save button 🖫 on the Quick Access toolbar to save the changes made to the document.

In Addition

Changing Spelling Options

Control spelling and grammar checking options at the Word Options dialog box with the Proofing option selected. Display this dialog box by clicking the Office button and then clicking the Word Options button that displays at the bottom of the drop-down list. At the Word Options dialog box, click *Proofing* at the left side of the dialog box. With options in the dialog box, you can tell the spelling checker to ignore certain types of text, create custom dictionaries, show readability statistics, and hide spelling and/or grammar errors in the document.

Editing While Checking Spelling and Grammar

When checking a document, you can temporarily leave the Spelling and Grammar dialog box by clicking in the document. To resume the spelling and grammar check, click the Resume button, which was formerly the Ignore button.

Activity 1.6

Using AutoCorrect and Thesaurus

The AutoCorrect feature automatically detects and corrects some typographical errors, misspelled words, and incorrect capitalizations. In addition to correcting errors, you can use the AutoCorrect feature to insert frequently used text. Use the Thesaurus feature to find synonyms, antonyms, and related words for a particular word. Synonyms are words that have the same or nearly the same meaning, and antonyms are words with opposite meanings.

Project

You need to insert additional text in the History and Physical Examination document. To speed up the process, you will add an entry to AutoCorrect. You will also use Thesaurus to find synonyms for specific words in the document.

Columbia River General Hospital

1. With **WordMedS1-02.docx** open, click the Office button and then click the Word Options button located at the bottom of the drop-down list.

2. At the Word Options dialog box, click the *Proofing* option located at the left side of the dialog box and then click the AutoCorrect Options button in the *AutoCorrect options* section.

3. At the AutoCorrect dialog box with the AutoCorrect tab selected, type **tc** in the *Replace* text box and then press the Tab key.

4. Type **tachycardia** in the *With* text box and then click the Add button.

5. With the *tc* selected in the *Replace* text box, type **pl** and then press the Tab key.

6. With *tachycardia* selected in the *With* text box, type **pulmonary**, click the Add button, and then click OK to close the dialog box.

7. Click OK to close the Word Options dialog box.

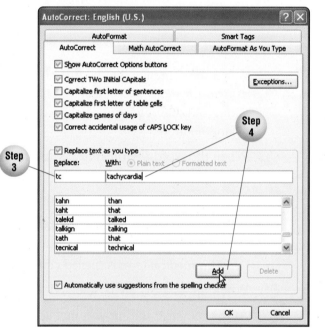

8. Press Ctrl + End to move the insertion point to the end of the document. Move the insertion point so it is positioned immediately right of the period after the sentence *The neurologic assessment was normal* (below the *NEUROLOGIC* heading) and then press the Enter key.

9. Type **DIAGNOSIS** and then press Shift + Enter.

    Shift + Enter is the New Line command.

FIGURE W1.2

> **DIAGNOSIS**
> Patient is diagnosed with deep vein thrombophlebitis in the left lower extremity and tc. This patient will be admitted. A pl ventilation perfusion scan is mandated by the presence of the tc. A baseline study needs to be done to exclude the presence of pl embolization. He will be treated with bed rest and anticoagulation. Further notation will be made as the case progresses. Appropriate studies for coagulopathy were performed.

10 Type the remaining text shown in Figure W1.2. (Type the text exactly as shown. AutoCorrect will correct *tc* to *tachycardia* and *pl* to *pulmonary*.)

11 Click anywhere in the word *done* located in the fourth sentence in the paragraph you just typed.

12 Click the Review tab and then click the Thesaurus button in the Proofing group.

13 At the Research task pane, position the mouse pointer on the word *completed* in the task pane list box, click the down-pointing arrow, and then click *Insert* at the drop-down list.

14 Close the Research task pane by clicking the Close button located in the upper right corner of the task pane.

15 Position the mouse pointer on the word *exclude* located in the fourth sentence in the paragraph you just typed and then click the *right* mouse button.

16 At the shortcut menu that displays, point to *Synonyms* and then click *rule out* at the side menu.

17 Click the Save button to save the document with the same name.

18 Click the Office button and then click the Word Options button. Click the *Proofing* option located at the left side of the dialog box and then click the AutoCorrect Options button.

19 At the AutoCorrect dialog box, type **pl** in the *Replace* text box.

> This selects the pulmonary entry in the list box.

20 Click the Delete button.

21 Type **tc** in the *Replace* text box and then click the Delete button.

22 Click OK to close the dialog box.

23 Click OK to close the Word Options dialog box.

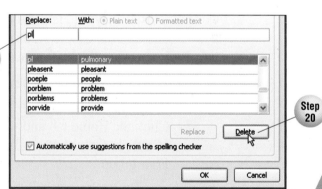

In Brief

Add AutoCorrect Entry
1. Click Office button, Word Options button.
2. Click *Proofing*.
3. Click AutoCorrect Options.
4. Type text in *Replace* text box.
5. Type text in *With* text box.
6. Click Add button.
7. Click OK.
8. Click OK.

Use Thesaurus
1. Click in desired word.
2. Click Review tab.
3. Click Thesaurus button.
4. Click down-pointing arrow at right of desired word.
5. Click *Insert*.

In Addition

Using the Research Task Pane

Depending on the word you are looking up, the words in the Research task pane list box may display followed by *(n.)* for *noun*, *(adj.)* for *adjective*, or *(adv.)* for *adverb*. As you look up synonyms for various words, click the Previous search button or click the Next search button to display the next search in the sequence. You can also click the down-pointing arrow at the right side of the Next search button to display a list of words for which you have looked up synonyms.

Activity 1.7

Using the Help Feature; Highlighting Text

Microsoft Word includes a Help feature that contains information on Word features and commands. For example, you might want to find information on Word's highlighting feature. With the Help feature, you can find and print the information about the Text Highlight Color button located in the Font group in the Home tab. This button allows you to highlight important information electronically, similar to the way you might highlight sentences in books, magazines, and papers with a marker or highlighter pen.

Project

You want to identify specific text in the History and Physical Examination document for your supervisor to review. You will use the Help feature to search for and print information on highlighting text and then highlight specific text in the document.

1. With **WordMedS1-02.docx** open, click the Microsoft Office Word Help button ⓦ located in the upper right corner of the screen.

2. At the Word Help window, type **highlight text** in the text box and then press Enter.

3. Click *Apply or remove highlighting* in the list box.

   This displays information on applying and removing highlighting in the Word Help window.

4. Read the information that displays in the Word Help window and then click the Print button located toward the top of the window. At the Print dialog box, click the Print button.

5. Close the Word Help window by clicking the Close button ☒ located in the upper right corner of the window.

6. Press Ctrl + Home to move the insertion point to the beginning of the document.

7. Click the Home tab and then click the Text Highlight Color button ab located in the Font group.

   The insertion point now displays with a pen icon attached.

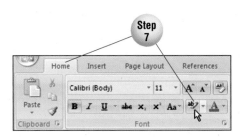

8. Select the sentence *Dr. Melina at the North Shore Medical Clinic saw him and an ultrasound was performed demonstrating clear evidence for deep venous thrombosis.* located toward the end of the HISTORY OF PRESENT ILLNESS section.

9 Select the sentence *Dr. Melina requested a consultation by Dr. St. Claire, a physician at North Shore Medical Center, who confirmed the diagnosis of deep venous thrombosis.* that displays below the *CONSULTATION* heading.

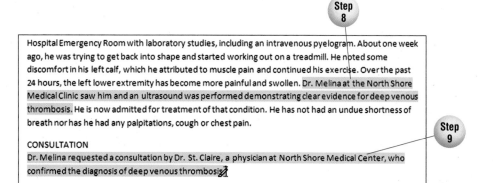

Step 8

Hospital Emergency Room with laboratory studies, including an intravenous pyelogram. About one week ago, he was trying to get back into shape and started working out on a treadmill. He noted some discomfort in his left calf, which he attributed to muscle pain and continued his exercise. Over the past 24 hours, the left lower extremity has become more painful and swollen. Dr. Melina at the North Shore Medical Clinic saw him and an ultrasound was performed demonstrating clear evidence for deep venous thrombosis. He is now admitted for treatment of that condition. He has not had an undue shortness of breath nor has he had any palpitations, cough or chest pain.

CONSULTATION
Dr. Melina requested a consultation by Dr. St. Claire, a physician at North Shore Medical Center, who confirmed the diagnosis of deep venous thrombosis.

Step 9

10 Click the Text Highlight Color button [ab] in the Font group to turn off highlighting.

11 Click the Text Highlight Color button arrow and then click No Color at the palette.

12 Select the sentence *Dr. Melina at the North Shore Medical Clinic saw him and an ultrasound was performed demonstrating clear evidence for deep venous thrombosis.*

This removes the highlighting from the sentence.

Step 11

Calibri (Body) 11 A A

B *I* U abe x₂ x² Aa ab A

Font

HISTORY OF
Mr. Lowell i
thromboph
problems u

No Color
Stop Highlighting

13 Click the Text Highlight Color button arrow and then click the yellow color (first color from the left in the top row).

14 Click the Text Highlight Color button [ab] to turn off highlighting.

15 Click the Save button [💾] on the Quick Access toolbar to save the document.

In Addition

Getting Additional Help

Microsoft Office includes the shortcut key, F1, which you can press to display the Word Help window. Many of the dialog boxes contain a Help button that displays with a question mark and is located in the upper right corner of the dialog box (immediately left of the Close button). Click this button and the Word Help window opens with information pertaining to the dialog box.

Activity 1.8

Changing Document Views

By default, a document generally displays in Print Layout view. You can change this default to Full Screen Reading, Web Layout, Outline, or Draft. You can also change the zoom percentage for viewing a document. In Print Layout view, you can show and/or hide white space at the top and bottom of each page. With the Zoom button in the View tab and the Zoom slider bar on the Status bar, you can change the percentage of display.

Project Your supervisor as well as Dr. Lipinski will be reviewing the History and Physical Examination document so you decide to experiment with various views to determine the best view for reviewing on screen.

1. With **WordMedS1-02.docx** open, press Ctrl + Home to move the insertion point to the beginning of the document and then change to Draft view by clicking the View tab and then clicking the Draft button in the Document Views group.

   You can also change to the Draft view by clicking the Draft button located in the View area near the right side of the Status bar.

2. Click the Print Layout button in the Document Views group.

3. Change the zoom by clicking the Zoom button in the Zoom group in the View tab. At the Zoom dialog box, click *75%* in the *Zoom to* section and then click OK.

   You can also display the Zoom dialog box by clicking the percentage that displays at the left side of the Zoom slider bar.

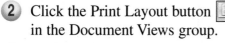

4. Return the view percentage to 100% by positioning the mouse pointer on the button on the Zoom slider bar and then dragging the button to the right until *100%* displays at the left side of the bar.

5. To save space on the screen, you decide to remove the white and blue space that displays at the top and bottom of each page. To do this, position the mouse pointer on the blue space at the top of the page until the pointer turns into the hide white space icon and then double-click the left mouse button.

6. Scroll through the document and then redisplay the white and blue space at the top and bottom of each page. To do this, position the mouse pointer on the black line at the top of the page until the pointer turns into a show white space icon and then double-click the left mouse button.

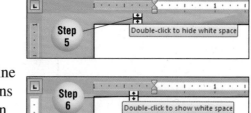

7. Click the Full Screen Reading button in the Document Views group and then navigate in the document using the commands shown in Table W1.5.

   Full Screen Reading view displays a document for easy viewing and reading. You can also display the document in Full Screen Reading view by clicking the Full Screen Reading button located in the View area on the Status bar.

⑧ Return to Print Layout view by clicking the Close button located in the upper right corner of the screen.

⑨ Click the *Document Map* check box in the Show/Hide group in the View tab.

> The navigation pane displays at the left side of the screen and displays the title of the document as well as the initials that display at the end of the document.

⑩ Click the initials *SL:SN* to display the page containing the initials.

⑪ Click the *Document Map* check box to remove the check mark and turn off the display of the navigation pane.

⑫ Press Ctrl + Home, click the *Thumbnails* check box in the Show/Hide group to display miniatures of each page of the document in the navigation pane, and then click the page 2 thumbnail.

⑬ Click the *Thumbnail* check box to turn off the display of the navigation pane.

⑭ Click the Two Pages button ⧉ in the Zoom group to display two pages on the screen and then click the One Page button ⧉ in the Zoom group.

⑮ Click the Page Width button ⧉ in the Zoom group to display the document so the width of the page matches the width of the window.

⑯ Drag the button on the Zoom slider bar or click the Zoom Out button ⊖ or Zoom In button ⊕ until *100%* displays at the left side of the bar.

TABLE W1.5 Navigating in Full Screen Reading View

Press this key	To complete this action
Page Down or spacebar	Move to next page or section.
Page Up or Backspace key	Move to previous page or section.
Right Arrow	Move to next page.
Left Arrow	Move to previous page.
Home	Move to first page in document.
End	Move to last page in document.
Esc	Return to previous view.

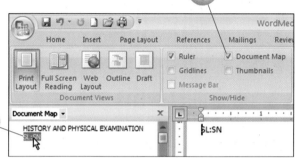

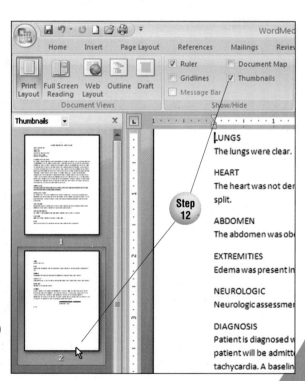

In Brief

Display Draft View
1. Click View tab.
2. Click Draft button in Document Views group.
OR
Click Draft button in View area.

Display Full Screen Reading View
1. Click View tab.
2. Click Full Screen Reading button in Document Views group.
OR
Click Full Screen Reading button in View area.

In Addition

Hiding the Ribbon

If you want to view more of your document on the screen, you can hide the ribbon by double-clicking the active tab. The tabs remain on the screen but the groups and commands are removed. Redisplay the ribbon by double-clicking any tab.

Activity 1.9

Previewing and Printing a Document

Before printing a document, previewing a document may be useful. Word's Print Preview feature displays the document on the screen as it will appear when printed. With this feature, you can view a partial page, single page, multiple pages, or zoom in on a particular area of a page. With the options available at the Print dialog box, you can specify the number of copies to print and also specific pages for printing.

Project
You are ready to print certain sections of the History and Physical Examination document. But first you will preview the document on screen.

1. With **WordMedS1-02.docx** open, press Ctrl + Home to move the insertion point to the beginning of the document.

2. Click the Office button 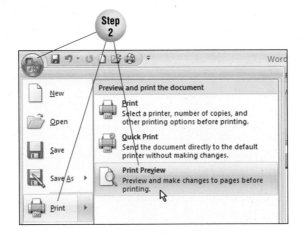, point to *Print*, and then click *Print Preview*.

    This displays the **WordMedS1-02.docx** document in Print Preview.

Step 2

3. Click the Next Page button in the Preview group to display the next page in the document.

4. Click the Two Pages button in the Zoom group to display both pages of the document.

5. Click the One Page button.

6. Click the Close Print Preview button.

7. Display the Print dialog box by clicking the Office button and then clicking *Print* at the drop-down list.

⑧ At the Print dialog box, print only page 2 by clicking in the *Pages* text box in the *Page range* section and then typing **2**.

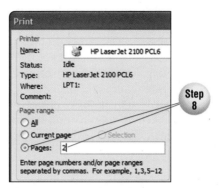

⑨ Click OK.

⑩ Move the insertion point to the beginning of the heading *Name: Samuel Lowell*. Select text from the location of the insertion point to immediately below the paragraph in the HISTORY OF PRESENT ILLNESS section.

⑪ Click the Office button 🔘 and then click *Print* at the drop-down list.

⑫ At the Print dialog box, click the *Selection* option in the *Page range* section.

⑬ Click OK.

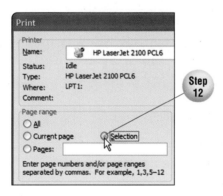

In Addition

Printing a Range of Pages

With the *Pages* option in the *Page range* section of the Print dialog box, you can identify a specific page, multiple pages, and/or a range of pages for printing. If you want specific multiple pages printed, use a comma to indicate *and* and use a hyphen to indicate *through*. For example, to print pages 2 and 5, you would type **2,5** in the *Pages* text box. To print pages 6 through 10, you would type **6-10**. You can print specific pages using both the comma and the hyphen. For example, to print pages 2 and 5 *and* pages 7 through 9, you would type **2,5,7-9**.

Activity 1.10

Inserting the Date, Time, and Quick Parts; Closing a Document

Insert the current date and/or time with options at the Date and Time dialog box. The Date and Time dialog box contains a list of date and time options in the *Available formats* list box. If the *Update automatically* option at the Date and Time dialog box does not contain a check mark, the date and/or time are inserted in the document as normal text that can be edited in the normal manner. You can also insert the date and/or time as a field in a document. The advantage to inserting the date or time as a field is that you can update the field with the Update Field key, F9. Insert the date and/or time as a field by inserting a check mark in the *Update automatically* check box. Word also contains a Quick Parts button with options for inserting pre-designed building blocks to help you build a document.

Project

You are satisfied with the recent revisions to the History and Physical Examination document. You need to identify the document as confidential, insert the date and time, and then close the document.

1. With **WordMedS1-02.docx** open, press Ctrl + End to move the insertion point to the end of the document.

2. Type **Date:** and then press the spacebar once.

3. Click the Insert tab and then click the Date & Time button 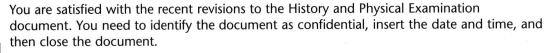 in the Text group.

4. At the Date and Time dialog box, click the third option from the top in the *Available formats* list box. (Your date will vary from what you see below.)

5. Click in the *Update automatically* check box to insert a check mark and then click OK to close the dialog box.

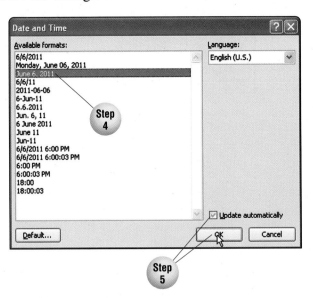

6. Press Shift + Enter, type **Time:**, and then press the spacebar once.

7. Click the Date & Time button.

8 At the Date and Time dialog box, click the option that will insert the time in numbers with the hour, minutes, and seconds (for example, *6:01:48 PM*). Make sure the *Update automatically* check box contains a check mark and then click OK to close the dialog box.

> This option may be the fourteenth or fifteenth from the top in the *Available formats* list box.

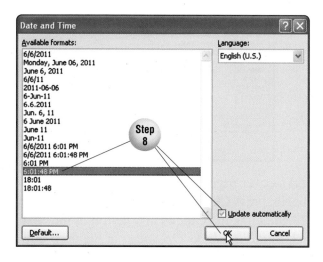

9 Print only page 2 of the document.

10 You want to identify the document as confidential and decide to insert a building block that displays the word *CONFIDENTIAL* as a watermark (a lightened image that displays behind text). To begin, click the Quick Parts button [Quick Parts ▾] in the Text group in the Insert tab and then click *Building Blocks Organizer* at the drop-down list.

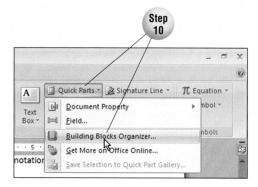

11 At the Building Blocks Organizer dialog box, click the *Gallery* column heading.

> This sorts the building blocks alphabetically by gallery.

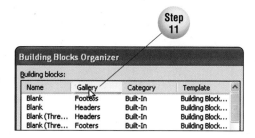

continues

12 Scroll to the end of the list box, click *CONFIDENTIAL 1* in the list box, and then click the Insert button.

> You will not see the entire name of the quick part in the list box. Click a *CONFIDENT* option in this list box and the name of the quick part displays in the lower right corner of the dialog box below the preview section.

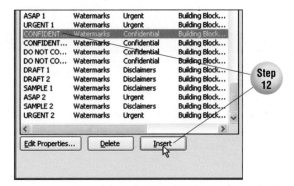

13 You need to insert a cover page for the document and decide to use a predesigned cover page. To begin, press Ctrl + Home to move the insertion point to the beginning of the document, click the Quick Parts button in the Text group in the Insert tab, and then click *Building Blocks Organizer* at the drop-down list.

14 At the Building Blocks Organizer dialog box, click *Cubicles* in the list box and then click the Insert button.

> Make sure you click the *Cubicles* cover page building block that displays *Cover Pages* in the Gallery column.

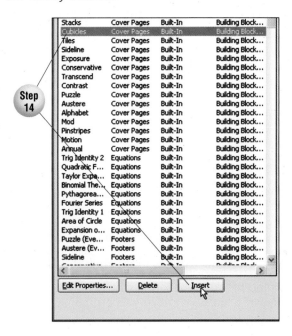

15 Click anywhere in the placeholder text *[Type the company name]* to select it and then type **Columbia River General Hospital**.

16 Click anywhere in the placeholder text *[Type the document title]* and then type **History and Physical Examination**.

17 Click anywhere in the placeholder text *[Type the document subtitle]*, click the placeholder tab, and then press the Delete key.

> Clicking an object tab selects that object.

In Brief

Display Date and Time Dialog Box
1. Click Insert tab.
2. Click Insert Date & Time button.

Display Building Blocks Organizer
1. Click Insert tab.
2. Click Quick Parts button.
3. Click *Building Blocks Organizer*.

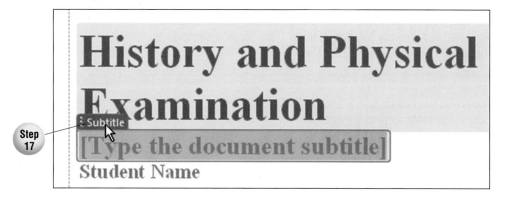

Step 17

History and Physical Examination

Subtitle

[Type the document subtitle]

Student Name

18 Click the text that displays below the title (might be a personal name or a school name), click the placeholder tab, and then type your first and last names.

19 Click anywhere in the placeholder text *[Year]*, click the placeholder tab, and then press the Delete key.

20 Press Ctrl + End to move the insertion point to the end of the document, click anywhere in the time text, and then press F9 to update the time.

> Pressing F9, the Update Field key, updates the time. You can also click the Update tab that displays above the selected time.

21 Click the Save button on the Quick Access toolbar and then click the Quick Print button.

22 Close the document by clicking the Office button and then clicking *Close* at the drop-down list.

In Addition

Sorting Data in the Building Blocks Organizer

The Building Blocks Organizer dialog box provides a single location where you can view all of the pre-designed building blocks available in Word. You can sort the building blocks in the dialog box alphabet- ically by clicking the column heading. For example, to sort building blocks by name, click the *Name* column heading.

Activity 1.11

Creating a Document Using a Template

Word includes a number of template documents formatted for specific uses. Each Word document is based on a template document with the *Normal* template the default. With Word templates, you can easily create a variety of documents such as letters, faxes, and awards, with specialized formatting. Templates are available in the *Templates Categories* section of the New Document dialog box. You can choose an installed template or choose from a variety of templates available online. You must be connected to the Internet to download the online templates.

Project

Your supervisor at North Shore Medical Clinic has asked you to send a letter requesting information on interpreting services.

1. Click the Office button 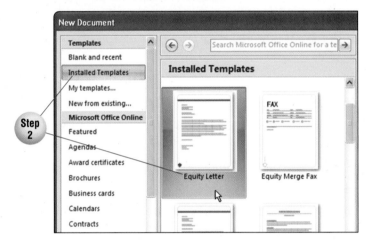 and then click *New* at the drop-down list.

2. At the New Document dialog box, display available templates by clicking *Installed Templates* in the *Templates* section, scroll through the list of installed templates, and then click the *Equity Letter* template.

3. Click the Create button that displays in the lower right corner of the dialog box.

4. Click the placeholder text *[Pick the date]* and then type the current date. (If you use words as part of your date, the date will automatically change to numbers when you click outside the placeholder.)

5. Select the name that displays below the date and then type your first and last names.

6. Click the placeholder text *[Type the sender company name]* and then type **North Shore Medical Clinic**.

7. Click the placeholder text *[Type the sender company address]*, type **7450 Meridian Street, Suite 150**, press the Enter key, and then type **Portland, OR 97202**.

8. Click the placeholder text *[Type the recipient name]* and then type **Community Interpreting Services**.

9. Click the placeholder text *[Type the recipient address]*, type **4525 Lawrence Street**, press the Enter key, and then type **Portland, OR 97216**.

10. Click the placeholder text *[Type the salutation]* and then type **Ladies and Gentlemen:**.

11 Click on any character in the three paragraphs of text in the body of the letter and then type the text shown in Figure W1.3.

12 Click the placeholder text *[Type the closing]* and then type **Sincerely,**.

13 Select the current name below *Sincerely,* and then type your first and last names.

In Brief

Create Document Using Template
1. Click Office button, click *New*.
2. Click *Installed Templates*.
3. Click desired template.
4. Click Create button.

6/7/2011

Student Name
North Shore Medical Clinic
7450 Meridian Street, Suite 150
Portland, OR 97202

Community Interpreting Services
4525 Lawrence Street
Portland, OR 97216

Ladies and Gentlemen:

At North Shore Medical Clinic, our goal is to provide the best possible medical care for our patients. Since some of our patients are non-English speakers, we occasionally need interpreting services. Up to this point, we have been hiring interpreters from various agencies. We recently determined that we would like to contract with one agency to provide all interpreting services at our clinic.

We are interested in learning about all interpreting services available at your agency and would like a representative to contact us to schedule a face-to-face meeting. Please call our clinic at 503-555-2330 and ask for the clinic director. We look forward to working with your agency.

Step 11

14 Click the placeholder text *[Type the sender title]* and then type **Medical Office Assistant**.

15 Click the Save button 💾 on the Quick Access toolbar.

16 At the Save As dialog box, type **WordMedS1-03** and then press Enter.

17 Click the Quick Print button 🖨 on the Quick Access toolbar.

18 Close the document by clicking the Office button 🔘 and then clicking *Close* at the drop-down list.

FIGURE W1.3 Step 11

At North Shore Medical Clinic, our goal is to provide the best possible medical care for our patients. Since some of our patients are non-English speakers, we occasionally need interpreting services. Up to this point, we have been hiring interpreters from various agencies. We recently determined that we would like to contract with one agency to provide all interpreting services at our clinic.

We are interested in learning about all interpreting services available at your agency and would like a representative to contact us to schedule a face-to-face meeting. Please call our clinic at 503-555-2330 and ask for the clinic director. We look forward to working with your agency.

In Addition

Using Online Templates

If you are connected to the Internet, Microsoft offers a number of predesigned templates you can download. Templates are grouped into categories and the category names display in the *Microsoft Office Online* section of the New Document dialog box. Click the desired template category in the list box and available templates display at the right. Click the desired template and then click the Download button.

Activity
1.12

Managing Documents

As you continue working with documents, consider document management tasks such as creating a folder and copying, moving, and deleting documents. You can complete many document management tasks at the Open dialog box on one document or selected documents. By default, Word saves a file as a Word document and adds the extension *.docx* to the name. With the *Save as type* option at the Save As dialog box, you can save a document in a different format such as a Web page, a plain text file, a rich text format, or an earlier version of Word.

Project

To manage your documents, you decide to create a folder for the various types of documents you prepare. You will create a folder named H&P in which you will save all history and physical examination documents.

Columbia River General Hospital

① Click the Open button 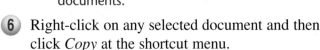 on the Quick Access toolbar.

② At the Open dialog box with WordMedS1 the active folder, click the Create New Folder button on the dialog box toolbar.

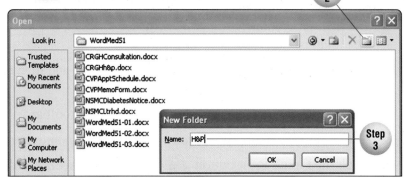

③ At the New Folder dialog box, type **H&P** and then press Enter.

The new folder becomes the active folder.

④ Click the Up One Level button on the Open dialog box toolbar to return to the previous folder.

⑤ Click the document ***CRGHh&p.docx*** in the Open dialog box list box, hold down the Ctrl key, click ***WordMedS1-02.docx***, click ***WordMedS1-03.docx***, and then release the Ctrl key.

Use the Ctrl key to select nonadjacent documents. Use the Shift key to select adjacent documents.

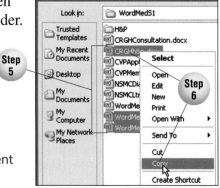

⑥ Right-click on any selected document and then click *Copy* at the shortcut menu.

⑦ Double-click the *H&P* file folder.

File folders display in the *Open dialog box* list box before documents. File folders display preceded by a file folder icon and documents display preceded by a document icon.

⑧ Position the mouse pointer in a white portion of the *Open dialog box* list box, click the *right* mouse button, and then click *Paste* at the shortcut menu.

The copied documents are inserted in the H&P folder.

9 You need to send the **WordMedS1-02.docx** document to a colleague that uses Word 2003, so you need to save the document in that format. At the Open dialog box with the H&P folder active, double-click *WordMedS1-02.docx*.

10 Click the Office button and then click *Save As*. At the Save As dialog box, type **WordMedS1-02Wd2003** in the *File name* text box.

11 Click the down-pointing arrow at the right side of the *Save as type* list box and then click *Word 97-2003 Document (*.doc)*.

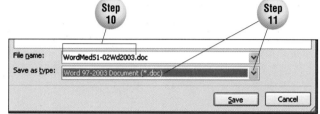

You can also save a document in Word 2003 format by clicking the Office button, pointing to the *Save As* option, and then clicking *Word 97-2003 Document*.

12 Click the Save button located in the lower right corner of the dialog box and then close the document.

If a compatibility checker message displays, click the Continue button.

13 Display the Open dialog box and then click the Up One Level button on the dialog box toolbar.

14 Rename the H&P folder. To do this, right-click on the folder name and then click *Rename* at the shortcut menu. Type **H&PEDocs** and then press Enter.

The new folder name replaces the original folder name. You can also rename a folder by clicking the Tools button, clicking *Rename*, and then typing the new folder name.

15 Delete the H&PEDocs folder by clicking once on the folder to select it and then clicking the Delete button on the dialog box toolbar. At the message asking if you are sure you want to delete the folder and all its contents, click the Yes button.

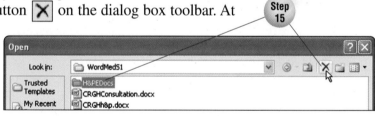

16 Close the Open dialog box.

17 Exit Word by clicking the Close button located in the upper right corner of the screen.

You can also exit Word by clicking the Office button and then clicking the Exit Word button.

In Brief

Create Folder
1. Click Open button on Quick Access toolbar.
2. Click Create New Folder button.
3. Type folder name.
4. Press Enter.

Save Document in Different Format
1. Open document.
2. Click Office button, *Save As*.
3. Type document name.
4. Change *Save as type* option to desired format.
5. Click Save button.

In Addition

Saving a Document for Viewing but Not Editing

If you want to send a document to someone so they can view it but not edit it, consider saving the document in the PDF or XPS file format or as a Web page. Documents saved in the PDF and XPS file formats can be viewed in a variety of software and these formats preserve the page layout of the document. Save a document as a Web page and the document can be viewed in a Web browser. This format, however, does not preserve the page layout of the document.

Features Summary

Feature	Ribbon Tab, Group	Button	Quick Access Toolbar	Office Button Drop-down List	Keyboard Shortcut
AutoCorrect dialog box				Word Options, Proofing, AutoCorrect Options	
close				Close	Ctrl + F4
date	Insert, Text	Date & Time			Shift + Alt + D
Document Map	View, Show/Hide	✔ Document Map			
Draft view	View, Document Views				
exit Word		✖		Exit Word	
Full Screen Reading view	View, Document Views				
Help		⊘			F1
new document			🗋	New, Blank document	Ctrl + N
New Document dialog box				New	
open			📂	Open	Ctrl + O
Print dialog box				Print	Ctrl + P
print document			🖨		
Print Layout view	View, Document Views				
Print Preview				Print, Print Preview	
Quick Parts	Insert, Text	Quick Parts ▾			
redo an action			↻		
Save As dialog box				Save As	F12
save document			💾		Ctrl + S
Spelling & Grammar	Review, Proofing	ABC			F7
Thesaurus	Review, Proofing	Thesaurus			Shift + F7
thumbnails	View, Show/Hide	✔ Thumbnails			
time	Insert, Text	Date & Time			Shift + Alt + T
undo an action			↺ ▾		
Word Options dialog box				Word Options	

Knowledge Check

Completion: In the space provided at the right, write in the correct term, command, or option.

1. This button displays as a Microsoft Office logo.

2. This toolbar contains buttons for commonly used commands.

3. This area on the screen contains tabs and commands divided into groups.

4. Use this keyboard command to move the insertion point to the beginning of the document.

5. To select a sentence, hold down this key and then click anywhere in the sentence.

6. To begin checking the spelling and grammar in a document, click this tab and then click the Spelling & Grammar button in the Proofing group.

7. This feature automatically detects and corrects some typographical errors.

8. Use this feature to find synonyms for a word.

9. Display a document in this view for easy viewing and reading.

10. The Print Layout button is located in this group in the View tab.

11. Predesigned cover pages and watermarks are located in this dialog box.

12. Available templates display in this dialog box.

13. Click this button on the Open dialog box toolbar to display the New Folder dialog box.

14. Select nonadjacent documents at the Open dialog box by holding down this key while clicking each document.

Skills Review

Review 1   Moving the Insertion Point, Scrolling, and Inserting Text

1. Open **CRGHConsultation.docx**.
2. Save the document with Save As and name it **WordMedS1-R1**.
3. Practice moving the insertion point to the following locations:
   a. Move the insertion point to the end of the document.
   b. Move the insertion point back to the beginning of the document.
   c. Scroll to the end of the document.
   d. Scroll back to the beginning of the document.
   e. Move the insertion point to the beginning of the second page.
   f. Move the insertion point to the beginning of the document.
4. Move the insertion point to the beginning of the date *04/25/2011* located toward the beginning of the document, type **Date of Admission:**, and then press the spacebar once.
5. Move the insertion point to the beginning of the date *06/05/1936*, type **Date of Birth:**, and then press the spacebar once.
6. Save **WordMedS1-R1.docx**.

Review 2   Selecting and Deleting Text

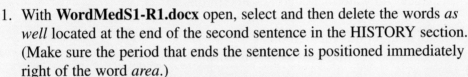

1. With **WordMedS1-R1.docx** open, select and then delete the words *as well* located at the end of the second sentence in the HISTORY section. (Make sure the period that ends the sentence is positioned immediately right of the word *area*.)
2. Select and then delete the words *was brought to the Emergency Room by her husband and* located in the fourth sentence in the HISTORY section.
3. Select and then delete the sentence *Review of systems is unremarkable* (the second paragraph in the HISTORY section).
4. Undo the deletion.
5. Redo the deletion.
6. Select and then delete the last sentence in the HISTORY section (*The rest of her social and family history is noted on the admission report.*).
7. Undo the deletion.
8. Deselect the text.
9. Save **WordMedS1-R1.docx**.

Review 3   Checking the Spelling and Grammar in a Document

1. With **WordMedS1-R1.docx** open, move the insertion point to the beginning of the document.
2. Complete a spelling and grammar check on the document. (The following medical terms are spelled correctly: *intertrochanteric, trochanter, nontender,* and *ecchymosis*.)
3. Save **WordMedS1-R1.docx**.

Review 4 Creating an AutoCorrect Entry; Using Thesaurus; Inserting the Date and Time and a Cover Page

Columbia River General Hospital

1. With **WordMedS1-R1.docx** open, add the following to the AutoCorrect dialog box: insert *ic* in the *Replace* text box and *intertrochanteric* in the *With* text box and insert *tr* in the *Replace* text box and *trochanter* in the *With* text box.
2. Move the insertion point to the blank line above the RECOMMENDATIONS heading (below the EXAMINATION section) and then type the text shown in Figure W1.4. ***Hint: Press Shift + Enter after typing X-RAY and after typing IMPRESSION.***
3. Use Thesaurus and make the following changes:
   a. Change *aware* in the first sentence of the EXAMINATION section to *alert*.
   b. Change *unidentified* located toward the end of the HISTORY section to *unknown*.
4. Move the insertion point to the end of the document, insert the current date (you choose the format), press Shift + Enter, and then insert the current time (you choose the format).
5. Delete the AutoCorrect entries for *ic* and *tr*.
6. Insert the *Stacks* cover page. ***Hint: Choose the Stacks cover page at the Building Blocks Organizer dialog box.***
7. Click in the placeholder text *[Type the document title]* and then type **Consultation Report**.
8. Click in the placeholder text *[Type the document subtitle]* and then type **ID# 09232**.
9. Select the name that displays below the subtitle and then type your first and last names.
10. Save, print, and then close **WordMedS1-R1.docx**.

FIGURE W1.4 Review 4

X-RAY
Review of x-rays demonstrates a comminuted right ic hip fracture with comminution of the greater tr, as well as lesser tr.

IMPRESSION
Right comminuted ic hip fracture, noninsulin dependent diabetes mellitus, and hypercholesterolemia.

Review 5 Creating a Fax Using a Template

North Shore Medical Clinic

1. Use the Equity Fax template (located in the *Installed Templates* section of the New document dialog box with *Installed Templates* selected; you may need to scroll down the list to display this template) and then type text in placeholders as indicated:
   a. *[Type the recipient name]*   = **Andres Diaz**
   b. Select the text that displays after the *From:* heading and then type your first and last names.
   c. *[Type the recipient fax number]*   = **503-555-0988**
   d. *[Type number of pages]*   = **Cover page plus 1 page**
   e. *[Type the recipient phone number]* = **503-555-0900**
   f. *[Pick the date]*   = **05.28.2011**
   g. *[Type text]* (located after *Re:*)   = **Interpreting Services and Fees**
   h. Click the *[Type text]* placeholder that displays after *CC:*, click the placeholder tab, and then delete the placeholder.
   i. Click in the square that displays immediately left of *Please Comment* and then type the letter **X**.

j. *[Type comments]* = **Interpreting services and fees are shown on the following document.**

2. Save the completed fax and name it **WordMedS1-R2**.
3. Print and then close **WordMedS1-R2.docx**.

Skills Assessment

Assessment 1 Inserting Text in a Document

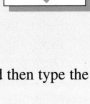

1. Open **NSMCDiabetesNotice.docx**.
2. Save the document with Save As and name it **WordMedS1-A1**.
3. In the first paragraph of text, make the following changes:
   a. Change the day from *Thursday* to *Wednesday*.
   b. Change the date from *20* to *19*.
   c. Change the time from *7:30 to 9:00* to *7:00 to 8:30*.
4. Press Ctrl + End to move the insertion point to the end of the document and then type the information shown in Figure W1.5.
5. Save, print, and then close **WordMedS1-A1.docx**.

FIGURE W1.5 Assessment 1

> The presentation will include information on the prevalence of diabetes among people of different age and ethnic groups, health complications related to diabetes, and treatment and prevention of diabetes. For more information on the presentation, please contact Lee Elliott.

Assessment 2 Preparing a Memo

1. Open **CVPMemoForm.docx**.
2. Save the document with Save As and name it **WordMedS1-A2**.
3. Insert the following information after the specified heading:

To:	**All Front Office Staff**
From:	**Sydney Larsen, Office Manager**
Date:	(Insert current date)
Re:	**Well-child Checkup Appointments**

4. Move the insertion point below the *Re:* heading and then write the body of the memo using the following information (write the information in paragraph form—do not use bullets):
   • With the recent hiring of Dr. Joseph Yarborough, pediatric specialist, we will be scheduling additional well-child checkup appointments.
   • Schedule appointments at the ages of 2 weeks and 2, 4, 6, 12, 18, and 24 months.
   • Appointment length is generally 20 minutes.
   • Schedule well-child checkup appointments for Dr. Yarborough on Tuesdays and Thursdays.
   • Evening hours for appointments with Dr. Yarborough will be added next month.
5. Complete a spelling and grammar check on the memo.
6. Save, print, and then close **WordMedS1-A2.docx**.

Assessment 3 Adding Text to a Clinic Patient Information Document

1. Open **CVPApptSchedule.docx**.
2. Save the document with Save As and name it **WordMedS1-A3**.
3. Create an AutoCorrect entry that inserts *Appointments* when you type *Aps*.
4. Insert the following text in the document:
   a. Move the insertion point to the beginning of the second paragraph (begins with *These are short visits . . .*), type **Acute Illness Aps (20 minutes)**, and then press Shift + Enter. (The AutoCorrect feature will insert *Appointments* when you press the spacebar after typing *Aps*.)
   b. Move the insertion point to the beginning of the paragraph that begins *These appointments, available within one week . . .* , type **Routine Aps (20 minutes)**, and then press Shift + Enter.
   c. Move the insertion point to the beginning of the paragraph that begins *Physical examination appointments are usually . . .* , type **Physical Examination Aps (30 minutes)**, and then press Shift + Enter.
   d. Move the insertion point to the beginning of the paragraph that begins *All children should be seen . . .* , type **Well-child Checkup Aps (20 minutes)**, and then press Shift + Enter.
5. Complete a spelling and grammar check on the document.
6. Move the insertion point to the end of the document and then insert the current date and time.
7. Delete the AutoCorrect entry *Aps*.
8. Insert the DRAFT 1 watermark
9. Save, print, and then close **WordMedS1-A3.docx**.

Assessment 4 Locating Online Training Resources

1. Display the Word Help window, scroll to the end of the window, and then click the *Training* hyperlink that displays below the heading *More on Office Online*. (If this heading does not appear in your window, click the Connection Status button in the lower right corner of the Help window and then click *Show content from Office Online*.)
2. Look at the Microsoft Office Online training home page and learn about the available training resources.
3. Using the information you learn, prepare a memo to your instructor describing at least three interesting training resources available at the Web page.
4. Save the memo and name it **WordMedS1-A4**.
5. Print and then close **WordMedS1-A4.docx**.

Assessment 5 Researching a Company Selling a Medical Spell Checking Dictionary

1. As you learned in Activity 1.5, the Word standard spell checking dictionary does not contain many medical terms. Most medical offices, clinics, and hospitals that prepare medical documents and forms add a supplemental medical spell checking dictionary. One of the most popular is Stedman's. As the medical office assistant at North Shore Medical Clinic, your supervisor has asked you to locate information about the Stedman's

medical spell checking dictionary. Using the Internet, go to the Stedman home page at www.stedmans.com. (If this Web site is not available, search for another company that sells a medical spell checking dictionary and visit the company's home page.)

2. After looking at the information at the Stedman's Web site, prepare a memo to your supervisor, Lee Elliott, Office Manager, and include information on the medical dictionary including Web address, price, features, and how to order.
3. Save the completed memo and name it **WordMedS1-A5**.
4. Print and then close **WordMedS1-A5.docx**.

Marquee Challenge

Challenge 1 Preparing a Presurgery Letter to Doctor

1. Open **NSMCLtrhd.docx** and then save the document with Save As and name it **WordMedS1-C1**.
2. Type the letter as shown in Figure W1.6.
3. Save, print, and then close **WordMedS1-C1.docx**.

Challenge 2 Preparing a Patient Chart Note

1. Open **NSMCLtrhd.docx** and then save the document with Save As and name it **WordMedS1-C2**.
2. Type the chart notes as shown in Figure W1.7.
3. Save, print, and then close **WordMedS1-C2.docx**.

FIGURE W1.6 Challenge 1

North Shore Medical Clinic
7450 Meridian Street, Suite 150
Portland, OR 97202
(503) 555-2330

Date: _____

Dear Doctor _____:

Our mutual patient _____, D.O.B _____, is scheduled for
surgery on _____. Please assist us by providing the following information:

      Pathology report
      Copy of most recent EKG
      New lab work (Basic Metabolic Panel, HCT/Hemoglobin, Protime/INR, K+)
      Clearance for surgery

The surgeon would like the patient to stop Coumadin as soon as possible prior to surgery. Please let us
know if instructing the patient to do so is safe and how long the patient can be off the medication.

Please fax requested information to us as soon as possible. Our fax number is (503) 555-2335. If you
have any questions, please call the clinic at (503) 555-2330.

Sincerely,

Darrin Lancaster, CMA
Medical Assistant

WordMedS1-C1.docx

North Shore Medical Clinic
7450 Meridian Street, Suite 150
Portland, OR 97202
(503) 555-2330

PATIENT: Grace Montgomery
DATE OF VISIT: 04/07/2011

SUBJECTIVE
Patient is complaining of itching and a rash that began about three weeks ago, starting on the hands and arms and spreading to the chest and back. She is currently taking Benadryl at bedtime with little relief. She stated that she has tried a new perfume after her shower for the past three or four days.

OBJECTIVE
GENERAL APPEARANCE: Normal.
VITAL SIGNS: Temperature 98.6 degrees, blood pressure 140/74, weight 145, height 5 feet 6 inches, heart rate 74, respirations 22.
SKIN: Patient has a smooth, erythematous rash over her neck extending over her trunk and back. She has a confluent, erythematous rash extending to fingertips on her upper extremities. Wheals with petechiae are noted in the antecubital fossae bilaterally.

ASSESSMENT
Contact dermatitis, secondary to allergy to perfume.

PLAN
Avoid use of any perfume or perfumed soap.
Wash or dry-clean all clothing and linens exposed to suspected perfume.
Take diphenhydramine (Benadryl) 25 mg q6 h x 3 days.

_____

Jonathon Melina, MD

JM:SN

Date: (Insert current date)
Time: (Insert current time)

Word SECTION 2

Formatting Characters and Paragraphs

Skills

- Apply fonts and font effects
- Use Format Painter
- Repeat a command
- Align text in paragraphs
- Indent text
- Change line and paragraph spacing
- Insert bullets and numbering
- Insert symbols and special characters
- Set tabs and tabs with leaders
- Add borders and shading to text
- Insert a page border
- Apply styles and Quick Styles sets

Projects Overview

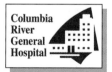
Edit and format a document on heart disease.

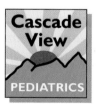
Edit and format a document on well-child checkup appointment recommendations and suggestions and prepare a document containing information on clinic hours.

Edit and format a document on diabetes, edit and format a document on how to request medical records, prepare a letter to the local community college indicating the availability of an internship, prepare a memo describing Word features, prepare a job announcement, and prepare a flyer advertising a free diabetes presentation.

Activity 2.1

Applying Formatting with the Font Group and the Mini Toolbar

The appearance of a document in the document screen and how it looks when printed is called the *format*. Use buttons in the Font group in the Home tab to apply character formatting to text. The top row contains buttons for changing the font and font size and increasing and decreasing the size of the font. The bottom row contains buttons for applying formatting such as bold, italics, underlining, superscript, and subscript. The default font used by Word is Calibri. Change this default with the Font button in the Font group. Microsoft Word has taken some commonly used commands and placed them on the Mini toolbar. The Mini toolbar displays in a faded manner when you select text and then becomes solid when you point to it.

Project

Your supervisor at Columbia River General Hospital has asked you to format and edit an informational document on heart disease. You decide to improve the appearance of the document by applying different types of fonts and effects to the text.

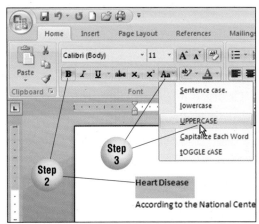

1. Open **CRGHHeartDisease.docx** and then save the document and name it **WordMedS2-01**.

2. Select *Heart Disease* and then click the Bold button **B** in the Font group in the Home tab.

3. With *Heart Disease* still selected, click the Change Case button **Aa** in the Font group and then click *UPPERCASE* at the drop-down list.

   Use options at the Change Case drop-down list to specify the case of selected text.

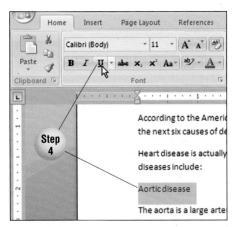

4. Select *Aortic disease* and then click the Underline button **U** in the Font group.

5. Select and then underline the remaining headings: *Arrhythmia (abnormal heart rhythm), Cardiomyopathy (heart muscle disease), Congenital heart disease, Coronary artery disease, Heart failure, Heart valve disease, Pericardial disease,* and *Vascular disease*.

6. Select the words *abnormal heart rhythm* located in the parentheses after the word *Arrhythmia*, point to the Mini toolbar that displays above the selected text, and then click the Italic button **I** on the Mini toolbar.

   The Mini toolbar displays in a faded manner until you point to it and then it becomes solid. The toolbar disappears when you move the mouse pointer away from it and when you click a button on the toolbar.

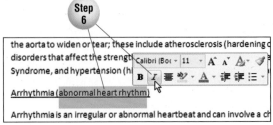

7. Select the words *heart muscle disease* located in the parentheses after the word *Cardiomyopathy* and then click the Italic button *I* on the Mini toolbar.

8. Select the entire document by clicking the Select button in the Editing group in the Home tab and then clicking *Select All* at the drop-down list.

9. Click the Font button arrow in the Font group. Hover the mouse pointer over various typefaces in the drop-down gallery and notice how the text in the document reflects the selected font.

> This feature is referred to as **live preview** and provides you with an opportunity to see how the document will appear with font formatting before making a final choice.

10. Scroll down the gallery and then click *Times New Roman*.

11. Click the Font Size button arrow and then click *12* at the drop-down gallery.

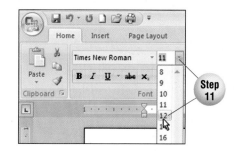

12. Click the Font Color button arrow and then click *Dark Blue* at the color gallery (second color from the *right* in the *Standard Colors* row).

13. Deselect the text by clicking in the document outside of selected text.

14. Save and then print **WordMedS2-01.docx**.

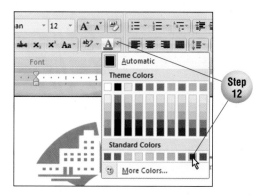

In Addition

Using Typefaces

A typeface is a set of characters with a common design and shape and can be decorative or plain and either monospaced or proportional. Word refers to typeface as **font**. A monospaced typeface allots the same amount of horizontal space for each character while a proportional typeface allots a varying amount of space for each character. Proportional typefaces are divided into two main categories: **serif** and **sans serif**. A serif is a small line at the end of a character stroke. Consider using a serif typeface for text-intensive documents because the serifs help move the reader's eyes across the page. Use a sans serif typeface for headings, headlines, and advertisements. Microsoft Word 2007 includes six new typefaces designed for extended on-screen reading. These typefaces include the default, Calibri, as well as Cambria, Candara, Consolas, Constantia, and Corbel. Calibri, Candara, and Corbel are sans serif typefaces; Cambria and Constantia are serif typefaces; and Consolas is monospaced.

Activity 2.2

Using the Font Dialog Box and Format Painter; Repeating a Command

In addition to buttons in the Font group, you can apply font formatting with options at the Font dialog box. With options at this dialog box, you can change the font, font size, and font style; change the font color; choose an underlining style; and apply formatting effects. Once you apply font formatting to text, you can copy that formatting to different locations in the document using the Format Painter. If you apply formatting to text in a document and then want to apply the same formatting to other text, use the Repeat command. Repeat a command by pressing the F4 function key.

Project The changes you made to the heart disease document have enhanced the readability and visual appeal of the text. Now you will turn your attention to the headings.

1. With **WordMedS2-01.docx** open, press Ctrl + Home to move the insertion point to the beginning of the page and then select the entire document by pressing Ctrl + A.

    Ctrl + A is the keyboard shortcut to select the entire document.

2. Click the Font group dialog box launcher.

    The dialog box launcher displays as a small button containing a diagonal arrow.

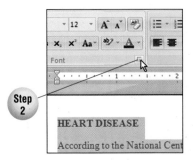

3. At the Font dialog box, click *Cambria* in the *Font* list box (you will need to scroll up the list box to display this option) and then click *11* in the *Size* list box.

4. Click the down-pointing arrow at the right side of the *Font color* option and then click *Black, Text 1* (second choice from the left in the top row).

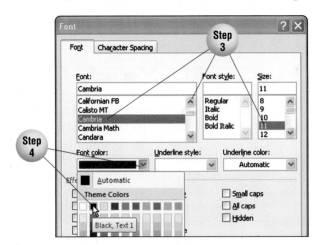

5 Click OK to close the dialog box.

6 Select the heading *HEART DISEASE* that displays towards the beginning of the document and then click the Font group dialog box launcher.

7 At the Font dialog box, click *Candara* in the *Font* list box (you will need to scroll down the list box to display this option), click *14* in the *Size* list box (you will need to scroll down the list box to display *14*), and then click *Shadow* in the *Effects* section.

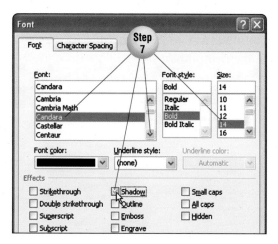

8 Click OK to close the Font dialog box.

9 With the heading still selected, click once on the Format Painter button in the Clipboard group in the Home tab.

> When Format Painter is active, the mouse pointer displays with a paintbrush attached.

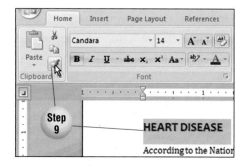

continues

10 Scroll down the document and then select the heading *HEART DISEASE FACTS*.

> Since you clicked once on the Format Painter button, selecting the heading will apply the formatting from the first heading and also turn off Format Painter.

11 Select the heading *Aortic disease* and then click the Font group dialog box launcher.

12 Click *Candara* in the *Font* list box (you will need to scroll down the list box to display this option), click *Bold* in the *Font style* list box, and then click *14* in the *Size* list box (you will need to scroll down the list box to display *14*).

13 Click the down-pointing arrow at the right side of the *Underline style* option and then click *(none)* at the drop-down list.

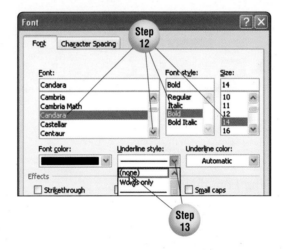

14 Click OK to close the dialog box and then deselect the heading.

15 Click once on any character in the heading *Aortic disease* and then double-click the Format Painter button ![icon] in the Clipboard group in the Home tab.

> When Format Painter is active, the mouse pointer displays with a paintbrush attached.

16 Select the heading *Arrhythmia (abnormal heart rhythm)*.

> With Format Painter active, selecting text applies formatting.

17 Select individually the remaining headings *Cardiomyopathy (heart muscle disease), Congenital heart disease, Coronary artery disease, Heart failure, Heart valve disease, Pericardial disease,* and *Vascular disease.*

18 Click once on the Format Painter button ⬚ in the Clipboard group to turn off Format Painter.

19 Select the text *National Center for Chronic Disease Prevention and Health Promotion* located in the first paragraph of text and then click the Font group dialog box launcher.

20 At the Font dialog box, click *Shadow* in the *Effects* section and then click OK to close the dialog box.

21 Select the text *American Heart Association* that displays in the second paragraph and then press the F4 function key.

> Pressing F4 repeats the previous command and applies the shadow effect to selected text.

22 Select the text *Marfan Syndrome* located in the first paragraph in the *Aortic disease* section and then press F4.

23 Save **WordMedS2-01.docx**.

In Addition

Font Keyboard Shortcuts

Along with buttons in the Font group and the Font dialog box, you can apply character formatting with the following keyboard shortcuts.

Font Group Button	Keyboard Shortcut	Font Group Button	Keyboard Shortcut
Font	Ctrl + Shift + F	Italic	Ctrl + I
Font Size	Ctrl + Shift + P	Underline	Ctrl + U
Grow Font	Ctrl + >	Subscript	Ctrl + =
Shrink Font	Ctrl + <	Superscript	Ctrl + Shift + +
Bold	Ctrl + B	Change Case	Shift + F3

Activity 2.3

Aligning Text in Paragraphs

Paragraphs of text in a document are aligned at the left margin by default. This default alignment can be changed to center alignment (used for titles, headings, or other text you want centered), right-aligned (used for addresses, date, time, or other text you want aligned at the right margin), and justified (used for text you want aligned at both the left and right margins such as text in a report or book). Change paragraph alignment with buttons in the Paragraph group in the Home tab, the *Alignment* option at the Paragraph dialog box, or with shortcut keys. You can use the keyboard shortcut Ctrl + Q to remove formatting from the paragraph in which the insertion point is located. If you want to remove character formatting and paragraph formatting from selected text, click the Clear Formatting button in the Font group in the Home tab.

Project

You decide to improve the appearance of the heart disease document by changing text alignment.

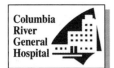
Columbia River General Hospital

1. With **WordMedS2-01.docx** open, center the title *HEART DISEASE* by positioning the insertion point on any character in the title and then clicking the Center button in the Paragraph group in the Home tab.

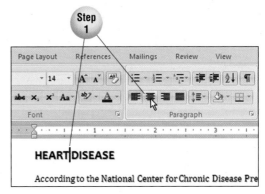
Step 1

2. Click on any character in the title *HEART DISEASE FACTS* (located toward the middle of page 2 after the *HEART DISEASE* section) and then click the Center button.

3. Press Ctrl + Home to move to the beginning of the document and then select from the middle of the paragraph *Heart disease is actually a number of…* (third paragraph in the document) to the end of the document.

   The entire paragraph does not have to be selected, only a portion.

4. Click the Justify button in the Paragraph group.

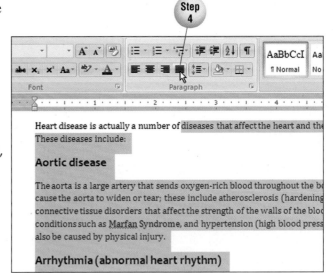
Step 4

5. Move the insertion point to any character in the title *HEART DISEASE FACTS* and then click the Center button.

   When you justified the text, the *HEART DISEASE FACTS* title was moved to the left.

6. Press Ctrl + End to move the insertion point to the end of the document and then press the Enter key.

7. Click the Center button in the Paragraph group.

8. Click the Bold button in the Font group to turn on bold formatting, type your first and last names, and then click the Bold button to turn off bold formatting.

9 Press Shift + Enter.

10 Type **Date:**, press the spacebar, and then press Alt + Shift + D.

Alt + Shift + D is the shortcut key to insert the current date.

11 Press Shift + Enter, type **Time:**, press the spacebar, and then press Alt + Shift + T.

Alt + Shift + T is the shortcut key to insert the current time.

12 Press the Enter key.

13 Remove the center paragraph formatting (returning to left alignment) by pressing the shortcut key Ctrl + Q.

When you press Ctrl + Q, paragraph formatting such as line spacing and paragraph spacing is removed from the selected text.

14 After looking at the centered text you just typed, you decide to remove the formatting and try other formatting. To do this, first select the three lines of text you just typed.

15 Click the Clear Formatting button 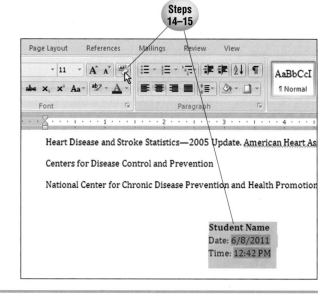 in the Font group in the Home tab.

The Clear Formatting button removes any paragraph formatting and character formatting applied to the text. Since you pressed Ctrl + Q in Step 13, paragraph formatting was removed from the selected text. Clicking the Clear Formatting button also removed character formatting.

16 With the three lines still selected, click the Align Text Right button in the Paragraph group, click the Font button arrow and click *Candara* at the drop-down gallery, and then click the Font Size button arrow and click *10* at the drop-down gallery.

17 Deselect the text and then save **WordMedS2-01.docx**.

In Addition

Options for Changing Alignment

You can change paragraph alignment with the *Alignment* option at the Paragraph dialog box. Display the Paragraph dialog box by clicking the Paragraph group dialog box launcher. At the Paragraph dialog box, click the down-pointing arrow at the right of the *Alignment* option and then click the desired alignment at the drop-down list. You can also change alignment with the following shortcut keys:

Alignment	Keyboard Shortcut
Left	Ctrl + L
Center	Ctrl + E
Right	Ctrl + R
Justified	Ctrl + J

Activity 2.4

Indenting Text

To draw attention to specific text in a document, consider indenting the text. Indenting might include indenting the first line of text in a paragraph, indenting all lines of text in a paragraph, and indenting the second and subsequent lines of a paragraph (called a hanging indent). Several methods are available for indenting text including buttons in the Paragraph group in the Home tab, markers on the Ruler, options at the Paragraph dialog box with the Indents and Spacing tab selected, and shortcut keys.

Project

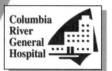

You have decided to highlight certain paragraphs of information in the heart disease document to improve the visual appearance. Indenting seems preferable to other formatting choices such as changing the font.

1. With **WordMedS2-01.docx** open, click anywhere in the paragraph below the *Aortic disease* heading.

2. Position the mouse pointer on the Left Indent marker on the Ruler, shown in Figure W2.1, hold down the left mouse button, drag the marker to the 0.5-inch mark on the Ruler, and then release the mouse button.

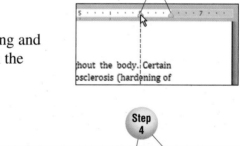

> A ScreenTip displays with *Left Indent* in a box when you position the mouse pointer on the Left Indent marker. To position a marker on the Ruler at a precise measurement, hold down the Alt key while dragging the marker.

FIGURE W2.1 Ruler Indent Markers

First Line Indent | Left Indent | Hanging Indent | Right Indent

3. Drag the Right Indent marker on the Ruler to the 6-inch mark.

4. Click anywhere in the paragraph below the *Arrhythmia (abnormal heart rhythm)* heading and then click the Increase Indent button in the Paragraph group in the Home tab.

> This indents text 0.5 inches from the left margin.

5. Drag the Right Indent marker on the Ruler to the 6-inch mark.

6. Click anywhere in the paragraph below *Cardiomyopathy (heart muscle disease)* and then click the Page Layout tab. In the *Indent* section in the Paragraph group, click in the *Left* text box and then type **0.5**. Click the up-pointing arrow at the right side of the *Right* text box until *0.5"* displays.

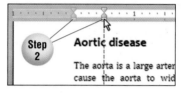

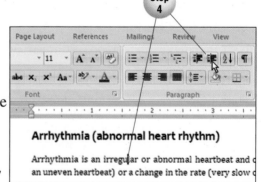

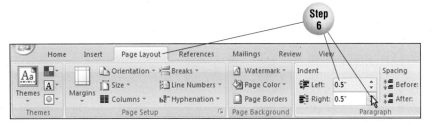

(7) Click anywhere in the paragraph below the *Congenital heart disease* heading and then change the left and right indents using the Paragraph dialog box. To begin, click the Paragraph group dialog box launcher.

(8) At the Paragraph dialog box, click the up-pointing arrow at the right of the *Left* option in the *Indentation* section until *0.5″* displays in the text box.

(9) Click the up-pointing arrow at the right of the *Right* option in the *Indentation* section until *0.5″* displays in the text box.

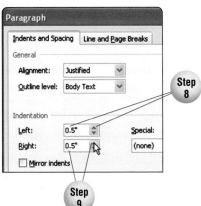

(10) Click OK to close the Paragraph dialog box.

(11) Click anywhere in the paragraph below the *Coronary artery disease* heading and then press F4.

(12) Indent the paragraph of text below each of the headings *Heart failure, Heart valve disease, Pericardial disease,* and *Vascular disease* by clicking in each paragraph and then pressing F4.

(13) Click anywhere in the first paragraph of text below the title *HEART DISEASE* (the paragraph that begins *According to the National Center for Heart Disease*).

(14) Drag the First Line Indent marker to the 0.5-inch mark on the Ruler and then drag the Hanging Indent marker to the 1-inch mark on the Ruler.

> This creates a hanging indent paragraph.

(15) Click anywhere in the second paragraph of text below the title *HEART DISEASE*, click the Home tab, click the Increase Indent button in the Paragraph group, and then press Ctrl + T.

> Ctrl + T is the keyboard shortcut to create a hanging indent paragraph. For additional keyboard shortcuts, refer to the In Addition at the bottom of this page.

(16) Save **WordMedS2-01.docx**.

In Addition

Indenting Text Using Keyboard Shortcuts

Indentation	Keyboard Shortcut
Indent text from left margin	Ctrl + M
Decrease indent from left margin	Ctrl + Shift + M
Create a hanging indent	Ctrl + T
Remove hanging indent	Ctrl + Shift + T

Activity 2.5

Changing Line and Paragraph Spacing

By default, line spacing is set at 1.15. This default line spacing can be changed with the Line spacing button in the Paragraph group in the Home tab, keyboard shortcuts, or with the *Line spacing* and *At* options at the Paragraph dialog box. Control spacing above and below paragraphs with options at the Line spacing button drop-down list, the Spacing Before and Spacing After buttons in the Paragraph group in the Page Layout tab, or with the *Before* and/or *After* options at the Paragraph dialog box with the Indents and Spacing tab selected. Word contains a number of predesigned formats grouped into style sets called Quick Styles. Some of these styles display in the Styles group in the Home tab. With the No Spacing style, you can remove some of the default formatting in a Word document. Either click the No Spacing style and then type text or select text and then click the No Spacing style. Clicking the No Spacing style changes the line spacing to 1, removes spacing after paragraphs, and removes any character formatting applied to selected text.

Project

Your supervisor needs the heart disease document in a few hours. You decide to make a few spacing changes in the document before printing the final version.

1. With **WordMedS2-01.docx** open, select the entire document by pressing Ctrl + A.

2. Click the Line spacing button in the Paragraph group in the Home tab and then click *1.5* at the drop-down list.

3. Deselect the text and then scroll through the document. After viewing the document in 1.5 line spacing, you decide to decrease the line spacing to 1.3. To begin, press Ctrl + A to select the entire document, click the Line spacing button, and then click *Line Spacing Options* at the drop-down list.

4. Type **1.3** in the *At* text box in the *Spacing* section of the Paragraph dialog box.

   > The Paragraph dialog box also contains a *Line spacing* option. Click the down-pointing arrow at the right side of the option and a drop-down list displays with spacing choices.

5. Click OK to close the dialog box and then deselect the text.

6. You decide to single space the text in the *HEART DISEASE FACTS* section. To do this, select from the beginning of the heading *HEART DISEASE FACTS* to the end of the document.

7. Click the Line spacing button and then click *1.0* at the drop-down list.

   > Choosing this option changes the line spacing to single for the selected paragraphs of text. You can also change line spacing with keyboard shortcuts. Press Ctrl + 1 to change to single spacing, Ctrl + 2 to change to double spacing, and Ctrl + 5 to change to 1.5 line spacing.

8. Change spacing before and after a paragraph by clicking anywhere in the *Aortic disease* heading and then clicking the Page Layout tab.

9. Click once on the up-pointing arrow at the right side of the *After* text box in the Paragraph group. (This inserts *12 pt* in the box.) Click in the *Before* text box (this

selects *0 pt*), type **15**, and then press Enter. (When you press Enter, the measurement displays as *3 pt*.)

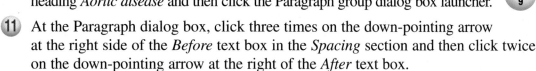

Step 9

⑩ After looking at the spacing before and after the heading, you decide to remove the spacing. To do this, make sure the insertion point is positioned in the heading *Aortic disease* and then click the Paragraph group dialog box launcher.

⑪ At the Paragraph dialog box, click three times on the down-pointing arrow at the right side of the *Before* text box in the *Spacing* section and then click twice on the down-pointing arrow at the right of the *After* text box.

  Both the *Before* and *After* text boxes should display *0 pt*.

⑫ Click OK to close the Paragraph dialog box.

⑬ Click anywhere in the heading *Arrhythmia (abnormal heart rhythm)* and then press F4.

  Pressing F4 repeats the paragraph before and after spacing.

⑭ Click individually in each of the remaining headings [*Cardiomyopathy (heart disease), Congenital heart disease, Coronary artery disease, Heart failure, Heart valve disease, Pericardial disease,* and *Vascular disease*] and then press F4.

⑮ You decide that you do not like the look of the justified paragraph and want to change to left alignment. To do this, select all the text in the *HEART DISEASE* section, except the title, click the Home tab, and then click the Align Text Left button in the Paragraph group.

⑯ Select all the text in the *HEART DISEASE FACTS* section, except the title and the right-aligned text, and then click the Align Text Left button in the Paragraph group.

⑰ You also decide you want to remove the hanging indents. To do this, select the two paragraphs of text below the *HEART DISEASE* title, press Ctrl + Shift + T, and then click the Decrease Indent button 🔽 in the Paragraph group.

⑱ Press Ctrl + End to move the insertion point to the end of the document and then click the No Spacing style in the Styles group in the Home tab.

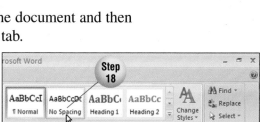

Step 18

⑲ Click the Align Text Right button, change the font to 10-point Candara, type **North Shore Medical Clinic**, press the Enter key, and then type **Heart Disease Document**.

⑳ Press Ctrl + Home to move the insertion point to the beginning of the document and then press the Enter key once.

㉑ Save, print, and then close **WordMedS2-01.docx**.

Step 11

In Brief
Change Line Spacing
1. Click Line spacing button.
2. Click desired line spacing option.
OR
1. Click Line spacing button.
2. Click *Line Spacing Options*.
3. Type desired line spacing in *At* text box.
4. Click OK.

In Addition

Spacing Above or Below Paragraphs

Spacing above or below paragraphs is added in points. A vertical inch contains approximately 72 points and a half inch contains approximately 36 points. For example, to add 9 points of spacing below selected paragraphs, click the Page Layout tab or display the Paragraph dialog box with the Indents and Spacing tab selected. Select the current measurement in the *After* text box and then type 9. You can also click the up-pointing or down-pointing arrows to increase or decrease the amount of spacing before or after paragraphs.

Activity 2.6

Inserting Bullets and Numbering

If you want to draw the reader's attention to a list of items, consider inserting a bullet before each item. Insert a bullet before items in a list using the Bullets button in the Paragraph group in the Home tab. If a list of items is in a sequence, consider inserting numbers before each item. Insert a number before sequenced items using the Numbering button in the Paragraph group.

Project

Dr. St. Claire has asked you to edit and format a document on diabetes. The medical staff will provide this informational document to patients who have been diagnosed with diabetes or are interested in learning more about diabetes. To improve the readability of the document, you decide to insert numbering and bullets to specific paragraphs.

① Open **NSMCDiabetes.docx**.

② Save the document with Save As and name it **WordMedS2-02**.

③ Select the three paragraphs of text below the *Types of Diabetes* heading.

④ Click the Numbering button in the Paragraph group in the Home tab.

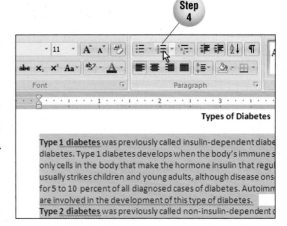

? PROBLEM

If you click the wrong button, immediately click the Undo button.

⑤ Position the insertion point at the end of the third numbered paragraph and then press the Enter key.

Pressing the Enter key automatically inserts the number *4.* and indents the insertion point.

⑥ Type the first four words *Other types of diabetes* as shown in Figure W2.2, click the Bold button to turn off bold, and then type the remaining text shown in Figure W2.2.

Because the first words of the numbered paragraphs were bolded, Word automatically turned on bold when you inserted the new paragraph.

FIGURE W2.2

> **Other types of diabetes** result from specific genetic conditions (such as maturity-onset diabetes of youth), surgery, drugs, malnutrition, infections, and other illnesses. Such types of diabetes may account for 1 to 5 percent of all diagnosed cases of diabetes.

diabetes have a 20 to 50 percent chance of developing diabetes in the following 5- to 10-year period.
4. **Other types of diabetes** result from specific genetic conditions (such as maturity-onset diabetes of youth), surgery, drugs, malnutrition, infections, and other illnesses. Such types of diabetes may account for 1 to 5 percent of all diagnosed cases of diabetes.

7 Select the four lines of text below the *Heart Disease and Stroke* heading and then click the Bullets button 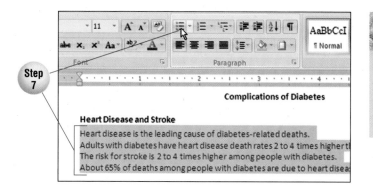 in the Paragraph group.

> Clicking the Bullets button in the Paragraph group inserts a round bullet before each paragraph.

In Brief

Insert Numbers
1. Select text.
2. Click Numbering button.

Insert Bullets
1. Select text.
2. Click Bullets button.

8 With the text still selected, you decide to replace the round bullet with a custom bullet. To do this, click the down-pointing arrow to the right of the Bullets button arrow and then click a bullet in the *Bullet Library* section that interests you.

> Bullet choices at the Bullets button drop-down list vary depending on the most recent bullets selected.

9 Select the text below the *High Blood Pressure* heading and then press F4.

> Pressing F4 repeats the last command (inserting bullets).

10 Continue selecting text below each of the remaining headings (*Blindness*, *Kidney Disease*, *Nervous System Disease*, *Amputations*, *Dental Disease*, *Complications of Pregnancy*, and *Other Complications*) and pressing F4.

11 Save **WordMedS2-02.docx**.

In Addition

Inserting Multilevel List Numbering

Use the Multilevel List button in the Paragraph group in the Home tab to specify the type of numbering for paragraphs of text at the left margin, first tab, second tab, and so on. Apply predesigned multilevel numbering to text in a document by clicking the Multilevel List button and then clicking the desired numbering style at the drop-down gallery.

Creating Numbered and/or Bulleted Text

If you type 1., press the spacebar, type a paragraph of text, and then press the Enter key, Word indents the number approximately 0.25 inch and then hang indents the text in the paragraph approximately 0.5 inch from the left margin. Additionally, 2. is inserted 0.25 inch from the left margin at the beginning of the next paragraph. You can insert bullets as you type by beginning a paragraph with the symbol *, >, or -. Type one of the symbols, press the spacebar, type the text, and then press Enter and Word converts the symbol to a bullet. Word converts the asterisk symbol to a round bullet, the greater than symbol to an arrow, and the hyphen symbol to hyphen bullet.

Turning Off Automatic Numbering and/or Bulleting

If you do not want automatic numbering or bulleting in a document, turn off the features at the AutoCorrect dialog box with the AutoFormat As You Type tab selected. Display this dialog box by clicking the Office button and then clicking the Word Options button. At the Word Options dialog box, click the *Proofing* option and then click the AutoCorrect Options button. At the AutoCorrect dialog box, click the AutoFormat As You Type tab. Click the *Automatic numbered lists* check box and/or *Automatic bulleted lists* check box to remove the check mark.

Activity 2.7

Inserting Symbols and Special Characters

You can insert special symbols such as é, ö, and Ā with options at the Symbol palette or at the Symbol dialog box. Display the Symbol palette by clicking the Insert tab and then clicking the Symbol button in the Symbols group. Click the desired symbol to insert it in the document. To display additional symbols, display the Symbol dialog box by clicking the Symbol button and then clicking the *More Symbols* option. Click the desired symbol at the dialog box, click the Insert button, and then click the Close button. At the Symbol dialog box with the Symbols tab selected, you can change the font and display different symbols. Click the Special Characters tab at the dialog box and a list displays containing special characters and the keyboard shortcuts to insert the characters.

Project

You need to include a registered trademark symbol after the organization name *American Diabetes Association* and insert Spanish text indicating that the diabetes document is available in Spanish. You will use the Symbol dialog box to insert the registered trademark and type text in Spanish.

1. With **WordMedS2-02.docx** open, move the insertion point to the end of the document.

2. Position the insertion point immediately after *Association*.

3. Click the Insert tab, click the Symbol button Ω, and then click *More Symbols* at the bottom of the palette.

4. At the Symbol dialog box, click the Special Characters tab.

5. At the Symbol dialog box with the Special Characters tab selected, click the ® symbol in the *Character* list box.

6. Click the Insert button and then click the Close button.

7. Press Ctrl + End to move the insertion point to the end of the document.

8. Type the text shown in Figure W2.3 up to the é in *También*. To insert the é symbol, click the Symbol button Ω and then click *More Symbols*.

The text in Figure W2.3 is Spanish and translates as *(Also available in Spanish)*.

9. At the Symbol dialog box with the Symbols tab selected, click the down-pointing arrow at the right of the *Font* list box and then click *(normal text)* at the drop-down list. [You may need to scroll up to see this option. Skip this step if *(normal text)* is already selected.]

10. Scroll down the list box until the eleventh row is visible and then click the é symbol (the ninth symbol from the left).

11. Click the Insert button and then click the Close button.

12. Type the text shown in Figure W2.3 up to the *ñ* symbol, click the Symbol button Ω and then click *More Symbols*.

13. At the Symbol dialog box, click the *ñ* symbol (first option from the left in the twelfth row).

14. Click the Insert button and then click the Close button.

15. Type the remaining text in Figure W2.3.

16. Save **WordMedS2-02.docx**.

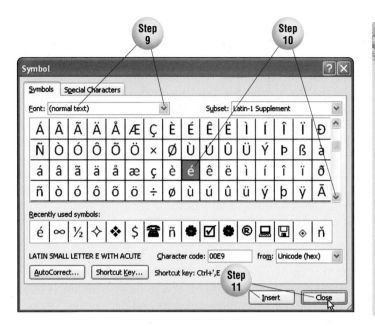

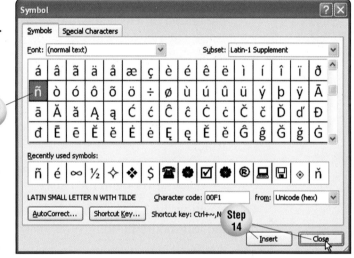

In Brief

Insert Symbol
1. Click Insert tab.
2. Click Symbol button.
3. Click *More Symbols*.
4. Click desired symbol.
5. Click Insert button.
6. Click Close button.

Insert Special Character
1. Click Insert tab.
2. Click Symbol button.
3. Click *More Symbols*.
4. Click Special Characters tab.
5. Click desired character.
6. Click Insert button.
7. Click Close button.

FIGURE W2.3

(También disponible en español.)

In Addition

Inserting Symbols with Keyboard Shortcuts

Another method for inserting symbols in a document is to use a keyboard shortcut. Click a symbol at the Symbol dialog box and the keyboard shortcut displays toward the bottom of the dialog box. For example, click the ø symbol and the keyboard shortcut *Ctrl+/,O* displays toward the bottom of the dialog box. To insert the ø symbol in a document using the keyboard shortcut, hold down the Ctrl key and then press the / key. Release the Ctrl key and then press the o key. Not all symbols contain a keyboard shortcut.

Inserting Symbols Using the Palette

When you click the Symbol button in the Symbols group, a drop-down palette displays with symbol choices. The palette displays the most recently used symbols. If the palette contains the desired symbol, click the symbol and it is inserted in the document.

Activity 2.8

Setting Tabs

Word offers a variety of default settings including left tabs set every 0.5 inch. You can set your own tabs using the Ruler or at the Tabs dialog box. Use the Ruler to set, move, and delete tabs. The default tabs display as tiny vertical lines along the bottom of the Ruler. With a left tab, text aligns at the left edge of the tab. The other types of tabs that can be set on the Ruler are center, right, decimal, and bar. The small button at the left side of the Ruler is called the Alignment button. Each time you click the Alignment button, a different tab

or paragraph alignment symbol displays. To set a tab, display the desired alignment button on the Ruler and then click on the Ruler at the desired position. Four types of tabs can be set with leaders. (Leaders cannot be used with a bar tab.) Leaders are useful in documents where you want to direct the reader's eyes across the page. Leaders can be periods, hyphens, or underlines. Tabs with leaders are set with options at the Tabs dialog box. At the Tabs dialog box, you can chose the type of tab, the type of leader, and enter a tab position measurement.

Project

Dr. St. Claire has done some additional research on diabetes and has asked you to include the information in the document. You think that the information would be understandable and easy to read if set in three columns and decide that setting tabs would make the most sense.

1. With **WordMedS2-02.docx** open, move the insertion point to the end of the paragraph of text below the *Statistics on Diabetes* heading and then press the Enter key twice.

2. Type the paragraph of text (first sentence) shown in Figure W2.4 and then press the Enter key twice.

3. Make sure the left tab symbol ⌊ displays in the Alignment button at the left side of the Ruler.

   If the Ruler is not displayed, turn it on by clicking View and then *Ruler*.

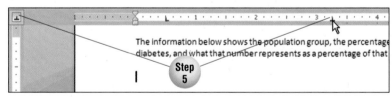

4. Position the arrow pointer below the 0.5-inch mark on the Ruler and then click the left mouse button.

5. Click once on the Alignment button located at the left side of the Ruler to display the center tab symbol ⊥, position the arrow pointer below the 3.25-inch mark on the Ruler, and then click the left mouse button.

6. Click once on the Alignment button located at the left side of the Ruler to display the right tab symbol ⌟, position the arrow pointer below the 6-inch mark on the Ruler, and then click the left mouse button.

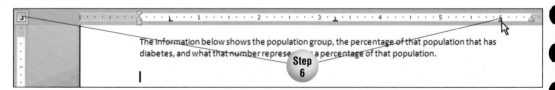

7. Type the text shown in Figure W2.4, pressing the Tab key before typing each tabbed entry. Make sure you bold and underline the text as shown in the figure and that you press the Tab key before typing the entry in the first column.

FIGURE W2.4

The information below shows the population group, the percentage of that population that has diabetes, and what that number represents as a percentage of that population.

Population	Number with diabetes	Percentage
Under 20	210 thousand	0.26%
20 and older	18 million	8.70%
Men 20 and older	8.7 million	8.70%
Women 20 and older	9.3 million	8.70%

In Brief

Set a Tab on the Ruler
1. Display desired alignment symbol on Alignment button.
2. Click on Ruler at desired position.

Set a Tab at the Tabs Dialog Box
1. Click Paragraph group dialog box launcher.
2. At Paragraph dialog box, click Tabs button.
3. Type tab measurement.
4. Click desired alignment.
5. Click desired leader (if any).
6. Click Set.
7. Click OK.

8 After typing the last entry in the third column, press the Enter key and then press Ctrl + Q, the shortcut key to remove paragraph formatting.

> Pressing Ctrl + Q removes the tabs you set from the Ruler.

9 You decide to add leaders to the center and right tabs. To begin, select the text you typed at the left, center, and right tabs *except* the headings (***Population***, ***Number with diabetes***, and ***Percentage***).

10 Click the Paragraph group dialog box launcher.

11 At the Paragraph dialog box, click the Tabs button that displays in the lower left corner.

12 At the Tabs dialog box, click *3.25″* in the *Tab stop position* section, click *2....* in the *Leader* section, and then click the Set button.

13 Click *6″* in the *Tab stop position* section, click *2....* in the *Leader* section, and then click the Set button.

14 Click OK to close the dialog box.

15 Position the insertion point immediately following the first *8.70%* in the ***Percentage*** column and then press the Enter key.

16 Press the Tab key, type **60 and older**, press the Tab key, type **8.6 million**, press the Tab key, and then type **18.30%**.

17 Save **WordMedS2-02.docx**.

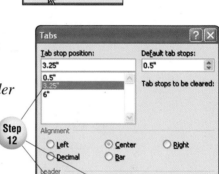

In Addition

Moving a Tab

Move a tab on the Ruler by positioning the mouse pointer on the tab symbol on the Ruler. Hold down the left mouse button, drag the symbol to the new location on the Ruler, and then release the mouse button.

Deleting a Tab

Delete a tab from the Ruler by positioning the arrow pointer on the tab symbol. Hold down the left mouse button, drag the symbol down into the document screen, and then release the mouse button.

Setting a Decimal Tab

Set a decimal tab for column entries you want aligned at the decimal point. To set a decimal tab, click the Alignment button located at the left side of the Ruler until the decimal tab symbol displays and then click on the desired position on the Ruler.

Clearing Tabs at the Tabs Dialog Box

At the Tabs dialog box, you can clear an individual tab or all tabs. To clear all tabs, click the Clear All button. To clear an individual tab, specify the tab position and then click the Clear button.

Activity 2.9

Adding Borders and Shading

Insert a border around text and/or apply shading to text in a paragraph or selected text with the Border button and Shading button in the Paragraph group in the Home tab or at the Borders and Shading dialog box. At the Borders and Shading dialog box with the Borders tab selected, you can specify the border type, style, color, and width. Click the Shading tab and the dialog box contains options for choosing a fill color and pattern style. Click the Page Border tab and the dialog box contains options for applying a page border.

Project

To add visual appeal and increase readability of the diabetes document, you decide to add borders to specific text, apply shading behind the title, and apply a border and shading to the information in tabbed columns.

① With **WordMedS2-02.docx** open, select the numbered paragraphs of text below the heading *Types of Diabetes*.

② Click the Border button arrow in the Paragraph group in the Home tab and then click *Outside Borders* at the drop-down list.

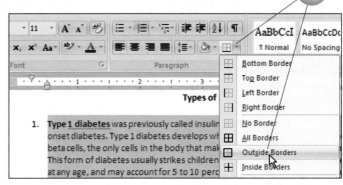

The name of the button changes depending on the border choice you previously selected at the button drop-down list.

③ Select the title *UNDERSTANDING DIABETES* and then change the font size to 16 points and turn on bold.

④ Click anywhere in the title, click the Shading button arrow, and then click *More Colors* at the drop-down gallery.

⑤ At the Colors dialog box with the Standard tab selected, click the light purple color as shown at the right.

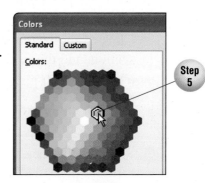

⑥ Click OK to close the Colors dialog box.

⑦ Select text from the sentence that begins *The information below shows the population group...* through the line of text containing the column entries *Women 20 and older*, *9.3 million*, and *8.70%*.

⑧ Click the Border button arrow and then click *Borders and Shading* at the bottom of the drop-down list.

⑨ At the Borders and Shading dialog box with the Borders tab selected, click the down-pointing arrow at the right of the *Style* list box until the first double-line option displays and then click the double-line option.

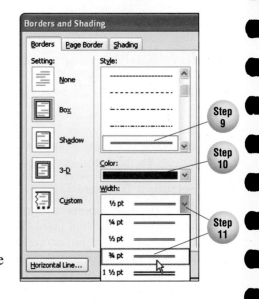

10 Click the down-pointing arrow at the right of the *Color* list box and then click the *Dark Blue* option (second option from the *right* in the Standard Colors section).

11 Click the down-pointing arrow at the right of the *Width* list box and then click *¾ pt* at the drop-down list.

12 Click the Shading tab.

13 Click the down-pointing arrow at the right side of the *Fill* option and then click *More Colors* at the drop-down list.

14 At the Colors dialog box, click the same light purple color you chose in Step 5.

15 Click OK to close the Colors dialog box.

16 With the Borders and Shading dialog box displayed, insert a page border around all pages in the document. To do this, click the Page Border tab.

> You can also display the Borders and Shading dialog box with the Page Border tab selected by clicking the Page Layout tab and then clicking the Page Borders button in the Page Background group.

17 Click the *Shadow* option in the *Setting* section. Click the down-pointing arrow at the right side of the *Color* option and then click *Dark Blue* in the *Standard Colors* section (second option from the *right*).

18 Click the down-pointing arrow at the right side of the *Width* option and then click *2 ¼ pt* at the drop-down list.

19 Click OK to close the Borders and Shading dialog box.

20 Select the entire document and then change the font to Corbel.

21 Save, print, and then close **WordMedS2-02.docx**.

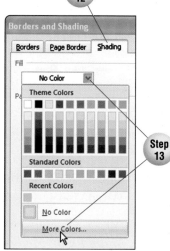

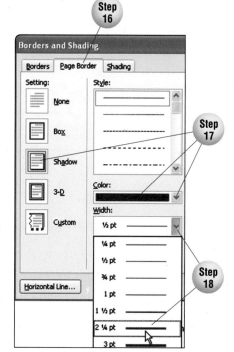

In Addition

Inserting Horizontal Lines

Word includes a horizontal line feature that inserts a graphic horizontal line in a document. To display the Horizontal Line dialog box, display the Borders and Shading dialog box with any tab selected and then click the Horizontal Line button [Horizontal Line...] located toward the bottom of the dialog box. Click the desired horizontal line in the list box and then click OK and the line is inserted in the document.

Applying Styles and Quick Styles Sets

The Styles group in the Home tab contains a number of predesigned styles you can apply to text in a document. In a previous section, you applied the No Spacing style to remove some of the default formatting provided in a Word document. The Styles group contains a number of other styles. To display additional styles, click the More button that displays at the right side of the Styles group. Apply a style by clicking the desired style in the drop-down list. A Word document contains a number of predesigned formats grouped into style sets called Quick Styles. Display the available Quick Styles sets by clicking the Change Styles button in the Styles group in the Home tab and then pointing to *Style Set*. Choose a Quick Styles set and the styles visible in the Styles group change to reflect the set. With options at the Change Styles drop-down list, you can apply a different color to styles and change the style font.

Project You have been asked by Douglas Brown, legal counsel, to format a document that explains records storage and maintenance. You decide to apply styles to enhance the visual appeal of the document.

Columbia River General Hospital

1. Open **CRGHMaintainRecords.docx** and then save the document and name it **WordMedS2-03**.

2. Apply a heading style to the title by clicking on any character in the title *Maintaining Medical Records* and then clicking the *Heading 1* style that displays in the Styles group in the Home tab.

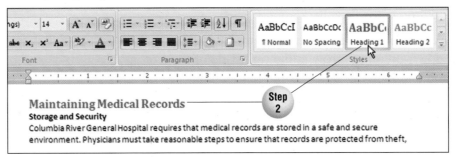

3. Click on any character in the heading *Storage and Security* and then click the *Heading 2* style.

> The Heading 1 and Heading 2 styles apply both paragraph and character formatting. Some styles will apply only paragraph formatting and other will apply only character formatting.

4. Apply the Heading 2 style to the remaining headings *Creating a Patient Profile* and *Creating Progress Notes*.

5. Apply a Quick Styles set to the document by clicking the Change Styles button in the Styles group in the Home tab, pointing to *Style Set*, and then clicking *Formal* at the drop-down list.

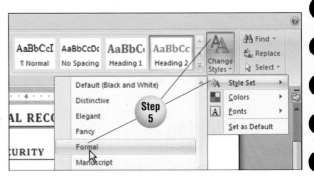

> With the Formal Quick Styles set applied to the document, the heading styles change the font and font color of the text, add spacing before and after the heading, and insert a bottom border. The Formal Quick Styles set also changes the font and font size of the body text in the document.

6 After looking at the formatting applied by the Formal Quick Styles set, you decide to change the color so it better reflects the color of the hospital logo. To do this, click the Change Styles button in the Styles group, point to *Colors*, and then click *Oriel* at the side menu.

7 You decide that you want to change the font applied by the Formal Quick Styles set. To do this, click the Change Styles button, point to *Fonts*, scroll down the side menu, and then click *Foundry*.

8 Apply a character style to text in the document. To begin, select the text *safe and secure environment* that displays in the first paragraph of text in the *Storage and Security* section and then click the More button that displays at the right side of the styles in the Styles group.

9 At the drop-down gallery, click the *Subtle Emphasis* style.

10 Change the style applied to the title of the document by clicking on any character in the title *MAINTAINING MEDICAL RECORDS* and then clicking the *Title* style in the Styles group.

> If the Title style is not visible in the Styles group, click the More button at the right side of the styles and then click *Title* at the drop-down gallery.

11 Save, print, and then close **WordMedS2-03.docx**.

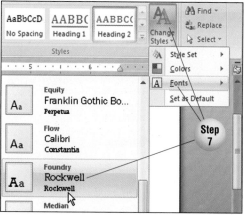

In Brief

Apply a Quick Style
1. Position insertion point at desired location.
2. Click style in Styles group or click More button and then click desired style.

Change Quick Styles Set
1. Click Change Styles button.
2. Point to *Style Set*.
3. Click desired set.

Change Quick Styles Set Colors
1. Click Change Styles button.
2. Point to *Colors*.
3. Click desired color set.

Change Quick Styles Set Fonts
1. Click Change Styles button.
2. Point to *Fonts*.
3. Click desired font set.

In Addition

Displaying the Styles Window

The Styles group in the Home tab contains a number of styles you can apply to a document. To view additional styles provided by Word display the Styles window by clicking the Styles group dialog box launcher. The Styles window displays available styles. Styles that apply paragraph formatting display followed by a paragraph symbol (¶), styles that apply paragraph and character formatting display followed by a paragraph symbol and the **a** character, and styles that apply only character formatting display followed by the **a** character. Close the Styles window by clicking the Close button (contains an X) located in the upper right corner of the window.

Displaying All Styles

The Styles window displays some of the most commonly used styles but not all of the predesigned styles. To display all styles, click the Styles group dialog box launcher and then click *Options* (located in the lower right corner) at the Styles window. At the Styles Pane Options dialog box, click the down-pointing arrow at the right side of the *Select styles to show* option box and then click *All styles* at the drop-down list. Click OK to close the dialog box. All styles are now available in the Styles window.

Features Summary

Feature	Ribbon Tab, Group	Button	Keyboard Shortcut
1.5 line spacing	Home, Paragraph		Ctrl + 5
align text left	Home, Paragraph		Ctrl + L
align text right	Home, Paragraph		Ctrl + R
bold	Home, Font		Ctrl + B
border	Home, Paragraph		
bullets	Home, Paragraph		
center	Home, Paragraph		Ctrl + E
change case	Home, Font		Shift + F3
change styles	Home, Styles		
clear formatting	Home, Font		
decrease indent	Home, Paragraph		Ctrl + Shift + M
double line spacing	Home, Paragraph		Ctrl + 2
font	Home, Font	Calibri (Body)	
font color	Home, Font		
Font dialog box	Home, Font		Ctrl + Shift + F
font size	Home, Font	11	Ctrl + Shift + P
Format Painter	Home, Clipboard		
hanging indent			Ctrl + T
highlight	Home, Font		
increase indent	Home, Paragraph		Ctrl + M
insert symbol	Insert, Symbols		
italics	Home, Font		Ctrl + I
justify	Home, Paragraph		Ctrl + J
line spacing	Home, Paragraph		
numbering	Home, Paragraph		
Paragraph dialog box	Home, Paragraph		
remove hanging indent			Ctrl + Shift + T
shading	Home, Paragraph		
single line spacing	Home, Paragraph		Ctrl + 1

continues

Feature	Ribbon Tab, Group	Button	Keyboard Shortcut
styles	Home, Styles		
Styles window	Home, Styles	🔲	
Tabs dialog box	Home, Paragraph OR Page Layout, Paragraph	🔲 , Tabs...	
underline	Home, Font	U ▾	Ctrl + U

Knowledge Check

Completion: In the space provided at the right, write in the correct term, command, or option.

1. The Bold button is located in this group in the Home tab.
2. Click this button in the Font group and then click the *UPPERCASE* option to change selected text to uppercase letters.
3. Press these keys on the keyboard to italicize selected text.
4. Repeat a command by pressing this function key.
5. Click this button in the Paragraph group in the Home tab to align text at the right margin.
6. Click this button in the Font group in the Home tab to remove paragraph formatting and character formatting from selected text.
7. Indent text from the left margin by dragging the Left Indent marker on this.
8. The Line spacing button displays in this group in the Home tab.
9. Click this button in the Paragraph group in the Home tab to number selected paragraphs.
10. Display the Symbol palette by clicking this tab and then clicking the Symbol button in the Symbols group.
11. This is the name of the button that displays at the left side of the Ruler.
12. Set tabs at the Tabs dialog box or using this.
13. These can be added to a tab to help guide the reader's eyes across the page.
14. Insert a page border with options at this dialog box with the Page Border tab selected.
15. A document contains a number of predesigned formats grouped into sets called this.

Skills Review

Review 1 Applying Fonts; Using the Format Painter

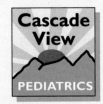

1. Open **CVPWell-Child.docx**.
2. Save the document with Save As and name it **WordMedS2-R1**.
3. Select the entire document and then change the font to Constantia.
4. Select the title *WELL-CHILD APPOINTMENTS*, change the font to 16-point Candara bold, and then deselect the text.
5. Select the heading *Appointment Recommendations*, change the font to 14-point Candara bold, and then deselect the heading.
6. Using Format Painter, change the font to 14-point Candara bold for the remaining headings (*Appointment Services*, *Appointment Suggestions*, *Immunizations*, and *Child Development Assessment*).
7. Save **WordMedS2-R1.docx**.

Review 2 Applying Font Effects; Using the Repeat Command

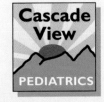

1. With **WordMedS2-R1.docx** open, select the last paragraph of text in the document (the text in parentheses), change the font size to 10, and apply small caps effect. ***Hint: The small caps feature is located in the* Effects *section of the Font dialog box.***
2. Select the title *WELL-CHILD APPOINTMENTS* and then apply a shadow effect.
3. Select the heading *Appointment Recommendations* and then apply a shadow effect.
4. Use the Repeat command to apply the shadow effect to the remaining headings in the document (*Appointment Services*, *Appointment Suggestions*, *Immunizations*, and *Child Development Assessment*).
5. Save **WordMedS2-R1.docx**.

Review 3 Aligning and Indenting Text; Changing Line and Paragraph Spacing

1. With **WordMedS2-R1.docx** open, position the insertion point anywhere in the paragraph below the heading *Appointment Recommendations*, change the paragraph alignment to Justify, and indent the paragraph 0.25 inch from the left margin.
2. Position the insertion point anywhere in the last paragraph of text in the document (the text in parentheses) and then change the paragraph alignment to Center.
3. Select the entire document and then change to 1.15 line spacing.
4. Click anywhere in the heading *Appointment Recommendations* and then change the paragraph spacing after to 6 points.
5. Use the Repeat command to insert 6 points of spacing after the remaining headings (*Appointment Services*, *Appointment Suggestions*, *Immunizations*, and *Child Development Assessment*).
6. Save **WordMedS2-R1.docx**.

Review 4 Inserting Bullets and Numbers

1. With **WordMedS2-R1.docx** open, select the seven lines of text below the *Appointment Services* heading and then insert bullets.
2. Select the paragraphs of text below the heading *Appointment Suggestions* and then insert numbering.
3. Move the insertion point to the end of the second numbered paragraph, press the Enter key, and then type **Take snacks with you for young children in case you have to wait for your appointment.**
4. Save **WordMedS2-R1.docx**.

Review 5 Setting Tabs

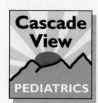

1. With **WordMedS2-R1.docx** open, move the insertion point a double-space below the paragraph of text in the *Immunizations* section (the paragraph that begins *Cascade View Pediatrics schedule for immunizations …*) and then create the tabbed text shown in Figure W2.5 with the following specifications. (Type the text as shown in the figure.)
   a. Set a left tab at the 1.5-inch mark on the Ruler.
   b. Set a right tab at the 5-inch mark on the Ruler.
   c. Type the column headings (*Vaccine* and *Shots/Doses*) bolded and underlined at the appropriate tabs.
   d. Before typing the column entries, display the Tab dialog box and add leaders to the right tab.
   e. Type the remainder of the text shown in Figure W2.5.
2. Save **WordMedS2-R1.docx**.

FIGURE W2.5 Review 5

Vaccine	Shots/Doses
Hepatitis B	3 shots
DTaP	5 shots
Hib	4 shots
Pneumococcal (PCV)	4 shots
Polio	4 shots
Measles-Mumps-Rubella	2 shots
Varicella (chicken pox)	1 shot
Influenza*	1 or 2 doses
Hepatitis A**	2 shots

*Two doses are recommended for children receiving the influenza vaccine for the first time.

**The hepatitis A vaccine is recommended only in certain areas where infection rates are highest.

Review 6 Adding Borders and Shading

1. With **WordMedS2-R1.docx** open, select the tabbed text you just typed (including the blank line above the column headings, the sentences after the asterisks, and the blank line below the sentences) and then insert a border and shading of your choosing.
2. Click on any character in the title *WELL-CHILD APPOINTMENTS* and then apply a shading of your choosing. (The shading will span from the left to the right margin.)
3. Insert a page border of your choosing to the document. (If possible, match the color of the page border with the colors in the letterhead and/or title shading.)
4. Save **WordMedS2-R1.docx**.

Review 7 Inserting Symbols

1. With **WordMedS2-R1.docx** open, move the insertion point to the end of the document.
2. Change the font to Candara, the font size to 11, and the line spacing to single. Type the following text at the left margin:
   >®2011 Cascade View Pediatrics
   >Raphaël Severin, MD
3. Save, print, and then close **WordMedS2-R1.docx**.

Review 8 Applying Styles

1. Open **CysticFibrosis.docx** and then save the document with Save As and name it **WordMedS2-R2**.
2. Apply the Heading 1 style to the title *Cystic Fibrosis* and apply the Heading 2 style to the headings *Cause, Diagnosis,* and *Symptoms of Cystic Fibrosis*.
3. Apply the *Modern* Quick Styles set to the document.
4. Change the Quick Styles set color to Foundry.
5. Change the Quick Styles set font to Flow.
6. Insert in the document a page border of your choosing. Apply a color to the page border that matches or complements the colors of the Quick Styles set.
7. Save, print, and then close **WordMedS2-R2.docx**.

Skills Assessment

Assessment 1 Changing Fonts; Aligning and Indenting Text; and Changing Paragraph Spacing

1. Open **NSMCRequestInfo.docx**.
2. Save the document with Save As and name it **WordMedS2-A1**.
3. Select the entire document and then change the font to Cambria and the font size to 12.
4. Set the title *MEDICAL RECORDS* in 14-point Constantia bold.
5. Set the heading *How to Request a Copy of Your Medical Records* in 12-point Constantia bold, add a shadow effect, and then change the spacing after the paragraph to 6 points (instead of 10 points).
6. Use Format Painter to format the remaining headings shown below in 12-point Constantia bold with shadow effect and with 6 points of space below the heading.
   Information from Your Medical Records
   Submitting a Request
   Additional Information about Medical Records
   Mailing Medical Records
   Reproduction Charges
   Sending Records to Another Medical Facility
   Processing Time
   Picking up Medical Records
7. Center-align the title, MEDICAL RECORDS, and then apply paragraph shading of your choosing to the title.
8. Select the four lines of text below the paragraph of text in the *How to Request a Copy of Your Medical Records* section (*AIDS/HIV* through *Fertility treatment*) and then apply bullets.
9. Indent 0.5 inch from the left margin all the lines of text in the *Submitting a Request* section *except* the first paragraph (the paragraph that begins *Once you have completed ...*).
10. Move the insertion point to the end of the document and then type the following text at the left margin (press Shift + Enter after typing the first line of text):
    ®2011 North Shore Medical Clinic
    Maria Cárdenas, MD
11. Save and then print **WordMedS2-A1.docx**.
12. Apply the Heading 1 style to the title *Medical Records* and apply the Heading 2 style to the headings (*How to Request a Copy of Your Medical Records, Information from Your Medical Records, Submitting a Request, Additional Information about Medical Records, Mailing Medical Records, Reproduction Charges, Sending Records to Another Medical Facility, Processing Time,* and *Picking Up Medical Records*).
13. Apply the Fancy Quick Styles set, change the Quick Styles color to Oriel, and change the Quick Styles font to Foundry.
14. Select the entire document and then click the Italic button to remove italic formatting.
15. Save, print, and then close **WordMedS2-A1.docx**.

Assessment 2 Preparing and Formatting a Letter

1. Open **NSMCLtrhd.docx**.
2. Save the letterhead document with Save As and name it **WordMedS2-A2**.
3. Click the *No Spacing* style. (This removes the 10 points of spacing after paragraphs and changes the line spacing to single.)
4. You have been asked by your supervisor to send a letter to the local community college indicating that a medical office assistant internship is available. Send the letter to Mrs. Janelle Meyers, Medical Assistant Program, Columbia River Community College, Third Avenue North, Portland, OR 97301, and include the following:
   - In the first paragraph, tell Mrs. Meyers that your clinic has an opening for a medical office assistant intern for 15 hours a week for minimum wage with flexible hours.
   - In the second paragraph tell Mrs. Meyers that the intern will be trained in specific areas and then include the following in a numbered list: registering patients, typing memos and correspondence, filing correspondence and some medical records, make photocopies, and scheduling appointments.
   - In the third paragraph, tell Mrs. Meyers that she can contact Lee Elliott at the clinic. Provide the clinic name, address, and telephone number.
   - End the letter with the complimentary close *Sincerely* and type your name four lines below *Sincerely*.
5. After typing the letter, select the letter text and then change to a font other than Calibri.
6. Change the numbered list to a bulleted list.
7. Save, print, and then close **WordMedS2-A2.docx**.

Assessment 3 Setting Leader Tabs

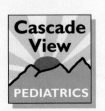

1. Open **CVPLtrhd.docx**.
2. Save the document with Save As and name it **WordMedS2-A3**.
3. Type the text shown in Figure W2.6.
4. After typing the text, select the document and then change the font to Cambria.
5. Save, print, and then close **WordMedS2-A3.docx**.

FIGURE W2.6 Assessment 3

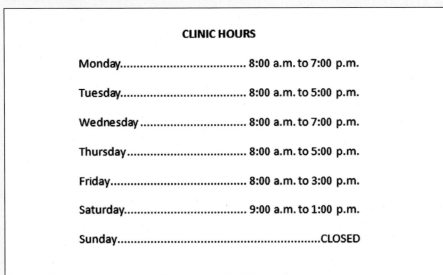

CLINIC HOURS

Monday.. 8:00 a.m. to 7:00 p.m.

Tuesday.. 8:00 a.m. to 5:00 p.m.

Wednesday .... 8:00 a.m. to 7:00 p.m.

Thursday...................................... 8:00 a.m. to 5:00 p.m.

Friday.. 8:00 a.m. to 3:00 p.m.

Saturday...................................... 9:00 a.m. to 1:00 p.m.

Sunday...CLOSED

Assessment 4 Finding Information on the Widow/Orphan Feature and Keeping Text Together

1. Your supervisor at North Shore Medical Clinic, Lee Elliott, has asked you to learn about the widow/orphan feature and how to keep paragraphs of text together on the same page. (You can find this information by typing **insert a page break** in the Word Help window and then clicking the *Insert a page break* hyperlink.)

HELP

2. She would like you to prepare a memo to all medical office staff that contains information on the two features with the following specifications.
   a. Open the **NSMCMemoForm.docx** document and then save it with Save As and name it **WordMedS2-A4**.
   b. Create a Subject for the memo.
   c. Write a paragraph discussing the widow/orphan feature.
   d. Write a paragraph discussing how to keep paragraphs of text together on the same page.
3. Save, print, and then close **WordMedS2-A4.docx**.

Assessment 5 Hyphenating Words in a Document

1. In some Word documents, the right margin may appear ragged. If the paragraph alignment is changed to Justify, the right margin will appear even, but extra spaces are added throughout the line. In these situations, hyphenating long words that fall at the end of the text line provides the document with a more balanced look. Use Word's Help feature to learn how to automatically and manually hyphenate words in a document. *Hint: To learn about hyphenation, display the Word Help window, type* insert hyphen, *press the Enter key, and then click the* <u>Insert a hyphen</u> *hyperlink.*

HELP

2. Open **WordMedS2-A1.docx**.
3. Save the document with Save As and name it **WordMedS2-A5**.
4. Manually hyphenate words in the document.
5. Save, print, and then close **WordMedS2-A5.docx**.

Assessment 6 Locating Information and Writing a Memo

1. Using the Internet, visit the Web site of the American Association of Medical Assistants (AAMA) at www.aama-ntl.org. At the Web site, discover the following information:
   • Mission of the AAMA
   • Administrative duties of a medical assistant
   • Salaries and benefits of a medical assistant
   • Any other information you find interesting
2. Using one of Word's memo template forms, create a memo to your instructor explaining the information you found at the Web site.
3. Save the completed memo and name it **WordMedS2-A6**.
4. Print and then close **WordMedS2-A6.docx**.

Marquee Challenge

Challenge 1 Preparing a Job Announcement

1. Open **NSMCLtrhd.docx** and then save the document with Save As and name it **WordMedS2-C1**.
2. Click the *No Spacing* style, change the font to 12-point Cambria, and then type the job announcement shown in Figure W2.7. Change the font size for the title to 14 and apply paragraph shading as shown.
3. Save, print, and then close **WordMedS2-C1.docx**.

Challenge 2 Preparing a Flyer for a Diabetes Presentation

1. At a blank document, change the spacing after paragraphs to 0 pt, change the font to Cambria, and then create the flyer shown in Figure W2.8.
2. Save the completed flyer and name the document **WordMedS2-C2**.
3. Print and then close **WordMedS2-C2.docx**.

North Shore Medical Clinic
7450 Meridian Street, Suite 150
Portland, OR 97202
(503) 555-2330

JOB ANNOUNCEMENT

JOB TITLE.. Medical Office Assistant
STATUS ....Full-time employment
SALARY ....Depending on experience
CLOSING DATE .... March 1, 2011

JOB SUMMARY
- Register new patients; assist with form completion
- Retrieve charts
- Enter patient data into computer database
- Maintain and file medical records
- Schedule patients
- Call patients with appointment reminders
- Answer telephones and route messages
- Call and/or fax pharmacy for prescription order refills
- Mail lab test results to patients
- Perform other clerical duties as required

REQUIRED SKILLS
- Keyboarding (35+ wpm)
- Knowledge of Microsoft Word, Excel, and PowerPoint
- Thorough understanding of medical terms
- Excellent grammar and spelling skills
- Excellent customer service skills

EDUCATION
- High school diploma
- Post-secondary training as a medical office assistant, CMA or RMA preferred
- CPR certification

For further information, contact Lee Elliott at (503) 555-2330.

Understanding

DIABETES

Please join Dr. Käri St. Claire from North Shore Medical Clinic as she presents *Understanding Diabetes*. At this informative presentation, she will discuss:

- Types of diabetes
- Statistics on diabetes
- Complications of diabetes
- Living with diabetes
- Developing self-management skills

When .... Wednesday, October 19
Time .... 7:00 p.m. to 8:30 p.m.
Where .... Columbia River General Hospital
Location .... Room 224
Cost .... FREE!

Sponsored by the
Greater Portland Healthcare Workers Association

Word SECTION 3

Formatting and Enhancing a Document

Skills

- Find and replace text and formatting
- Reveal formatting
- Cut, copy, and paste text
- Use the Clipboard task pane to copy and paste items
- Change page margins and orientation
- Apply a theme
- Customize page and page background
- Insert page numbers, headers, and footers
- Insert a page break and a section break
- Create and modify newspaper columns
- Insert, size, and move images
- Insert, size, and move WordArt
- Insert a file into an existing file
- Insert and customize shapes and text boxes
- Prepare an envelope
- Prepare labels

Student Resources

Before beginning this section:
1. Copy to your storage medium the WordMedS3 subfolder from the Unit3Word folder on the Student Resources CD.
2. Make WordMedS3 the active folder.

In addition to containing the data files needed to complete section work, the Student Resources CD contains model answers in PDF format for each of the projects in this section; model answers for end-of-section exercises are not provided.

Projects Overview

Edit, format, and reorganize a child development assessment form; format and add visual appeal to a monthly newsletter; enhance the visual appeal of a parenting class flyer; format and add visual appeal to a patient confidentiality document; prepare an envelope and mailing labels; prepare a notice and two announcements; and format a document on Fifth disease.

Format and add visual appeal to a document on writing and maintaining medical records.

Prepare an envelope and mailing labels, and format and add visual appeal to a document on fibromyalgia.

Activity 3.1

Finding and Replacing Text

Use the Find and Replace feature to find specific text and replace with other text. For example, you can use abbreviations for common phrases when entering text and then replace the abbreviations with the actual text later, or you can set up standard documents with generic names and replace the names with other names to make a personalized document. You can also find and replace some formatting. These options are available at the Find and Replace dialog box with the Replace tab selected.

Project

Sydney Larsen has asked you to proofread the Assessment of Child Development form parents fill out before each well-child appointment at Cascade View Pediatrics. Your review identifies some spelling and grammar errors that you will correct using the Find and Replace feature.

1. Open the **CDAssessment.docx** document and then save the document with Save As and name it **WordMedS3-01**.

2. After looking over the document, you realize that *development* is misspelled as *developement* throughout the document. You decide to use the Find and Replace feature to correct this spelling error. To begin, click the Replace button ab Replace in the Editing group in the Home tab.

3. At the Find and Replace dialog box with the Replace tab selected, type **developement** in the *Find what* text box and then press the Tab key.

   Pressing the Tab key moves the insertion point to the *Replace with* text box.

4. Type **development** in the *Replace with* text box and then click the Replace All button located toward the bottom of the dialog box.

   Clicking the Replace All button replaces all occurrences of the text in the document. If you want control over what is replaced in a document, click the Replace button to replace text or click the Find Next button to move to the next occurrence of the text.

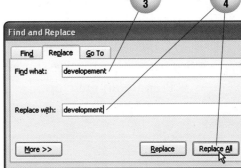

PROBLEM

If the *Replace with* text box does not display, click the Replace tab.

5. At the message telling you that three replacements were made, click the OK button.

6. Click the Close button to close the Find and Replace dialog box.

7. Looking at the document, you realize that *well-baby* should be *well-child*. To begin, display the Find and Replace dialog box by clicking the Replace button in the Editing group.

8. At the Find and Replace dialog box with the Replace tab selected, type **well-baby** in the *Find what* text box.

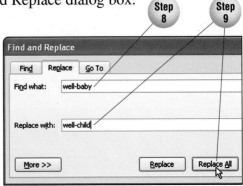

In Brief
Find and Replace Text
1. Click Replace button in Editing group in Home tab.
2. Type find text.
3. Press Tab key.
4. Type replace text.
5. Click Replace All button.

9. Press the Tab key, type **well-child** in the *Replace with* text box, and then click the Replace All button.

10. At the message telling you that two replacements were made, click the OK button.

11. Click the Close button to close the Find and Replace dialog box.

12. Select the title *ASSESSMENT OF CHILD DEVELOPMENT*, change the font to 16-point Candara bold, change the alignment to center, and then add 12 points of spacing after the paragraph.

13. Select the subtitle *Ages Newborn to Three Years*, change the font to 14-point Candara bold, change the alignment to center, and then add 9 points of spacing after the paragraph.

14. Change the font to 12-point Candara bold for the headings *Child Development – Talking* and *Child Development – Hearing*.

15. Save **WordMedS3-01.docx**.

In Addition

Options at the Expanded Find and Replace Dialog Box

The Find and Replace dialog box contains a variety of check boxes with options you can choose for completing a find and replace. To display these options, click the More button located at the bottom of the dialog box. This causes the Find and Replace dialog box to expand as shown at the right. The options are described below.

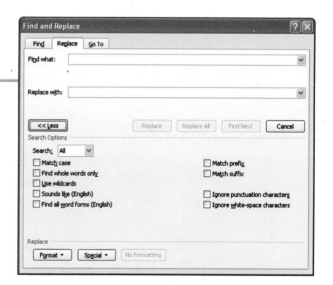

Option	Action
Match case	Exactly match the case of the search text. For example, if you search for *Book*, Word will stop at *Book* but not *book* or *BOOK*.
Find whole words only	Find a whole word, not a part of a word. For example, if you search for *her* and did *not* select *Find whole words only*, Word would stop at t*her*e, *her*e, *her*s, and so on.
Use wildcards	Search for wildcards, special characters, or special search operators.
Sounds like	Match words that sound alike but are spelled differently such as *know* and *no*.
Find all word forms	Find all forms of the word entered in the *Find what* text box. For example, if you enter *hold*, Word will stop at *held* and *holding*.
Match prefix	Find only those words that begin with the letters in the *Find what* text box. For example, if you enter *per*, Word will stop at words such as *perform* and *perfect* but skip over words such as *super* and *hyperlink*.
Match suffix	Find only those words that end with the letters in the *Find what* text box. For example, if you enter *ly*, Word will stop at words such as *accurately* and *quietly* but skip over words such as *catalyst* and *lyre*.
Ignore punctuation characters	Ignore punctuation within characters. For example, if you enter *US* in the *Find what* text box, Word will stop at *U.S.*
Ignore white-space characters	Ignore spaces between letters. For example, if you enter *F B I* in the *Find what* text box, Word will stop at *FBI*.

Activity 3.2

Revealing Formatting; Finding and Replacing Formatting

Display formatting applied to specific text in a document at the Reveal Formatting task pane. Display this task pane using the keyboard shortcut Shift + F1. The Reveal Formatting task pane displays font, paragraph, and section formatting applied to text where the insertion point is positioned or to selected text. With options at the Find and Replace dialog box with the Replace tab selected, you can search for specific formatting or characters containing specific formatting and replace with other characters or formatting.

Project

After reviewing the Assessment of Child Development form, you decide that the headings would look better set in a different font and font color. To display the formatting applied to specific text, you will use the Reveal Formatting task pane and then find and replace font formatting.

Cascade View
PEDIATRICS

① With **WordMedS3-01.docx** open, press Ctrl + Home to move the insertion point to the beginning of the document and then press Shift + F1.

> Pressing Shift + F1 displays the Reveal Formatting task pane with information on the formatting applied to the title. Generally, a minus symbol precedes *Font* and *Paragraph* and a plus symbol precedes *Section* in the *Formatting of selected text* section. Click the minus symbol to hide any items below a heading and click the plus symbol to reveal items. Some items in the Reveal Formatting task pane are hyperlinks. For example, click the *Font* hyperlink and the Font dialog box displays. Use these hyperlinks to make changes to the document formatting.

② Click anywhere in the paragraph of text below the subtitle and look at the Reveal Formatting task pane to determine the formatting.

③ Click anywhere in the heading *Child Development – Talking* and then notice the formatting applied to the text.

④ Close the Reveal Formatting task pane by clicking the Close button located in the upper right corner of the task pane.

⑤ Find text set in 12-point Candara bold and replace it with text set in 13-point Cambria bold and in dark blue color. To begin, position the insertion point at the beginning of the document and then click the Replace button 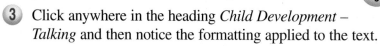 in the Editing group.

⑥ At the Find and Replace dialog box, press the Delete key. (This deletes any text that displays in the *Find what* text box.)

⑦ Click the More button. (If a check mark displays in the *Find all word forms* check box, click the option to remove the mark.)

⑧ Click the Format button located at the bottom of the dialog box and then click *Font* at the drop-down list.

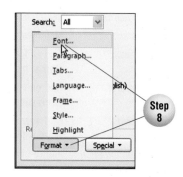

In Brief
Reveal Formatting
1. Click in desired text.
2. Press Shift + F1.

9) At the Find Font dialog box, change the *Font* to *Candara*, the *Font style* to *Bold*, and the *Size* to *12*, and then click OK to close the dialog box.

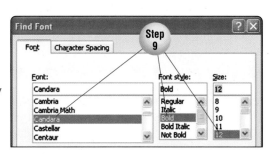

10) At the Find and Replace dialog box, press the Tab key and then press the Delete key. (This removes any text in the *Replace with* text box.)

11) Click the Format button located at the bottom of the dialog box and then click *Font* at the drop-down list.

12) At the Replace Font dialog box, change the *Font* to *Cambria*, the *Font style* to *Bold*, the *Size* to *13*, and the *Font color* to Dark Blue, and then click OK to close the dialog box.

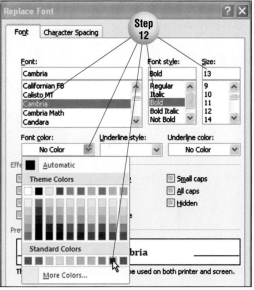

> To change the font size to 13, select the existing text in the *Size* text box and then type 13.

13) At the Find and Replace dialog box, click the Replace All button. At the message telling you that the search of the document is complete and two replacements were made, click OK.

14) With the Find and Replace dialog box open and the insertion point positioned in the *Find what* text box, click the No Formatting button (located toward the bottom of the dialog box). Press the Tab key to move the insertion point to the *Replace with* text box and then click the No Formatting button. (This deletes any font formatting that displays in the *Find what* and *Replace with* text boxes.)

15) With the Find and Replace dialog box open, find all text set in 12-point Calibri bold and replace with 11-point Cambria bold in dark blue.

> Twelve replacements should be made.

16) At the Find and Replace dialog box with the insertion point positioned in the *Find what* text box, click the No Formatting button. Press the Tab key and then click the No Formatting button. Click the Less button and then click the Close button.

17) Select the title *ASSESSMENT OF CHILD DEVELOPMENT* and the subtitle *Ages Newborn to Three Years* and then change the font to 16-point Cambria bold and the font color to Dark Blue.

18) Save **WordMedS3-01.docx**.

In Addition

Comparing Formatting

Along with displaying formatting applied to text, you can use the Reveal Formatting task pane to compare formatting of two text selections to determine what formatting is different. To compare formatting, display the Reveal Formatting task pane and then select the first instance of formatting to be compared. Click the *Compare to another selection* check box to insert a check mark and then select the second instance of formatting to compare. Any differences between the two selections will display in the *Formatting differences* list box.

Activity 3.3

Cutting, Copying, and Pasting Text; Using Paste Special

With the Cut, Copy, and Paste buttons in the Clipboard group in the Home tab, you can move and/or copy words, sentences, or entire sections of text to other locations in a document. You can cut and paste text or copy and paste text within the same document or between documents. Specify the formatting of pasted text with options at the Paste Special dialog box. Use options at the dialog box to specify how you want text pasted in the document.

Project

After consulting with Deanna Reynolds, the child development specialist at Cascade View Pediatrics, Sydney Larsen has asked you to reorganize the Assessment of Child Development form and include additional information from other sources.

1. With **WordMedS3-01.docx** open, move the *Child Development – Hearing* section above the *Child Development – Talking* section. Begin by selecting from the beginning of the *Child Development – Hearing* heading to the end of the document.

2. Click the Cut button ✂ in the Clipboard group in the Home tab.

    This places the text in a special location within Word called the "Clipboard."

    ? PROBLEM

    If you click the wrong button, immediately click the Undo button.

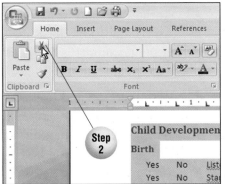

3. Position the insertion point at the beginning of the heading *Child Development – Talking* and then click the Paste button 📋 in the Clipboard group in the Home tab.

    A Paste Options button 📋 displays below the pasted text. Click this button and options display for specifying the formatting of the pasted text. The default setting keeps source formatting for the pasted text. You can choose to match the destination formatting, keep only the text and not the formatting, or display the Word Options dialog box with options for specifying defaults for pasted text.

4. Copy text from another document and paste it in the Assessment of Child Development document. To begin, open **CDSpecialistQuestions.docx**.

5. Select the line containing the text *Child's Name: _____* and the two lines of text below and then click the Copy button 📋 in the Clipboard group.

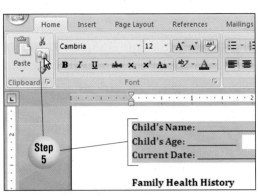

6. Click the button on the Taskbar representing **WordMedS3-01.docx**.

7. Position the insertion point at the end of the first paragraph of text (the paragraph that begins *Before you bring your child to the next...*) and then press the Enter key twice.

8. Click the Paste button 📋 in the Clipboard group.

9 Hover the mouse pointer over the Paste Options button (displays in the lower right corner of the copied text) until the button displays with a down-pointing arrow and then click the button.

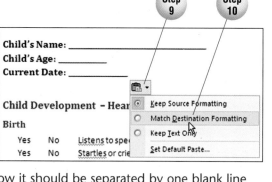

10 At the Paste Options drop-down list, click the *Match Destination Formatting* option.

> The copied text and the heading below it should be separated by one blank line (a double space).

11 Click the button on the Taskbar representing **CDSpecialistQuestions.docx**.

12 Move the insertion point to the end of the document and then select the heading *Additional Information* and the paragraph of text below the heading.

13 Click the Copy button [icon] in the Clipboard group.

14 Click the button on the Taskbar representing **WordMedS3-01.docx**.

15 Move the insertion point to the end of the document a double space below the last line of text and then press Ctrl + Q to remove formatting.

16 Paste the copied text into the document without the formatting by clicking the Paste button arrow and then clicking *Paste Special* at the drop-down list.

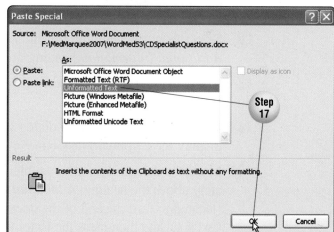

17 At the Paste Special dialog box, click *Unformatted Text* in the *As* list box and then click OK.

18 Set the heading *Additional Information* in 11-point Cambria bold in dark blue color.

19 Save **WordMedS3-01.docx**.

In Brief

Cut and Paste Text
1. Select text.
2. Click Cut button in Clipboard group.
3. Move insertion point to desired position.
4. Click Paste button in Clipboard group.

Copy and Paste Text
1. Select text.
2. Click Copy button in Clipboard group.
3. Move insertion point to desired position.
4. Click Paste button in Clipboard group.

Display Paste Special Dialog Box
1. Cut or copy text.
2. Click Paste button arrow.
3. Click *Paste Special*.
4. Click desired format in *As* list box.
5. Click OK.

In Addition

Moving and Copying Text with the Mouse

You can move selected text using the mouse. To do this, select the text with the mouse and then move the I-beam pointer inside the selected text until the I-beam pointer turns into an arrow pointer. Hold down the left mouse button, drag the arrow pointer (displays with a gray box attached) to the location where you want the selected text inserted, and then release the button. You can copy and move selected text by following similar steps. The difference is that you need to hold down the Ctrl key while dragging with the mouse. With the Ctrl key down, a box containing a plus symbol displays near the gray box by the arrow pointer.

Activity 3.4

Using the Clipboard Task Pane

Using the Clipboard task pane, you can collect up to 24 different items and then paste them in various locations in a document. Display the Clipboard task pane by clicking the Clipboard group dialog box launcher. Cut or copy an item and the item displays in the Clipboard task pane.

If the item is text, the first 50 characters display. Paste an item by positioning the insertion point at the desired location and then clicking the item in the Clipboard task pane. When all desired items are inserted, click the Clear All button located in the upper right corner of the task pane.

Project Sydney Larsen wants you to include additional information from the Child Development Specialist Questionnaire form. You will use the Clipboard to copy sections of text from the questionnaire document and paste them into the Assessment of Child Development form.

1. Make sure **WordMedS3-01.docx** and **CDSpecialistQuestions.docx** are open.

2. Make the **CDSpecialistQuestions.docx** document active and then display the Clipboard task pane by clicking the Clipboard group dialog box launcher. If any items display in the Clipboard task pane, click the Clear All button located in the upper right corner of the task pane.

3. Select from the beginning of the *Family Health History* heading to just above (on the blank line) the next heading (*Feeding/Oral Behavior*) and then click the Copy button in the Clipboard group.

   Notice how the copied item is represented in the Clipboard task pane.

4. Select from the beginning of the *Feeding/Oral Behavior* heading to just above the *Sleep* heading and then click the Copy button.

5. Select from the beginning of the *Sleep* heading to just above the *Your Child's Health* heading and then click the Copy button.

6. Select from the beginning of the *Feelings and Moods* heading to just above the *Additional Information* heading and then click the Copy button.

7. Click the button on the Taskbar representing **WordMedS3-01.docx**.

8. Click the Clipboard group dialog box launcher to display the Clipboard task pane.

9. Move the insertion point to the blank line immediately above the heading *Additional Information* (located toward the end of the document), press Ctrl + Q, and then press the Enter key once.

10. Click the item in the Clipboard task pane representing *Feelings and Moods*.

11. Click the Paste Options button and then click *Match Destination Formatting*.

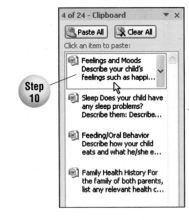

Step 10

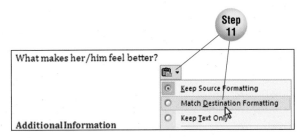

Step 11

12 With the insertion point positioned on the blank line immediately above the heading *Additional Information*, click the item in the Clipboard task pane representing *Feeding/Oral Behavior*.

13 Click the Paste Options button and then click *Match Destination Formatting*.

14 With the insertion point positioned on the blank line immediately above the heading *Additional Information*, paste the item representing *Sleep*.

15 Click the Paste Options button and then click *Match Destination Formatting*.

16 Click the Clear All button located in the upper right corner of the Clipboard task pane.

17 Close the Clipboard task pane by clicking the Close button located in the upper right corner of the task pane.

18 Click the button on the Taskbar representing **CDSpecialistQuestions.docx** and then close the document.

This displays the **WordMedS3-01.docx** document.

19 Set the headings *Feelings and Moods, Feeding/Oral Behavior*, and *Sleep* in 11-point Cambria bold in dark blue color.

20 Select the title *ASSESSMENT OF CHILD DEVELOP-MENT* and the subtitle *Ages Newborn to Three Years*, click the Shading button arrow, and then click the *Aqua, Accent 5, Lighter 60%* option.

21 Apply Aqua, Accent 5, Lighter 80% shading to the headings *Child Development – Hearing* and *Child Development – Talking*.

22 Save **WordMedS3-01.docx**.

In Brief

Use Clipboard Task Pane
1. Click Clipboard group dialog box launcher.
2. Select text.
3. Click Copy button.
4. Select and copy any additional items.
5. Move insertion point to desired position.
6. Click item in Clipboard task pane representing desired item.
7. Paste any other desired items from Clipboard task pane.
8. Click Clear All button.

Step 16   Step 17

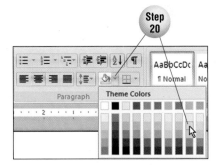

Step 20

In Addition

Clipboard Task Pane Options

Click the Options button located toward the bottom of the Clipboard task pane and a pop-up menu displays with five options as shown at the right. Insert a check mark before those options that you want active. For example, you can choose to display the Clipboard task pane automatically when you cut or copy text, press Ctrl + C twice to display the Clipboard task pane, cut and copy text without displaying the Clipboard task pane, display the Office Clipboard icon on the Taskbar when the Clipboard is active, and display the status message near the Taskbar when copying items to the Clipboard.

Activity 3.5

Changing Page Margins, Orientation, and Size; Applying a Theme

In Word, a page contains a number of defaults such as a page size of 8.5 inches by 11 inches; top, bottom, left, and right margins of one inch; a portrait page orientation; and a page break after approximately nine inches of vertical text on a page. Change these default settings with buttons in the Page Setup group in the Page Layout tab. You can apply formatting to a document using a theme. A theme applies formatting in much the same way as the Quick Style sets. A document theme is a set of formatting choices that include a color theme (a set of colors), a font theme (a set of heading and body text fonts), and an effects theme (a set of lines and fill effects). Apply a theme with buttons in the Themes group in the Page Layout tab.

Project

To further format the Assessment of Child Development form you will change the document margins, orientation, and page size and then customize and add visual appeal by applying a theme.

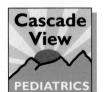

1. With **WordMedS3-01.docx** open, change the margins by clicking the Page Layout tab, clicking the Margins button in the Page Setup group, and then clicking the *Office 2003 Default* option at the drop-down list.

   The *Office 2003 Default* option changes the left and right margins to 1.25, which is the default for Word 2003.

2. Change the page orientation by clicking the Orientation button in the Page Setup group in the Page Layout tab and then clicking *Landscape* at the drop-down list.

   By default, a page is set in portrait orientation. At this orientation, Word considers a page 8.5 inches wide and 11 inches tall. Change to landscape orientation and Word considers a page 11 inches wide and 8.5 inches tall. You can also change page orientation at the Page Setup dialog box with the Margins tab selected.

3. With the document in landscape orientation, you decide to make changes to the margins. To begin, click the Margins button in the Page Setup group in the Page Layout tab and then click the *Custom Margins* option that displays at the bottom of the drop-down list.

4. At the Page Setup dialog box with the Margins tab selected, click the down-pointing arrow at the right side of the *Bottom* option until *1"* displays. Click the up-pointing arrow at the right side of the *Left* option until *1.5"* displays.

   You can also change a margin measurement by selecting the measurement and then typing the new measurement.

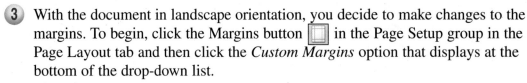

5. Select the current measurement in the *Right* text box and then type **1.5**.

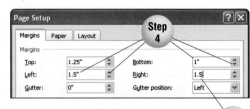

6 Click OK to close the Page Setup dialog box.

7 Apply a theme to the document by clicking the Themes button [Aa] in the Themes group and then clicking *Flow* at the drop-down gallery.

> Apply formatting to an entire document using a theme. A document theme is formatting that includes a font theme, a color theme, and an effects theme.

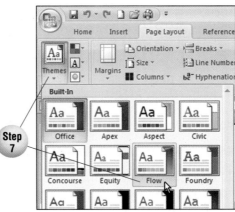

8 You like the color of the theme but you decide to change the font. To do this, click the Theme Fonts button [A ▾] in the Themes group and then click *Apex*.

9 You decide to experiment with paper size by clicking the Size button [▯] in the Page Setup group and then clicking the *Legal* option at the drop-down list.

> Your drop-down list may display differently than what you see in the image below and at the right.

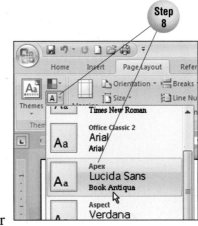

10 Scroll through the document and notice how the document is affected by the Legal page size. After looking at the document you decide to return to the default page size. To do this, click the Size button [▯] in the Page Setup group and then click *Letter* at the drop-down list.

11 Return the margins to the default by clicking the Margins button [▯] and then clicking *Normal* at the drop-down list.

12 Return the orientation to Portrait by clicking the Orientation button [▤] and then clicking *Portrait* at the drop-down list.

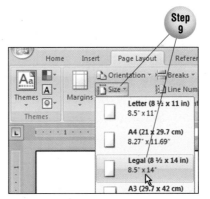

13 Save **WordMedS3-01.docx**.

In Brief

Changing Margins
1. Click Page Layout tab.
2. Click Margins button.
3. Click desired option.

Changing Orientation
1. Click Page Layout tab.
2. Click Orientation button.
3. Click desired orientation option.

Changing Page Size
1. Click Page Layout tab.
2. Click Size button.
3. Click desired size option.

Apply a Theme
1. Click Page Layout tab.
2. Click Themes button.
3. Click desired theme.

In Addition

Applying a Theme

In Step 7, you applied a theme to the document. A theme is a set of formatting choices that includes a color theme (a set of colors), a font theme (a set of heading and body text fonts), and an effect theme (a set of lines and fill effects). Built-in themes available in Microsoft Word are also available in Excel, PowerPoint, and Outlook. Having these themes available across applications allows you to "brand" business files such as documents, workbooks, and presentations with a consistent and uniform appearance.

Activity 3.6

Customizing the Page and Page Background

The Page Background group in the Page Layout tab contains buttons you can use to insert a watermark, change the page color, and insert a page border. In an activity in Section 1, you applied a watermark to a document using options at the Building Blocks Organizer dialog box. You can also apply a watermark with the Watermark button. In a project in Section 2, you applied a page border to a document. You can also apply a page border using the Page Borders button in the Page Background group. The Pages group in the Insert tab contains buttons for adding a cover page, a blank page, and a page break.

Project

To add visual appeal to the Assessment of Child Development document, you will apply page color and a page border. You will add a cover page at the beginning of the document and identify the document as a draft by inserting a watermark.

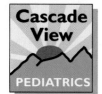

1. With **WordMedS3-01.docx** open, press Ctrl + Home.

2. Insert a watermark by clicking the Page Layout tab, clicking the Watermark button [A] Watermark ▾ in the Page Background group, scrolling down the drop-down list, and then clicking the *DRAFT 1* option.

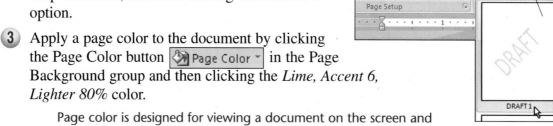

3. Apply a page color to the document by clicking the Page Color button 🎨 Page Color ▾ in the Page Background group and then clicking the *Lime, Accent 6, Lighter 80%* color.

   Page color is designed for viewing a document on the screen and does not print.

4. Click the Page Borders button ▢ Page Borders in the Page Background group.

5. At the Borders and Shading dialog box with the Page Border tab selected, click the down-pointing arrow at the right side of the *Art* option box. Scroll down the list of page borders and then click the art border option shown at right. Click OK to close the dialog box.

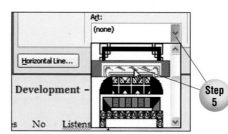

6. Move the insertion point to the beginning of the heading *Feelings and Moods* and then insert a hard page break by clicking the Insert tab and then clicking the Page Break button 📄 Page Break in the Pages group.

   You can also insert a hard page break with the keyboard shortcut Ctrl + Enter or by clicking the Page Layout tab, clicking the Breaks button 📄 Breaks ▾ in the Page Setup group, and then clicking *Page* at the drop-down list.

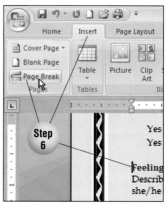

7. Save and then print **WordMedS3-01.docx**. (The page background color does not print.)

(8) After looking at the printed document, you decide to make some changes. Remove the page color by clicking the Page Layout tab, clicking the Page Color button 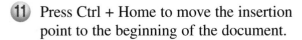 in the Page Background group, and then clicking the *No Color* option.

(9) Remove the page border by clicking the Page Borders button, clicking *None* in the *Setting* section of the Borders and Shading dialog box, and then clicking OK.

(10) Delete the page break you inserted by positioning the insertion point on the blank line below the text on page 3 and then pressing the Delete key twice.

(11) Press Ctrl + Home to move the insertion point to the beginning of the document.

(12) Insert a cover page by clicking the Insert tab, clicking the Cover Page button in the Pages group, and then clicking *Pinstripes* at the drop-down list. (You will need to scroll down the list to display this cover page.)

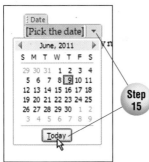

Step 8

Step 12

(13) Click in the placeholder text *[Type the document title]* and then type **Assessment of Child Development**.

(14) Click in the placeholder text *[Type the document subtitle]* and then type **Ages Newborn to Three Years**.

(15) Click in the placeholder text *[Pick the date]*, click the down-pointing arrow at the right of the placeholder, and then click the Today button to insert the current date.

(16) Click in the placeholder text *[Type the company name]* and then type **Cascade View Pediatrics**.

(17) Select the name that displays below *Cascade View Pediatrics* and then type your first and last names.

(18) Save **WordMedS3-01.docx**.

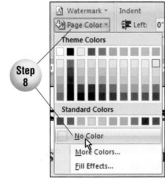

Step 15

In Addition

Inserting a Blank Page

The Pages group in the Insert tab contains a Blank Page button. Click this button to insert a blank page at the position of the inserting point. Inserting a blank page can be useful as a spaceholder in a document when you want to insert an illustration, graphic, or figure.

Activity 3.7

Inserting Page Numbering, Headers, and Footers

Insert page numbering in a document with options from the Page Number button or in a header or footer. Click the Page Number button in the Header & Footer group in the Insert tab and a drop-down list displays with options for inserting page numbers at the top or bottom of the page or in the page margins, removing page numbers, and formatting page numbers. Text that appears at the top of every page is called a *header* and text that appears at the bottom of every page is referred to as a *footer*. Headers and footers are common in manuscripts, textbooks, reports, and other publications. Insert a predesigned header in a document with the Header button in the Header & Footer group in the Insert tab. Insert a predesigned footer in the same manner as a header. Headers and footers are visible in Print Layout view but not Draft view. Predesigned headers and footers contain formatting which you can customize.

Project

Insert identifying information in the document using a header and footer and insert page numbering in the Assessment of Child Development document.

1. With **WordMedS3-01.docx** open, move the insertion point to the beginning of the title *ASSESSMENT OF CHILD DEVELOPMENT* at the top of the second page (*not* on the cover page).

   When a document contains a cover page, you generally insert page elements such as page numbers, headers, and footers on the first page *after* the cover page.

   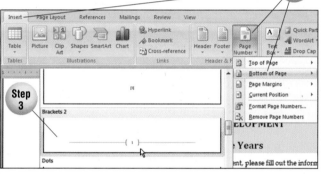

2. Number pages at the bottom of each page by clicking the Insert tab, clicking the Page Number button in the Header & Footer group, and then pointing to *Bottom of Page*.

3. At the gallery of predesigned page numbers, scroll down the list and then click the *Brackets 2* option.

4. Double-click in the body of the document and then scroll through the document and notice how the page numbers display toward the bottom of each page except the cover page.

5. Remove page numbering by clicking the Insert tab, clicking the Page Number button in the Header & Footer group, and then clicking *Remove Page Numbers* at the drop-down list.

6. Insert a header in the document by clicking the Header button in the Header & Footer group, scrolling down the header list, and then clicking the *Pinstripes* header.

   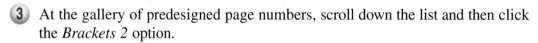

   Notice how the document title you entered in the cover page is inserted in the header.

7. Double-click in the body of the document.

   This makes the document active and dims the header.

8 Insert a footer in the document by clicking the Insert tab, clicking the Footer button in the Header & Footer group, scrolling down the footer list, and then clicking the *Pinstripes* footer.

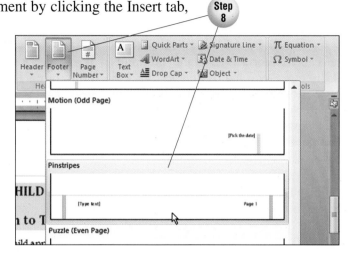

Step 8

9 Click in the placeholder text *[Type text]* and then type your first and last names.

10 Double-click in the body of the document and then scroll through the document and notice how the header and footer appear on each page except the cover page.

11 Remove the header by clicking the Insert tab, clicking the Header button in the Header & Footer group, and then clicking the *Remove Header* option at the drop-down list.

12 Edit the footer by clicking the Insert tab, clicking the Footer button in the Header & Footer group, and then clicking *Edit Footer* at the drop-down list.

13 Press Ctrl + A to select all of the text in the footer and then change the font to 10-point Calibri bold.

14 Double-click in the document.

15 Remove the watermark by clicking the Page Layout tab, clicking the Watermark button, and then clicking the *Remove Watermark* option at the drop-down list.

16 Press Ctrl + End to display the end of the document. If the document flows on to the fifth page, delete extra blank lines in the *Sleep* section until text no longer displays on the fifth page.

17 Save, print, and then close **WordMedS3-01.docx**.

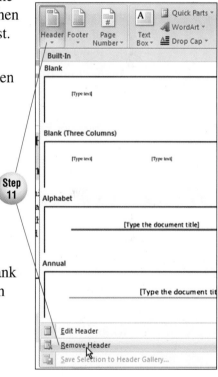

Step 11

In Brief

Insert Page Numbers
1. Click Insert tab.
2. Click Page Number button.
3. Point to desired location.
4. Click desired option at drop-down gallery.

Insert Header
1. Click Insert tab.
2. Click Header button.
3. Click desired option at drop-down gallery.

Insert Footer
1. Click Insert tab.
2. Click Footer button.
3. Click desired option at drop-down gallery.

In Addition

Creating Your Own Header or Footer

You can create your own header or footer using the *Edit Header* or *Edit Footer* options from the drop-down list. For example, to create a header, click the Insert tab, click the Header button, and then click *Edit Header* at the drop-down list. This displays a Header pane in the document and also displays the Header & Footer Tools Design tab with buttons and options for editing the header. Make the desired edits to the header with options in the tab and then close the header window by clicking the Close Header and Footer button located in the Close group in the Header & Footer Tools Design tab.

Activity 3.8

Inserting a Section Break; Creating and Modifying Newspaper Columns

To increase the ease with which a person can read and understand groups of words (referred to as the *readability* of a document), consider setting text in the document in newspaper columns. Newspaper columns contain text that flows up and down on the page. Create newspaper columns with the Columns button in the Page Layout tab or with options at the Columns dialog box. If you want to apply column formatting to only a portion of a document, insert a section break in the document. Insert a section break in the document with options at the Breaks button drop-down list.

Project

Sydney Larsen has asked you to format the monthly newsletter into columns and to apply some formatting to improve the visual appeal of the newsletter.

1. Open **CVPNewsletter.docx** and then save the document with Save As and name it **WordMedS3-02**.

2. Position the insertion point at the beginning of the first heading, *Pediatrician Joins CVP*.

3. Insert a continuous section break by clicking the Page Layout tab, clicking the Breaks button in the Page Setup group, and then clicking *Continuous* in the *Section Breaks* section.

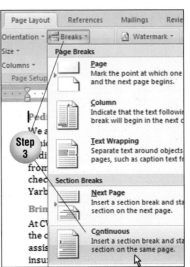

   The section break is not visible in Print Layout view. A continuous section break separates the document into sections but does not insert a page break. Click one of the other three options in the *Section Breaks* section of the Breaks button drop-down list if you want to insert a section break that begins a new page.

4. Click the Draft button in the View section of the Status bar.

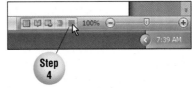

   The View section on the Status bar is located toward the bottom right corner of the screen. You can also display Draft view by clicking the View tab and then clicking the Draft button in the Document Views section.

5. With the insertion point positioned below the section break, format the text below the section break into three newspaper columns by clicking the Columns button in the Page Setup group in the Page Layout tab and then clicking *Three* at the drop-down list.

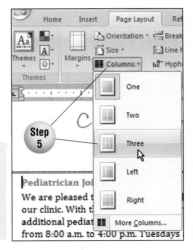

   Formatting text into columns automatically changes the view to Print Layout.

PROBLEM

If the second and third columns of text align with the title, click the Undo button. Make sure the insertion point is positioned at the beginning of the first paragraph of text (not the beginning of the document) and then create the columns.

6 As you view the document, you decide that the three columns are too narrow, so you decide to set the text in two columns and also add a line between. To do this, click in the heading *Pediatrician Joins CVP* and then display the Columns dialog box by clicking the Columns button in the Page Setup group and then clicking *More Columns* at the drop-down list.

7 At the Columns dialog box, click *Two* in the *Presets* section.

8 Slightly decrease the spacing between the two columns by clicking once on the down-pointing arrow at the right of the *Spacing* option in the *Width and spacing* section.

> Make sure *0.4″* displays in the *Spacing* text box.

9 Make sure a check mark displays in the *Equal column width* check box. If not, click the option to insert a check mark.

> This option, when activated, makes the two columns the same width.

10 Click the *Line between* option to insert a check mark.

> Choosing the *Line between* option inserts a line between the two columns. The Preview section of the dialog box provides a visual representation of the columns.

11 Click OK to close the dialog box.

12 Press Ctrl + End to move the insertion point to the end of the document. Looking at the columns, you decide to balance the two columns. To do this, click the Breaks button in the Page Setup group and then click *Continuous* in the *Section Breaks* section.

13 Save, print, and then close **WordMedS3-02.docx**.

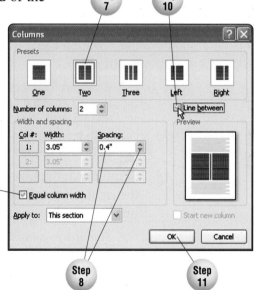

In Addition

Changing Column Width

One method for changing column width in a document is to drag the column marker on the horizontal ruler. To change the width (and also the spacing) of columns of text, position the arrow pointer on the left or right edge of a column marker on the horizontal ruler until it turns into a double-headed arrow pointing left and right. Hold down the left mouse button, drag the column marker to the left or right to make the column of text wider or narrower, and then release the mouse button. Hold down the Alt key while dragging the column marker and measurements display on the horizontal ruler.

Activity 3.9

Inserting, Sizing, and Moving Images in a Document

Office 2007 includes a gallery of media images you can insert in a document such as clip art, photographs, and movie images, as well as sound clips. Specify and insert images in a document with options at the Clip Art task pane. You can also insert a picture or image from a specific file location with options at the Insert Picture dialog box. You can move, size, and customize an inserted image or picture with buttons in the Picture Tools Format tab.

Project

Deanna Reynolds has asked you to enhance a document created for her parenting classes. You decide to add clip art images to the document and apply some additional formatting to enhance the visual appeal.

1. Open **CVPParentClasses.docx** and then save the document with Save As and name it **WordMedS3-03**.

2. You know that images in a document can generally improve its visual appeal, so you decide to add an image of a parent and child. To begin, display the Clip Art task pane by clicking the Insert tab and then clicking the Clip Art button in the Illustrations group.

   This displays the Clip Art task pane at the right side of the screen.

3. At the Clip Art task pane, type **toddler** in the *Search for* text box and then click the Go button. (If text displays in the *Search for* text box, select the text and then type **toddler**.)

   If you are connected to the Internet, a message may display asking if you want to include thousands of clip art images and photos from Microsoft Office Online. Check with your instructor to determine if you should click the Yes button or the No button.

4. Scroll down the images and then click the image shown at the right. (If this image is not available, choose another image related to *toddler*.)

   The image is inserted in the document, it is selected (sizing handles display around the image), and the Picture Tools Format tab displays as shown in Figure W3.1.

FIGURE W3.1 Picture Tools Format Tab

5. Close the Clip Art task pane by clicking the Close button located in the upper right corner of the task pane.

6. With the image selected, click the Text Wrapping button 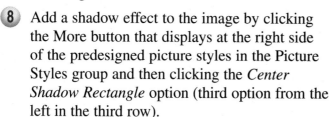 in the Arrange group in the Picture Tools Format tab and then click *Tight* at the drop-down list.

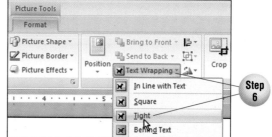

7. Click in the *Shape Height* box in the Size group, type **1.9**, and then press Enter.

    > When you change the height measurement, the width measurement is automatically changed to maintain the proportions of the image.

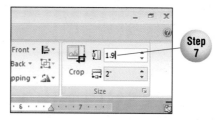

8. Add a shadow effect to the image by clicking the More button that displays at the right side of the predesigned picture styles in the Picture Styles group and then clicking the *Center Shadow Rectangle* option (third option from the left in the third row).

9. Move the image by positioning the arrow pointer on the image until the pointer displays with a four-headed arrow attached, holding down the mouse button, dragging the image so it is positioned as shown in Figure W3.2, and then releasing the mouse button.

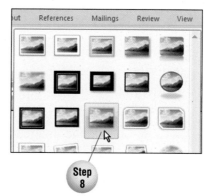

10. Click outside the image to deselect it.

11. Position the insertion point at the beginning of the bulleted list.

12. Click the Insert tab and then click the Clip Art button in the Illustrations group.

13. At the Clip Art task pane, make sure *toddler* displays in the *Search for* text box as well as the images associated with *toddler*. (If *toddler* does not display, select any existing text in the *Search for* text box and then type **toddler**.)

14. Click the image shown at the right. (If this image is not available, choose another image related to *toddler*.)

15. Close the Clip Art task pane by clicking the Close button located in the upper right corner of the task pane.

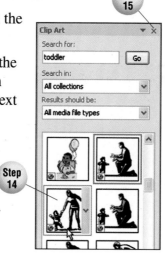

continues

16 With the image selected, click the Text Wrapping button and then click *Square* at the drop-down list.

17 Click the down-pointing arrow at the right side of the *Shape Height* box in the Size group until *1.3* displays in the box.

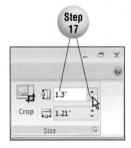

18 Add a shadow effect to the image by clicking the More button that displays at the right side of the predesigned picture styles in the Picture Styles group and then clicking the *Center Shadow Rectangle* option (third option from the left in the third row).

19 Move the image by positioning the arrow pointer on the image until the pointer displays with a four-headed arrow attached, holding down the left mouse button, dragging the image so it is positioned as shown in Figure W3.2, and then releasing the mouse button.

20 Click outside the image to deselect it.

21 Move the insertion point to the end of the document and then insert the Cascade View Pediatrics logo. To begin, click the Insert tab and then click the Picture button ![icon] in the Illustrations group.

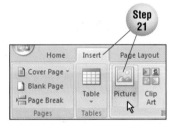

22 At the Insert Picture dialog box, display the folder where your data documents are located and then double-click *CVPLogo.jpg*.

23 With the image selected, click the Text Wrapping button and then click *Tight* at the drop-down list.

24 With the image still selected, hold down the Shift key and then drag one of the corner sizing handles (circles) to reduce the size of the logo so it displays as shown in Figure W3.2. If necessary, move the logo to the position shown in the figure.

> Holding down the Shift key while increasing or decreasing the size of an image maintains the proportions of the image. When you insert the image, it will display on the second page. Make sure you decrease the size so the logo fits on the first page.

25 Save, print, and then close **WordMedS3-03.docx**.

FIGURE W3.2 Completed **WordMedS3-03.docx** Document

In Brief

Insert Clip Art Image
1. Click Insert tab.
2. Click Clip Art button.
3. Type category information in *Search for* text box.
4. Click Go button.
5. Click desired clip art image.

Insert Picture
1. Click Insert tab.
2. Click Picture button.
3. Navigate to desired folder.
4. Double-click desired picture file.

CASCADE VIEW PEDIATRICS
Basic Parenting Course

Presented by Deanna Reynolds
Child Development Specialist

Parenting is a full-time job and wondering about your child's behaviors and your responsibilities as a parent are normal. You may have asked yourself:

- What can I do when my child misbehaves?
- Is my child's development and behavior "normal"?
- What is the difference between punishment and discipline?
- How can I improve the way I communicate with my child?
- How can I help my child learn to make good choices?

Deanna Reynolds, Child Development Specialist at Cascade View Pediatrics, will cover these questions as well as others in a four-week course designed to help you better handle the challenges of parenting:

When	Monday and Wednesday
Beginning	Monday, March 7
Ending	Wednesday, March 30
Time	7:00 p.m. to 8:30 p.m.
Where	Cascade View Pediatrics
Location	Suite 150, Room 3
Cost	$85

For more information on this important parenting class and to sign up for the class, call (503) 555-7753. You can also read more about the classes and register online by visiting the Cascade View Pediatrics web site at www.emcp.cvpeds.com.

Cascade View PEDIATRICS

In Addition

Formatting an Image with Buttons in the Picture Tools Format Tab

Images inserted in a document can be formatted in a variety of ways, which might include adding fill color and border lines, increasing or decreasing the brightness or contrast, choosing a wrapping style, and cropping the image. Format an image with buttons in the Picture Tools Format tab as shown in Figure W3.1. With buttons in the Adjust group you can control the brightness and contrast of the image; recolor the image; change to a different image; reset the image to its original size, position, and color; and compress the picture. Compress a picture to reduce resolution or discard extra information to save room on the hard drive or to reduce download time. Use buttons in the Picture Styles group to apply a predesigned style, insert a picture border, or apply a picture effect. The Arrange group contains buttons for positioning the image, wrapping text around the image, and aligning and rotating the image. Use options in the Size group to crop the image and specify the height and width of the image.

Activity 3.10

Inserting, Sizing, and Moving WordArt in a Document; Inserting a File

Use the WordArt application to distort or modify text to conform to a variety of shapes. Consider using WordArt to create a company logo, letterhead, flier title, or heading. With WordArt, you can change the font, style, and alignment of text; use different fill patterns and colors; customize border lines; and add shadow and three-dimensional effects. You can size and move selected WordArt text. In some situations, you may want to insert one file into another. Do this at the Insert File dialog box.

Project

The Health Insurance Portability and Accountability Act of 1996 (HIPAA) requires that healthcare providers adopt and adhere to policies and procedures that protect the patient's privacy regarding disclosure of sensitive health information. Cascade View Pediatrics has established clear guidelines for patient confidentiality. Sydney Larsen has asked you to compile a document with information on patient confidentiality and enhance the document with WordArt for more impact.

1. Open **CVPHIPAA.docx** and then save the document with Save As and name it **WordMedS3-04**.

2. Press Ctrl + End to move the insertion point to the end of the document.

3. Insert a file into the current document by clicking the Insert tab, clicking the Object button arrow (located in the Text group), and then clicking *Text from File* at the drop-down list.

4. At the Insert File dialog box, navigate to the folder containing your data documents and then double-click *CVPRules.docx*.

5. Select the paragraphs of text in the document and then insert bullets by clicking the Bullets button in the Paragraph group in the Home tab.

6. Move the insertion point to the beginning of the document and then insert WordArt by clicking the Insert tab and then clicking the WordArt button in the Text group.

7. At the WordArt button drop-down list, click the third option from the left in the third row (*WordArt style 15*).

8. At the Edit WordArt Text dialog box, type **Important** and then click OK to close the dialog box.

   Blue sizing handles display around the selected WordArt, and the WordArt Tools Format tab is active as shown in Figure W3.3.

FIGURE W3.3 WordArt Tools Format Tab

9 Increase the width of the WordArt text by positioning the mouse pointer on the middle right sizing handle until the pointer turns into a double-headed arrow pointing left and right. Hold down the left mouse button, drag to the right to approximately the 5-inch mark on the horizontal ruler, and then release the mouse button.

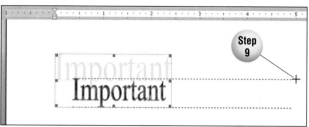

Step 9

> When you release the mouse button, the WordArt will stretch out to approximately the 5.5-inch mark on the horizontal ruler.

10 Click the Text Wrapping button ☒ Text Wrapping ▾ in the Arrange group in the WordArt Tools Format tab and then click *Square* at the drop-down list.

Step 10

11 Click the Shape Fill button arrow in the WordArt Styles group in the WordArt Tools Format tab and then click *Aqua, Accent 5, Darker 25%* at the drop-down gallery.

12 Click the Shape Outline button arrow in the WordArt Styles group and then click Dark Red in the *Standard Colors* section of the drop-down gallery.

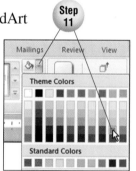

Step 11

Step 12

13 Drag the WordArt text so it is centered between the left and right margins. To do this, position the mouse pointer on the WordArt text until the pointer displays with a four-headed arrow attached. Hold down the left mouse button, drag the WordArt text to the desired position, and then release the mouse button.

> Make sure that the heading *Patient Confidentiality Rules* displays below the WordArt text and not at the right side.

14 Click outside the WordArt text box to deselect it.

15 Save **WordMedS3-04.docx**.

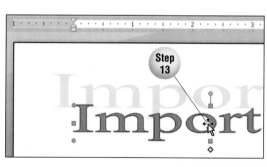

Step 13

In Brief

Insert File into Another
1. Click Insert tab.
2. Click Object button arrow in Text group and then click *Text from File*.
3. At Insert File dialog box, double-click desired document.

Insert WordArt
1. Click Insert tab.
2. Click WordArt button.
3. At WordArt button drop-down list, double-click desired option.
4. At Edit WordArt Text dialog box, type desired text.
5. Click OK.

In Addition

Changing the Font and Font Size

The font for WordArt text will vary depending on the choice you make at the WordArt button drop-down list. You can change the font at the Edit WordArt Text dialog box. Display this dialog box by clicking the Edit Text button in the Text group in the WordArt Tools Format tab. At the Edit WordArt Text dialog box, click the down-pointing arrow at the right side of the *Font* option and then click the desired font at the drop-down list. Change the font size by clicking the down-pointing arrow at the right side of the *Size* text box. The Edit WordArt Text dialog box also contains a Bold button and an Italic button you can click to apply the specific formatting.

Activity 3.11

Inserting and Customizing Shapes and Text Boxes

With the Shapes button in the Insert tab, you can draw a variety of shapes and lines and then customize the shapes or lines with options in the Drawing Tools Format tab. Use the Text Box button to draw a box and then type text inside the box. Customize a text box with buttons on the Text Box Tools Format tab. You can size and move a drawn object or text box in the same manner as an image or WordArt text.

Project

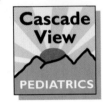

To enhance further the patient confidentiality rules document and to emphasize the priority of maintaining confidentiality, you decide to add a shape containing text at the bottom of the document.

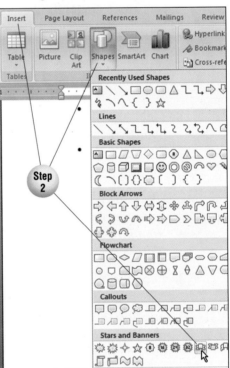

1. With **WordMedS3-04.docx** open, press Ctrl + End to move the insertion point to the end of the document.

2. Draw the banner shape shown in Figure W3.4. To do this, click the Insert tab, click the Shapes button in the Illustrations group, and then click the *Up Ribbon* shape in the *Stars and Banners* section (ninth option from the left in the top row of the section).

FIGURE W3.4 Up Ribbon Banner Shape

Patient confidentiality is a top priority at Cascade View Pediatrics!

3. Position the mouse pointer (displays as crosshairs) below the text at approximately the 1-inch mark on the horizontal ruler and the 6.5-inch mark on the vertical ruler. Hold down the left mouse button, drag down and to the right until the banner is approximately 5 inches wide and 1.5 inches high, and then release the mouse button.

This inserts the shape in the document and makes active the Drawing Tools Format tab as shown in Figure W3.5.

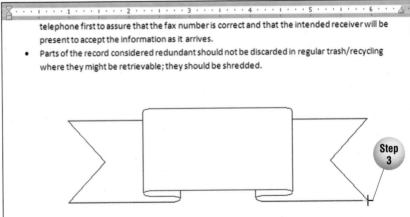

telephone first to assure that the fax number is correct and that the intended receiver will be present to accept the information as it arrives.

- Parts of the record considered redundant should not be discarded in regular trash/recycling where they might be retrievable; they should be shredded.

FIGURE W3.5 Drawing Tools Format Tab

In Brief

Draw a Shape
1. Click Insert tab.
2. Click Shapes button.
3. Click desired shape.
4. Drag with mouse to draw shape.

Draw a Text Box
1. Click Insert tab.
2. Click Text Box button.
3. Click *Draw Text Box* option.
4. Drag with mouse to draw text box.

④ Fill the banner with light aqua color by clicking the Shape Fill button arrow in the Shape Styles group in the Drawing Tools Format tab and then clicking *Aqua, Accent 5, Lighter 60%* in the drop-down gallery.

⑤ Draw a text box inside the shape by clicking the Insert tab, clicking the Text Box button in the Text group, and then clicking the *Draw Text Box* option at the drop-down list option.

⑥ Position the mouse pointer (displays as crosshairs) inside the banner, hold down the left mouse button, drag to create a text box similar to the one shown at the right, and then release the mouse button.

⑦ Change the font size to 12, turn on bold, change to center alignment, and then type **Patient confidentiality is a top priority at Cascade View Pediatrics!**

⑧ Remove fill from the text box by clicking the Text Box Tools Format tab, clicking the Shape Fill button arrow, and then clicking *No Fill* at the drop-down gallery.

> When you remove the fill from the text box, the fill shape is visible. Removing the fill causes the text box to appear to be part of the shape.

⑨ Remove the outline around the text box by clicking the Shape Outline button arrow and then clicking *No Outline* at the drop-down gallery.

⑩ Deselect the text box by clicking outside the banner and text box.

⑪ Save, print, and then close **WordMedS3-04.docx**.

In Addition

Drawing Lines

With options at the Shapes button drop-down list, you can draw lines or enclosed shapes. To draw a line, click an option in the Lines group and the mouse pointer changes to crosshairs. Position the crosshairs in the document and then drag with the mouse to draw the line. If you want to draw a straight horizontal or vertical line, hold down the Shift key while dragging with the mouse.

Drawing Enclosed Shapes

If you choose a shape in the *Lines* section of the drop-down list, the shape you draw is considered a line drawing. If you choose an option in the other sections of the drop-down list, the shape you draw is considered an enclosed shape. When drawing an enclosed shape, you can maintain the proportions of the shape by holding down the Shift key while dragging with the mouse to create the shape.

Activity 3.12

Preparing an Envelope

Word automates the creation of envelopes with options at the Envelopes and Labels dialog box with the Envelopes tab selected. At this dialog box, type a delivery address and a return address. If you enter a return address, Word will ask you before printing if you want to save the new return address as the default return address. Answer yes if you want to use the return address for future envelopes or answer no if you will use a different return address for future envelopes.

Project Deanna Reynolds has asked you to mail a Basic Parenting Course flyer to Lowell Quasim, Education Coordinator at Columbia River General Hospital.

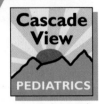

1. Click the New button on the Quick Access toolbar to display a blank document.

    If the New button does not display on the Quick Access toolbar, click the Customize Quick Access Toolbar button that displays at the right side of the toolbar and then click *New* at the drop-down list.

2. Click the Mailings tab and then click the Envelopes button in the Create group.

3. At the Envelopes and Labels dialog box with the Envelopes tab selected, type the following name and address in the *Delivery address* text box. (Press Enter at the end of each line, except the last line containing the city name, state, and ZIP code.)

    Mr. Lowell Quasim
    Education Coordinator
    Columbia River General Hospital
    4550 Fremont Street
    Portland, OR 97045

4. Click in the *Return address* text box and then type the following name and address. (If any text displays in the *Return address* text box, select and then delete it.)

    Deanna Reynolds
    Cascade View Pediatrics
    350 North Skagit
    Portland, OR 97505

5. Click the Add to Document button.

    Clicking the Add to Document button inserts the envelope in the document. You can also send the envelope directly to the printer by clicking the Print button.

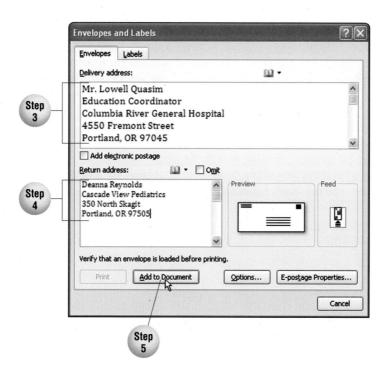

Step 3

Step 4

Step 5

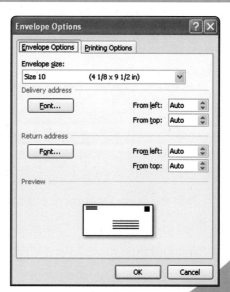

In Brief

Prepare Envelope
1. Click Mailings tab.
2. Click Envelopes button.
3. Type delivery address.
4. Type return address.
5. Click either Add to Document button or Print button.

(6) At the message asking if you want to save the new return address as the default address, click the No button.

(7) Save the document and name it **WordMedS3-05**.

(8) Print and then close **WordMedS3-05.docx**. *Note: Manual feed of the envelope may be required. Please check with your instructor.*

In Addition

Customizing Envelopes

With options at the Envelope Options dialog box shown at the right, you can customize an envelope. Display this dialog box by clicking the Options button at the Envelopes and Labels dialog box with the Envelopes tab selected. At the Envelope Options dialog box, you can change the envelope size, change the font for the delivery and return addresses, and specify the positioning of the addresses in relation to the left and top edges of the envelope.

Activity 3.13

Preparing Mailing Labels

Use Word's Labels feature to print text on mailing labels, file labels, disk labels, or other types of labels. You can create labels for printing on a variety of pre-defined labels, which you can purchase at an office supply store. With the Labels feature, you can create a sheet of mailing labels with the same name and address or enter a different name and address on each label. Create a label with options at the Envelopes and Labels dialog box with the Labels tab selected.

Project

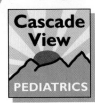

You will create a sheet of mailing labels containing the Cascade View Pediatrics name and address and then create mailing labels for sending the Basic Parenting Course flyer to various professionals and clinics in the area.

1. Click the New button on the Quick Access toolbar to display a blank document.

   You can also press Ctrl + N to display a blank document.

2. Click the Mailings tab and then click the Labels button in the Create group.

3. Type the following information in the *Address* text box. (Press Enter at the end of each line, except the last line containing the city name, state, and ZIP code.)

   Cascade View Pediatrics
   350 North Skagit
   Portland, OR 97505

4. Click the Options button.

5. At the Label Options dialog box, click the down-pointing arrow at the right side of the *Label vendors* list box and then click *Avery US Letter*.

6. Click the down-pointing arrow at the right side of the *Product number* list box, click *5630* in the list box, and then click OK to close the dialog box.

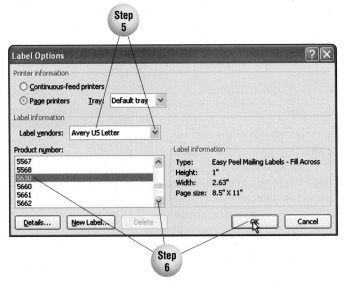

7. Click the New Document button at the Envelopes and Labels dialog box.

8. Save the document and name it **WordMedS3-06**.

9. Print and then close **WordMedS3-06.docx**.

   The number of labels printed on the page varies depending on the label selected at the Label Options dialog box.

10 Click the Mailings tab and then click the Labels button in the Create group.

11 At the Envelopes and Labels dialog box, click the New Document button.

12 At the document, type the first name and address shown in Figure W3.6 in the first label. Press the Tab key twice to move the insertion point to the next label and then type the second name and address shown in Figure W3.6. Continue in this manner until you have typed all of the names and addresses in Figure W3.6.

13 Save the document and name it **WordMedS3-07**.

14 Print and then close **WordMedS3-07.docx**.

15 Close the blank document.

FIGURE W3.6 Mailing Labels for Step 12

Paul Watanabe
Division Street Clinic
5330 Division Street
Portland, OR 97255

Nora Reeves
Community Counseling
1235 North 122nd Avenue
Portland, OR 97230

Dr. Thomas Wickstrom
Columbia Mental Health Center
550 Columbia Boulevard
Portland, OR 97305

Christina Fuentes
Parenting Services
210 Martin Luther King Way
Portland, OR 97403

In Addition

Customizing Labels

Click the Options button at the Envelopes and Labels dialog box with the Labels tab selected and the Label Options dialog box displays as shown at the right. At this dialog box, choose the type of printer, the desired label vendor, and the product number. This dialog box also displays information about the selected label such as type, height, width, and paper size. When you select a label, Word automatically determines label margins. If, however, you want to customize these default settings, click the Details button at the Label Options dialog box.

Features Summary

Feature	Ribbon Tab, Group	Button	Keyboard Shortcut
Clip Art task pane	Insert, Illustrations		
Clipboard task pane	Home, Clipboard		
copy selected text	Home, Clipboard		Ctrl + C
cut selected text	Home, Clipboard		Ctrl + X
Find and Replace dialog box with Find tab selected	Home, Editing		Ctrl + F
Find and Replace dialog box with Replace tab selected	Home, Editing		Ctrl + H
Envelopes and Labels dialog box with Envelopes tab selected	Mailings, Create		
Envelopes and Labels dialog box with Labels tab selected	Mailings, Create		
footer	Insert, Header & Footer		
header	Insert, Header & Footer		
Insert Picture dialog box	Insert, Illustrations		
page border	Page Layout, Page Background	Page Borders	
page break	Insert, Pages	Page Break	Ctrl + Enter
page color	Page Layout, Page Background	Page Color	
page margins	Page Layout, Page Setup		
page number	Insert, Header & Footer		
page orientation	Page Layout, Page Setup		
Page Setup dialog box	Page Layout, Page Setup		
page size	Page Layout, Page Setup		
paste selected text	Home, Clipboard		Ctrl + V
Paste Special dialog box	Home, Clipboard	Paste, Paste Special	
Reveal Formatting task pane			Shift + F1
theme	Page Layout, Themes		
watermark	Page Layout, Page Background	Watermark	
continuous section break	Page Layout, Page Setup	Breaks, Continuous	

Knowledge Check

Completion: In the space provided at the right, write in the correct term, command, or option.

1. Click this button at the Find and Replace dialog box to replace all occurrences of text.
2. Click this button at the Find and Replace dialog box to display additional options.
3. This is the keyboard shortcut to display the Reveal Formatting task pane.
4. The Cut button is located in this group in the Home tab.
5. Click this button to insert selected text in the document.
6. Click this to display the Clipboard task pane.
7. Click this tab to display the Margins button.
8. This is the default measurement for the top, bottom, left, and right margins.
9. This is the default page orientation.
10. This is the default page size.
11. A document theme is a set of formatting choices that includes a font theme, an effects theme, and this.
12. This is the keyboard shortcut to insert a page break.
13. The Breaks button is located in this group in the Page Layouts tab.
14. Insert a footer by clicking the Footer button in this group in the Insert tab.
15. The Clip Art button displays in this group in the Insert tab.
16. Click this button in the Picture Tools Format tab to choose a wrapping style.
17. Click this button in the Insert tab to display the Insert Picture dialog box.
18. When changing the size of an image, maintain the image proportions by holding down this key while dragging a corner sizing handle.
19. To display the Envelopes and Labels dialog box, click this tab and then click the Envelopes button or the Labels button.

Skills Review

Review 1 Finding and Replacing Text; Cutting and Pasting Text

1. Open **CRGHMedicalRecords.docx**.
2. Save the document with Save As and name it **WordMedS3-R1**.
3. Find every occurrence of *crgh* and replace it with *Columbia River General Hospital*.
4. Select the heading *Modifying Medical Records*, the paragraph of text below it, and the blank line below the paragraph and then move the selected text to the end of the document.
5. Save **WordMedS3-R1.docx**.

Review 2 Collecting and Pasting Text

1. With **WordMedS3-R1.docx** open, open the document named **CRGHRecMaintenance.docx**.
2. Turn on the display of the Clipboard task pane. Make sure the Clipboard task pane is empty.
3. At the **CRGHRecMaintenance.docx** document, select and then copy text from the beginning of the heading *Storage and Security* to the blank line just above the heading *Creating a Patient Profile*.
4. Select and then copy text from the beginning of the heading *Creating a Patient Profile* to the blank line just above the heading *Creating Progress Notes*.
5. Select and then copy text from the heading *Creating Progress Notes* to the end of the document.
6. Make **WordMedS3-R1.docx** the active document.
7. Turn on the display of the Clipboard task pane.
8. Move the insertion point to the end of the document and then paste the text (matching destination formatting) that begins with the heading *Creating Progress Notes*.
9. With the insertion point positioned at the end of the document, paste the text (matching destination formatting) that begins with the heading *Creating a Patient Profile*.
10. With the insertion point positioned at the end of the document, paste the text (matching destination formatting) that begins with the heading *Storage and Security*.
11. Clear the contents of the Clipboard task pane and then close the task pane.
12. Save **WordMedS3-R1.docx**.
13. Make **CRGHRecMaintenance.docx** the active document and then close it.

Review 3 Inserting Page Numbers; Changing Margins; Changing Page Orientation

1. With **WordMedS3-R1.docx** open, insert page numbers that print at the bottom of each page using the *Plain Number 2* option.
2. Change the page orientation to landscape.
3. Change the top and bottom margins to 1.5 inches.
4. Save and then print **WordMedS3-R1.docx**.

Review 4 Inserting a Footer and Applying a Theme

1. With **WordMedS3-R1.docx** open, change the page orientation to portrait and then change the left and right margins to 1 inch.
2. Remove the page numbering. *Hint: Do this with the* **Remove Page Numbers** *option at the Page Number button drop-down list.*
3. Insert the Alphabet footer. When the footer is inserted in the document, click the placeholder text *[Type text]* and then type **Creating and Maintaining Medical Records**. *Hint: Double-click in the document to return to the document.*
4. Apply the Heading 1 style to the title *COLUMBIA RIVER GENERAL HOSPITAL* and apply the Heading 2 style to the following headings: *Legal Department, Creating and Maintaining Medical Records, Creating Medical Records, Modifying Medical Records, Creating Progress Notes, Creating a Patient Profile,* and *Storage and Security.*
5. Apply the *Formal* Quick Styles set to the document.
6. Apply the *Origin* theme to the document.

7. Change the theme color set to *Oriel*.
8. Save **WordMedS3-R1.docx**.

Review 5 Inserting WordArt and Drawing a Shape and a Text Box

1. With **WordMedS3-R1.docx** open, move the insertion point to the beginning of the document, press the Enter key twice, and then move the insertion point back to the beginning of the document.
2. Insert the WordArt shown in Figure W3.7. (At the WordArt button drop-down list, select the fifth WordArt option from the left in the second row.)
3. With the WordArt selected, change the text wrapping to Tight and then size the WordArt by typing **0.6** in the *Shape Height* box and typing **6** in the *Shape Width* box. Move the WordArt so it is positioned as shown in Figure W3.7.
4. Move the insertion point to the end of the document and then use the *Bevel* shape in the *Basic Shapes* section of the Shapes button drop-down list to draw the shape shown in Figure W3.8. Change the height of the shape to *1.5*, the width to *4*, and add light blue fill (*Blue, Accent 2, Lighter 60%*).
5. Draw a text box inside the shape, remove the shape fill and outline from the text box, and then center and type the text shown in Figure W3.8. If necessary, move the shape and the text box inside the shape so they are centered between the left and right margins.
6. Save **WordMedS3-R1.docx**.

FIGURE W3.7 WordArt for Review 5

FIGURE W3.8 Shape for Review 5

For further information on managing your medical records, please contact Douglas Brown in the Legal Department at (503) 555-2045

Review 6 Formatting Text in Columns

1. With **WordMedS3-R1.docx** open, move the insertion point to the blank line below the last paragraph of text (above the shape) and then insert a continuous section break.
2. Move the insertion point to the beginning of the first paragraph of text (the text that begins *At Columbia River General Hospital, physicians are…*) and then insert a continuous section break.
3. Format text into two columns with a line between and *0.4"* spacing between columns.
4. Save, print, and then close **WordMedS3-R1.docx**.

Review 7 Inserting an Image

1. Open **NSMCPrenatalCare.docx** and then save the document with Save As and name it **WordMedS3-R2**.
2. Insert a clip art image of a pregnant woman as shown in Figure W3.9. (If this image is not available, choose another image showing a pregnant woman.) Change the text wrapping for the image to *Tight*, change the height of the image to *2.5"*, and apply the *Drop Shadow Rectangle* picture style to the image. (This image is the fourth icon from the left in the Picture Styles group in the Picture Tools Format tab.) Position the clip art as shown in Figure W3.9.
3. Save, print, and then close **WordMedS3-R2.docx**.

FIGURE W3.9 Review 7

North Shore Medical Clinic
7450 Meridian Street, Suite 150
Portland, OR 97202
(503) 555-2330

TAKING CARE OF YOURSELF

Prenatal Care Guidelines

- Stop smoking and avoid consistent or prolonged exposure to second-hand smoke.
- Stop all alcohol and recreational drug use.
- Limit your caffeine intake to the equivalent of one cup of coffee a day.
- Eat a healthy, well-balanced diet.
- Drink approximately eight glasses of water daily.
- Participate in moderate exercise regularly.
- Sleep seven to eight hours a night.
- Take your prenatal vitamins daily.
- Avoid taking any over-the-counter or prescribed medication unless your physician knows you are taking them.
- Avoid contact with noxious chemicals such as household cleaners, paint, varnish, and hair dye.
- Avoid changing kitty litter and wear gloves when gardening to decrease exposure to infections that may be present in cat litter and soil.
- All meat, poultry, fish, and seafood should be well cooked.
- Limit your intake of fish purchased in stores and restaurants to six to twelve ounces per week.

Review 8 Preparing an Envelope

1. At a blank document, prepare an envelope with the return and delivery addresses shown in Figure W3.10, and add the envelope to the document.
2. Save the document and name it **WordMedS3-R3**.
3. Print and then close **WordMedS3-R3.docx**. (Manual feed may be required.)

FIGURE W3.10 Review 8

North Shore Medical Clinic
7450 Meridian Street
Suite 150
Portland, OR 97202

Jennifer Cruz
Women's Health Center
142 Southeast Powell Boulevard
Portland, OR 97334

Review 9 Preparing Mailing Labels

1. At a blank document, prepare a sheet of mailing labels for the following name and address using the Avery 5630 mailing labels.

   North Shore Medical Clinic
   7450 Meridian Street
   Suite 150
   Portland, OR 97202
2. Save the mailing label document and name it **WordMedS3-R4**.
3. Print and then close **WordMedS3-R4.docx**.

Skills Assessment

Assessment 1 Formatting a Document on Fibromyalgia

1. Open **Fibromyalgia.docx** and then save the document with Save As and name it **WordMedS3-A1**.
2. Open **FM.docx** and then copy individually the three sections (*Triggers and Metabolism*, *Symptoms*, and *Diagnosing Fm*), including the blank line below each section, to the Clipboard task pane.
3. Make **WordMedS3-A1.docx** the active document and then paste the sections from the **FM.docx** document into the **WordMedS3-A1.docx** document, matching the destination formatting so the sections are in the following order: *What Is Fibromyalgia?*, *Symptoms*, *Diagnosing Fm*, *Causes of Fm*, *Triggers and Metabolism*, and *Treatment*.
4. Make **FM.docx** the active document and then close it.

5. With **WordMedS3-A1.docx** the active document, search for all occurrences of *fm* and replace with *fibromyalgia*. (Make sure the *Match case* option at the expanded Find and Replace dialog box does not contain a check mark.)

6. Select the heading *What Is Fibromyalgia?*, click the Bold button, and then insert 6 points of space after the heading.

7. Use Format Painter to apply bold formatting and insert 6 points of space after headings to the remaining headings: *Symptoms, Diagnosing Fibromyalgia, Causes of Fibromyalgia, Triggers and Metabolism,* and *Treatment*.

8. Search for all occurrences of 11-point Candara bold and replace with 12-point Corbel bold.

9. Change the left and right margins to 1.5 inches.

10. Delete the title *FACTS ABOUT FIBROMYALGIA* and then create the title *Facts about Fibromyalgia* as WordArt with these specifications: use WordArt style 8 (second option in the second row in the WordArt button drop-down list), change the shape fill to black, and change the height to *0.5"* and the width to *5.5"*.

11. Insert the *Conservative* footer.

12. Move the insertion point to the end of the document and then insert a continuous section break.

13. Move the insertion point to the beginning of the heading *What Is Fibromyalgia?* and then insert a continuous section break.

14. Format the text into two columns with a line between and change the spacing between columns to *0.6"*.

15. Save, print, and then close **WordMedS3-A1.docx**.

Assessment 2 Creating an Announcement

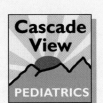

1. Open **CVPLtrhd.docx** and then save the document with Save As and name it **WordMedS3-A2**.

2. Using a shape of your choosing, draw a shape in the middle of the document and then insert the following information in the shape inside a text box (you determine the font and font size of the text):

Congratulations!
Lindsay Levy
Employee of the Month

3. Add fill to the shape and text box that is a complementary color to the letterhead image. Remove the outline around the text box so the text appears to be inside the shape (and not a text box).

4. Save, print, and then close **WordMedS3-A2.docx**.

Assessment 3 Preparing a Notice

1. Open **CVPLtrhd.docx** and then save the document with Save As and name it **WordMedS3-A3**.
2. Use the information shown in Figure W3.11 to create a notice of a support group with the following specifications:
   a. Set the text in a font and font color that is complementary to the color and font style of the letterhead.
   b. Format the heading *Support Group for New Moms* differently than the paragraph that follows.
   c. Set the text regarding dates, times, and location in tabbed columns and consider using leaders.
   d. Insert a clip art image related to mothers and babies.
3. Save, print, and then close **WordMedS3-A3.docx**.

FIGURE W3.11 Assessment 3

Support Group for New Moms

You and your baby are invited to meet other new moms and learn about parenting your newborn. Discussion topics include infant feeding, sleep patterns, newborn personalities, and child development. Support activities and educational sessions are coordinated by Deanna Reynolds, Child Development Specialist at Cascade View Pediatrics. The support group for new moms will provide you with opportunities to meet other new moms while sharing the joys, frustrations, successes, and challenges of motherhood. Join us weekly until your baby is six months old.

    When: Monday evenings
    Time: 7:00 p.m. to 8:30 p.m.
    Location: Cascade View Pediatrics
    Room: Conference Room 3B
    Cost: $25 per month

Assessment 4 Preparing Mailing Labels

1. Prepare return mailing labels with the following information:
   > **Columbia River General Hospital**
   > **Education Department**
   > **4550 Fremont Street**
   > **Portland, OR 97045**
2. Save the labels document and name it **WordMedS3-A4**.
3. Print and then close **WordMedS3-A4.docx**.

Assessment 5 Finding Information on Flipping and Copying Objects

1. Use Word's Help feature to learn how to flip objects and copy objects.
2. At a blank document, create the document shown in Figure W3.12. Create the arrow at the left by clicking the Shapes button and then clicking the Striped Right Arrow in the *Block Arrows* section. Format the arrow with dark red fill as shown. Copy and flip the arrow to create the arrow at the right side. Create the text in a text box.
3. Save the completed document and name it **WordMedS3-A5**.
4. Print and then close **WordMedS3-A5.docx**.

HELP

FIGURE W3.12 Assessment 5

Our clinic will be
CLOSED
November 25, 2011

Assessment 6 Locating Information and Creating a Banner

1. Using the Internet, search for a hospital near you. When you find the Web site for the hospital, locate the hospital address and telephone number.
2. Using the information you find on the hospital, create a banner using a shape and insert the hospital name, address, and telephone number inside the banner.
3. Save the banner document and name it **WordMedS3-A6**.
4. Print and then close **WordMedS3-A6.docx**.

Assessment 7 Locating Information on Chickenpox

1. Using the Internet, search for information on chickenpox. Find information on the symptoms, treatment, incubation period, and infectious period of chickenpox.
2. Using the information you find, create a document that contains information on the four areas listed above: symptoms, treatment, incubation period, and infectious period.
3. Add any enhancements you feel will improve the visual appeal of the document such as a clip art image, WordArt, or a shape.
4. Save the document and name it **WordMedS3-A7**.
5. Print and then close **WordMedS3-A7.docx**.

Marquee Challenge

Challenge 1 Preparing a Class Announcement Document

1. Open **CVPLtrhd.docx** and then save the document with Save As and name it **WordMedS3-C1**.

2. Create the class announcement as shown in Figure W3.13. *Hint: Search for images matching the word* baby *to find the clip art image shown in Figure W3.13. If this image is not available, choose another image related to babies.* Set the text in 12-point Constantia and the title in 18-point Constantia.

3. Save, print, and then close **WordMedS3-C1.docx**.

FIGURE W3.13 Challenge 1

Cascade View Pediatrics

350 North Skagit ☐ Portland, OR 97505 ☐ (503) 555-7700

BABY CARE CLASS

Deanna Reynolds, Child Development Specialist for Cascade View Pediatrics, is offering a one-day class on basic baby care. This five-hour class offers basic survival techniques to care for your newborn. During this informative class, you will learn about newborn characteristics, infant milestones, bathing and hygiene, diapering, crying and comforting, sleeping, and recognizing signs of illness in your newborn. This class is ideal for first-time parents.

Date...Saturday, April 9

Time....................................9:00 a.m. to 2:00 p.m.

Location...........................Cascade View Pediatrics

Room......................................Conference Room 2

Cost $70

For more information, contact
Deanna Reynolds at (503) 555-7705

Challenge 2 Preparing a Fact Sheet on Fifth Disease

1. Open **FifthDisease.docx** and then save the document with Save As and name it **WordMedS3-C2**.
2. Format the document so it appears as shown in Figure W3.14. Insert the page border, the WordArt, and clip art image as shown. (To insert the clip art, search for images related to *doctor*. If this image is not available, choose a similar clip art image.)
3. Save, print, and then close **WordMedS3-C2.docx**.

Cascade View PEDIATRICS

FIGURE W3.14 Challenge 2

Fifth Disease

Fifth disease (also called *erythema infectiosum*) is an infection common in children between the ages of 5 and 15. It produces a red rash on the face that spreads to the trunk, arms, and legs. Fifth disease is actually a viral illness caused by a virus called parvovirus B19. Most children recover from Fifth disease in a short time with no complications.

Symptoms

Fifth disease begins with a low-grade fever, headache, body aches, and mild cold-like symptoms such as a stuffy or runny nose. These symptoms pass and the illness seems to be gone but in 7 to 10 days a red rash on the cheeks appears, making the face look like it has been slapped. (This is why the disease is called *slapped cheek syndrome*.) The rash spreads to other parts of the body and red blotches expand down the trunk, arms, and legs. The rash may last from one to three weeks and may recur over weeks to months.

Contagiousness

A person with Fifth disease is most contagious before the rash appears and probably no longer contagious after the rash begins. Fifth disease spreads easily from person to person in fluids from the nose, mouth, and throat of someone with the infection and especially through large droplets from coughs and sneezes. It can also spread through sharing a drinking glass and from mother to fetus. Once someone is infected with the virus, they develop immunity to it and more than likely will not become infected again.

Treatment

Since a virus causes Fifth disease, it cannot be treated with antibiotics. Antiviral medicines do exist but none that will treat Fifth disease. No specific medication or vaccine is available and treatment is limited to relieving the symptoms.

Complications

Most children with Fifth disease recover without any complications and usually feel well by the time the rash appears. The infection, however, is more serious for children with HIV or blood disorders such as sickle cell anemia or hemolytic anemia. The virus can temporarily slow down or stop the body's production of the oxygen-carrying red blood cells, causing anemia.

Prevention

To help prevent your child from being infected with the virus, encourage your child to use good hygiene including frequent hand washing, disposing of tissues, and not sharing eating utensils with a sick person.

Challenge 3 Preparing a Cascade View Pediatrics Newsletter

1. Open **CVPNewsletter.docx** and then save the document with Save As and name it **WordMedS3-C3**.
2. Format the document so it appears as shown in Figure W3.15. If the clip art images are not available, choose similar images. The page border can be found in the *Art* drop-down list (about two-thirds of the way down the list) at the Borders and Shading dialog box with the Page Border tab selected. Change the page border color to aqua.
3. Save, print and then close **WordMedS3-C3.docx**.

FIGURE W3.15 Challenge 3

Cascade View Pediatrics
January 2011 Newsletter

Pediatrician Joins CVP

We are pleased to announce that Dr. Joseph Yarborough, Pediatric Specialist, has joined our clinic. With the addition of Dr. Yarborough to our staff, we are able to accommodate additional pediatric appointments. He will be taking appointments Monday through Friday from 8:00 a.m. to 4:00 p.m. Tuesdays and Thursdays have been reserved for well-child checkup appointments. Evening hours for well-child checkup appointments with Dr. Yarborough will be available next month.

Bring Your Insurance Card

At CVP, we deal with over 25 different insurance plans! No insurance plan is the same as the other and each has different co-pays, allowables, and deductibles. We do our best to assist you with insurance questions but you are responsible for knowing what your insurance covers. To help us with insurance issues, please bring your insurance card with you every time you visit the clinic. This may seem inconvenient but when we do not check insurance coverage with every visit, our billing accuracy declines by 10 percent.

Benefits of Lycopene

Lycopene is an antioxidant that is abundant in red tomatoes and processed tomato products. Antioxidants like lycopene neutralize free radicals, which can damage cells in the body. Research has shown that lycopene may help prevent macular degeneration (a common cause of blindness in the elderly), prostate cancer and some other forms of cancer, and heart disease.* To consume the recommended amount of at least 5 to 10 mg of lycopene per day, consider eating the following foods:

- Spaghetti sauce, ½ cup, approximately 28.1 mg of lycopene
- Tomato juice, 1 cup, approximately 25.0 mg of lycopene
- Tomato paste, 2 tablespoons, approximately 13.8 mg of lycopene
- Tomato soup, 1 cup, approximately 9.7 mg of lycopene

Other foods to consider that contain lycopene include watermelon, pink grapefruit, chili sauce, seafood sauce, and ketchup.

*Discuss medical conditions or problems with your doctor. Good nutrition is not a substitute for medical treatment and a doctor's care.

Well-Child Appointments

When you bring your child for a well-child checkup appointment, the doctor will be checking your child's progress and growth. During the visit, your doctor will weigh your child, measure his or her length and head circumference, and plot the information on your child's own growth chart. The doctor will perform a physical examination, paying special attention to any previous problems. You will be able to ask your doctor questions about how you are doing with your child and seek advice on what to expect during the coming months. Your child will receive immunizations during some visits.

Word

SECTION 4

Formatting with Special Features

Skills

- Create, edit, and modify merge documents
- Sort and filter records in a data source
- Merge envelopes
- Create, format, and modify a table
- Create a form for handwritten entries
- Create a form and save it as a template
- Fill in and print a form document
- Edit a form template
- Create and fill in a form with a form field drop-down list

Student Resources

Before beginning this section:
1. Copy to your storage medium the WordMedS4 subfolder from the Unit3Word folder on the Student Resources CD.
2. Make WordMedS4 the active folder.

In addition to containing the data files needed to complete section work, the Student Resources CD contains model answers in PDF format for each of the projects in this section; model answers for end-of-section exercises are not provided.

Projects Overview

Prepare a main document reminding parents to schedule a well-child checkup appointment and create a data source using the Mail Merge wizard; edit the main document and input text during a merge; and create and format a calendar.

Prepare a main document advising people of upcoming parent education classes and create a data source using the Mail Merge wizard; merge envelopes; and prepare a template document for gathering information on secondary payer information.

Sort and filter data source records by ZIP code and by last name; filter records in a data source and then print a letter for patients living in Lake Oswego; prepare and print merged envelopes; insert a table in a fact sheet on caffeine and then format the table; create a patient post-operative call sheet using tables; prepare a template document for updating patient information; prepare a main document advising patients of childbirth education classes and create a data source using the Mail Merge wizard; create and format a medical questionnaire; create and format a table containing information on airfare from Portland to Chicago; create a treadmill test form; prepare a pre-op questions document.

Activity 4.1

Merging Documents

Word includes a Mail Merge wizard you can use to create customized letters, envelopes, labels, directories, e-mail messages, and faxes. The Mail Merge wizard guides you through six steps to create customized documents, including steps on selecting a document type to executing the final merge. Generally, a merge requires two documents—the *data source* and the *main document*. The data source document contains the variable information that will be inserted in the main document. Before creating a data source document, determine what type of correspondence you will be creating and the type of information you will need to insert in the correspondence. Variable information in a data source document is saved as a *record*. A record contains all of the information for one unit (for example, a person, family, customer, client, or business). A series of fields makes one record, and a series of records makes a data source document.

Project

Your supervisor, Sydney Larsen, has asked you to create a main document reminding parents to schedule a well-child checkup appointment and create a data source containing parent and patient information.

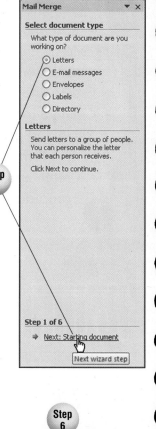

1. At a blank document click the Mailings tab, click the Start Mail Merge button 📄 in the Start Mail Merge group and then click the *Step by Step Mail Merge Wizard* option that displays at the bottom of the drop-down list.

    This displays the Mail Merge task pane.

2. At the first wizard step at the Mail Merge task pane, make sure *Letters* is selected in the *Select document type* section and then click the *Next: Starting document* hyperlink located toward the bottom of the task pane.

3. At the second wizard step, make sure *Use the current document* is selected in the *Select starting document* section of the task pane and then click the *Next: Select recipients* hyperlink.

4. At the third wizard step, click *Type a new list* in the *Select recipients* section and then click the *Create* hyperlink.

    At the New Address List dialog box, the Mail Merge wizard provides you with a number of predesigned fields. You can use these predesigned fields as well as create your own custom fields.

5. Delete the fields you do not need. Begin by clicking the Customize Columns button located toward the bottom left corner of the dialog box.

6. At the Customize Address List dialog box, click *Company Name* to select it and then click the Delete button.

7. At the message asking if you are sure you want to delete the field, click the Yes button.

8. Complete steps similar to those in Steps 6 and 7 to delete the following fields: *Address Line 2*, *Country or Region*, *Home Phone*, *Work Phone*, and *E-mail Address*.

9 Click the Add button.

> If the Mail Merge wizard predesigned fields do not provide for all variable information, create your own custom field.

10 At the Add Field dialog box, type **Child** and then click OK.

11 Click the OK button to close the Customize Address List dialog box.

12 At the New Address List dialog box, type **Mr. and Mrs.** in the Title column, and then press the Tab key.

> This moves the insertion point to the *First Name* column. Press Shift + Tab to move to a previous column.

13 Type **William** and then press the Tab key. Type **Nordyke** and then press the Tab key. Type **12330 South 32nd** and then press the Tab key. Type **Portland** and then press the Tab key. Type **OR** and then press the Tab key. Type **97233** and then press the Tab key. Type **Lillian** and then press the Tab key.

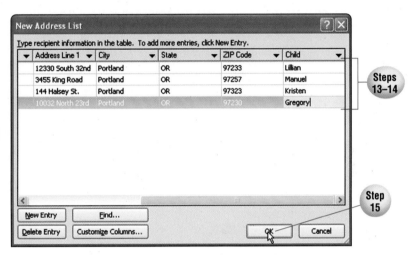

14 With the icon point positioned in the *Title* column, complete steps similar to those in Steps 12 and 13 to enter the information for the three other patients shown in Figure W4.1.

FIGURE W4.1 Patient Information

Title	Mr. and Mrs.	*Title*	Ms.
First Name	William	*First Name*	Stephanie
Last Name	Nordyke	*Last Name*	Walker
Address Line 1	12330 South 32nd	*Address Line 1*	3455 King Road
City	Portland	*City*	Portland
State	OR	*State*	OR
ZIP Code	97233	*ZIP Code*	97257
Child	Lillian	*Child*	Manuel
Title	Mr. and Mrs.	*Title*	Mr.
First Name	Arnold	*First Name*	James
Last Name	Goldman	*Last Name*	Hutton
Address Line 1	144 Halsey St.	*Address Line 1*	10032 North 23rd
City	Portland	*City*	Portland
State	OR	*State*	OR
ZIP Code	97323	*ZIP Code*	97230
Child	Kristen	*Child*	Gregory

continues

15. After entering all of the information for the last client in Figure W4.1, click the OK button located in the bottom right corner of the New Address List dialog box.

16. At the Save Address List dialog box, click the down-pointing arrow at the right of the *Save in* option box. At the drop-down list that displays, click the location of your *WordMedS4* folder and then double-click the *WordMedS4* folder.

17. Click in the *File name* text box, type **CVPPatients**, and then press Enter.

18. At the Mail Merge Recipients dialog box, check to make sure all four entries are correct and then click the OK button.

19. Click the *Next: Write your letter* hyperlink in the Mail Merge task pane.

20. At the fourth wizard step, click the Home tab and then click the No Spacing style in the Styles group. Press the Enter key six times, type **February 7, 2011** as shown in Figure W4.2, and then press the Enter key five times.

21. Insert the address fields by clicking the *Address block* hyperlink located in the *Write your letter* section of the task pane.

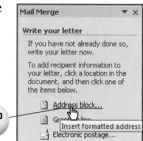

FIGURE W4.2 Main Document

February 7, 2011

«AddressBlock»

«GreetingLine»

Please contact Cascade View Pediatrics and schedule a well-child checkup appointment for «Child». At Cascade View Pediatrics, we recommend that children are seen by a pediatrician at the ages of 2 weeks and 2, 4, 6, 12, 18, and 24 months. Your child may require immunizations so plan at least 60 minutes for the appointment.

Your child's well-child appointment consists of a routine physical examination; vision, hearing, and speech screening; testing for anemia and lead poisoning; and immunizations. Additional services may include developmental testing, nutrition and social assessment, and guidance and parenting education.

To schedule a well-child appointment, please call our clinic at (503) 555-7700 or stop by our clinic at 350 North Skagit.

Sincerely,

Sydney Larsen
Office Manager

XX:Well-ChildMainDoc.docx

---

22 At the Insert Address Block dialog box, click the OK button.

23 Press the Enter key twice and then click the *Greeting line* hyperlink located in the *Write your letter* section of the task pane.

24 At the Insert Greeting Line dialog box, click the down-pointing arrow at the right of the option box containing the comma (the box to the right of the box containing *Mr. Randall*). At the drop-down list, click the colon.

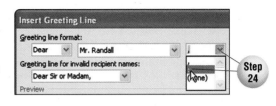

25 Click OK to close the Insert Greeting Line dialog box.

26 Press the Enter key twice and then type the letter shown in Figure W4.2 to the location of the *Child* field. Insert the field by clicking the *More items* hyperlink in the *Write your letter* section of the task pane.

27 At the Insert Merge Field dialog box, click *Child* in the *Fields* list box, click the Insert button, and then click the Close button.

28 Type the remainder of the letter as shown in Figure W4.2.

29 When you are finished typing the letter, click the *Next: Preview your letters* hyperlink.

30 At the fifth wizard step, look over the letter that displays in the document window and make sure the information has merged properly and then click the *Next: Complete the merge* hyperlink.

31 At the sixth wizard step, click the *Edit individual letters* hyperlink.

32 At the Merge to New Document dialog box, make sure *All* is selected and then click the OK button.

33 Save the merged letters in the normal manner and name the document **Well-ChildApptLetters**.

34 Close **Well-ChildApptLetters.docx**.

35 At the sixth wizard step, save the main document in the normal manner and name it **Well-ChildMainDoc**.

36 Close **Well-ChildMainDoc.docx**.

In Brief

Merge Documents
1. Click Mailings tab.
2. Click Start Mail Merge button.
3. Click *Step by Step Mail Merge Wizard* option.
4. At Step 1, identify document type.
5. At Step 2, select starting document.
6. At Step 3, select recipients (create or open data source).
7. At Step 4, type document.
8. At Step 5, preview merged documents.
9. At Step 6, merge to new document or printer.

In Addition

Using Buttons in the Mailing Tab to Create Merge Documents

In addition to the Step by Step Mail Merge Wizard, you can use buttons in the Mailings tab to create merge documents. To do this, click the Mailings tab, click the Start Mail Merge button, and then click the type of main document you want to create from the drop-down list. Create a data source file by clicking the Select Recipients button in the Start Mail Merge group in the Mailings tab and then clicking *Type New List* at the drop-down list. At the New Address List dialog box, use the predesigned fields or edit the fields. You can also use an existing data source by clicking the Select Recipients button and then clicking the *Use Existing List* option at the drop-down list.

Activity
4.2

When you complete the six Mail Merge wizard steps, you create a data source document and a main document. The data source document is associated with the main document. If you need to edit the main document, open it in the normal manner, and make the required changes. Changes you make to the data source document are saved automatically. If you want to save edits made to a main document, you must save the changes. In some situations, you may not need to keep all variable information in a data source file. Insert a Fill-in field at the location in the main document where you want to input variable information during a merge.

Project

Sydney Larsen has asked you to customize the well-child checkup appointments letters to identify the specific appointment.

1. Open **Well-ChildMainDoc.docx**. If a message displays telling you that opening the document will run an SQL command, click Yes.

2. Click the Mailings tab.

3. Edit the first paragraph so it displays as shown in Figure W4.3. To insert the *«Child»* field, click the Insert Merge Field button ⊞ arrow in the Write & Insert Fields group and then click *Child* at the drop-down list.

   The name, Lillian, rather than the field, will display in the document because the Mail Merge wizard automatically merges the letter.

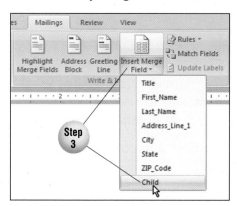

4. To insert a Fill-in field for *(Checkup)*, click the Rules button ▣ in the Write & Insert Fields group and then click *Fill-in* at the drop-down list.

FIGURE W4.3 Edited Paragraph

According to our records, «Child» is due for (Checkup). Please contact Cascade View Pediatrics and schedule the well-child checkup appointment. Your child may require immunizations so plan at least 60 minutes for the appointment.

5 At the Insert Word Field: Fill-in dialog box, type **Insert specific well-child checkup appointment** in the *Prompt* text box and then click OK.

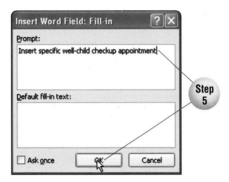

Step
5

6 At the Microsoft Office Word dialog box with *Insert specific well-child checkup appointment* displayed in the upper left corner, type **(Checkup)** and then click OK. Type or edit the remainder of the paragraph so it displays as shown in Figure W4.3.

Step
6

7 Edit some of the records in the data source. To begin, click the Edit Recipient List button [icon] in the Start Mail Merge group.

8 At the Mail Merge Recipients dialog box, click the file name **CVPPatients.mdb** in the *Data Source* list box and then click the Edit button that displays below the list box.

9 At the Edit Data Source dialog box, click on any character in the address *3455 King Road* (in the record for Stephanie Walker) and then type **6795 32nd Street**.

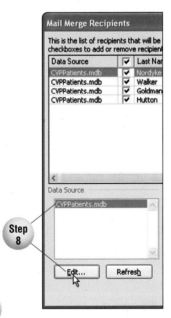

Step
8

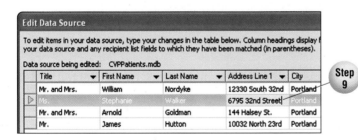

Step
9

continues

10 Click on any character in the ZIP code *97257* (you will need to scroll to the right to display the *ZIP Code* column) and then type **97239**.

11 Click the New Entry button and then type the following in the specified fields:

Title	**Mr.**
First Name	**Hayden**
Last Name	**Milovich**
Address Line 1	**19443 144th Place**
City	**Portland**
State	**OR**
ZIP Code	**97340**
Child	**Paulina**

12 Delete the record for James Hutton by clicking in the gray square at the beginning of the record for James Hutton and then clicking the Delete Entry button.

13 At the message asking if you want to delete the entry, click the Yes button.

14 At the Edit Data Source dialog box, click the OK button. At the message asking if you want to update your recipient list, click the Yes button.

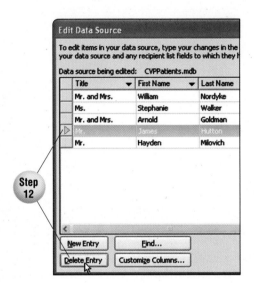

Step 12

15 Click OK to close the Mail Merge Recipients dialog box.

16 Click the Finish & Merge button in the Finish group in the Mailings tab and then click the *Edit Individual Documents* option at the drop-down list.

Step 16

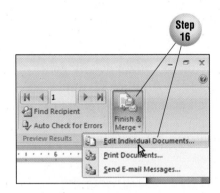

17 At the Merge to New Document dialog box, make sure *All* is selected and then click OK.

18 When Word merges the main document with the first record, a dialog box displays with the message *Insert specific well-child checkup appointment* and the text *(Checkup)* is selected. At this dialog box, type **her two-week checkup** and then click OK.

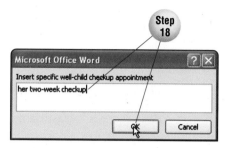

Step
18

19 At the dialog box, type **his 10-month checkup** (over *her two-week checkup*) and then click OK.

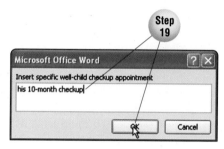

Step
19

20 At the dialog box, type **her 12-month checkup** and then click OK.

21 At the dialog box, type **her four-month checkup** and then click OK.

22 Save the merged letters in the normal manner in the WordMedS4 folder on your storage medium and name the document **Well-ChildEditedLtrs**.

23 Print and then close **Well-ChildEditedLtrs.docx**.

This document will print four letters.

24 Save and then close **Well-ChildMainDoc.docx**.

In Brief

Edit Data Source
1. Open main document.
2. Click Mailings tab.
3. Click Edit Recipient List button.
4. Click data source file name in *Data Source* list box.
5. Click Edit button.
6. At Edit Data Source dialog box, make necessary changes.
7. Click OK.
8. Click Yes at message.
9. Click OK.

In Addition

Editing a Data Source Using the Mail Merge Wizard

In addition to editing a data source by opening the main document and then clicking the Edit Recipient List button, you can edit a data source using the Mail Merge wizard. To do so, open a main document, click the Mailings tab, click the Start Mail Merge button, and then click the *Step by Step Mail Merge Wizard* option. This series of actions causes the Mail Merge wizard to open at the third step. At this step, click the *Edit recipient list* hyperlink. At the Mail Merge Recipients dialog box, click the data source file name in the *Data Source* list box, click the Edit button, and then make the necessary edits to the fields in the records at the Edit Data Source dialog box.

Activity 4.3

Sorting Records in a Data Source

To organize records in a data source, you can sort records in ascending and descending order. To sort records in a data source, click the Mailings tab, click the Select Recipients button, and then click *Use Existing List*. At the Select Data Source dialog box, navigate to the folder that contains the data source file you want to use and then double-click the file. Click the Edit Recipient List button in the Start Mail Merge group in the Mailings tab, and the Mail Merge Recipients dialog box displays. Click the field column heading to sort data in ascending order in a specific field. To perform additional sorts, click the down-pointing arrow at the right side of the field column heading and then click the desired sort order. You can refine a sort with options at the Filter and Sort dialog box.

Project

Lee Elliott has asked you to sort data source records by last name, city, and ZIP code.

1. Open **NSMCMainDoc.docx**. If a message displays telling you that opening the document will run an SQL command, click the Yes button.

    If a message displays telling you that Word cannot find the data source, click the Mailings tab, click the Select Recipients button in the Start Mail Merge group, and then click *Use Existing List* at the drop-down list. At the Select Data Source dialog box, navigate to the WordMedS4 folder on your storage medium and then double-click the file named **NSMCPatientsDS.mdb**.

2. If the Select Data Source dialog box displays, navigate to the WordMedS4 folder on your storage medium and then double-click the file named **NSMCPatientsDS.mdb**.

3. Sort records in the data source attached to this main document alphabetically. To begin, click the Mailings tab and then click the Edit Recipient List button in the Start Mail Merge group.

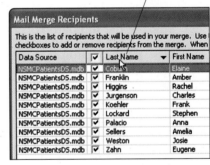

Step 4

4. At the Mail Merge Recipients dialog box, click the *Last Name* column heading.

    This sorts the last names in ascending alphabetical order.

5. Scroll to the right to display the *City* field, click the down-pointing arrow at the right side of the *City* column heading, and then click the *Sort Descending* option at the drop-down list.

    This sorts the city names in descending alphabetical order.

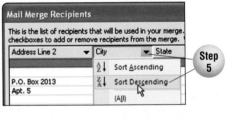

Step 5

6. Sort by ZIP code and then by last name. To begin, click the *Sort* hyperlink located in the *Refine recipient list* section.

7. At the Filter and Sort dialog box with the Sort Records tab selected, click the down-pointing arrow at the right side of the *Sort by* option box and then click *ZIP Code* at the drop-down list.

    You will need to scroll down the list to display *ZIP Code*.

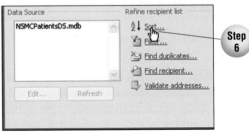

Step 6

8 Make sure *Last Name* displays in the *Then by* option box.

9 Click OK to close the Filter and Sort dialog box.

10 Click OK to close the Mail Merge Recipients dialog box.

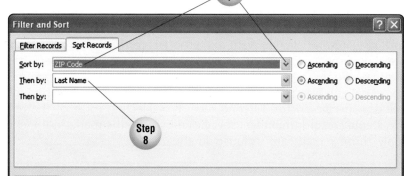

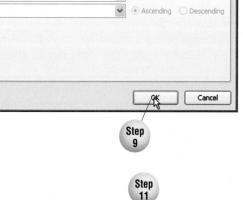

11 Make sure the Preview Results button 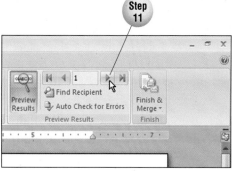 in the Preview Results group in the Mailings tab is active (displays with an orange background) and then preview each letter by clicking the Next Record button in the Preview Results group. Keep clicking the Next Record button until the last letter (the tenth) displays.

12 Click the Finish & Merge button in the Finish group in the Mailings tab and then click *Edit Individual Documents* at the drop-down list.

13 At the Merge to New Document dialog box, click the OK button.

14 Save the merged letters document and name it **WordMedS4-01**.

15 Print only the first page of **WordMedS4-01.docx**.

16 Close **WordMedS4-01.docx**.

17 Close **NSMCMainDoc.docx** without saving the changes.

In Brief

Complete a Sort
1. Open main document.
2. Click Mailings tab.
3. Click Edit Recipient List button.
4. Click desired column heading.

OR
1. Open main document.
2. Click Mailings tab.
3. Click Edit Recipient List button.
4. Click *Sort* hyperlink.
5. Specify fields for sorting.
6. Click OK.

In Addition

Clearing Sort Data

If you sort data in a data source file by clicking a column heading, the sort information will display if you open the Filter and Sort dialog box. Also, if you identify fields for sorting at the Filter and Sort dialog box, that sort information will display the next time you open the dialog box. If you want to complete a new sort at the Filter and Sort dialog box, first click the Clear All button that displays in the lower left corner of the dialog box.

Activity 4.4

Filtering Records

If you have created a main document and a data source document to create personalized form letters, situations may arise where you want to merge the main document with specific records in the data source. For example, you may want to send a letter to patients living in a particular city or patients seeing a specific doctor. Filtering records allows you to identify records that meet specific criteria and only those records are included in the merge. One method for filtering records is to display the Mail Merge Recipients dialog box and then insert or remove check marks from specific records. If you will be selecting only a few check boxes, click the check box at the right of the *Data Source* column heading. This removes the check marks from all of the check boxes. If you will be selecting most of the records in the data source, leave the marks in the check boxes.

Project

You know that you will need to identify specific records for mailing different types of letters. You decide that you want to experiment with selecting specific records and then merge and print a letter for those patients living in Lake Oswego.

1. Open **NSMCMainDoc.docx**. If a message displays telling you that opening the document will run an SQL command, click Yes.

    If a message displays telling you that Word cannot find the data source, click the Mailings tab, click the Select Recipients button in the Start Mail Merge group, and then click *Use Existing List* at the drop-down list. At the Select Data Source dialog box, navigate to the WordMedS4 folder on your storage medium and then double-click the file named **NSMCPatientsDS.mdb**.

2. If the Select Data Source dialog box displays, navigate to the WordMedS4 folder on your storage medium and then double-click the file named **NSMCPatientsDS.mdb**.

3. Click the Mailings tab and then click the Edit Recipient List button in the Start Mail Merge group.

4. At the Mail Merge Recipients dialog box, click the check box at the right of the *Data Source* column heading.

    This removes the check mark from the check box preceding each record.

5. Select the records of those individuals coming to the clinic for dermatology reasons by clicking the check box preceding the names *Zahn*, *Sellers*, *Higgins*, *Koehler*, and *Coburn*.

6. Click OK to close the Mail Merge Recipients dialog box.

7. Click the Next Record ▶ and/or Previous Record ◀ buttons to view the merged letters.

8. Select the records of those patients living in the city of Lake Oswego. Begin by clicking the Edit Recipient List button in the Start Mail Merge group.

9. At the Mail Merge Recipients dialog box, click the check box at the right of the *Data Source* column heading.

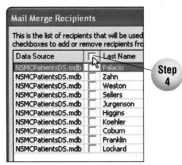

10. Click the check box preceding the patients *Koehler* and *Lockard*.

11. Click OK to close the Mail Merge Recipients dialog box.

12. View the merged letter and then click the Previous Record button ◀ to view the other merged letter.

13. Send the merged letters directly to the printer by clicking the Finish & Merge button 📄 in the Finish group in the Mailings tab and then clicking *Print Documents* at the drop-down list.

14. Click OK at the Merge to Printer dialog box and then click OK at the Print dialog box.

    Two letters will print.

15. Close **NSMCMainDoc.docx** without saving the changes.

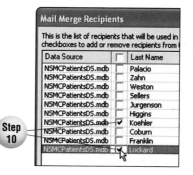

In Brief

Filter Records
1. Open main document.
2. Click Mailings tab.
3. Click Edit Recipient List button.
4. At Mail Merge Recipients dialog box, select specific records by inserting/removing check marks.
5. Click OK.

In Addition

Filtering Records Using the Filter and Sort Dialog Box

Using check boxes to select specific records is useful in a data source containing a limited number of records, but may not be practical in a data source containing many records. In a large data source, use options from the Filter and Sort dialog box with the Filter Records tab selected as shown below to select for merging with the main document records, that meet certain criteria. Display this dialog box by clicking the *Filter* hyperlink in the *Refine recipient list* section of the Mail Merge Recipients dialog box. When you select a field from the *Field* drop-down list, Word automatically inserts *Equal to* in the *Comparison* option box. You can make other com-

parisons. Clicking the down-pointing arrow to the right of the *Comparison* option box causes a drop-down list to display with these additional options: *Not equal to, Less than, Greater than, Less than or equal, Greater than or equal, Is blank, Is not blank, Contains,* and *Does not contain*. Use one of these options to create a select equation. For example, select all customers with a ZIP code higher than 97439 by clicking *ZIP Code* at the *Field* drop-down list. Click the down-pointing arrow at the right of the *Comparison* option box, click *Greater than*, and then type 97439 in the *Compare to* text box.

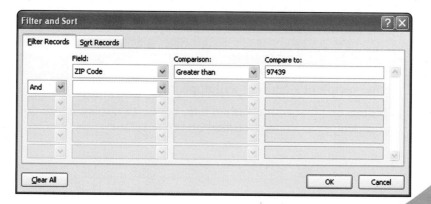

Activity 4.5

Preparing Envelopes Using the Mail Merge Wizard

If you create a letter as a main document and then merge it with a data source document, more than likely you will need properly addressed envelopes in which to send the letters. The Mail Merge wizard guides you through the steps for creating and printing envelopes.

Project Before mailing letters to clinic patients, you need to prepare and print the envelopes. You decide the most efficient method for printing the envelopes is to use the Mail Merge wizard.

1. At a blank document, click the Mailings tab, click the Start Mail Merge button, and then click the *Step by Step Mail Merge Wizard* option.

2. At the first wizard step at the Mail Merge task pane, click the *Envelopes* option in the *Select document type* section and then click the <u>Next: Starting document</u> hyperlink.

3. At the second wizard step, make sure the *Change document layout* option is selected in the *Select starting document* section and then click the <u>Next: Select recipients</u> hyperlink located toward the bottom of the task pane.

4. At the Envelope Options dialog box, make sure the envelope size is *10* and then click OK.

5. At the third wizard step, make sure the *Use an existing list* option is selected in the *Select recipients* section and then click the <u>Browse</u> hyperlink located in the *Use an existing list* section.

6. At the Select Data Source dialog box, change the *Look in* option to the WordMedS4 folder on your storage medium.

7. Double-click **CVPPatients.mdb** in the *Select Data Source* list box.

   Notice that **CVPPatients.mdb** is an Access database file and an Access icon displays before the file name.

8. At the Mail Merge Recipients dialog box, click OK.

9. Click the <u>Next: Arrange your envelope</u> hyperlink.

10. At the fourth wizard step, click in the approximate location in the envelope in the document window where the recipient's address will appear.

    This causes a box with a dashed blue border to display. If you do not see this box, try clicking in a different location on the envelope.

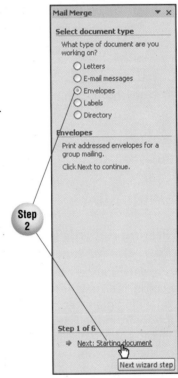

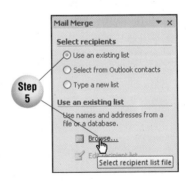

(11) Click the *Address block* hyperlink located in the *Arrange your envelope* section of the task pane.

(12) At the Insert Address Block dialog box, click OK.

> This inserts the field «AddressBlock» inside the box in the envelope.

(13) Click the *Next: Preview your envelopes* hyperlink.

(14) At the fifth wizard step, view the first merged envelope.

> To view the other envelopes, click the button located toward the top of the task pane containing the two right-pointing arrows.

(15) Click the *Next: Complete the merge* hyperlink.

(16) At the sixth wizard step, click the *Edit individual envelopes* hyperlink.

(17) At the Merge to New Document dialog box, make sure *All* is selected and then click the OK button.

(18) Save the merged envelopes in the normal manner in the WordMedS4 folder on your storage medium and name the document **CVPPatientEnvs**.

(19) Print **CVPPatientEnvs.docx**.

> This document will print four envelopes. Check with your instructor about specific steps for printing envelopes. You may need to hand feed envelopes into your printer.

(20) Close **CVPPatientEnvs.docx**.

(21) At the sixth wizard step, save the envelope main document in the normal manner in the WordMedS4 folder and name it **CVPEnvMainDoc**.

(22) Close **CVPEnvMainDoc.docx**.

Step 11

Mail Merge

Arrange your envelope

If you have not already done so, lay out your envelope now.

To add recipient information to your envelope, click a location in the document, and then click one of the items below.

- Address block...
    Insert formatted address
- Gr...
- Electronic postage...

Step 16

Mail Merge

Complete the merge

Mail Merge is ready to produce your envelopes.

To personalize your envelopes, click "Edit Individual Envelopes." This will open a new document with your merged envelopes. To make changes to all the envelopes, switch back to the original document.

Merge

- Print...
- Edit individual envelopes...
    Merge to new document

In Brief

Merge Envelopes

1. Click Mailings tab, click Start Mail Merge button, and then click *Step by Step Mail Merge Wizard* option.
2. At Step 1, click *Envelopes*.
3. At Step 2, click *Change document layout*.
4. At Envelope Options dialog box, click OK.
5. At Step 3, click *Browse* hyperlink.
6. Navigate to folder containing data source and then double-click data source document name.
7. At Mail Merge Recipients dialog box, click OK.
8. At Step 4, click in envelope, and then click *Address block* hyperlink.
9. At Insert Address Block dialog box, click OK.
10. At Step 5, view merged envelopes.
11. At Step 6, merge to new document or printer.

In Addition

Preparing a Directory Using the Mail Merge Wizard

When merging letters, envelopes, or mailing labels, a new form is created for each record. For example, if the data source document that is merged with a letter contains eight records, eight letters are created. If the data source document that is merged with a mailing label contains 20 records, 20 labels are created. In some situations, you may want merged information to remain on the same page. This is useful, for example, when creating a list such as a directory or address list. Use the Mail Merge wizard to create a merged directory.

Activity 4.6

Creating and Modifying a Table

Word's Table feature is useful for displaying data in columns and rows. You can create a table using the Table button in the Insert tab or with options at the Insert Table dialog box. Once you specify the desired numbers of rows and columns, Word displays the table and you are ready to enter information in the cells. A *cell* is the "box" created by the intersection of a row and a column. In a table, press the Tab key to move the insertion point to the next cell or press Shift + Tab to move the insertion point to the previous cell.

Project Lee Elliott has asked you to edit a fact sheet on caffeine. You will open the fact sheet and then insert additional information about caffeine and insert the information in a table for easy viewing.

North Shore Medical Clinic

1. Open **NSMCCaffeine.docx** and then save the document and name it **WordMedS4-02**.

2. Press Ctrl + End to move the insertion point to the end of the document.

3. Display the Insert Table dialog box by clicking the Insert tab, clicking the Table button in the Tables group, and then clicking the *Insert Table* option.

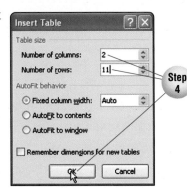
Step 4

4. At the Insert Table dialog box, type **2** in the *Number of columns* text box, press the Tab key, type **11** in the *Number of rows* text box, and then click OK to close the dialog box.

   You can also create a table by clicking the Table button and then dragging in the drop-down grid until the desired numbers of columns and rows are selected.

5. Type the text in cells as shown in Figure W4.4. Press the Tab key to move the insertion point to the next cell or press Shift + Tab to move the insertion point to the previous cell. To move the insertion point to different cells within the table using the mouse, click in the desired cell. After typing the last entry in the table, *20 mg*, do not press the Tab key. This action will insert another row. If this happens, immediately click the Undo button.

FIGURE W4.4 Step 5

Drink/Food	Amount of Caffeine
Brewed coffee	115 mg
Pepsi	38 mg
Coca-Cola	34 mg
Diet Coke	45 mg
Mountain Dew	55 mg
Tea (leaf or bag)	50 mg
Iced tea	70 mg
Cocoa beverage	4 mg
Milk chocolate	6 mg
Dark chocolate	20 mg

6. After typing the table, you realize that you need to include a column that identifies the specific amount of the food or drink. To do this, click in the cell containing the text *Amount of Caffeine*, click the Table Tools Layout tab, and then click the Insert Left button in the Rows & Columns group.

In Brief

Create a Table
1. Click Insert tab.
2. Click Table button.
3. Click *Insert Table*.
4. At Insert Table dialog box, type desired number of columns.
5. Press the Tab key.
6. Type desired number of rows.
7. Click OK.
OR
1. Click Insert tab.
2. Click Table button.
3. Drag in grid to select desired number of columns and rows.

7. Click in the top cell of the new column, type **Amount of Drink/Food**, and then press the Down Arrow key. Type the amounts in the remaining cells as shown in Figure W4.5. (Press the Down Arrow key to move to the next cell down.)

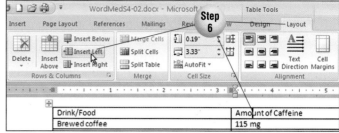

8. Delete the *Cocoa beverage* row. To do this, click anywhere in the text *Cocoa beverage*, click the Table Tools Layout tab, click the Delete button in the Rows & Columns group, and then click *Delete Rows* at the drop-down list.

FIGURE W4.5 Step 7

Amount of Drink/Food	Amount
5 ounces	115 mg
12 ounces	38 mg
12 ounces	34 mg
12 ounces	45 mg
12 ounces	55 mg
8 ounces	50 mg
12 ounces	70 mg
5 ounces	4 mg
1 ounce	6 mg
1 ounce	20 mg

9. Insert a row above *Drink/Food* by clicking anywhere in the text *Drink/Food* and then clicking the Insert Above button in the Rows & Columns group.

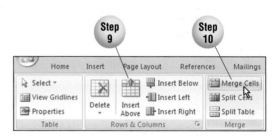

10. With the new top row selected, merge the cells by clicking the Merge Cells button in the Merge group.

11. Type **CAFFEINE CHART** in the top row.

12. Select all cells in the table by clicking the table move handle that displays in the upper left corner of the table (square with a four-headed arrow inside).

> You can also select all cells in a table by clicking the Table Tools Layout tab, clicking the Select button in the Table group, and then clicking *Select Table* at the drop-down list.

13. Click the Home tab, change the font to Cambria, the font size to 12, and then click outside the table to deselect it.

14. Save **WordMedS4-02.docx**.

In Addition

Another Method for Creating a Table

In addition to creating a table with options at the Insert Table dialog box, you can create a table using the Table button drop-down grid. To do so, click the Insert tab, click the Table button, and click and drag the mouse pointer down and to the right until the desired number of columns and rows are selected and the numbers above the grid display the desired numbers of columns and rows.

Activity 4.7

Changing the Table Layout

In the previous activity, you added a column and a row and deleted a row using buttons in the Table Tools Layout tab. This tab contains additional buttons for customizing the table layout, such as for changing cell size, alignment, direction, and margins; sorting data; and converting a table to text. When you create a table, columns are the same width and rows are the same height. The width of columns depends on the number of columns as well as the document margins. You can change column width and row height using a variety of methods including dragging the gridlines. You can apply formatting to text in cells by selecting text or selecting multiple cells and then applying formatting.

Project

The Caffeine Chart table needs adjustments to improve its appearance. You will increase and decrease column widths, increase the height of a row, and apply formatting to the entire table and to specific cells in the table.

1. With **WordMedS4-02.docx** open, position the mouse pointer on the gridline between the first and second columns until the pointer turns into a double-headed arrow pointing left and right with a short double line between. Hold down the left mouse button, drag to the left until the table column marker displays on the 1.5-inch mark on the horizontal Ruler, and then release the mouse button.

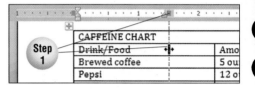

2. Following the same procedure, drag the gridline between the second and third columns to the left until the table column marker displays on the 3.5-inch mark on the horizontal Ruler.

3. Drag the gridline at the far right side of the table to the left until the table column marker displays on the 5.25-inch mark on the Ruler.

4. Position the mouse pointer on the gridline between the first and second row until the pointer turns into a double-headed arrow pointing up and down with a short double line between. Hold down the left mouse button, drag down approximately 0.25-inch on the vertical Ruler, and then release the mouse button.

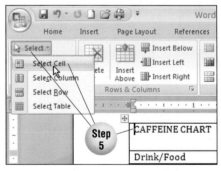

5. Click the top cell containing the text *CAFFEINE CHART*, click the Select button in the Table group in the Table Tools Layout tab, and then click *Select Cell* at the drop-down list.

6. Apply character formatting by clicking the Home tab, clicking the Bold button in the Font group, clicking the Font Size button, and then clicking *16* at the drop-down list.

7. With the cell still selected, horizontally and vertically center the text in the cell by clicking the Table Tools Layout tab and then clicking the Align Center button in the Alignment group.

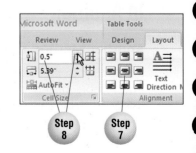

8 Increase the height of the top row by clicking the up-pointing arrow at the right side of the *Table Row Height* measurement box in the Cell Size group in the Table Tools Layout tab until *0.5"* displays.

9 Click in the cell containing the text *Drink/Food*.

10 Click the Select button in the Table group and then click *Select Row* at the drop-down list.

11 Format the text in the row by pressing Ctrl + B to apply bold formatting and then clicking the Align Bottom Center button in the Alignment group in the Table Tools Layout tab.

12 Position the mouse pointer in the cell containing the first entry of the text *5 ounces*, hold down the left mouse button, drag down and to the right to the cell containing the text *20 mg*, and then release the mouse button.

13 With the cells selected, click the Align Bottom Center button in the Alignment group.

14 Click anywhere outside the table to deselect the cells.

15 Center the table between the left and right margins. To begin, click the Properties button in the Table group in the Table Tools Layout tab.

16 At the Table Properties dialog box with the Table tab selected, click the *Center* option in the *Alignment* section.

17 Click OK to close the dialog box.

18 Save **WordMedS4-02.docx**.

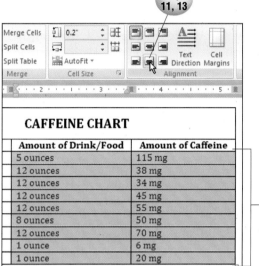

Steps 11, 13

CAFFEINE CHART

Amount of Drink/Food	Amount of Caffeine
5 ounces	115 mg
12 ounces	38 mg
12 ounces	34 mg
12 ounces	45 mg
12 ounces	55 mg
8 ounces	50 mg
12 ounces	70 mg
1 ounce	6 mg
1 ounce	20 mg

Step 12

Step 16

In Brief

Increase/Decrease Column/Row

1. Position mouse pointer on gridline until it turns into double-headed arrow.
2. Hold down left mouse button, drag to desired position, then release mouse button.

In Addition

Selecting Cells with the Keyboard

As an alternative to using the mouse, you can also select cells using keyboard shortcuts by completing the following steps:

To select	Press
the next cell's contents	Tab
the preceding cell's contents	Shift + Tab
the entire table	Alt + 5 (on the numeric keypad with Num Lock off)
adjacent cells	Hold Shift key and then press an arrow key repeatedly.
a column	Position insertion point in top cell of column, hold down the Shift key, and then press Down Arrow key until column is selected.

Activity 4.8

Changing the Table Design

The Table Tools Design tab contains a number of options for enhancing the appearance of the table. With options in the Table Styles group, apply a predesigned style that applies color and border lines to a table. Maintain further control over the predesigned style formatting applied to columns and rows with options in the Table Style Options group. For example, if your table contains a total row, you would insert a check mark in the *Total Row* option. Apply additional design formatting to cells in a table with the Shading and Borders buttons in the Table Styles group. Draw a table or draw additional rows and/or columns in a table by clicking the Draw Table button in the Draw Borders group. Click this button and the mouse pointer turns into a pencil. Drag in the table to create the desired columns and rows. Click the Erase button and the mouse pointer turns into an eraser. Drag through the column and/or row lines you want to erase in the table.

Project

You will add final touches to the Caffeine Chart table by applying border, shading, and table styles formatting.

① With **WordMedS4-02.docx** open, click anywhere in the table and then select the entire table by clicking the table move handle that displays in the upper left corner of the table.

② With the table selected, click the Table Tools Design tab, click the Borders button arrow, and then click *Borders and Shading* at the drop-down list.

This displays the Borders and Shading dialog box with the Borders tab selected.

③ At the dialog box, click the *Grid* option in the *Setting* section, scroll down the *Style* list box, and then click the first thick/thin option (see image at the right).

④ Click the down-pointing arrow at the right of the *Color* option box and then click *Purple, Accent 4, Darker 25%* at the drop-down palette.

⑤ Click OK to close the Borders and Shading dialog box.

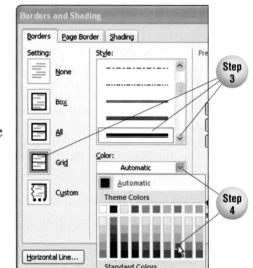

⑥ Select the second row in the table, click the Shading button arrow, and then click *Olive Green, Accent 3, Lighter 80%* at the drop-down palette.

⑦ Save and then print **WordMedS4-02.docx**.

⑧ Make sure the insertion point is positioned in the table and then apply a table style to the table. Begin by clicking the More button that displays at the right of the table style icons in the Table Styles group.

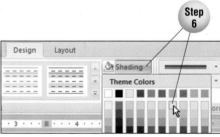

This displays a drop-down gallery of style choices.

9. Scroll down the list of table styles and then click the *Medium Shading 1 – Accent 1* option (second option from the left in the fourth row in the *Built-In* section).

> Notice the color and border style formatting and also notice how the style changed the border and shading formatting you applied earlier.

10. Experiment with an additional style by clicking the More button at the right of the table style icons in the Table Styles group, scrolling down the drop-down gallery, and then clicking the *Medium Shading 1 – Accent 4* option (fifth option from the left in the fourth row in the *Built-In* section).

11. Change the formatting by clicking the *Banded Rows* option in the Table Style Options group to remove the check mark. Click the *Banded Columns* option to insert a check mark. Click the *Header Row* option to remove the check mark and click the *First Column* option to remove the check mark.

12. Save, print, and then close **WordMedS4-02.docx**.

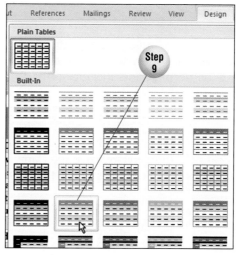

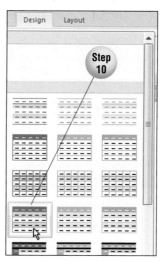

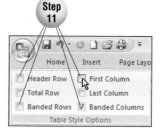

In Addition

Sorting in a Table

Sort text in a table alphabetically, numerically, or by date with options at the Sort dialog box shown at the right. Display this dialog box by positioning the insertion point in a cell in the table and then clicking the Sort button in the Data group in the Table Tools Layout tab. Make sure the column you want to sort is selected in the *Sort by* option and then click OK. If the first row in the table contains data such as headings that you do not want to include in the sort, click the *Header row* option in the *My list has* section of the Sort dialog box. If you want to sort specific cells in a table, select the cells first and then click the Sort button.

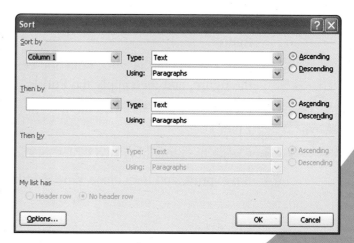

Activity 4.9

Creating a Form for Handwritten Entries

Forms are a major part of a patient's medical records. Forms come in a variety of types in a medical office or hospital and include forms that require patients to enter handwritten informa- tion and forms that require the medical office assis- tant or hospital worker to enter information at the computer. When creating forms for entering hand- written information, consider using tables to improve the readability of the form.

Project

One of your job duties is to call patients after they have received day surgery. You realize that creating a form will improve the clarity and completeness of the information you gather from the patients. You decide to use the Table feature to create boxes for handwritten entries.

1. Open **NSMCLtrhd.docx** and then save the document and name it **WordMedS4-03**.

2. Click the No Spacing style in the Styles group in the Home tab, change the font to 12-point Cambria, and then press the Enter key twice.

3. Create the form shown in Figure W4.6. To begin, type the title **POST-OPERATIVE CALL RECORD**, centered and bolded.

4. Press the Enter key twice and then change the paragraph alignment back to left.

5. Create a table with four rows and four columns by clicking the Insert tab, clicking the Table button, dragging the mouse pointer down and to the right until four rows and four columns are selected in the grid and *4x4 Table* displays above the grid, and then releasing the left mouse button.

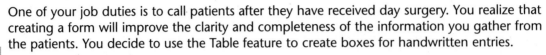

6. Type the text in the cells as shown in Figure W4.6. Bold and center the column heading text as shown. (The shading in the row is Purple, Accent 4, Lighter 80%.)

7. After creating the first table, press Ctrl + End to move the insertion point below the table.

8. Press the Enter key and then type the text below the first table as shown in Figure W4.6.

9. Create the second table with six rows and four columns as shown in the figure.

10. Decrease or increase the size of the columns so they match what you see in the figure.

11. Type the text in the cells, bold and center the column heading text as shown in the figure, and then apply the Purple, Accent 4, Lighter 80% shading as shown.

12. Press Ctrl + End to move the insertion point below the table and then press the Enter key.

13. Create the remaining two tables as shown in Figure W4.6.

14. Save, print, and then close **WordMedS4-03.docx**.

FIGURE W4.6 Form for Handwritten Entries

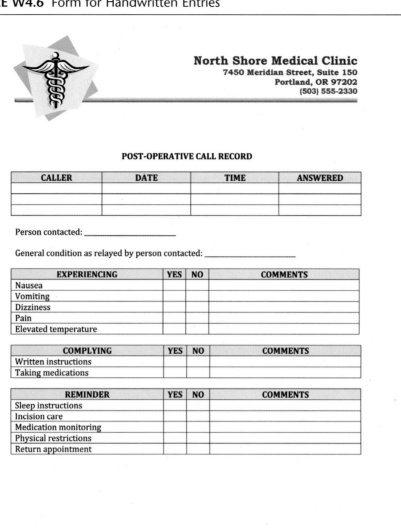

North Shore Medical Clinic
7450 Meridian Street, Suite 150
Portland, OR 97202
(503) 555-2330

POST-OPERATIVE CALL RECORD

CALLER	DATE	TIME	ANSWERED

Person contacted: _____

General condition as relayed by person contacted: _____

EXPERIENCING	YES	NO	COMMENTS
Nausea			
Vomiting			
Dizziness			
Pain			
Elevated temperature			

COMPLYING	YES	NO	COMMENTS
Written instructions			
Taking medications			

REMINDER	YES	NO	COMMENTS
Sleep instructions			
Incision care			
Medication monitoring			
Physical restrictions			
Return appointment			

In Addition

Customizing Cell Size

When you create a table, the column widths are equal as are the row heights. You can customize the width of columns and the height of rows with buttons in the Cell Size group in the Table Tools Layout tab. Use the *Table Row Height* measurement box to increase or decrease the height of rows and use the *Table Column Width* measurement box to increase or decrease the width of columns. The Distribute Rows button distributes equally the height of selected rows and the Distribute Columns button distributes equally the width of selected columns. You can also change column width using the move table column markers on the horizontal ruler. To do this, position the mouse pointer on a marker until the pointer turns into a left-and-right arrow and then drag the marker to the desired position. Hold down the Shift key while dragging a table column marker and the horizontal ruler remains stationary while the table column marker moves. Hold down the Alt key while dragging a table column marker and measurements display on the horizontal ruler.

Activity 4.10

Creating a Form and Saving It as a Template

Many businesses use preprinted forms that are generally filled in by hand or using a computer. These forms require additional storage space and also cost the company money. With Word's form feature, you can create your own forms, eliminating the need for preprinted forms. You can insert text boxes, check boxes, and pull-down lists. A form is created as a template so that when someone fills in the form, they are working on a copy of the form, not the original. The original is the template document

that is saved as a protected document. When a form is created from the template form document that has been protected, information can be typed only in the fields designated when the form was created. Word provides a Legacy Tools button in the Developer tab with options for inserting a text box, check box, or other form fields into a form template document. Turn on the display of the Developer tab at the Word Options dialog box. Generally, a form is created based on the default template document (called the *Normal* template).

Project

You are responsible for checking in patients as they arrive and updating their records, if necessary. You decide to create a form with fields for updating records, which can be used to enter revised patient data at the computer.

1. Display the Developer tab. Begin by clicking the Office button and then clicking the Word Options button located toward the bottom of the drop-down list.

2. At the Word Options dialog box, click the *Show Developer tab in the Ribbon* check box to insert a check mark and then click OK to close the dialog box.

The Developer tab displays at the right of the View tab.

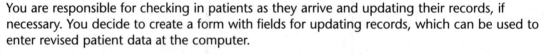
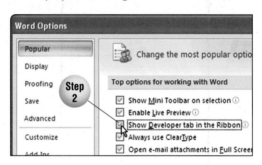

3. Create the form document shown in Figure W4.7. Begin by clicking the Office button and then clicking *New*.

4. At the New Document dialog box, click *My templates* in the *Templates* section.

5. At the New dialog box, if necessary, click the *Blank Document* template in the list box, click *Template* in the *Create New* section, and then click OK.

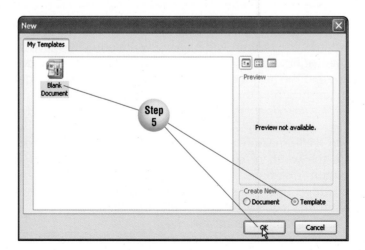

FIGURE W4.7 Template Form

Cascade View Pediatrics

Patient Update

Patient Name: ▢   Patient Number: ▢

Address: ▢   City: ▢   State: ▢   Zip: ▢

Telephone: ▢   Medical Insurance: ▢

Check the appropriate box identifying with whom the patient lives.

☐ Both Parents   ☐ Mother

☐ Father   ☐ Other – Specify: ▢

Guardian Information	**Guardian Information**
Relationship: ▢	Relationship: ▢
Name: ▢	Name: ▢
Address: ▢	Address: ▢
City: ▢ State: ▢ Zip: ▢	City: ▢ State: ▢ Zip: ▢
Home Telephone: ▢	Home Telephone: ▢

⑥ Insert a document into the blank template document. To begin, click the Insert tab, click the Object button arrow, and then click *Text from File* at the drop-down list.

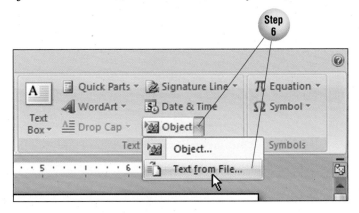

⑦ At the Insert File dialog box, navigate to the WordMedS4 folder on your storage medium and then double-click ***CVPPatientForm.docx***.

This inserts a document containing a table with cells containing patient information categories. Please refer to Figure W4.7.

continues

8 Position the mouse pointer immediately right of the text *Patient Name:* and then click the left mouse button. This positions the insertion point one space to the right of the colon after *Patient Name:*.

9 Click the Developer tab, click the Legacy Tools button 🔧 in the Controls group, and then click the Text Form Field button ab| at the drop-down palette.

The text form field displays as a shaded area in the cell.

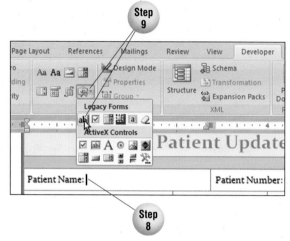

10 Refer to Figure W4.7 and then insert text form fields in the remaining cells as shown in the figure. To insert the check boxes in the *Check the appropriate box identifying with whom the patient lives.* section, click in the desired cell, click the Legacy Tools button in the Controls group, and then click the Check Box Form Field button ☑ in the *Legacy Forms* section.

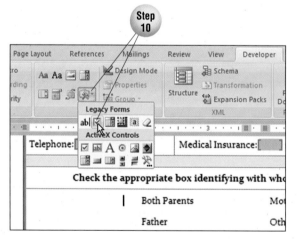

11 Protect the template document by clicking the Protect Document button 🔒 in the Protect group in the Developer tab.

12 At the Restrict Formatting and Editing task pane, click in the *Allow only this type of editing in the document:* check box, click the down-pointing arrow at the right of the option box in the *Editing restrictions* section, and then click *Filling in forms* at the drop-down list.

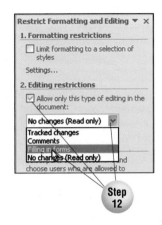

Step 12

13 Click the Yes, Start Enforcing Protection button and then click OK at the Start Enforcing Protection dialog box. (Creating a password is optional.)

14 Close the Restrict Formatting and Editing task pane by clicking the Close button that displays in the upper right corner of the task pane.

15 Save the document and name it **XXXUpdateTemplate** (in the Templates default folder). (Use your initials in place of the *XXX*.)

16 Print and then close **XXXUpdateTemplate.dotx**.

    The text box form field and check box form field shading do not print.

In Brief

Create Form Document
1. Click Office button, click *New*.
2. At New Document dialog box, click *My Templates*.
3. At New dialog box, click *Blank Document* template in list box.
4. Click *Template* in *Create New Section*.
5. Click OK.
6. Click Developer tab.
7. Type document clicking the Legacy Tools button and then clicking the Text Form Field button to insert a text form field or clicking the Legacy Tools button and then clicking the Check Box Form Field button to insert a check box.
8. Click Protect Document button.
9. Click *Allow only this type of editing in the document* check box.
10. Click down-pointing arrow at right of option in *Editing restrictions* section and then click *Filling in forms*.
11. Click Yes, Start Enforcing Protection button.
12. Click OK at Start Enforcing Protection dialog box.

In Addition

Planning the Form Layout

When planning the form layout, consider these points:
- Group like items together in the form as this makes providing complete and accurate information easier for the person filling in the form.
- Place the most important information at the top of the form to increase the likelihood of obtaining the desired information.
- Use fonts, colors, lines, and graphics purposefully and sparingly as overuse of such design elements tends to clutter a form and make it difficult to read.
- Use white space and lines to separate sections and clearly identify each section.

Activity 4.11

Filling in and Printing a Form Document

After you create, protect, and save a template form document, you can use it to create a personalized form document. When you open a protected form template document, the insertion point is automatically inserted in the first form field. Type the information for the data field and then press the Tab key to move the insertion point to the next form field. You can move the insertion point to a preceding form field by pressing Shift + Tab. To fill in a check box form field, click in the check box or move the insertion point to the check box and then press the spacebar. Complete the same steps to remove an *X* from a check box form field.

Project
A patient that is a minor child has arrived at the clinic for an appointment. You enter the updated information for the patient and her parents using the Update Template form.

1. Create a form with the **XXXUpdateTemplate.dotx** form template (where *XXX* indicates your initials). To begin, click the Office button and then click *New* at the drop-down list.

2. At the New Document dialog box, click *My templates* in the *Templates* section.

3. At the New dialog box, click *XXXUpdateTemplate.dotx*, make sure *Document* is selected in the *Create New* section, and then click OK.

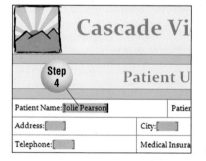

4. Word displays the form document with the insertion point positioned in the first form field after *Patient Name:*. Type the name **Jolie Pearson** as shown below and in Figure W4.8.

5. Press the Tab key to move to the next form field.

6. Fill in the remaining text and check box form fields as shown in Figure W4.8. Press the Tab key to move the insertion point to the next form field. Press Shift + Tab to move the insertion point to the preceding form field. To insert the *X* in a check box, click in the check box, or move the insertion point to the check box, and then press the spacebar.

7. When the form is completed, save the document in the WordMedS4 folder on your storage medium and name it **WordMedS4-04**.

8. Print and then close **WordMedS4-04.docx**.

FIGURE W4.8 Filled-in Form

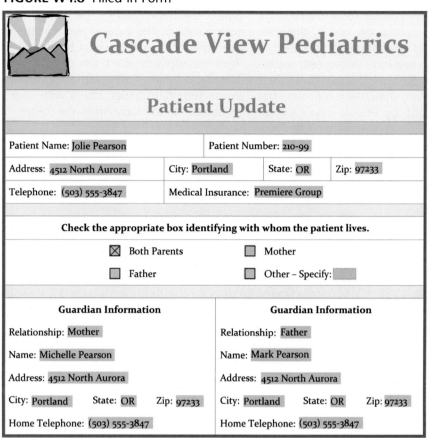

Cascade View Pediatrics

Patient Update

Patient Name: Jolie Pearson   Patient Number: 210-99

Address: 4512 North Aurora   City: Portland   State: OR   Zip: 97233

Telephone: (503) 555-3847   Medical Insurance: Premiere Group

Check the appropriate box identifying with whom the patient lives.

☒ Both Parents   ☐ Mother

☐ Father   ☐ Other – Specify:

Guardian Information	**Guardian Information**
Relationship: Mother	Relationship: Father
Name: Michelle Pearson	Name: Mark Pearson
Address: 4512 North Aurora	Address: 4512 North Aurora
City: Portland State: OR Zip: 97233	City: Portland State: OR Zip: 97233
Home Telephone: (503) 555-3847	Home Telephone: (503) 555-3847

In Brief

Fill in Form
1. Click Office button, click *New*.
2. At New Document dialog box, click *My templates*.
3. At New dialog box, click desired template document.
4. Click OK.
5. Type text to insert text or press spacebar to insert check mark.
6. Press Tab key to move to next field or press Shift + Tab to move to previous field.

In Addition

Customizing Text Form Field Options

To change options for a text form field, select the text form field and then click the Properties button in the Controls group in the Developer tab. This displays the Text Form Field Options dialog box shown at the right. At this dialog box, you can change the type of text inserted in the form field, type default text, specify a maximum length for a form field, and apply formatting options.

Customizing Check Box Form Field Options

You can customize check box form field options at the Check Box Form Field Options dialog box shown at the right. Display this dialog box by selecting a check box form field and then clicking the Properties button in the Controls group in the Developer tab. At the dialog box, you can specify options such as the check box size and default value.

Editing a Form Template

When you create and protect a form template, the text in the template cannot be changed. If you need to make changes to a form document, unprotect the document and then make the changes. After making the changes, protect the document again. Word, by default, saves a template document in the Templates folder. The loca-tion of this folder varies depending on your system configuration. The *Look in* panel at the left side of the Open dialog box should contain the *Trusted Templates* option. Click the option to display the Templates folder. If your template does not display in the Templates folder, check with your instructor to determine the location of the folder.

Project After using the Update Template form a couple of times, you realize that you need to add additional fields.

1. Click the Open button on the Quick Access toolbar.

2. Click the *Trusted Templates* option in the *Look in* panel located at the left side of the Open dialog box.

3. Double-click ***XXXUpdateTemplate.dotx*** in the list box (where ***XXX*** indicates your initials).

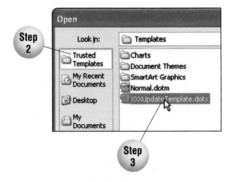

4. Unprotect the template document by clicking the Developer tab and then clicking the Protect Document button in the Protect group.

5. At the Restrict Formatting and Editing task pane, click the Stop Protection button that displays at the bottom of the task pane.

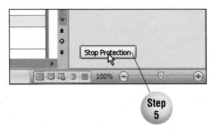

Insert a new row at the bottom of the table. To do this, click in one of the cells in the bottom row, click the Table Tools Layout tab, and then click the Insert Below button in the Rows & Columns group.

Click in the new cell in the first column, type **Work Telephone:** and then press the spacebar.

Insert a text form field by clicking the Developer tab, clicking the Legacy Tools button, and then clicking the Text Form Field button in the drop-down palette.

Press the Tab key (this moves the insertion point to the new cell in the second column), type **Work Telephone:**, press the spacebar, and then insert a text form field.

Protect the document by clicking the Yes, Start Enforcing Protection button in the task pane.

Click OK at the Start Enforcing Protection dialog box.

Close the Restrict Formatting and Editing task pane.

Save **XXXUpdateTemplate.dotx**.

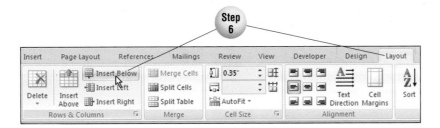

Step 6

Step 10

Brief

Edit Form Template
1. Open template.
2. Click Developer tab.
3. Click Protect Document button.
4. Click Stop Protection button in task pane.
5. Make desired changes.
6. Click the Yes, Start Enforcing Protection button in task pane.
7. Click OK at Start Enforcing Protection dialog box.

In Addition

Using Buttons in the Developer Tab Controls Group

The Controls group in the Developer tab contains two text control buttons, the Rich Text button and the Text button. The Text button inserts a plain text content control that takes on the format of the text that surrounds it. The Rich Text button inserts a content control that supports unique formatting for the content control but is most commonly used when the data entered will be used in or linked to another file or document. Use the Picture Content Control button to insert a picture content control in a form and use the Date Picker button to insert a date content control. Click the Properties button in the Controls group to change the properties of the selected content control.

Activity 4.13

Creating and Filling in a Form with a Drop-Down Form Field

Some fields in a form may require the person entering the information to choose from specific options, rather than typing the information. You can create a field with multiple choices using the Drop-Down Form Field button. After inserting a drop-down form field, click the Properties button in the Controls group in the Developer tab and the Drop-Down Form Field Options dialog box displays. Use options at this dialog box to type the options you want displayed. A drop-down form field in a form document displays as a gray box with a down-pointing arrow at the right side of the box. When entering data in a form, click the down-pointing arrow and then click the desired option at the drop-down list.

Project

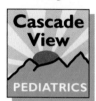

After looking at the Patient Update form, you realize that the field after the *Medical Insurance:* text should be changed to a drop-down form field since your clinic accepts medical insurance from three healthcare companies.

1. With **XXXUpdateTemplate.dotx** open, unprotect the template document by clicking the Developer tab and then clicking the Protect Document button. At the task pane, click the Stop Protection button.

2. Change a text form field to a drop-down form field. Begin by clicking the text form field immediately right of *Medical Insurance:* and then pressing the Delete key.

   This removes the text form field from the cell.

3. Click the Developer tab, click the Legacy Tools button in the Controls group, and then click the Drop-Down Form Field button ▥.

4. Click the Properties button 🖳 in the Controls group.

   This displays the Drop-Down Form Field Options dialog box.

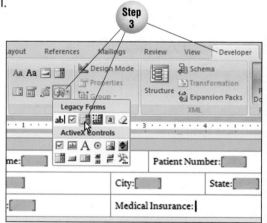

5. At the Drop-Down Form Field Options dialog box, type **Health Plus America** in the *Drop-down item* text box and then click the Add button.

6. Type **Premiere Group** in the *Drop-down item* text box and then click the Add button. Type **Healthwise Cooperative** and then click the Add button. Type **Self Insured** and then click the Add button.

7. Click OK to close the Drop-Down Form Field Options dialog box.

8. Protect the template by clicking the Yes, Start Enforcing Protection button in the task pane and then clicking OK at the Start Enforcing Protection dialog box.

9. Close the Restrict Formatting and Editing task pane.

10. Save and then close **XXXUpdateTemplate.dotx**.

(11) Fill in the form as shown in Figure W4.9. To begin, click the Office button and then click New at the drop-down list. At the New Document dialog box, click *My templates* in the *Templates* section. At the New dialog box, click **XXXUpdateTemplate.dotx**, make sure *Document* is selected in the *Create New* section, and then click OK.

(12) Fill in the text and check boxes as shown in Figure W4.9. Press the Tab key to move to the next field or press Shift + Tab to move to the previous field. To fill in the drop-down form field, click the down-pointing arrow at the right of the *Medical Insurance:* option box and then click *Healthwise Cooperative* at the drop-down list.

(13) Save the completed form and name it **WordMedS4-05**.

(14) Print and then close **WordMedS4-05.docx**.

In Brief

Insert Drop-Down Form Field
1. Click Developer tab.
2. Click Legacy Tools button.
3. Click Drop-Down Form Field button.

Display Drop-Down Form Field Options Dialog Box
1. Select drop-down form field.
2. Click Properties button in Controls group in Developer tab.

FIGURE W4.9 Filled-in Form

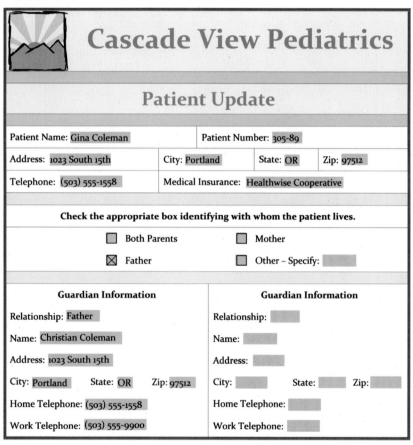

In Addition

Filling in a Drop-down List

When filling in a drop-down form field, make the field active and then complete one of the following steps:
- Click the down-pointing arrow at the right side of the form field.
- Press F4.
- Press Alt + Down Arrow key.

When you choose one of the methods, a drop-down list displays with choices for the field. Click the desired choice or press the Up or Down arrow to select the desired choice and then press the Enter key.

Features Summary

Feature	Ribbon Tab, Group	Button	Option
Mail Merge wizard	Mailings, Start Mail Merge		Step by Step Mail Merge Wizard
table	Insert, Tables		
delete column	Table Tools Layout, Rows & Columns		Delete Columns
delete row	Table Tools Layout, Rows & Columns		Delete Rows
insert column	Table Tools Layout, Rows & Columns	or	
insert row	Table Tools Layout, Rows & Columns	or	
Table Properties dialog box	Table Tools Layout, Table		
table styles	Table Tools Design, Table Styles		
protect document	Developer, Protect		
Word Options dialog box		, Word Options	
New Document dialog box			New
text form field	Developer, Controls	, ab|	
drop-down form field	Developer, Controls	,	
check box form field	Developer, Controls	,	

Knowledge Check

Completion: In the space provided at the right, write in the correct term, symbol, or command.

1. A merge generally takes two documents—the main document and this.

2. To start the Mail Merge wizard, click the Mailings tab, click the Start Mail Merge button, and then click this option at the drop-down list.

3. The Mail Merge wizard guides you through this number of steps to prepare merge documents.

4. Insert this field in a main document at the location where you want to insert variable information during a merge.

5. Click this hyperlink in the Mail Merge Recipients dialog box to display the Filter and Sort dialog box with the Sort Records tab selected.

6. You can create a table using the Table button in this tab.

7. Press this key to move the insertion point to the next cell in a table.

8. Press these keys to move the insertion point to the previous cell in a table.

9. To insert a row in a table above the current row, click this button in the Rows & Columns group in the Table Tools Layout tab.

10. Center a table between the left and right margins with the *Center* option in the *Alignment* section in this dialog box.

11. Apply predesigned table styles with options in the Table Styles group in this tab.

12. The Legacy Tools button is located in the Controls group in this tab.

13. Click the Protect Document button and this task pane displays.

14. To fill in a check box form field, make the check box active and then press this key on the keyboard.

15. Click this button in the Legacy Tools drop-down palette to insert a shaded area identifying a location for users to enter text in a form.

16. Use this button in the Legacy Tools drop-down palette to insert a field with multiple choices.

Skills Review

Review 1 Creating and Merging Letters

Columbia River General Hospital

1. Look at the information in Figure W4.10 and Figure W4.11. Use the Mail Merge wizard to prepare six letters using the information shown in the figures. When completing the steps, consider the following:
   a. At Step 3, create a data source document using the information shown in Figure W4.10. (Enter the records in this order—*Watanabe, Reeves, Torres, Wickstrom, O'Leary,* and *Fuentes.*) Save the data source document in the WordMedS4 folder on your storage medium and name it **CRGHEducationList**.

Mr. Paul Watanabe
Division Street Clinic
5330 Division Street
Portland, OR 97255

Ms. Nora Reeves
Community Counseling
1235 North 122nd Avenue
Portland, OR 97230

Mr. Ramon Torres
Youth and Family Services
8904 McLoughlin Boulevard
Oak Grove, OR 97267

Dr. Thomas Wickstrom
Columbia Mental Health Center
550 Columbia Street
Portland, OR 97305

Ms. Suzanne O'Leary
Family Counseling Center
100 Center Street
Oak Grove, OR 97268

Dr. Christina Fuentes
Parenting Services
210 Martin Luther King Way
Portland, OR 97403

b. At Step 4, type the letter shown in Figure W4.11. Insert a Fill-in field for the *(School)* field. (You determine the prompt message.)

c. At Step 6, click the *Edit individual letters* hyperlink in the task pane.

d. At the Merge to New Document dialog box, make sure *All* is selected and then click the OK button.

e. When merging the letters, type the following in the specific record:

Record 1	**Jefferson Elementary School**
Record 2	**Jefferson Elementary School**
Record 3	**Evergreen Elementary School**
Record 4	**Jefferson Elementary School**
Record 5	**Evergreen Elementary School**
Record 6	**Jefferson Elementary School**

2. Save the merged letters in the normal manner in the WordMedS4 folder on your storage medium and name the document **CRGHEduationLetters**.

3. Print and then close **CRGHEducationLetters.docx**. (This document will print six letters.)

4. Save the main document in the normal manner in the WordMedS4 folder on your storage medium and name it **CRGHEducationMainDoc**.

5. Close **CRGHEducationMainDoc.docx**.

FIGURE W4.11 Review 1, Letter

February 2, 2011

«AddressBlock»

«GreetingLine»

The staff in the Education Department at Columbia River General Hospital has prepared parent education classes designed for parents of children between the ages of 5 and 10. Classes focus on a commonsense approach to parenting and provide parents with practical ideas about setting limits and teaching children to make responsible choices. Parents are given ideas and techniques that can be used at home to help children develop decision-making and problem-solving skills.

Qualified family counselors will teach the classes, which will begin Monday, March 7, and end Wednesday, April 6. Classes will be held from 7:00 to 8:30 p.m. at (School). Cost for the classes is based on a sliding-fee scale. For more information on these parenting classes and how parents can register, as well as directions to the school, please call me at (503) 555-2500.

Sincerely,

Laura Latterell
Education Director

XX:CRGHEducationLetters.docx

Review 2 Preparing Envelopes

1. Use the Mail Merge wizard to prepare envelopes for the letters created in Review 1.
2. Specify **CRGHEducationList.mdb** as the data source document.
3. Save the merged envelope document in the WordMedS4 folder on your storage medium and name the document **CRGHEducationEnvs**.
4. Print and then close the **CRGHEductionEnvs.docx** document. (Manual feed may be required.)
5. Close the envelope main document without saving the document.

Review 3 Creating Chart Notes Using a Table

1. Open **NSMCLtrhd.docx** and then save the document with Save As and name it **WordMedS4-R3**.
2. Click the No Spacing style, change the font to Constantia, and add 12 points of spacing above paragraphs. *Hint: Add 12 points of spacing above paragraphs by clicking the Line spacing button in the Paragraph group in the Home tab and then clicking* **Add Space Before Paragraph** *at the drop-down list.*
3. Create a table with 2 columns and 20 rows.
4. Select and then merge each row (individually) as shown in Figure W4.12. *Hint: To merge cells, select the cells and then click the Merge Cells button in the Merge group in the Table Tools Layout tab.*
5. Type the text in cells as shown in Figure W4.12.

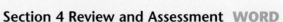

6. Change the font size to 16 and turn on bold for the title *CHART NOTES* and change to center alignment.
7. Apply Purple, Accent 4, Lighter 60% shading to the top row. **Hint: Do this with the Shading button in the Table Styles group in the Table Tools Design tab.**
8. Save, print, and then close **WordMedS4-R3.docx**.

FIGURE W4.12 Review 3

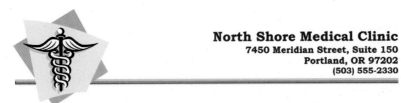

North Shore Medical Clinic
7450 Meridian Street, Suite 150
Portland, OR 97202
(503) 555-2330

CHART NOTES	
NAME	DOB
DATE	AGE
Reason for visit:	
B/P	PULSE
SHEENT	
Neck	
Lungs	
Cardiovascular	
Abdomen	
Genitourinary	
Musculoskeletal	
Neurologic/Psychiatric	
Lab/x-rays	
Impressions:	
Plan:	

Review 4 Preparing a Form

1. Create the form shown in Figure W4.13 as a template. Begin by clicking the Office button and then clicking *New*. At the New Document dialog box, click *My templates* in the *Templates* section. At the New dialog box, click the *Blank Document* template in the list box, click *Template* in the *Create New* section, and then click OK.
2. At the template, insert the document named **CRGHSecPayerForm.docx**. *Hint: Insert the file by clicking the Insert tab, clicking the Object button arrow, and then clicking* **Text from File**. *At the Insert File dialog box, navigate to the WordMedS4 folder on your storage medium and then double-click* **CRGHSecPayerForm.docx**.
3. Insert the text form fields and check box form fields as shown in Figure W4.13. For the *Name of Insurance Company:* cell, insert a drop-down form field with these options: *Assure Medical*, *Premiere Group*, *Sound Medical*, *Health Plus*, and *First Choice*.
4. Protect the document.
5. Save the template with the name **XXXCRGHSPFormTemplate**. (Use your initials in place of the *XXX*.)
6. Close **XXXCRGHSPFormTemplate.dotx**.
7. Create a form document with the **XXXCRGHSPFormTemplate.dotx** template. Begin by clicking the Office button and then clicking *New*. At the New Document dialog box, click *My templates* in the *Templates* section. At the New dialog box, click **XXXCRGHSPFormTemplate.dotx** and then click OK.
8. Insert the following data in the specified fields:
   Patient Name: **Wyatt Johnston**
   Patient Number: **839488**
   Address: **3107 North Cedar Street**
   City: **Portland**
   State: **OR**
   Zip: **97429**
   Telephone: **(503) 555-4775**
   Date of Birth: **05/15/1975**
   Insert a check mark in the *Yes* check box for the first question and insert a check mark in the *No* check box for each of the second through sixth questions.
   Name of Insurance Company: Choose *Health Plus* from the drop-down list
   Telephone Number: **1-800-555-3995**
   Name of Policy Holder: **Wyatt Johnston**
   Policy Number: **RT-90338**
9. Save the document with the name **WordMedS4-R4**.
10. Print and then close **WordMedS4-R4.docx**.

Columbia
River
General
Hospital

Columbia River General Hospital
4550 Fremont Street ● Portland, Oregon 97045 ● (503) 555-2000

SECONDARY PAYER FORM

Patient Name: Patient Number:

Address: City: State: Zip:

Telephone: Date of Birth:

Please answer the following questions related to your illness or injury:

Yes	No	
☐	☐	Is illness/injury due to an automobile accident?
☐	☐	Is illness/injury due to an accident covered by Worker's Compensation?
☐	☐	Does the Black Lung Program cover this illness?
☐	☐	Are you eligible for coverage under the Veterans Administration?
☐	☐	If under 65, do you have Medicare coverage due to a disability?
☐	☐	Do you have coverage under a spouse's health insurance plan?

Name of Insurance Company: Telephone Number:

Name of Policy Holder: Policy Number:

Skills Assessment

Assessment 1 Creating and Merging Letters

1. Use the Mail Merge wizard to create the letter shown in Figure W4.14 and merge it with the **NSMCPatientsDS.mdb** data source document with the following specifications:

   a. At Step 3, browse to the WordMedS4 folder and then double-click *NSMCPatientsDS.mdb*. With the records displayed in the Mail Merge Recipients dialog box, add the following record:

Title	**Mrs.**
First Name	**Lola**
Last Name	**Solberg**
Address Line 1	**23100 North Tillicum**
Address Line 2	(leave blank)
City	**Portland**
State	**OR**
ZIP Code	**97402**
Home Phone	**(503) 555-3437**
Specialty	**Obstetrics**

   b. With the Mail Merge Recipients dialog box displayed, identify only those records containing a specialty of *Obstetrics*.

   c. At Step 4, type the letter shown in Figure W4.14.

   d. At Step 6, click the *Edit individual letters* hyperlink in the task pane.

   e. At the Merge to New Document dialog box, make sure *All* is selected and then click the OK button.

2. Save the merged letters in the normal manner in the WordMedS4 folder on your storage medium and name the document **NSMCChildbirthClassLtrs**.

3. Print and then close **NSMCChildbirthClassLtrs.docx**. (Three letters should print.)

4. Save the main document in the normal manner in the WordMedS4 folder on your storage medium and name it **NSMCChildbirthMainDoc**.

5. Close **NSMCChildbirthMainDoc.docx**.

September 15, 2011

«AddressBlock»

«GreetingLine»

North Shore Medical Clinic is partnering with the Education Department at Columbia River General Hospital and offering childbirth education classes. A certified nurse practitioner teaches the classes at various times during the year. Participants in the class meet once a week for six weeks.

You can register for the classes directly with Columbia River General Hospital by calling the Education Department at (503) 555-2500 or by contacting us at (503) 555-2330. The fee for the classes is $75 payable directly to the hospital.

Sincerely,

Lee Elliott
Office Manager

XX:NSMCChildbirthClassLtrs.docx

Assessment 2 Modifying and Formatting a Calendar

1. Open **CVPCalendar.docx** and then save it with Save As and name it **WordMedS4-A2**.
2. Delete one of the rows in the calendar.
3. Select the entire table and then change the row height to *1.2"*. ***Hint: Do this with the* Table Row Height *measurement box in the Cell Size group in the Table Tools Layout tab.***
4. With the table still selected, change the font to 10-point Candara.
5. Position the insertion point in any cell in the second row and then change the row height to *0.2"*.
6. Merge the cells in the top row.
7. Select the top row (one cell), change the font size to 26, turn on bold, click the Align Center button in the Alignment group in the Table Tools Layout tab, apply the light aqua shading (*Aqua, Accent 5, Lighter 60%*), and then type the text shown in the cell in Figure W4.15.
8. Select the second row, change the font size to *11*, turn on bold, click the Align Center button in the Alignment group in the Table Tools Layout tab, apply the light aqua shading (*Aqua, Accent 5, Lighter 80%*), and then type the text shown in the second row in Figure W4.15.
9. Type the text in each cell as shown in Figure W4.15.
10. Save, print, and then close **WordMedS4-A2.docx**.

FIGURE W4.15 Assessment 2

Cascade View Pediatrics

350 North Skagit ☐ Portland, OR 97505 ☐ (503) 555-7700

Parenting Classes
March 2011

Sunday	Monday	Tuesday	Wednesday	Thursday	Friday	Saturday
		1	2	3	4 Mom & Baby 9:30 to 11:00 a.m.	5
6	7 Basic Parenting 7:00 to 8:30 p.m.	8	9 Basic Parenting 7:00 to 8:30 p.m.	10	11 Mom & Baby 9:30 to 11:00 a.m.	12
13	14 Basic Parenting 7:00 to 8:30 p.m.	15	16 Basic Parenting 7:00 to 8:30 p.m.	17	18 Mom & Baby 9:30 to 11:00 a.m.	19
20	21 Basic Parenting 7:00 to 8:30 p.m.	22	23 Basic Parenting 7:00 to 8:30 p.m.	24	25 Mom & Baby 9:30 to 11:00 a.m.	26
27	28 Basic Parenting 7:00 to 8:30 p.m.	29	30 Basic Parenting 7:00 to 8:30 p.m.	31		

Assessment 3 Formatting and Filling in a Medical Questionnaire

1. Create the form shown in Figure W4.16 as a template. Begin by clicking the Office button and then clicking *New*. At the New Document dialog box, click *My templates* in the *Templates* section. At the New dialog box, click the Blank Document template in the list box, click *Template* in the *Create New* section, and then click OK.
2. At the template, insert the document named **NSMCMedHistory.docx**. *Hint: Insert the file by clicking the Insert tab, clicking the Object button arrow, and then clicking* **Text from File**. *At the Insert File dialog box, navigate to the WordMedS4 folder on your storage medium and then double-click* **NSMCMedHistory.docx**.

3. Press Ctrl + End and then create the third table in the medical history document as shown in Figure W4.16. Use the other two tables in the document as a guideline for formatting the third table. After creating the table, insert the text form fields and check boxes in all three tables as shown in the figure.
4. Protect the document.
5. Save the template with the name **XXXNSMCMedHistoryTemplate**. (Use your initials in place of the *XXX*.)
6. Close **XXXNSMCMedHistoryTemplate.dotx**.
7. Create a form document with the **XXXNSMCMedHistoryTemplate.dotx** template. Begin by clicking the Office button and then clicking *New*. At the New Document dialog box, click *My templates* in the *Templates* section. At the New dialog box, click ***XXXNSMCMedHistoryTemplate.dotx*** and then click OK.
8. Fill in the first table with the following information:
   a. Patient's name is *Sean Joslin*, his patient ID number is *5423*, and his insurance is *Premiere Group*. Insert the current date in the *Date:* field.
   b. Click the *Yes* box after the *Prior operations?* question and then insert the information *Appendectomy, 2004* in the *Specify:* field.
   c. Click the *No* box for the next two questions.
   d. Click the *Yes* box after the *Current medications?* question and then insert the information *Prilosec, Tylenol* in the *List:* field.
9. Fill in the second table with the following information:
   a. Click the check boxes in the *Mother* column for *Asthma* and *Eczema/dermatitis*.
   b. Click the check box in the *Father* column for *High blood pressure*.
   c. Click the check boxes in the *Relative* column for *Arthritis*, *Cancer*, *Heart disease*, and *High blood pressure*.
10. Fill in the third table with the following information:
    a. Click the *Yes* box after the *Currently employed?* question and then insert the information *Firefighter* in the *Occupation:* field.
    b. Click the *No* box for the next three questions.
    c. Click the *Yes* box after the *Married?* question.
11. Save the document with the name **WordMedS4-A3**.
12. Print and then close **WordMedS4-A3.docx**.

MEDICAL HISTORY QUESTIONNAIRE			

Patient Name:		Patient ID#:	
Insurance:		Date:	

PAST MEDICAL HISTORY			
	Yes	No	
Prior operations?	☐	☐	Specify:
Prior major illness?	☐	☐	Specify:
Allergies to medications?	☐	☐	List:
Current medications?	☐	☐	List:

FAMILY HISTORY			
	Mother	Father	Relative
Allergies	☐	☐	☐
Arthritis	☐	☐	☐
Asthma	☐	☐	☐
Cancer	☐	☐	☐
Diabetes	☐	☐	☐
Eczema/dermatitis	☐	☐	☐
Heart disease	☐	☐	☐
High blood pressure	☐	☐	☐
Lung disease	☐	☐	☐
Other:			

SOCIAL HISTORY			
	Yes	No	
Currently employed?	☐	☐	Occupation:
Pregnant?	☐	☐	
Smoke tobacco?	☐	☐	Daily quantity:
Drink alcohol?	☐	☐	Daily quantity:
Married?	☐	☐	

Assessment 4 Converting a Table to Text

1. Use Word's Help feature to learn how to convert a table to text.
2. Open **Table.docx**.
3. Save the document with Save As and name it **WordMedS4-A4**.
4. Convert the table to text separating text with tabs.
5. Save, print, and then close **WordMedS4-A4.docx**.

HELP

Assessment 5 Locating Information and Writing a Memo

1. Two doctors from the clinic are traveling to Chicago for a medical conference. Lee Elliott has asked you to find information on round trip airfare from Portland to Chicago. For the departure date, use the first Monday of the next month and for the return date, use the first Saturday after the departure date. Use the Internet and an Internet travel company (such as Expedia or Travelocity) to search for flights. The doctors want to leave sometime between 9:00 a.m. and noon and return sometime between noon and 3:00 p.m.

2. Open **NSMCMemoForm.docx** and then, using the flight information you find, write a memo to Lee Elliott that includes a table containing information such as airline names, flight numbers, times, and cost. Format and modify the table so the information is attractive and easy to read.

3. Save the completed memo and name it **WordMedS4-A5**.

4. Print and then close **WordMedS4-A5.docx**.

Marquee Challenge

Challenge 1 Preparing a Treadmill Exercise Test Form

1. Open **NSMCLtrhd.docx** and then save it with Save As and name it **WordMedS4-C1**.

2. Change the spacing after paragraphs to 0 points.

3. Create the document shown in Figure W4.17.

4. Save, print, and then close **WordMedS4-C1.docx**.

Challenge 2 Preparing a Pre-operative Questions Form

1. Create the form shown in Figure W4.18 as a template.

2. At the template, insert the document named **NSMCPreOpQuestions.docx**.

3. Insert data in the table, format the table, and insert text form fields and check boxes so your form appears the same as the form in Figure W4.18.

4. Protect the document.

5. Save the template with the name **XXXNSMCPreOpQuestionsTemplate**. (Use your initials in place of the *XXX*.)

6. Close **XXXNSMCPreOpQuestionsTemplate.dotx**.

7. Create a form document with the **XXXNSMCPreOpQuestionsTemplate.dotx** template. You determine the information to insert in the form.

8. Save the document with the name **WordMedS4-C2**.

9. Print and then close **WordMedS4-C2.docx**.

North Shore Medical Clinic
7450 Meridian Street, Suite 150
Portland, OR 97202
(503) 555-2330

TREADMILL EXERCISE TEST

EXERCISE					
Stage (mph – grade)	**Blood Pressure**	**Heart Rate**	**Premature Beats**	**ST mm**	**ST slope**
AT REST					
Stage ½ (1.7 mph – 5%)					
Stage I (1.7 mph – 10%)					
Stage II (2.5 mph – 12%)					
Stage III (3.4 mph – 14%)					
Stage IV (4.2 mph – 16%)					
Stage V (5.0 mph – 18%)					
Stage VI (5.5 mph – 22%)					
Stage VII (6.0 mph – 22%)					

RECOVERY					
RECOVERY	**Blood Pressure**	**Heart Rate**	**Premature Beats**	**ST mm**	**ST slope**
IMMEDIATE					
1 Minute					
3 Minutes					
5 Minutes					
7 Minutes					

PRE-OPERATIVE QUESTIONS

Patient Name:		Patient ID#:	
Birth Date:		Surgery Date:	

Do you now have or have you ever had:

	Yes	No	
Anesthesia	☐	☐	When?
Difficulty with anesthesia	☐	☐	What?
A relative who has difficulty with anesthesia	☐	☐	What?
Asthma, bronchitis, emphysema, or other lung problems	☐	☐	
Abnormal chest x-ray	☐	☐	
Hypertension, chest pain, irregular heart beat	☐	☐	What?
Heart attack, heart murmur, abnormal EKG	☐	☐	What?
Bleeding or clotting problems	☐	☐	
Convulsions or seizures	☐	☐	
Stroke, muscle weakness, numbness, dizziness	☐	☐	
Hepatitis or jaundice	☐	☐	
Diabetes	☐	☐	
Kidney problems or blood in your urine	☐	☐	
Cortisone pills or injections	☐	☐	
Taking Coumadin, aspirin, ibuprofen or other blood thinner	☐	☐	
Taking prescription drugs	☐	☐	List:
Smoke tobacco	☐	☐	

Using Excel *in the* Medical Office

Introducing
Excel 2007

Microsoft Excel 2007 is a popular choice among individuals and companies to analyze and present data organized in columns and rows in a document called a *worksheet*. A worksheet is the electronic version of an accountant's ledger—only with a lot more power and versatility. Once a worksheet has been created you can perform a *what-if* analysis such as *What if medical supplies increase in price by 4%?* Changing a value in a worksheet causes Excel to automatically recalculate any other values dependent on the number you changed. In an instant your question is answered.

In Section 1, you will create new worksheets by entering labels, values, and formulas. To work efficiently you will learn to use tools such as the fill handle and copying techniques. Section 2 presents editing and formatting options with which you can improve a worksheet's appearance and correct errors. Section 3 introduces function formulas, visual elements such as charts, clip art, and drawing objects, page layout and print options, and data management features for working with lists.

In each of the three Excel sections, you will prepare medical worksheets for two clinics and a hospital as described below.

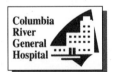

Cascade View Pediatrics is a full-service pediatric clinic that provides comprehensive primary pediatric care to infants, children, and adolescents.

North Shore Medical Clinic is an internal medicine clinic dedicated to providing exceptional care to all patients. The physicians in the clinic specialize in a number of fields including internal medicine, family practice, cardiology, and dermatology.

Columbia River General Hospital is an independent, not-for-profit hospital with the mission of providing high-quality, comprehensive care to patients and improving the health of members of the community.

Excel SECTION 1

Analyzing Data Using Excel

Skills

- Start Excel and identify features in the Excel window
- Enter labels and values
- Use the fill handle to enter a series
- Enter formulas
- Create a formula using Sum
- Copy a formula
- Test a worksheet for accuracy
- Apply the Accounting Number Format to values
- Right-align labels
- Use the Help feature
- Center a label across multiple columns
- Sort a range of cells
- Change the page orientation to landscape
- Preview and print a worksheet
- Save a workbook using Save and Save As
- Close a workbook and exit Excel
- Navigate a large worksheet using the mouse and the keyboard
- Jump to a specific cell using Go To
- Create a new workbook using a template

Student Resources

Before beginning this section:
1. Copy to your storage medium the ExcelMedS1 subfolder from the Unit4Excel folder on the Student Resources CD.
2. Make ExcelMedS1 the active folder.

In addition to containing the data files needed to complete section work, the Student Resources CD contains model answers in PDF format for each of the projects in this section; model answers for end-of-section exercises are not provided.

Projects Overview

Create a payroll worksheet, browse a supplies inventory and standard exam room cost report, create a time card, create a purchase order for medical supplies, and create an invoice for in-service training.

Complete an estimated travel expenses worksheet and calculate costs and registration fee for a medical seminar.

Edit an executive management salary report, calculate funds needed for a professional development budget, and prepare a surgery cost report.

197

Activity 1.1

Completing the Excel Worksheet Cycle

Information is created in Excel in a *worksheet* and is saved in a file called a *workbook*. A workbook can contain several worksheets. Imagine a worksheet as a page with horizontal and vertical lines drawn in a grid representing columns and rows. Data is entered into a *cell*, which is the intersection of a column with a row. Columns are lettered A to Z, AA to AZ, BA to BZ, and so on. The last column in the worksheet is labeled *XFD*. Rows are numbered 1, 2, 3, and so on. A column letter and a row number identify each cell. For example, A1 is the cell address for the intersection of column A with row 1. Each worksheet in Excel contains 16,384 columns and 1,048,576 rows. An Excel workbook initially contains three worksheets labeled Sheet1, Sheet2, and Sheet3. Additional sheets can be inserted as needed.

Project

You have been asked to update data in the Executive Management Salary Report for the Columbia River General Hospital by adding and editing data and viewing the impact of new data on cells used to calculate salary and benefit costs.

1. On the Windows XP desktop, click the Start button 🏁 *start* on the Taskbar.

2. Point to *All Programs.*

3. Point to *Microsoft Office.*

4. Click *Microsoft Office Excel 2007.*

   Depending on your operating system and/or system configuration, the steps you complete to open Excel may vary.

5. At the Excel screen, identify the various features by comparing your screen with the one shown in Figure E1.1. If necessary, maximize the Excel window. Depending on your screen resolution, your screen may vary slightly. Refer to Table E1.1 for a description of the screen features.

FIGURE E1.1 The Excel Screen

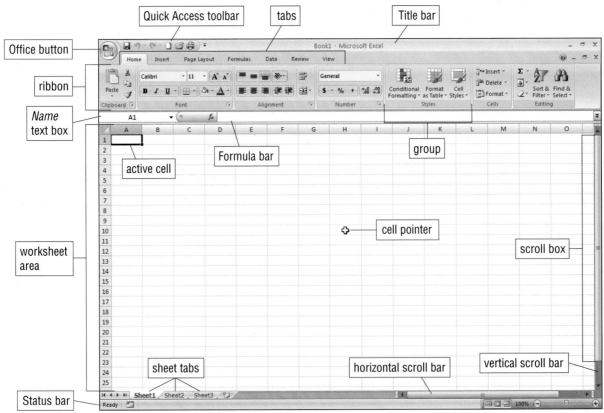

TABLE E1.1 Excel Screen Features

Feature	Description
Office button	Displays as a Microsoft Office logo and, when clicked, displays a list of document management actions, such as save or print, and a list of recently opened workbooks.
Quick Access toolbar	Contains buttons for commonly used commands which can be executed with a single mouse click.
tabs	Commands and features in the ribbon are organized into related groups which are accessed by clicking a tab name.
Title bar	Displays workbook name followed by Microsoft Excel.
ribbon	Area from which commands and features for performing actions on a cell or worksheet are accessed. Begin by selecting a tab and then choosing the command or feature.
Name text box	Displays the active cell address or name assigned to active cell.
Formula bar	Displays the contents stored in the active cell.
active cell	Location in the worksheet that will display typed data or that will be affected by a command.
worksheet area	Contains cells used to create the worksheet.
cell pointer	Select cells when you see this icon by clicking or dragging the mouse.
vertical and horizontal scroll bars	Used to view various parts of the worksheet beyond the current screen.
sheet tabs	Identifies the worksheets in the workbook. Use these tabs to change the active worksheet.
Status bar	Displays current mode, action messages, View buttons, and Zoom slider.

6. Click the Open button on the Quick Access toolbar.

If the Open button does not display on the Quick Access toolbar, click the Customize Quick Access Toolbar button that displays at the right side of the toolbar and then click *Open* at the drop-down list.

7. If necessary, navigate to the ExcelMedS1 folder on your storage medium.

To change to a different drive, click the down-pointing arrow at the right of the *Look in* list box and then select the correct drive or folder from the drop-down list. Double-clicking a folder name in the file list box changes the active folder.

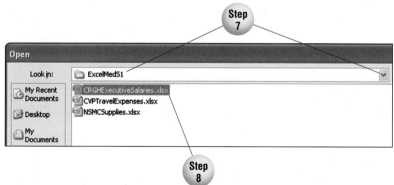

8. Double-click *CRGHExecutiveSalaries.xlsx*.

This workbook contains the salary and benefits report for the executive management team at Columbia River General Hospital. The formulas to sum the salaries and benefits have already been created. Notice some of the cells are empty. You will enter these values in Steps 11 through 14.

continues

9 Click the Office button and then click *Save As*.

> Use the *Save* option to save a file using the same name. If you want to keep the original workbook and save the workbook with the changes under a new name, use *Save As*.

10 At the Save As dialog box, make sure the ExcelMedS1 folder on your storage medium is the active folder, type **ExcelMedS1-01** in the *File name* text box, and then press Enter or click Save.

> Excel automatically adds the file extension *.xlsx* to the end of a workbook name. The *Save in* option at the Save As dialog box displays the active folder. If you need to make ExcelMedS1 the active folder, click the down-pointing arrow at the right of the *Save in* list box, navigate to the correct file storage location, and then double-click *ExcelMedS1* in the file list box.

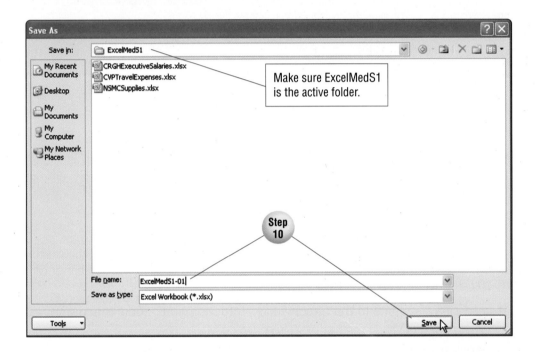

11 Move the cell pointer over the intersection of column F with row 8 (F8) and then click to make F8 the active cell.

12 Type **15400** and then press Enter.

> You do not need to type a comma in the thousands place. The column is formatted to insert the comma automatically. You will learn about formatting in Section 2. Notice that the entry in G8 has changed. This is because the formula created in G8 was dependent on F8. As soon as you enter a value in F8, any other dependent cells are automatically updated. Can you identify other cells that changed as a result of the new value in F8?

 PROBLEM

Typing mistake? Press Backspace to delete the characters at the left of the insertion point and then type the correct text

(13) Make E14 the active cell and then type **85000**.

(14) Make F14 the active cell, type **9275**, and then press Enter.

(15) Double-click the left mouse button in cell D14. Using the Right or Left Arrow keys, position the blinking insertion point immediately right of the comma, press the Backspace key to delete the comma, press the spacebar to insert a space, type *of*, and then press Enter.

> You noticed an inconsistency in the title for directors in column D. Double-clicking a cell opens the cell for editing. A blinking insertion point will appear inside the cell. Correct the entry using the arrow keys to move the insertion point, pressing the Backspace key or the Delete key to remove text, and then typing new text.

	E	F	G
Hospital			
Report			
12			
	Salary	Benefits	Total
	$ 155,000	$ 18,400	$ 173,400
	90,500	17,500	108,000
	110,750	18,400	129,150
	101,500	15,400	116,900
	95,475	14,650	110,125
	87,750	12,675	100,425
	85,000	9,275	94,275
	85,000	9,275	94,275
	85,000	9,275	94,275
	85,000	9,275	94,275
	$ 980,975	$134,125	$1,115,100

Step 12
Step 13
Step 14

In Brief

Start Excel
1. Click Start.
2. Point to *All Programs*.
3. Point to *Microsoft Office*.
4. Click *Microsoft Office Excel 2007*.

Open Workbook
1. Click Open button on Quick Access toolbar.
2. Navigate to storage medium and folder.
3. Double-click workbook name.

Save Workbook with New Name
1. Click Office button.
2. Click *Save As*.
3. Type new workbook name.
4. Click Save or press Enter.

Step 15

13	Mr.	William	Formet	Director of Planning
14	Mr.	Paul	Unraue	Director of Community Relations

(16) Click the Save button 🖫 on the Quick Access toolbar.

(17) Click the Quick Print button 🖨 on the Quick Access toolbar.

> If the Quick Print button does not display on the Quick Access toolbar, click the Customize Quick Access Toolbar button that displays at the right side of the toolbar and then click *Quick Print* at the drop-down list.

(18) Click the Office button and then click *Close* at the drop-down list.

> Excel displays a blank blue screen in the worksheet area when no workbooks are currently open.

In Addition

AutoComplete

The AutoComplete feature in Excel will complete text entries for you as you start to type a new entry in a cell. If the first few letters that you type match another entry in the column, Excel automatically fills in the remaining text. Press Tab or Enter to accept the text Excel suggests, or continue typing the correct text. You can turn off AutoComplete by clicking the Office button and then clicking the Excel Options button near the bottom right of the drop-down list. Click Advanced in the left pane of the Excel Options dialog box, click the *Enable AutoComplete for cell values* check box to clear the box, and then click OK.

Activity 1.2

Entering Labels and Values; Using Fill Options

A *label* is an entry in a cell that helps the reader relate to the values in the corresponding column or row. Labels are generally entered first when creating a new worksheet since they define the layout of the data in the columns and rows. By default, Excel aligns labels at the left edge of the column. A *value* is a number, formula, or function that can be used to perform calculations in the worksheet. By default, Excel aligns values at the right edge of the column. Take a few moments to plan or sketch out the layout of a new worksheet before entering labels and values. Decide the calculations you will need to execute and how to display the data so that it will be easily understood and interpreted.

Project

You need to create a new payroll worksheet for the hourly paid staff at the North Shore Medical Clinic. Begin by entering labels and values.

1 At the blank Excel screen, click the New button on the Quick Access toolbar to start a new blank workbook.

> If the New button does not display on the Quick Access toolbar, click the Customize Quick Access Toolbar button that displays at the right side of the toolbar and then click *New* at the drop-down list. Ctrl + N is the keyboard shortcut to begin a new blank workbook.

2 Type **Payroll** as the title for the new worksheet in A1.

> When you type a new entry in a cell, the entry appears in the Formula bar as well as within the active cell in the worksheet area. To end a cell entry, press Enter, move to another cell in the worksheet, or click the Enter button on the Formula bar.

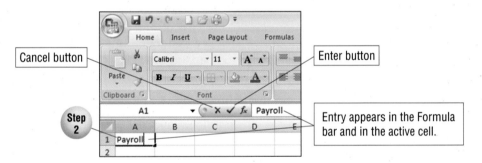

3 Press Enter.

? PROBLEM

If you catch a typing error after a cell has been completed, activate the cell, retype the entry, and press Enter, or double-click the cell to open the cell for editing.

4 With A2 the active cell, type **Week Ended: January 29, 2011** and then press Enter.

> Notice the entry in A2 is overflowing into columns B and C. You can allow a label to spill over into adjacent columns as long as you do not plan to enter other data in the overflow cells. In Section 2, you will learn how to adjust column widths.

5 Enter the remaining labels as shown below by making the appropriate cell active, typing the label, and then pressing Enter or clicking another cell. (Do not complete the labels for the days of the week beyond *Sun*, as this will be done in Steps 6–8.)

	A	B	C	D	E	F	G	H	I	J	K	L
1	Payroll											
2	Week Ended: January 29, 2011											
3										Total	Pay	Gross
4			Sun							Hours	Rate	Pay
5	Lancaster	Darrin										
6	Mitsui	Heather										
7	Elliott	Lee										
8	Melina	Jonathon										
9	St. Claire	Kari										
10	Cardenas	Maria										
11	DiSanto	Stephen										
12	Hydall	Patricia										
13	Greer	Katherine										
14	Freeman	Jason										
15	Monroe	Mele										
16	Hayden	Valerie										
17	Keyes	Scott										
18												
19	Total											

Step 4

Step 5

6 Click C4 to make the cell active.

A thick black border surrounds the active cell. A small black square displays at the bottom right corner of the active cell. This black square is called the *fill handle*. The fill handle is used to fill adjacent cells with the same data or consecutive data. The entries that are automatically inserted in the adjacent cells are dependent on the contents of the active cell. You will use the fill handle in C4 to automatically enter the remaining days of the week in D4 through I4.

Step 6

Step 7

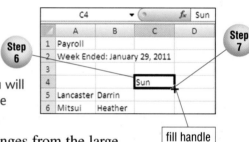

fill handle

7 Point at the fill handle in C4. The cell pointer changes from the large white cross to a thin black cross +.

8 Hold down the left mouse button, drag the pointer to I4, and then release the mouse.

The entries *Mon* through *Sat* appear in D4 to I4. As you drag the pointer to the right, a gray border surrounds the selected cells and a ScreenTip appears below the pointer indicating the label or value that will be inserted. When you release the left mouse button, the cells remain selected and the Auto Fill Options button appears.

Clicking the Auto Fill Options button causes a drop-down list to appear with various alternative actions for filling text or data into the cells.

	A	B	C	D	E	F	G	H	I	J
1	Payroll									
2	Week Ended: January 29, 2011									
3										Total
4			Sun	Mon	Tue	Wed	Thu	Fri	Sat	Hours
5	Lancaster	Darrin								
6	Mitsui	Heather								

Step 8

Auto Fill Options button

? PROBLEM

Mon through *Sat* does not appear? You probably dragged the mouse using the cell pointer instead of the fill handle. This action selects cells instead of filling them. Go back to Step 6 and try again.

continues

9 Click C5 to make the cell active.

10 Type **8** and then press the Right Arrow key.

11 Type **5** in D5 and then press the Right Arrow key.

12 Type the following values in the cells indicated:

E5   6
F5   8
G5   5
H5   0
I5   8

13 Make F5 the active cell.

14 Point at the fill handle in F5 and then drag the pointer down to F17.

This time the active cell contained a value. The value *8* is copied to the adjacent cells.

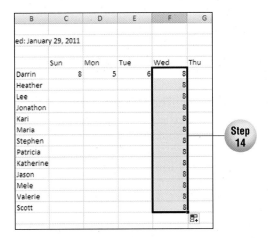

Step 14

15 Enter the remaining values for employee hours as shown below. Use the fill handle where there are duplicate values in adjacent cells to enter the data as efficiently as possible.

	A	B	C	D	E	F	G	H	I	J
1	Payroll									
2	Week Ended: January 29, 2011									
3										Total
4			Sun	Mon	Tue	Wed	Thu	Fri	Sat	Hours
5	Lancaster	Darrin	8	5	6	8	5	0	8	
6	Mitsui	Heather	0	8	6	8	7	5	0	
7	Elliott	Lee	8	8	0	8	7	7	0	
8	Melina	Jonathon	8	8	0	8	7	8	0	
9	St. Claire	Kari	0	8	0	8	8	7	0	
10	Cardenas	Maria	0	0	0	8	8	7	8	
11	DiSanto	Stephen	8	0	0	8	8	7	8	
12	Hydall	Patricia	8	0	0	8	8	7	8	
13	Greer	Katherine	8	6	8	8	0	0	8	
14	Freeman	Jason	0	5	8	8	6	0	8	
15	Monroe	Mele	5	6	8	8	0	8	0	
16	Hayden	Valerie	6	4	8	8	0	8	0	
17	Keyes	Scott	7	6	8	8	0	8	0	

Step 15

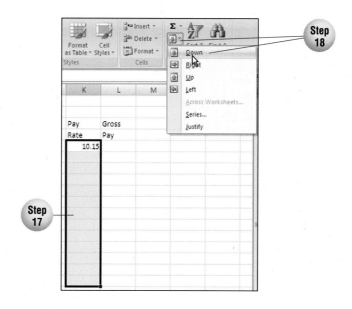

16. Click K5 to make the cell active, type **10.15**, and then press Enter.

17. Position the cell pointer over cell K5, hold down the left mouse button, drag down to K17, and then release the mouse.

    > A group of adjacent cells is referred to as a *range*. Select a range of cells when you want to perform an action on a group of cells.

18. With Home the active tab in the ribbon, click the Fill button arrow in the Editing group and then click *Down* at the drop-down list.

19. Click in any cell in the worksheet to deselect the range of cells in column K.

20. Click the Save button on the Quick Access toolbar.

21. At the Save As dialog box with ExcelMedS1 the active folder, type **ExcelMedS1-02** in the *File name* text box and then press Enter.

In Addition

More about the Fill Command

In this activity you used the fill handle to continue the days of the week and copy a static value to adjacent cells. The fill handle is versatile and can be used to enter a series of values, dates, times, or other labels as a pattern. The pattern is established based on the cells you select before dragging the fill handle. In the worksheet shown below, the cells in columns C through J were all populated using the fill handle. In each row, the first two cells in columns A and B were selected and then the fill handle dragged right to column J. Notice the variety of patterns used to extend a series.

Use the Auto Fill Options button drop-down list to control how the series is entered. After dragging the fill handle, the Auto Fill Options button is displayed at the end of the series. Pointing at the button causes the button to expand and display a down-pointing arrow. Click the down-pointing arrow and then select the desired fill action from the options in the drop-down list. By default, *Fill Series* is active.

	A	B	C	D	E	F	G	H	I	J	K	L	M
1	Examples Using the Fill Handle to Continue a Series in Adjacent Cells												
2	In each row below, the first two cells were selected and then the fill handle dragged right.												
3	1	2	3	4	5	6	7	8	9	10			
4	10	20	30	40	50	60	70	80	90	100			
5	9:00	10:00	11:00	12:00	13:00	14:00	15:00	16:00	17:00	18:00			
6	2008	2009	2010	2011	2012	2013	2014	2015	2016	2017			
7	1st Qtr	2nd Qtr	3rd Qtr	4th Qtr	1st Qtr	2nd Qtr	3rd Qtr	4th Qtr	1st Qtr	2nd Qtr			
8	Period 1	Period 2	Period 3	Period 4	Period 5	Period 6	Period 7	Period 8	Period 9	Period 10			
9													
10										Copy Cells			
11										⦿ Fill Series			
12										Fill Formatting Only			
13										Fill Without Formatting			
14													

Activity 1.3

Performing Calculations Using Formulas

A *formula* is entered into a cell to perform mathematical calculations in a worksheet. All formulas in Excel begin with the equals sign (=) as the first character. After the equals sign, the cell addresses that contain the values you want to calculate are entered between mathematical operators. The mathematical operators are + (addition), – (subtraction), * (multiplication), / (division), and ^ (exponentiation). An example of a valid formula is =A3*B3. The value in A3 is multiplied by the value in B3 and the result is placed in the formula cell. By including the cell address in the formula rather than typing the actual value, you can utilize the powerful recalculation feature in Excel. If you change a cell's content, the worksheet is automatically recalculated so that all values are current.

Project

To calculate total hours and gross pay for the first two medical office assistants listed in the payroll worksheet for the North Shore Medical Clinic, you will use two methods to enter formulas.

1. With **ExcelMedS1-02.xlsx** open, make J5 the active cell.

   Begin a formula by activating the cell in which you want the result placed.

2. Type **=c5+d5+e5+f5+g5+h5+i5** and then press Enter.

   The values in C5 through I5 are added and the result, *38*, is displayed in J5.

	A	B	C	D	E	F	G	H	I	J	K	L
1	Payroll											
2	Week Ended: January 29, 2011											
3										Total	Pay	Gross
4			Sun	Mon	Tue	Wed	Thu	Fri	Sat	Hours	Rate	Pay
5	Lancaster	Darrin	8	5	6	8	5	0	8	=c5+d5+e5+f5+g5+h5+i5		
6	Mitsui	Heather	0	8	6	8	7	5	0		10.15	

Step 2

Cell references in the formula bar are color-coded to the originating cell for quick reference and error checking.

3. Press the Up Arrow key to move the active cell back to J5.

   Notice that the result of the formula is displayed in the worksheet area and the formula used to calculate the result is shown in the Formula bar. Notice also that the column letters in cell addresses are automatically converted to uppercase.

4. Make J6 the active cell, type the formula **=c6+d6+e6+f6+g6+h6+i6**, and then press Enter.

   Seem like too much typing? A more efficient way to add a series of cells is available. This method will be introduced in the next activity after you learn the pointing method for entering formulas.

5. Make L5 the active cell.

   To calculate gross pay you need to multiply the total hours times the pay rate. In Steps 6–10, you will enter this formula using the pointing method.

6. Type the equals sign (=).

7 Click J5.

A moving dashed border (called a *marquee*) displays around J5, indicating it is the cell included in the formula, and the cell address is added to the formula cell (J5) with a blinking insertion point after the reference. Notice also that the Status bar displays the action *Point*.

? PROBLEM

Click the wrong cell by mistake? Simply click the correct cell, or press Esc to start the formula over again.

8 Type an asterisk (*).

The marquee surrounding cell J5 disappears and J5 is color-coded with the cell reference J5 within the formula cell.

9 Click K5.

10 Click the Enter button ✔ on the Formula bar.

The result 406 is displayed in L5. In Activity 1.6 you will learn how to display two decimal places for cells containing dollar values.

Marquee displays around cell K5 in Step 9.

11 Use the pointing method or type the formula **=j6*k6** to calculate the gross pay for Heather Mitsui in L6.

12 Click the Save button 💾 on the Quick Access toolbar.

In Brief

Enter Formula
1. Activate formula cell.
2. Type =.
3. Type first cell address.
4. Type operator symbol.
5. Type second cell address.
6. Continue Steps 3-5 until finished.
7. Press Enter or click Enter button.

Enter Formula Using Pointing Method
1. Activate formula cell.
2. Type =.
3. Click first cell.
4. Type operator symbol.
5. Click second cell.
6. Repeat Steps 3-5 until finished.
7. Press Enter or click Enter button.

J	K	L
Total	Pay	Gross
Hours	Rate	Pay
40	10.15	406
34	10.15	345.1

Step 11

In Addition

Order of Operations

If you include several operators in a formula, Excel calculates the result using the order of operations as follows: negations (e.g., –1) first, then percents (%), then exponentiations (^), then multiplication and division (* and /), and finally addition and subtraction (+ and –). If a formula contains more than one operator at the same level of precedence—for example, both an addition and a subtraction operation—Excel calculates the equation from left to right. To change the order of operations, use parentheses around the part of the formula you want calculated first.

Formula	Calculation
=B5*C5/D5	Both operators are at the same level of precedence—Excel would multiply the value in B5 times the value in C5 and then divide the result by the value in D5.
=(B5+B6+B7)*A10	Excel would add the values in B5 through B7 before multiplying times the value in A10.

Activity 1.4

Using the SUM Function

The formulas to calculate the hours worked by the first two employees were lengthy. A more efficient way to calculate the total hours for Darrin Lancaster in J5 would be to enter the formula =SUM(C5:I5). This formula includes one of Excel's built-in functions called SUM. A *function* is a preprogrammed formula. The structure of a formula utilizing a function begins with the equals sign (=), followed by the name of the function, and then the *argument*. Argument is the term given to the values identified within parentheses. In the example provided, the argument C5:I5 contains the starting cell and the ending cell separated by a colon (:). This is called a *range* and is used when the values to be added are located in a rectangular-shaped block of cells. Since the SUM function is used frequently, a Sum button is available in the Home tab.

Project

Lee Elliott, North Shore Medical Clinic's office manager, wants you to use a more efficient method of payroll calculation, so you will use Sum to complete the hours worked for the payroll worksheet.

① With **ExcelMedS1-02.xlsx** open, make J5 the active cell and then press the Delete key.

This deletes the formula in the cell. There was nothing wrong with the formula already entered in J5. You are deleting it so that the formulas in the completed worksheet will be consistent.

② Click the Sum button **Σ ▾** in the Editing group in the Home tab. (Do not click the down-pointing arrow at the right of the Sum button.)

A moving marquee surrounds cells C5 through I5 and a ScreenTip appears below the formula cell indicating the correct format for the SUM function. Excel enters the formula =SUM(C5:I5) in J5. The suggested range C5:I5 is selected within the formula so that you can highlight a different range with the mouse if the suggested range is not correct.

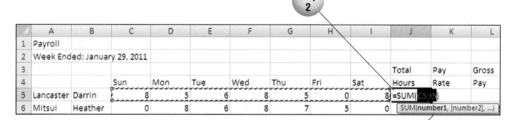

Step 2

ScreenTip displays correct format for SUM function.

③ Press Enter.

Since the range Excel suggests is the correct range, you can finish the formula by pressing Enter or by clicking the Enter button on the Formula bar.

④ With J6 the active cell, press the Delete key to delete the existing formula in the cell.

⑤ Click the Sum button. When Excel displays the formula =SUM(C6:I6), click the Enter button in the Formula bar.

⑥ Make J7 the active cell and then click the Sum button.

Notice this time the range of cells Excel is suggesting to add (J5:J6) is the wrong range. When you click the Sum button, Excel looks for multiple values in the cells immediately above the active cell. If no more than one value exists above the active cell, Excel looks in the cells to the left. In this case, there were multiple values above J7. You need to correct the range of cells that you want to add.

7 Position the cell pointer over C7, hold down the left mouse button, drag the pointer to the right to I7, and then release the mouse button.

Step 7

	A	B	C	D	E	F	G	H	I	J	K	L
1	Payroll											
2	Week Ended: January 29, 2011											
3										Total	Pay	Gross
4			Sun	Mon	Tue	Wed	Thu	Fri	Sat	Hours	Rate	Pay
5	Lancaster	Darrin	8	5	6	8	5	0	8	40	10.15	406
6	Mitsui	Heather	0	8	6	8	7	5	0	34	10.15	345.1
7	Elliott	Lee	8	8	0	8	7	7	0	=SUM(C7:I7		
8	Melina	Jonathon	8	8	0	8	7	8	0	SUM(number1, [number2], ...)		

8 Press Enter.

Now that you have seen how the Sum button operates, you already know that the suggested range for the next employee's total hours will be incorrect. In Step 9, you will select the range of cells *first* to avoid the incorrect suggestion.

9 Position the cell pointer in C8, hold down the left mouse button, drag the pointer to the right to J8, and then release the mouse button.

Notice you are including J8, the cell that will display the result, in the range of cells.

10 Click the Sum button.

The result, *39*, appears in cell J8.

	A	B	C	D	E	F	G	H	I	J
1	Payroll									
2	Week Ended: January 29, 2011									
3										Total
4			Sun	Mon	Tue	Wed	Thu	Fri	Sat	Hours
5	Lancaster	Darrin	8	5	6	8	5	0	8	40
6	Mitsui	Heather	0	8	6	8	7	5	0	34
7	Elliott	Lee	8	8	0	8	7	7	0	38
8	Melina	Jonathon	8	8	0	8	7	8	0	39

Steps 9–10

11 Click J8 and look in the Formula bar at the formula the SUM function created: *=SUM(C8:I8).*

Since Excel created the correct SUM formula from a range of selected cells, you decide to try calculating total hours for more than one employee in one step using the method employed in Steps 9 and 10 but with an expanded range.

12 Position the cell pointer in C9, hold down the left mouse button, drag the pointer down and right to J17, and then release the mouse button.

Steps 12–13

C	D	E	F	G	H	I	J
y 29, 2011							
							Total
Sun	Mon	Tue	Wed	Thu	Fri	Sat	Hours
8	5	6	8	5	0	8	40
0	8	6	8	7	5	0	34
8	8	0	8	7	7	0	38
8	8	0	8	7	8	0	39
0	8	0	8	8	7	0	31
0	0	0	8	8	7	8	31
8	0	0	8	8	7	8	39
8	0	0	8	8	7	8	39
8	6	8	8	0	0	8	38
0	5	8	8	6	0	8	35
5	6	8	8	0	8	0	35
6	4	8	8	0	8	0	34
7	6	8	8	0	8	0	37

13 Click the Sum button.

14 Click each of the cells starting with J9 and ending with J17 to confirm that the correct formulas appear in the Formula bar.

15 Click the Save button on the Quick Access toolbar.

Activity 1.5

Copying Formulas

Many times you may create a worksheet in which several formulas are basically the same. For example, in the payroll worksheet, the formula to total the hours for Darrin Lancaster is =SUM(C5:I5), for Heather Mitsui =SUM(C6:I6), and so on. The only difference between the two formulas is the row number. Whenever formulas are this similar, you can use the Copy and Paste feature to copy the formula from one cell to another. The cell containing the original formula is called the **source,** and the cell(s) to which the formula is copied is called the **destination.** When the formula is pasted, Excel automatically changes column letters or row numbers to reflect the destination location. By default, Excel assumes *relative addressing*—cell addresses update relative to the destination.

Project

To simplify your completion of the payroll worksheet for the North Shore Medical Clinic, you will copy formulas using two methods: Copy and Paste and the fill handle.

1. With **ExcelMedS1-02.xlsx** open, make L6 the active cell.

   This cell contains the formula *=J6*K6* to calculate the gross pay for Heather Mitsui. You will copy this formula to the remaining cells in column L to finish the *Gross Pay* column.

2. Click the Copy button in the Clipboard group in the Home tab.

   A moving marquee surrounds the active cell indicating the source contents are copied to the Clipboard, which is a temporary storage location. The source being copied is the formula *=J6*K6*—not the value *345.1*.

   marquee indicating source range

   Step 3

3. Select the range L7:L17. To do this, position the cell pointer over L7, hold down the left mouse button, drag the pointer down to L17, and then release the mouse button.

4. Click the Paste button in the Clipboard group in the Home tab. (Do not click the down-pointing arrow on the button.)

   Excel copies the formula to the selected cells, displays the results, and the Paste Options button appears. Clicking the Paste Options button will display a drop-down list with various alternatives for pasting the data. The moving marquee remains around the source cell and the destination cells remain highlighted. The moving marquee disappears as soon as you start another activity or press the Esc key.

   Step 4

   Paste Options button

5. Press the Esc key to remove the marquee and the Paste Options button, click L7, and then look at the entry in the Formula bar: *=J7*K7*.

   The row number in the source formula was increased by one to reflect the destination.

6. Use the Down Arrow key to check the remaining formulas in column L.

7. Make C19 the active cell.

8 Click the Sum button and then click the Enter button in the Formula bar.

> The SUM function inserts the formula *=SUM(C5:C18)*. Next, you will copy the formula using the fill handle.

9 Drag the fill handle in C19 right to L19.

> When the active cell contains a formula, dragging the fill handle causes Excel to copy the formula and change cell references relative to each destination location.

In Brief

Copy Formula
1. Activate source cell.
2. Click Copy button.
3. Select destination cell(s).
4. Click Paste button.

	A	B	C	D	E	F	G	H	I	J	K	L
1	Payroll											
2	Week Ended: January 29, 2011											
3										Total	Pay	Gross
4			Sun	Mon	Tue	Wed	Thu	Fri	Sat	Hours	Rate	Pay
5	Lancaster	Darrin	8	5	6	8	5	0	8	40	10.15	406
6	Mitsui	Heather	0	8	6	8	7	5	0	34	10.15	345.1
7	Elliott	Lee	8	8	0	8	7	7	0	38	10.15	385.7
8	Melina	Jonathon	8	8	0	8	7	8	0	39	10.15	395.85
9	St. Claire	Kari	0	8	0	8	8	7	0	31	10.15	314.65
10	Cardenas	Maria	0	0	0	8	8	7	8	31	10.15	314.65
11	DiSanto	Stephen	8	0	0	8	8	7	8	39	10.15	395.85
12	Hydall	Patricia	8	0	0	8	8	7	8	39	10.15	395.85
13	Greer	Katherine	8	6	8	8	0	0	8	38	10.15	385.7
14	Freeman	Jason	0	5	8	8	6	0	8	35	10.15	355.25
15	Monroe	Mele	5	6	8	8	0	8	0	35	10.15	355.25
16	Hayden	Valerie	6	4	8	8	0	8	0	34	10.15	345.1
17	Keyes	Scott	7	6	8	8	0	8	0	37	10.15	375.55
18												
19	Total		66	64	52	104	64	72	48	470	131.95	4770.5
20												

Step 9

PROBLEM

If the results do not appear in D19 through L19, you probably dragged the cell pointer instead of the fill handle. Click C19 and try again.

10 Make K19 the active cell and then press the Delete key.

> The sum of the *Pay Rate* column is not useful information.

11 Make D19 the active cell and look at the entry in the Formula bar: *=SUM(D5:D18)*.

> The column letter in the source formula was changed to reflect the destination.

12 Use the Right Arrow key to check the formulas in the remaining columns.

13 Click the Save button on the Quick Access toolbar.

In Addition

Copy and Paste versus Fill

What is the difference between Copy and Paste and the fill handle? When you use Copy, the contents of the source cell(s) are placed in the Clipboard. The data will remain in the Clipboard and can be pasted several times in the current worksheet, into any other worksheet that is open, or into an open document in another program. Use Copy and Paste when the formula is to be inserted more than once or into non-adjacent cells. Use the fill handle when the formula is only being copied to adjacent cells.

Activity 1.6

Testing the Worksheet; Improving the Worksheet Appearance; Sorting

When you have finished building the worksheet, verifying that the formulas you entered are accurate is a good idea. The worksheet could contain formulas that are correct in structure but not mathematically correct for the situation. For example, the wrong range may be included in a SUM formula, or parentheses missing from a multioperator formula may cause an incorrect result. Various methods can be employed to verify a worksheet's accuracy. One method is to create a proof formula in a cell beside or below the worksheet that will verify the totals. For example, in the payroll worksheet the *Total Hours* column can be verified by creating a formula that adds all of the hours for all of the employees.

Data in Excel can be rearranged by sorting rows in either ascending order or descending order. You can select a single column or define a custom sort to specify multiple columns that determine the sort order.

Project

North Shore Medical Clinic

To confirm the accuracy of your calculations in the payroll worksheet for the North Shore Medical Clinic, you will enter proof formulas to test the worksheet and then use two formatting options to improve the worksheet's appearance. Finally, you will sort the worksheet by last names.

1. With **ExcelMedS1-02.xlsx** open, make A21 the active cell.

2. Type **Hours**, press Alt + Enter, type **Proof**, and then press Enter.

   Alt + Enter is the command to insert a line break in a cell. This command is used when you want multiple lines within the same cell. The height of the row is automatically expanded to accommodate the multiple lines.

19	Total
20	
21	Hours
22	Proof

Step 2

3. Make B21 the active cell.

4. Click in the Formula bar, type **=sum(c5:i17)**, and then click the Enter button or press Enter. (Alternatively, you could click the Sum button and then drag the pointer across the range C5 through I17.)

   Excel displays the result, *470,* which verifies that your total hours in J19 is correct. Can you think of another formula that would have accomplished the same objective? *Hint: Think of the direction you added to arrive at the total hours in J19.*

Step 4

Typed range is color-coded for easy referencing and error checking.

	A	B	C	D	E	F	G	H	I	J
	SUM			fx	=sum(c5:i17)					
1	Payroll									
2	Week Ended: January 29, 2011									
3										Total
4			Sun	Mon	Tue	Wed	Thu	Fri	Sat	Hours
5	Lancaster	Darrin	8	5	6	8	5	0	8	40
6	Mitsui	Heather	0	8	6	8	7	5	0	34
7	Elliott	Lee	8	8	0	8	7	7	0	38
8	Melina	Jonathon	8	8	0	8	7	8	0	39
9	St. Claire	Kari	0	8	0	8	8	7	0	31
10	Cardenas	Maria	0	0	0	8	8	7	8	31
11	DiSanto	Stephen	8	0	0	8	8	7	8	39
12	Hydall	Patricia	8	0	0	8	8	7	8	39
13	Greer	Katherine	8	6	8	8	0	0	8	38
14	Freeman	Jason	0	5	8	8	6	0	8	35
15	Monroe	Mele	5	6	8	8	0	8	0	35
16	Hayden	Valerie	6	4	8	8	0	8	0	34
17	Keyes	Scott	7	6	8	8	0	8	0	37
18										
19	Total		66	64	52	104	64	72	48	470
20										
21	Hours Proof	m(c5:i17)								

PROBLEM

Didn't get 470? Then one of the cell entries is incorrect. Look through previous pages to see if the difference between 470 and your result equals a cell entry that you missed.

5 Make A22 the active cell.

6 Type **Gross**, press Alt + Enter, type **Pay Proof**, and then press Enter.

7 Make B22 the active cell.

> Since all of the employees are paid the same rate of pay, you can verify the *Gross Pay* column by multiplying the total hours times the pay rate.

8 Type **=j19*k5** and then press the Right Arrow key.

> The result, *4770.5*, confirms that the value in L19 is correct. The importance of testing a worksheet cannot be emphasized enough. Worksheets often contain important financial or statistical data that can form the basis for strategic business decisions.

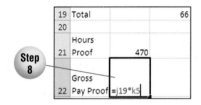

Step 8

19	Total	66
20		
21	Hours Proof	470
22	Gross Pay Proof	=j19*k5

9 Look at the completed worksheet shown below. Notice that some of the values in column L show no decimals while others show 1 or 2 decimal places. Also notice the labels do not align directly over the values below them.

Labels do not align directly over values.

	A	B	C	D	E	F	G	H	I	J	K	L
2	Week Ended: January 29, 2011											
3										Total	Pay	Gross
4			Sun	Mon	Tue	Wed	Thu	Fri	Sat	Hours	Rate	Pay
5	Lancaster	Darrin	8	5	6	8	5	0	8	40	10.15	406
6	Mitsui	Heather	0	8	6	8	7	5	0	34	10.15	345.1
7	Elliott	Lee	8	8	0	8	7	7	0	38	10.15	385.7
8	Melina	Jonathon	8	8	0	8	7	8	0	39	10.15	395.85
9	St. Claire	Kari	0	8	0	8	8	7	0	31	10.15	314.65
10	Cardenas	Maria	0	0	0	8	8	7	8	31	10.15	314.65
11	DiSanto	Stephen	8	0	0	8	8	7	8	39	10.15	395.85
12	Hydall	Patricia	8	0	0	8	8	7	8	39	10.15	395.85
13	Greer	Katherine	8	6	8	8	0	0	8	38	10.15	385.7
14	Freeman	Jason	0	5	8	8	6	0	8	35	10.15	355.25
15	Monroe	Mele	5	6	8	8	0	8	0	35	10.15	355.25
16	Hayden	Valerie	6	4	8	8	0	8	0	34	10.15	345.1
17	Keyes	Scott	7	6	8	8	0	8	0	37	10.15	375.55
18												
19	Total		66	64	52	104	64	72	48	470		4770.5
20												
21	Hours Proof	470										
22	Gross Pay Proof	4770.5										

Decimal places are not consistent.

continues

10 Select the range L5:L19.

These final steps in building a worksheet are meant to improve the appearance of cells. In column L, Excel uses up to 15 decimal places for precision when calculating values. Since the *Gross Pay* column represents a sum of money, you will format these cells to the Accounting format.

11 Click the Accounting Number Format button **$ ▾** in the Number group in the Home tab.

The Accounting Number format adds a dollar sign, a comma in the thousands place, and two decimal places to each value in the selection.

12 Make B22 the active cell and then click the Accounting Number Format button.

13 Select the range C3:L4.

As previously mentioned, labels are aligned at the left edge of a column while values are aligned at the right edge. In the next step, you will align the labels at the right edge of the column so they appear directly over the values they represent.

14 Click the Align Text Right button in the Alignment group in the Home tab.

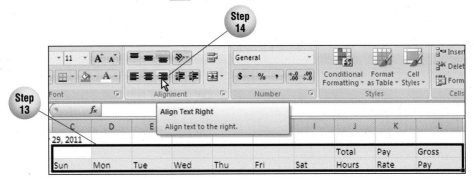

15 Click in any cell to deselect the range.

In the next steps, you will rearrange the names in the payroll worksheet so that they are in alphabetical order by last name.

16 Select the range A5:L17.

You are selecting the range before executing the sort command since you do not want to include the cells above and below the list of names in the sort action.

17 Click the Sort & Filter button in the Editing group in the Home tab.

18 Click *Sort A to Z* at the drop-down list.

19 Click in any cell to deselect the range. Compare your sorted worksheet to the one shown below.

	A	B	C	D	E	F	G	H	I	J	K	L
1	Payroll											
2	Week Ended: January 29, 2011											
3										Total	Pay	Gross
4			Sun	Mon	Tue	Wed	Thu	Fri	Sat	Hours	Rate	Pay
5	Cardenas	Maria	0	0	0	8	8	7	8	31	10.15	$ 314.65
6	DiSanto	Stephen	8	0	0	8	8	7	8	39	10.15	$ 395.85
7	Elliott	Lee	8	8	0	8	7	7	0	38	10.15	$ 385.70
8	Freeman	Jason	0	5	8	8	6	0	8	35	10.15	$ 355.25
9	Greer	Katherine	8	6	8	8	0	0	8	38	10.15	$ 385.70
10	Hayden	Valerie	6	4	8	8	0	8	0	34	10.15	$ 345.10
11	Hydall	Patricia	8	0	0	8	8	7	8	39	10.15	$ 395.85
12	Keyes	Scott	7	6	8	8	0	8	0	37	10.15	$ 375.55
13	Lancaster	Darrin	8	5	6	8	5	0	8	40	10.15	$ 406.00
14	Melina	Jonathon	8	8	0	8	7	8	0	39	10.15	$ 395.85
15	Mitsui	Heather	0	8	6	8	7	5	0	34	10.15	$ 345.10
16	Monroe	Mele	5	6	8	8	0	8	0	35	10.15	$ 355.25
17	St. Claire	Kari	0	8	0	8	8	7	0	31	10.15	$ 314.65
18												
19	Total		66	64	52	104	64	72	48	470		$4,770.50
20												
21	Hours Proof	470										
22	Gross Pay Proof	$4,770.50										

employees rearranged by last name

20 Click the Save button on the Quick Access toolbar.

In Addition

Rotating Text in Cells

The Alignment group in the Home tab contains an Orientation button, which can be used to rotate text within cells. Text can be rotated counterclockwise, clockwise, changed to a vertical alignment, rotated up vertically, or rotated down vertically. Often, text set in narrow columns is angled to improve the label appearance. In the screen shown at the right, the cells containing the days of the week in the payroll worksheet are angled counterclockwise.

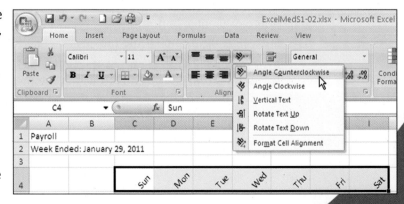

Activity 1.7

Using Help

An extensive online Help resource is available that contains information on Excel features and commands. Click the Microsoft Office Excel Help button located near the upper right corner of the screen (below the Minimize button on the Title bar) to open the Excel Help window. By default, the Help feature searches for an Internet connection. A message at the bottom right corner of the window will indicate whether Help will display information in Excel resources at Office Online or in the Offline Help file. Another method to use Help resources is to point to a button in the tab and then press function key F1.

Project

Lee Elliott, North Shore Medical Clinic's office manager, reviewed the payroll worksheet you created. Lee thinks the first two title rows would look better if they were centered over the columns in the worksheet. You will use the Help feature to look up the steps to do this.

1. With **ExcelMedS1-02.xlsx** open, make A1 the active cell.

   To center the title rows above the columns in the worksheet, you decide to browse the buttons in the Alignment group in the Home tab. The Merge & Center button in the group seems appropriate but you are not sure of the steps to work with this feature.

2. Point to the Merge & Center button in the Alignment group in the Home tab and read the information that displays in the ScreenTip.

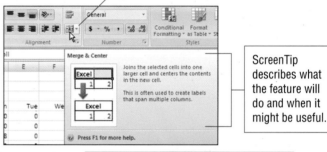

Step 2

ScreenTip describes what the feature will do and when it might be useful.

3. With the pointer still resting on the Merge & Center button, press function key F1.

4. Scroll down the Excel Help window, click the *Merge adjacent cells* hyperlink below the subtitle *What do you want to do?*, and then read the information describing the steps to merge cells. ***Note: If you are not connected to the Internet, your Help window may vary.***

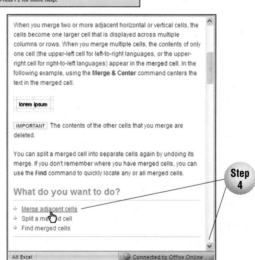

Step 4

5. Close the Excel Help window.

6. Select the range A1:L1 and then click the Merge & Center button in the Alignment group in the Home tab.

   A1 is merged across columns A through L and the text *Payroll* is automatically centered within the merged cell.

Step 6

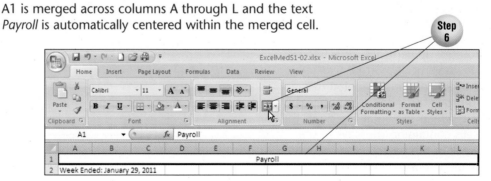

7 Select the range A2:L2 and then click the Merge & Center button.

The two titles in the payroll worksheet are now centered over the cells below them.

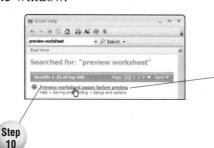

	A	B	C	D	E	F	G	H	I	J	K	L
1						Payroll						
2					Week Ended: January 29, 2011							
3										Total	Pay	Gross
4			Sun	Mon	Tue	Wed	Thu	Fri	Sat	Hours	Rate	Pay

Step 7

8 Click the Microsoft Office Excel Help button ⑦ located near the upper right corner of the screen (below the Minimize button on the Title bar).

You can also access Help resources by typing a search phrase and browsing related topics in the Help window.

9 With the insertion point positioned in the search text box, type **preview worksheet** and then click the Search button or press Enter.

10 Click the *Preview worksheet pages before printing* hyperlink and then read the information that displays in the window.

11 Close the Excel Help window.

12 Click the Save button on the Quick Access toolbar.

Step 9

Step 10

Since Microsoft Office Online is updated frequently, your search results list may vary, including the title or position in the list of this hyperlink.

In Addition

Using Offline Help

By default Excel checks for a live Internet connection when the Help feature is activated. If no connection is found, Excel displays the Help window shown at the right. Office Online provides additional resources such as online training and templates along with the most up-to-date information. You can disable online Help searches if you want to turn off the online access for reasons similar to the following:

- You are currently experiencing a slow Internet connection.
- You are working away from your normal site where you have to pay for Internet access.
- You are working away from your normal site and are concerned about privacy.

Click the down-pointing arrow to the right of the Search button and then click *Excel Help* in the *Content from this computer* section at the drop-down list to temporarily suspend online searches.

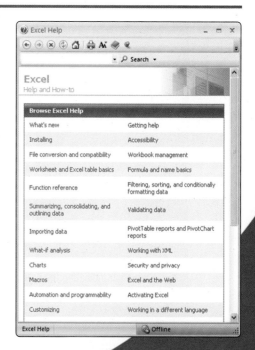

Activity 1.8

Previewing, Printing, and Closing a Workbook

Many times a worksheet is printed to have a paper copy, or *hard copy*, to file or to attach to a report. Large, complex worksheets are often easier to proofread and check from a paper copy. The Quick Print button on the Quick Access toolbar will print the active worksheet using default print options. Display the Print dialog box to modify print options. For example, if more than one worksheet exists in a workbook, open the Print dialog box by clicking the Office button and then *Print*. At the Print dialog box, change the *Print what* option to *Entire workbook*. Use Print Preview before printing to avoid wasted paper by checking in advance whether the entire worksheet will fit on one page, or to preview other page layout options.

Project

The payroll worksheet for the North Shore Medical Clinic is finished, so you want to preview the worksheet before printing a copy for the office manager.

1. With **ExcelMedS1-02.xlsx** open, make A24 the active cell and then type the student information your instructor has directed for printouts. For example, type your first and last names and then press Enter.

   Make sure you have checked if other identifying information such as your program or class number should be included.

2. Click the Office button, point to *Print*, and then click *Print Preview* to display the worksheet in the Print Preview window shown in Figure E1.2.

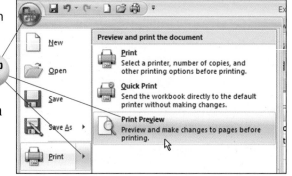

FIGURE E1.2 Print Preview Window

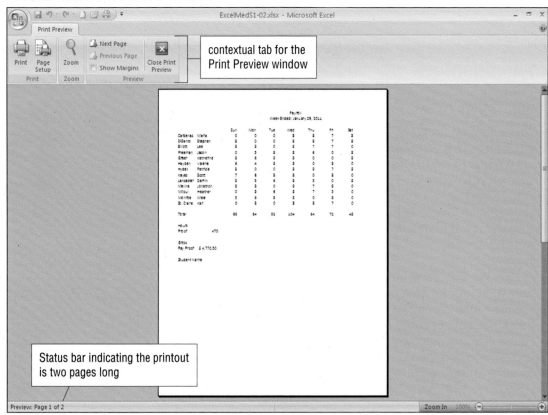

3 The Print Preview window displays a picture of what the printed page will look like. Notice the Status bar is indicating *Page 1 of 2*. Click the Next Page button in the Preview group in the Print Preview tab.

In Brief

Display Worksheet in Print Preview
1. Click Office button.
2. Point to *Print*.
3. Click *Print Preview*.

4 The second page of the printout appears showing the columns that could not fit on page 1. The mouse pointer displays as a magnifying glass 🔍 in the preview screen. Move the mouse pointer over the columns at the top left of page 2 and then click the left mouse button.

> This causes the display to enlarge so that you can read the data in the columns.

5 Click the mouse anywhere on the page to return to the full-page view and then click the Previous Page button in the Preview group.

6 Click the Page Setup button in the Print group.

> One method to reduce the printout to one page is to change the orientation of the paper from portrait to landscape. In **portrait** orientation, the page is printed on paper taller than it is wide. In **landscape** orientation, the data is rotated to print on paper that is wider than it is tall.

7 If necessary, click the Page tab in the Page Setup dialog box, click *Landscape* in the *Orientation* section, and then click OK.

> Print Preview updates to show the worksheet in landscape orientation. Notice that all of the columns now fit on one page.

8 Click the Print button in the Print group.

> Print Preview closes and the Print dialog box appears.

9 The default settings in the Print dialog box are to print one copy of all pages in the active sheet. Click OK.

10 If necessary, scroll right until you see the vertical dashed line between columns located to the right of the *Gross Pay* column.

> The dashed vertical line is a page break. Page breaks appear after you have used Print Preview or Print and indicate how much information from the worksheet can fit on a page.

11 Click the Save button on the Quick Access toolbar.

12 Click the Office button and then click *Close* at the drop-down list.

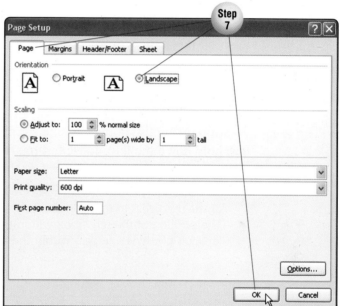

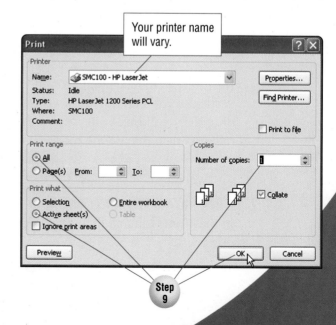

Activity
1.9

Navigating a Worksheet

Until now, you have been working with small worksheets that generally fit within the viewing area. Once worksheets become larger, you will need to scroll to the right or scroll down to locate cells with which you need to work. The horizontal and vertical scroll bars are used to scroll with the mouse. Scrolling using the scroll bars does not move the position of the active cell. You can also scroll using the arrow keys or with keyboard commands. Scrolling using the keyboard moves the active cell.

Project

To prepare for a visit from the medical supplies sales representative, you need to open and review the exam room standard supplies inventory report prepared by Lee Elliott, office manager for North Shore Medical Clinic.

1. Click the Open button on the Quick Access toolbar.

2. At the Open dialog box with ExcelMedS1 the active folder, double-click the workbook *NSMCSupplies.xlsx*.

3. Position the mouse pointer on the down scroll arrow at the bottom of the vertical scroll bar and then click the left mouse button a few times to scroll down the worksheet.

4. Position the mouse pointer on the right scroll arrow at the right edge of the horizontal scroll bar and then click the left mouse button a few times to scroll to the right.

5. Position the mouse pointer on the scroll box in the horizontal scroll bar, hold down the left mouse button, drag the scroll box to the left edge of the horizontal scroll bar, and then release the mouse button.

> The width or height of the scroll box indicates the proportional amount of the used cells in the worksheet that is visible in the current window. The position of the scroll box within the scroll bar indicates the relative location of the visible cells within the remainder of the worksheet.

Step 3

Step 4

Step 5

6. Position the mouse pointer on the scroll box in the vertical scroll bar, hold down the left mouse button, drag the scroll box to the top of the vertical scroll bar, and then release the mouse button.

> You are now back to viewing the beginning of the worksheet.

7. Click the Find & Select button in the Editing group in the Home tab and then click *Go To* at the drop-down list.

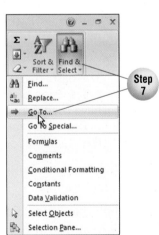

Step 7

⑧ At the Go To dialog box, type **n63** in the *Reference* text box and then click OK or press Enter.

> Cell N63, which is located at the bottom right edge of the worksheet, becomes the active cell. The total displayed is the sum of all the standard supplies required for the eight exam rooms at North Shore Medical Clinic.

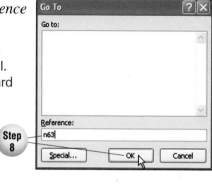

Step 8

In Brief

Go to Specific Cell
1. Click Find & Select button.
2. Click *Go To.*
3. Type cell address.
4. Click OK.

⑨ Press Ctrl + Home.

> Ctrl + Home makes A1 the active cell.

⑩ Press the Page Down button twice.

> Each time you press the Page Down key you move down one screen.

⑪ Press the Right Arrow key four times.

> Each time you press the Right Arrow key, you move the active cell one cell to the right.

⑫ Use the Up, Down, Left, and Right Arrow keys to practice moving around the worksheet.

> Holding down a directional arrow key causes the screen to scroll very quickly. Table E1.2 illustrates more keyboard scrolling techniques.

⑬ Click the Office button and then click Close to close **NSMCSupplies.xlsx**.

TABLE E1.2 Keyboard Movement Commands

Press	To move to
Arrow keys	one cell up, down, left, or right
Ctrl + Home	A1
Ctrl + End	last cell in worksheet
Home	beginning of row
Page Down	down one screen
Page Up	up one screen
Alt + Page Down	one screen to the right
Alt + Page Up	one screen to the left

In Addition

Viewing a Large Worksheet by Splitting the Window

You can split a worksheet into more than one window to facilitate viewing different sections of the worksheet at the same time. The split window allows you to view different sections of a large worksheet at the same time by scrolling in each window to different locations. For example, to view an item's price and total cost in the same window, you could split the window vertically as shown below. Each window contains a set of scroll bars to allow you to scroll to different areas within each window. To split a worksheet into two vertical windows, drag the split box [located immediately right of the right scroll arrow in the horizontal scroll bar to the position you want the split to occur. Drag the split bar back to the right edge of the screen to remove the split. Drag the split box at the top of the vertical scroll bar down to create a horizontal split.

	A	B	C	D	I	J	K	L	M	N
1	North Shore Medical Clinic			split bar	am Room Standard Cost					
2	Clinic Supplies Inventory Units and Price				Dermatology Room, WC - Women and Children's Room					
3	Item	Unit	Price	Standard Stock Qty	WC Room 4	DT Room 5	WC Room 6	WC Room 7	WC Room 8	Total Cost
4	Sterile powder-free synthetic gloves, size Small	per 100	35.95	4	71.90	71.90	71.90	71.90	71.90	575.20
5	Sterile powder-free synthetic gloves, size Mediu	per 100	35.95	4	71.90	71.90	71.90	71.90	71.90	575.20
6	Sterile powder-free synthetic gloves, size Large	per 100	35.95	4	71.90	71.90	71.90	71.90	71.90	575.20
7	Sterile powder-free latex gloves, size Small	per 100	16.25	4	32.50	32.50	32.50	32.50	32.50	260.00
8	Sterile powder-free latex gloves, size Medium	per 100	16.25	4	32.50	32.50	32.50	32.50	32.50	260.00

Activity
1.10

Creating a Workbook from a Template

Excel includes worksheets that are formatted and have text and formulas created for specific uses such as creating sales invoices, expenses, timecards, and financial statements. These preformatted work- sheets are called *templates*. Templates can be customized and saved with a new name to reflect individual company data. Additional tem- plates can be downloaded from Office Online.

Project

Darrin Lancaster has asked you to complete his time card. You decide to use a template to do this since the template has formulas already entered.

1. Click the Office button and then click *New* at the drop-down list.

2. At the New Workbook dialog box, click *Installed Templates* in the *Templates* list in the left pane.

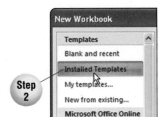

3. Scroll down the list of installed templates in the center pane and then double-click *Time Card*.

4. Scroll down the template to view the type of information required and the way the data is arranged on the page.

5. If necessary, click *C7* (next to *Employee*), type **Darrin Lancaster**, and then press Enter twice.

   Pressing Enter moves the active cell next to *[Street Address]* (C9) in the template.

6. Type **71 SW Oak Street** and then press Enter four times.

7. With the active cell next to *[City, ST ZIP Code]*, type **Portland, OR 97204** and then press Enter three times.

   The active cell moves next to *Week ending:* (C16).

8. Type **1/29/2011** and then click *G7* (next to *Manager:*).

   Notice the dates in the table below *Week ending* update once you change the date in C16.

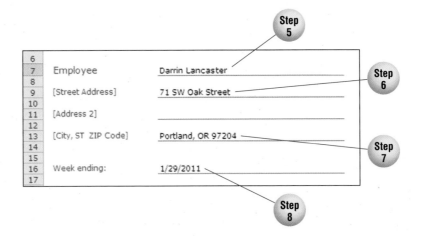

9 Type **Payne Dieter** and then press Enter twice.

Step 9

Manager:	Payne Dieter
Employee phone:	503 555 6217
Employee e-mail:	

Step 10

In Brief

Create Workbook from Template
1. Click Office button, then *New*.
2. Click *Installed Templates* or Office Online category.
3. Double-click desired template in center pane.
4. Fill in data or other information as needed.
5. Save, print, close.

10 With the active cell next to *Employee phone:*, type **503 555 6217** and then click D21.

11 Type the remaining entries in the time card as shown below by typing the value and then pressing Enter or clicking the next cell as needed. The cells in the shaded *Total* column, and *Total hours* and *Total pay* rows calculate automatically.

	C	D	E	F	G	H
20	Date	Regular Hours	Overtime	Sick	Vacation	Total
21	1/23/2011	8.00				8.00
22	1/24/2011	5.00				5.00
23	1/25/2011	6.00				6.00
24	1/26/2011	8.00				8.00
25	1/27/2011	5.00				5.00
26	1/28/2011					
27	1/29/2011	8.00				8.00
28		40.00				40.00
29		$ 10.15				
30		$ 406.00	$ -	$ -	$ -	$ 406.00

Step 11

12 Click the Save button.

13 At the Save As dialog box, navigate to the ExcelMedS1 folder on your storage medium, type **ExcelMedS1-03** in the *File name* text box and then press Enter.

14 Print and then close **ExcelMedS1-03.xlsx**.

In Addition

Templates from Microsoft Office Online

Microsoft maintains a Templates page on Office Online from which you can browse hundreds of pre-designed templates for all products in the Office 2007 suite. Browse for an Excel template in the *Microsoft Office Online* categories list in the left pane of the New Workbook dialog box, or click *Featured* in the Microsoft Office Online category, scroll to the bottom of the center pane, and then click the hyperlink to *Templates* below *More on Office Online*. At the Microsoft Office Online Templates Web page you can browse template categories or type a description of the template you need and search the site for available templates. Once you have located an appropriate template you can download the template to your computer.

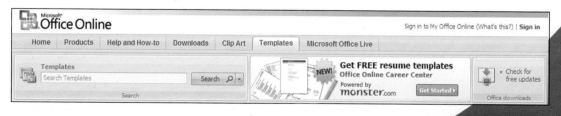

Features Summary

Feature	Ribbon Tab, Group	Button	Quick Access Toolbar	Office Button Drop-down List	Keyboard Shortcut
Accounting Number format	Home, Number	$			
align text left	Home, Alignment				
align text right	Home, Alignment				
close a workbook				Close	Ctrl + F4
copy	Home, Clipboard				Ctrl + C
exit Excel		X Exit Excel		Exit Excel	Alt + F4
fill down	Home, Editing				Ctrl + D
fill left	Home, Editing				
fill right	Home, Editing				Ctrl + R
fill up	Home, Editing				
Go To	Home, Editing				Ctrl + G
Help					F1
merge and center	Home, Alignment				
new workbook				New	Ctrl + N
open				Open	Ctrl + O
paste	Home, Clipboard				Ctrl + V
Print Preview				Print, Print Preview	Ctrl + F2
print using Print dialog box				Print	Ctrl + P
print using Quick Print					
save				Save	Ctrl + S
save with a new name				Save As	F12
sort	Home, Editing				
SUM function	Home, Editing	Σ			Alt + =
Templates				New	

Knowledge Check

Completion: In the space provided at the right, write in the correct term, command, or option.

1. This area contains commands and features for performing actions divided into tabs and groups.

2. This area displays the formula stored within the cell (not the result).

3. The cell pointer changes to this when pointing at the small black square at the bottom right corner of the active cell.

4. This would be the formula entry to divide the contents of cell C6 by the contents in cell C12.

5. This is the term for the method used to create a formula by typing the equals sign and operator symbols while clicking reference cells between the typed symbols.

6. This term is used to refer to the values identified within parentheses in the SUM function.

7. The SUM function button is located in this group in the Home tab.

8. Do this action if Excel suggests the wrong range after clicking the Sum button.

9. This button appears after copied cells are pasted into the destination range.

10. This is the term for the formulas entered beside or below a worksheet that are designed to verify the worksheet's accuracy.

11. This format adds a dollar sign, a comma in the thousands place, and two decimal places to each value in the selected range.

12. Click the Sort & Filter button in the Editing group in the Home tab and then click this option at the drop-down list to sort a list in ascending order.

13. This keyboard shortcut will open the Excel Help window when pointing to a button.

14. Display the active worksheet in Print Preview by clicking the Office button, pointing to this option, and then clicking *Print Preview*.

15. Open this dialog box to type a cell reference to which you want to move the active cell.

Skills Review

Review 1 Entering Labels and Values; Formatting Cells

North Shore Medical Clinic

1. Start a new workbook.
2. Create the worksheet shown in Figure E1.3. Use the fill handle whenever possible to facilitate data entry. Do not format cells since you will apply formatting options in Step 3 and in Review 3.
3. Select the range G12:G20 and then apply the Accounting Number format.
4. Deselect the range and then save the workbook as **ExcelMedS1-R1**.

FIGURE E1.3 Review 1 Worksheet

	A	B	C	D	E	F	G
1	North Shore Medical Clinic						
2	Purchase Order						
3							
4	Vendor:						
5	MedCare Medical Supplies			Telephone		Fax	
6	1913 NE 7th Avenue			503 555 4589		800 555 6315	
7	Portland, OR 97212-3906						
8							
9							
10							
11	Item				Order Qty	Unit	Price
12	Disposable shoe cover				1	per 300	37.75
13	Disposable bouffant cap				1	per 100	7.89
14	Disposable examination table paper				8	per roll	8.9
15	Disposable patient gown				8	per doz.	7.9
16	Disposable patient slippers				8	per doz.	4.27
17	Disposable skin staple remover				8	per doz.	92.4
18	Disposable skin stapler				8	per doz.	87.34
19	Disposable thermometer tips				8	per 100	4.12
20	Disposable earloop mask				8	per 50	5.61

Review 2 Entering and Copying Formulas; Using Sum

1. With **ExcelMedS1-R1.xlsx** open, create the following formulas by typing them in the Formula bar or the cell, using the pointing method, or clicking the Sum button:
   a. In cell H11 add the label **Line Total**.
   b. In cell H12, multiply the order quantity times the price by entering **=e12*g12**.
   c. Use the fill handle to copy the formula to cells H13:H20.
   d. In cell F22, add the label **Subtotal**.
   e. In cell H22, use Sum to add the range H12:H20.
   f. In cell F23, add the label **Shipping**.
   g. In cell H23, add the value **25**.
   h. In cell F24, add the label **Order Total**.
   i. In cell H24, calculate the purchase order total by entering **=h22+h23**.
2. Format H23 to the Accounting Number format.
3. Save **ExcelMedS1-R1.xlsx**.

Review 3 Improving the Appearance of the Worksheet; Previewing and Printing

1. With **ExcelMedS1-R1.xlsx** open, select the range A1:H1 and then click the Merge and Center button.
2. Merge and center A2 by completing steps similar to that in Step 1.
3. Select the range E11:H11 and then change the alignment to *Center*.
4. Select the range E12:E20 and then change the alignment to *Center*.
5. Make A9 the active cell, type the following label, and then press Enter.
   Terms: 1%/10, net 30 days. No substitutions.
6. Display the worksheet in the Print Preview. Magnify the display so that you can read the text and then print the worksheet.
7. Save **ExcelMedS1-R1.xlsx**.

Review 4 Using Help

1. With **ExcelMedS1-R1.xlsx** open, display the Excel Help window, type
   How do I add a background color?, in the search text box and then
   press Enter.
2. Click the *Apply or remove cell shading* hyperlink in the search results list.
3. Read the information displayed in the Excel Help window.
4. Close the Help window.
5. Select the range A11:H11 and then fill the range of cells with Aqua, Accent 5, Lighter
   60% using the button on the Formatting toolbar that you learned about using Help.
6. Select the range A1:A2 and fill the cells with Orange, Accent 6, Lighter 60%.
7. Deselect A1:A2.
8. Save, print, and then close **ExcelMedS1-R1.xlsx**.

Skills Assessment

Assessment 1 Adding Values and Formulas to a Worksheet

1. Open **CVPTravelExpenses.xlsx**.
2. Save the workbook with Save As and name it **ExcelMedS1-A1**.
3. You have been asked by Sydney Larsen, office manager at Cascade View
   Pediatrics, to calculate the estimated travel expenses for the American
   Academy of Pediatrics members who will be attending the International Pediatric
   Medical Conference in Toronto, Ontario, Canada, May 22–26. Sydney has already
   received quotations for airfare, hotel, and airport transfers. This information is summarized
   below.
   - Return airfare from Portland to Toronto $675.50 per person.
   - Sydney has negotiated a room rate of $1,270.00 per room for the entire duration with
     two persons per room.
   - Airport Transfer Limousine Service is a flat rate of $75.00 in Toronto and $55.00 in
     Portland.
   - All of the above prices include all taxes and are quoted in U.S. dollars.
   - Members attending the conference include:
     > Dr. Raphaël Severin
     > Dr. Joseph Yarborough
     > Dr. Beth Delaney
     > Deanna Reynolds, Child Development Specialist
4. Cascade View Pediatrics reimburses all traveling employees for food expenses at the
   rate of $70.00 per day.
5. Enter the appropriate values and formulas to complete the worksheet.
6. Make any formatting changes you think would improve the appearance of the worksheet.
7. Save, print, and then close **ExcelMedS1-A1.xlsx**.

Assessment 2 Creating a Workbook

1. Sydney Larsen, office manager of Cascade View Pediatrics, has asked you to prepare a cost and revenue estimate for a seminar on ADHD Treatment Strategies that Dr. Beth Delaney is hosting for the local chapter of the American Academy of Pediatrics. Cascade View Pediatrics will be billed for all expenses and reimbursed later by the local chapter. At the seminar, a registration fee is collected from each attending member. The cash received from this fee is turned over to the treasurer of the local chapter at the seminar. Create a new workbook that will calculate the total seminar costs and then calculate the registration fee that needs to be charged to each member using the following information.

   a. Click the New button on the Quick Access toolbar to open a blank workbook and then create a worksheet to summarize the seminar costs for 75 members using the following prices:
      * Rental fee for the meeting room at the Hilton Portland & Executive Tower is $250.00.
      * Rental fee for the audio-visual equipment Dr. Delaney needs for her presentation is $50.00 for the day.
      * Handouts, name badges, and other materials have been estimated at $25.00.
      * Morning coffee and refreshments are quoted at $2.75 per person.
      * Lunch is quoted at $7.92 per person.

   b. Calculate the total cost. In a separate row below the total cost, calculate the cost per member.

   c. The local chapter of the American Academy of Pediatrics collects $10.00 per member at each of these events for their general revenue fund. Below the cost per member, calculate the registration fee to be charged per member. The fee is the cost per member plus the $10.00 general revenue fund collection.

2. Two blank rows below the registration fee calculation, calculate the total registration fee receipts that will be collected at the seminar and given to the local treasurer.

3. Make any formatting changes you think would improve the appearance of the worksheet.

4. Save the workbook and name it **ExcelMedS1-A2**.

5. Print and then close **ExcelMedS1-A2.xlsx**.

Assessment 3 Creating a New Workbook

1. Laura Latterell, education director at Columbia River General Hospital, has asked you to prepare an estimate of the funds needed in the professional development budget for 2011. Professional development funding includes in-service sessions, continuing education course fees, and conference registration fees. All other related costs such as travel expenses are funded directly from each medical professional's department budget. Create a new workbook to calculate the total 2011 professional development budget. Include a subtotal for each category of funded professional development.

2. A survey of the department managers has provided the following information:
   * In-service training requests for 30 sessions throughout the year. Sessions are run by consultants Laura hires at the rate of $75.00 per session.
   * Continuing education courses:
         125 course requests for doctors at $500.00 per course
         60 course requests for nurses at $290.00 per course

30 course requests for respiratory therapists at $175.00 per course
25 course requests for anesthesiologists at $190.00 per course
20 course requests for radiologists at $175.00 per course
15 course requests for physical therapists at $180.00 per course
10 course requests for management staff at $150.00 per course
10 course requests for support staff at $145.00 per course

3. The hospital buys block registrations for the following conferences:

American Medical Association national annual conference	$7,500.00
American Academy of Nursing annual conference	$4,750.00
International Respiratory Congress	$5,100.00
Radiological Society of North America annual meeting	$5,150.00
American Society of Anesthesiologists annual conference	$3,800.00
American Physical Therapy Association annual conference	$2,775.00
American Hospital Association annual meeting	$4,950.00

4. Make any formatting changes you think would improve the appearance of the workbook.
5. Save the workbook and name it **ExcelMedS1-A3**.
6. Print and then close **ExcelMedS1-A3.xlsx**.

Assessment 4 Finding Information on Hiding Zero Values

1. Using Excel Help, find out how to display or hide zero values on an entire worksheet.
2. Open **NSMCSupplies.xlsx**.
3. Save the workbook with Save As and name it **ExcelMedS1-A4**.
4. Hide the zero values (display cells containing zeros as blank cells).
5. Change the page orientation to *Landscape*.
6. Display the Print dialog box, change the Print range to print page 1 to 1, and then click OK.

HELP

7. Save and then close **ExcelMedS1-A4.xlsx**.

Assessment 5 Locating and Completing Excel Training in Office Online

1. Display a new blank worksheet.
2. Open the Excel Help window.
3. Click the down-pointing arrow at the right of the Search button and then click *Excel Training* at the drop-down list.
4. Type **formulas** in the search text box and then click the Search button.
5. Click the hyperlink to one of the training courses that interests you.
6. Complete the online training course. *Note: You can skip through sections of the course that are teaching skills you have already mastered by clicking the next topic in the navigation pane.*
7. Close Internet Explorer when you have completed the course.
8. Close the Excel Help window and then close the worksheet.

Marquee Challenge

Challenge 1 Preparing a Surgery Average Cost Report

1. Create the worksheet shown in Figure E1.4.
2. Use the following information to complete the worksheet:
   a. Total average cost in column K is the sum of items starting with column F (Ward) and ending with column J (Pharmacy).
   b. Total cost of all cases in column L is column K (*Total Avg Cost*) times column D (*Cases*).
3. Format the values in columns K and L to Accounting Number format.
4. Add a grand total for all cases at the bottom of column L. Label the value appropriately.
5. Save the workbook and name it **ExcelMedS1-C1**.
6. Change the page setup to *Landscape* and then print the worksheet.
7. Close **ExcelMedS1-C1.xlsx**.

Challenge 2 Completing an Invoice

1. Create the worksheet shown in Figure E1.5 using the Invoice that calculates total template. *Note: You can download this template using the Invoices category at the New Workbook dialog box.*
2. Save the workbook and name it **ExcelMedS1-C2**.
3. Print and then close **ExcelMedS1-C2.xlsx**.

FIGURE E1.4 Challenge 1

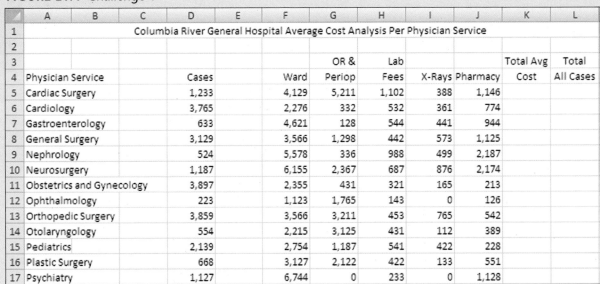

	A	B	C	D	E	F	G	H	I	J	K	L
1	Columbia River General Hospital Average Cost Analysis Per Physician Service											
2												
3							OR &	Lab			Total Avg	Total
4	Physician Service			Cases		Ward	Periop	Fees	X-Rays	Pharmacy	Cost	All Cases
5	Cardiac Surgery			1,233		4,129	5,211	1,102	388	1,146		
6	Cardiology			3,765		2,276	332	532	361	774		
7	Gastroenterology			633		4,621	128	544	441	944		
8	General Surgery			3,129		3,566	1,298	442	573	1,125		
9	Nephrology			524		5,578	336	988	499	2,187		
10	Neurosurgery			1,187		6,155	2,367	687	876	2,174		
11	Obstetrics and Gynecology			3,897		2,355	431	321	165	213		
12	Ophthalmology			223		1,123	1,765	143	0	126		
13	Orthopedic Surgery			3,859		3,566	3,211	453	765	542		
14	Otolaryngology			554		2,215	3,125	431	112	389		
15	Pediatrics			2,139		2,754	1,187	541	422	228		
16	Plastic Surgery			668		3,127	2,122	422	133	551		
17	Psychiatry			1,127		6,744	0	233	0	1,128		

North Shore Medical Clinic

INVOICE

7450 Meridian Street, Suite 150
Portland, OR 97202
Phone: (503) 555-2330; Fax: (503) 555-2335

DATE: (use current date)
INVOICE # A-128
FOR: *Educational Services*

Bill To:
Laura Latterell, Education Director
Columbia River General Hospital
4550 Fremont Street
Portland, OR 97045
(503) 555 2000 ext 2347

DESCRIPTION	AMOUNT
2 In-Service Training Sessions at $75.00 per session	$150.00
TOTAL	$ 150.00

Make all checks payable to North Shore Medical Clinic.
If you have any questions concerning this invoice, contact Lee Elliott, Office Manager at Extension 12.

THANK YOU FOR YOUR BUSINESS!

Excel SECTION 2

Editing and Formatting Worksheets

Skills

- Edit the content of cells
- Clear cells and cell formats
- Use proofing tools
- Insert and delete columns and rows
- Move and copy cells
- Use Paste Options to link cells
- Create formulas using absolute references
- Adjust column width and row height
- Change the font, size, style, and color of cells
- Apply numeric formats and adjust the number of
- decimal places
- Use Undo
- Change cell alignment and indentation
- Insert and edit comments
- Add borders and shading
- Copy formats using Format Painter
- Apply cell styles
- Find and replace cell entries and formats
- Freeze and unfreeze panes
- Change the zoom percentage
- View and modify page breaks

Student Resources

Before beginning this section:
1. Copy to your storage medium the ExcelMedS2 subfolder from the Unit4Excel folder on the Student Resources CD.
2. Make ExcelMedS2 the active folder.

In addition to containing the data files needed to complete section work, the Student Resources CD contains model answers in PDF format for each of the projects in this section; model answers for end-of-section exercises are not provided.

Projects Overview

Review the clinic's supplies inventory report and adjust page breaks.

Edit and format a laboratory requisitions billing report, edit and format research data for a medical conference presentation, research and create a workbook on healthcare costs, create a staffing worksheet for the neurology department, and create a radiology requisition form.

Edit and format a revenue summary report.

Activity 2.1

Editing and Clearing Cells; Using Proofing Tools

The contents of a cell can be edited directly within the cell or in the Formula bar. Clearing a cell can involve removing the cell contents, format, or both. The Spelling feature is a useful tool to assist with correcting typing errors within a worksheet. After completing a spelling check, you will still need to proofread the worksheet since the spelling checker will not highlight all errors and cannot check the accuracy of values. Other Proofing tools available include a Research feature to search for external information, a Thesaurus to find a word with similar meaning, and a Translate tool to translate a selected word into a different language.

Project

Sydney Larsen, office manager of Cascade View Pediatrics, has started a January revenue summary report for Dr. Joseph Yarborough. The report contains some typographical errors and needs updating after Sydney reviewed the day sheets from the medical accounting program. Sydney has asked you to correct the errors and finish the report. You will be working on this report through most of this section.

1. Open **CVPRevenue-Yarborough.xlsx**. *Note: This worksheet contains intentional spelling errors that will be corrected in this activity.*

2. Save the workbook with Save As in the ExcelMedS2 folder and name it **ExcelMedS2-01**.

3. Double-click E15.

    Double-clicking a cell inserts a blinking insertion point in the cell; *Edit* appears in the Status bar. The insertion point position varies depending on the location of the cell pointer when Edit mode is activated.

4. Press the Right or Left Arrow key as needed to move the insertion point between the *4* and *5* and then press the Delete key.

5. Type **3** and then press Enter.

6. Make E30 the active cell.

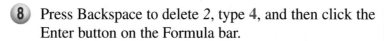

7. Move the pointer after *22* in the Formula bar and then click the left mouse button.

    The cell pointer changes to an I-beam pointer I when positioned in the Formula bar.

8. Press Backspace to delete *2*, type **4**, and then click the Enter button on the Formula bar.

9. Make A16 the active cell and then press Delete.

    Delete or Backspace clears only the contents of the cell; formats or comments applied to the cell remain in effect.

10. Select the range F7:F8. Click the Clear button [icon] in the Editing group in the Home tab and then click *Clear All* at the drop-down list.

    Clear All removes everything from a cell including formats or comments.

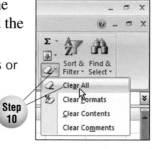

11. Press Ctrl + Home to make A1 the active cell.

(12) Click the Review tab in the ribbon and then click the Spelling button.

Spelling check begins at the active cell. Words within the worksheet that are not found in the dictionary are highlighted as potential errors. Use buttons in the Spelling dialog box to skip the word (Ignore Once or Ignore All), replace the word with the highlighted word in the *Suggestions* list box (Change), or add the word to the dictionary (Add to Dictionary) if spelled correctly.

(13) Click the Change button in the Spelling dialog box to instruct Excel to replace *assesment* with *assessment*.

Excel stops at the next row and flags the same spelling error. A quick glance down the worksheet reveals this word is frequently misspelled throughout the worksheet.

(14) Click the Change All button in the Spelling dialog box to replace all occurrences of *assesment* with *assessment*.

(15) Click the Change All button in the Spelling dialog box to replace *fomr* with *form*.

(16) Click OK at the message that the spelling check is complete.

(17) Make A29 the active cell.

(18) Click the Thesaurus button in the Proofing group in the Review tab.

Use the Thesaurus to replace a word in the worksheet with another word of similar meaning. Thesaurus is a feature within the Research task pane.

(19) Point to the word *replication* in the task pane word list, click the down-pointing arrow that appears, and then click *Insert* at the drop-down list.

The word *Photocopying* is replaced with *Replication* in A29.

(20) Click the Research button in the Proofing group to turn off the Research task pane.

(21) Save **ExcelMedS2-01.xlsx**.

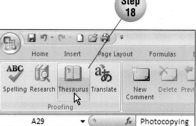

Step 13

Step 14

Step 18

Step 19

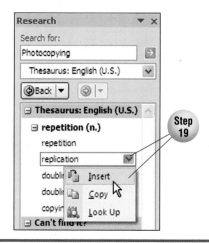

In Brief

Edit Cell
1. Double-click cell.
2. Insert and/or delete text.
3. Press Enter or click another cell.

Clear Cell
1. Click Clear button arrow in Home tab.
2. Click *Clear All*, *Clear Formats*, *Clear Contents*, or *Clear Comments*.

Spell Check
1. Click Review tab.
2. Click Spelling button.
3. Click Ignore Once, Ignore All, Change, or Add to Dictionary as required.

In Addition

Research Task Pane

You can use the Research task pane to search for information online without leaving the worksheet. For example, you can conduct an Internet search, look up information in online encyclopedias or business reference sites, or find a current stock quote using MSN Money Stock Quote. Choose the online source by clicking the down-pointing arrow at the right of the resources list box (located below the *Search for* text box).

Activity 2.2

Inserting and Deleting Columns and Rows

Insert rows or columns using options from the Insert button in the Home tab or from the context-sensitive shortcut menu that displays when you right-click a selected area. Inserted rows are placed above the active cell or selected rows and existing rows are shifted down. Columns are inserted left of the active cell or selected columns and existing columns are shifted right. When rows or columns are deleted, data automatically is shifted up or left to fill space and references in formulas are updated.

Project

Cascade View
PEDIATRICS

Sydney has provided you with new data that you need to insert into the worksheet. To improve the layout of the report, you decide to insert blank rows before each fee category and remove the blank row that was created when you deleted *Hospital physicals* in the last project.

1 With **ExcelMedS2-01.xlsx** open, position the cell pointer (displays as a right-pointing black arrow) over row indicator *18*, hold down the left mouse button, drag the mouse down over *19*, and then release the mouse.

> This selects rows *18* and *19*. Inserted rows are placed *above* the selected rows and columns are inserted to the *left*.

2 Click the Home tab, click the Insert button arrow [Insert ▾] in the Cells group, and then click *Insert Sheet Rows* at the drop-down list.

> Two blank rows are inserted. All rows below the inserted rows are shifted down.

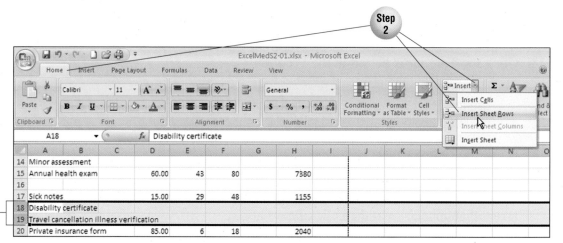

3 Click cell A18, type **Hearing assessment**, and then press Enter.

4 Type **Speech assessment** in cell A19 and then press Enter.

5 Type the data for hearing and speech assessment as follows:

D18 **26.50**	E18 **4**	F18 **2**
D19 **31.50**	E19 **7**	F19 **5**

6 Calculate the totals for hearing and speech assessment as follows:

H18	=(e18+f18)*d18
H19	=(e19+f19)*d19

	A	D	E	F	H	
16						
17	Sick notes	15.00	29	48	1155	Steps 3–6
18	Hearing assessment	26.50	4	2	159	
19	Speech assessment	31.50	7	5	378	

7 Position the cell pointer over row indicator *16* and then click the left mouse button to select the entire row.

8 Click the Delete button arrow in the Cells group and then click *Delete Sheet Rows* at the drop-down list.

> Row 16 is removed from the worksheet.

9 Select row 11. Hold down the Ctrl key, select rows 24 and 29, and then release the mouse and the Ctrl key.

> Hold down the Ctrl key to select multiple rows or columns that are not adjacent.

10 Position the pointer within any of the three selected rows, right-click to display the shortcut menu and Mini toolbar, and then click *Insert*.

11 Select column G and display the shortcut menu and Mini toolbar by positioning the cell pointer over column indicator letter *G* (displays as a down-pointing black arrow) and right-clicking the mouse.

12 At the shortcut menu, click *Delete*.

> Data in columns to the right of the deleted column are shifted left to fill in the space.

13 Click in any cell to deselect the column.

14 Save **ExcelMedS2-01.xlsx**.

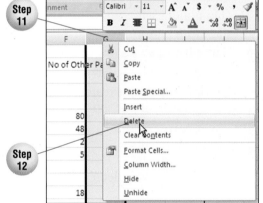

Mini toolbar

In Brief

Insert Rows or Columns
1. Select required number of rows or columns.
2. Click Insert button arrow.
3. Click *Insert Sheet Rows* or *Insert Sheet Columns*.

Delete Rows or Columns
1. Select rows or columns to be deleted.
2. Click Delete button arrow.
3. Click *Delete Sheet Rows* or *Delete Sheet Columns*.

In Addition

Inserting and Deleting Cells

In this activity, you selected entire rows and columns before inserting or deleting. This practice is the more common method when you need to add or delete data to a worksheet. Another method used less frequently is to insert new blank cells or delete a range of cells within the worksheet area. To insert new blank cells, select the range of cells you need to add and then click the Insert button in the Cells group, or click the Insert button arrow and then click *Insert Cells* at the drop-down list to display the dialog box shown at the right. Using the dialog box you can choose to shift existing cells right or down. Click the Delete button in the Cells group to delete a selected range of cells and shift up the cells below the deleted range. Click the Delete button arrow and then click *Delete Cells* to open the Delete dialog box with similar options as Insert.

Activity 2.3

Moving and Copying Cells

In Section 1 you learned how to use copy and paste to copy formulas in the payroll worksheet for the North Shore Medial Clinic. You can also use cut and paste to move the contents of a cell or range of cells to another location in the worksheet. The selected cells being cut or copied are called the *source*. The cell or range of cells that is receiving the source data is called the *destination*. If data already exists in the destination cells, Excel replaces the contents. Cells cut or copied to the Clipboard can be pasted more than once in the active workbook, in another workbook, or in another Office application.

Project

Continue to work on the report by moving cells and copying and linking cells using buttons from the toolbar and a method called *drag and drop*.

1. With **ExcelMedS2-01.xlsx** open, make A40 the active cell.

2. Click the Cut button ✂ in the Clipboard group in the Home tab.

   A moving marquee surrounds the source after you use Cut or Copy, indicating the cell contents have been placed in the Clipboard.

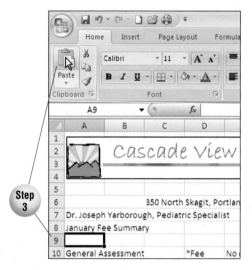

3. Make A9 the active cell and then click the Paste button 📋 in the Clipboard group. (Do not click the down-pointing arrow on the Paste button as this displays a drop-down list of Paste options.)

   Step 3

   The text is removed from A40 and placed in A9. In the next step, you will move a cell using a method called *drag and drop*.

4. Select A10.

5. Point at any one of the four borders surrounding the selected cell.

   Step 5

   When you point at a border, the pointer changes from the thick white cross to a white arrow with the move icon attached to it (four-headed arrow).

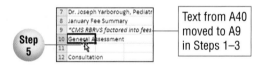

Text from A40 moved to A9 in Steps 1–3

6. Hold down the left mouse button, drag the cell down one row to A11, and then release the mouse.

   A gray border will appear as you drag, indicating the placement of the range when you release the mouse. The destination range displays in a ScreenTip below the gray border.

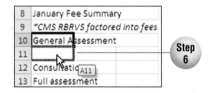

   Step 6

7. Make D34 the active cell.

   Dr. Yarborough charges the same fee for telephone prescription renewals and sick notes. He wants you to link the sick notes fee to the telephone prescription renewal fee. When the fee is changed, you will only need to update one of the two cells.

8 Click the Copy button 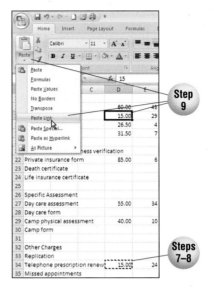 in the Clipboard group.

9 Make D17 the active cell, click the Paste button arrow in the Clipboard group, and then click *Paste Link* at the drop-down list.

> The source and destination cells are now linked. Linking the cells means that any change made to the source cell will automatically be applied to the destination cell.

10 Press Esc to remove the moving marquee from D34.

11 Make D34 the active cell and edit the value to *16.50*.

> Notice the value in D17 is also changed to 16.50 automatically.

12 Select E27:G27.

13 Point at any one of the four borders surrounding the selected range until the pointer displays as a white arrow with the move icon attached to it, hold down the Ctrl key, and then drag the mouse to E28:G28. Release the mouse button first and then release the Ctrl key.

> Holding down the Ctrl key while dragging copies cells.

14 Make D28 the active cell, type **30.00**, and then press Enter.

15 Save **ExcelMedS2-01.xlsx**.

In Brief

Move or Copy Cells
1. Select source cells.
2. Click Cut or Copy button.
3. Select starting destination cell.
4. Click Paste button.

Copy and Link Cells
1. Select source cells.
2. Click Copy button.
3. Select destination cell.
4. Click Paste button arrow.
5. Click *Paste Link*.

Step 9

Steps 7–8

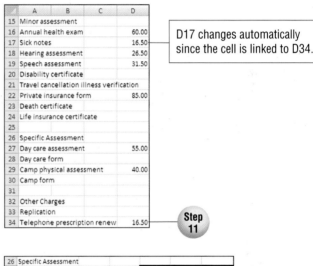

> D17 changes automatically since the cell is linked to D34.

Step 11

Step 13

In Addition

Paste Options

The Paste button arrow contains several options for controlling how cut or copied text is pasted into the destination. The list shown at the right includes options to paste *Formulas*, *Paste Values* (instead of source formulas), *No Borders* (borders in source cell are not duplicated), and *Transpose* (rows are converted to columns and vice versa). Click *Paste Special* to open the Paste Special dialog box with more paste options. The bottom of the Paste drop-down list contains hyperlink and picture options.

Activity 2.4

Creating Formulas with Absolute Addressing

In Section 1, when you copied and pasted formulas in the payroll worksheet, the cell addresses in the destination cells changed automatically *relative* to the destination row or column. The formulas in the payroll worksheet used **relative addressing**. Sometimes you need a cell address to remain fixed when it is copied to another location in the worksheet. To do this, the formulas must include **absolute addressing** for those cell addresses that you do not want changed. Make a cell address absolute by typing a dollar symbol ($) in front of the column letter or row number that cannot be changed. You can also use the function key F4 to toggle through variations of the address as relative, absolute, or mixed in which either the row is absolute and the column is relative or vice versa.

Project

Dr. Yarborough would like to increase his monthly revenue by approximately $1,500.00. You will add columns and create formulas in the January fee summary worksheet to find the percent increase needed in fees to achieve the doctor's goal.

1 With **ExcelMedS2-01.xlsx** open, make H10 the active cell and then type **New Fee**.

2 Make I10 the active cell and then type **New Total**.

3 Make H9 the active cell and then type **5%**.

> You want to reference a cell for the percent increase in case you need to try different values before you find the percent that will achieve the $1,500.00 increase. In the next steps you will create and copy formulas that will calculate revenue based on a 5% increase in fees.

4 Make H12 the active cell, type **=(d12*h9**, press function key F4, type **)+d12**, and then press Enter.

You will be copying this formula to the remaining rows and

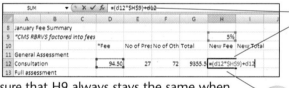

need to make sure that H9 always stays the same when the formula is duplicated. Pressing F4 causes Excel to insert dollar symbols in front of the row and column number immediately left of the insertion point—h9 becomes $H$9—an absolute address.

> Pressing F4 immediately after typing a cell reference inserts a dollar symbol ($) before the column letter and row number. A dollar symbol makes the reference absolute.

Step 4

5 Make I12 the active cell, type **=(e12+f12)*h12**, and then press Enter.

The formula to calculate the total revenue does not require an absolute reference. When the formula is copied, you want the row numbers to change relative to the destination cells.

Step 5

6 Make H16 the active cell, type the formula **=(d16*h9)+d16**, and then press Enter.

You can also type the dollar symbols into the formula rather than use F4. In the next steps you will copy and paste the formula to the other cells in column H.

Step 6

7. Make H16 the active cell and then click the Copy button in the Clipboard group in the Home tab.

8. Select the range H17:H19, hold down the Ctrl key, select H22, hold down the Ctrl key, select H27:H29, hold down the Ctrl key, and then select H34.

9. Click the Paste button in the Clipboard group. (Do not click the down-pointing arrow on the Paste button).

10. Press the ESC key to remove the moving marquee from H16.

11. Click H17 and then look at the Formula bar to see the formula that was pasted into the cell: =(D17*$H$9)+D17.

> Notice that the cell address containing the percent value (H9) did not change while the cell address that contains the original fee for sick notes (D17) changed relative to the destination (row 17).

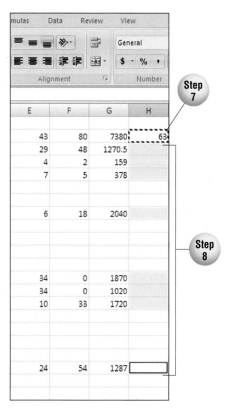

Step 7

Step 8

In Brief

Make Cell Address Absolute
With insertion point positioned just after cell address or with cell address selected in Formula bar, press F4.
OR
Type dollar symbols immediately preceding column letter and/or row number.

12. Click a few other cells in column H to view the formula. Notice in each cell, H9 remains the same while the cell address for column D always changes relative to the destination row.

13. Copy the New Total formula in I12 and paste it to I16:19, I22, I27:29, and I34 by completing steps similar to those in Steps 7–9.

14. Copy the formula in G38 and paste it to I38.

15. Make A40 the active cell and type **Increase in January Revenue:**.

16. Make I40 the active cell, type **=i38-g38**, and then press Enter.

> Notice the increased revenue (1324) is not close to the $1,500.00 goal.

17. Make H9 the active cell and edit the value to 6%.

18. Look at the updated value in I40. Notice that the increased revenue (1588.8) is now close to the goal.

19. Save **ExcelMedS2-01.xlsx**.

In Addition

More about Mixed Addressing

Excel can be instructed to fix only the row number or the column letter of a cell that is copied and pasted to another location. Following are more ways that a cell address can use absolute referencing. Pressing F4 repeatedly causes Excel to scroll through each of these variations for the selected cell address.

Example	Action
=$A$12*.01	Neither the column nor the row will change.
=$A12*.01	The column will remain fixed at column A, but the row will change.
=A$12*.01	The column will change, but the row remains fixed at row 12.
=A12*.01	Both the column and row will change.

Activity 2.5

Adjusting Column Width and Row Height

By default, columns are all the same width and rows are all the same height with columns set by default to a width of 8.43 characters (64 pixels) and rows to a height of 15 points (110 pixels). In some cases you do not have to increase the width when the text is too wide for the column, since labels "spill over" into the next cell if it is empty. Some column headings in the report are truncated because an entry exists in the column immediately to the right. Excel automatically adjusts the height of rows to accommodate the size of the text within the cells. Manually increasing the row height adds more space between rows, which can be used to improve readability or as a design technique to draw attention to a series of cells.

Project

To make the report more easily understood, you will adjust the column widths for columns in which the entire label is not currently visible and increase the height of the row containing the column headings.

1. With **ExcelMedS2-01.xlsx** open, make any cell in column E the active cell.

2. Click the Format button in the Cells group in the Home tab and then click *Column Width* at the drop-down list.

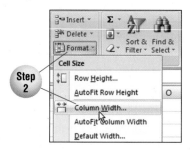

3. At the Column Width dialog box, type **23** and then click OK or press Enter.

   In the next step, you will adjust the width of column F using the mouse.

4. Position the mouse pointer on the boundary line in the column indicator row between columns F and G until the pointer changes to a vertical line with a left- and right-pointing arrow ✛.

5. Hold down the left mouse button, drag the boundary line to the right until *Width: 19.00 (138 pixels)* displays in the ScreenTip, and then release the mouse button.

   As you drag the boundary line to the right or left, a dotted line appears in the column in the worksheet area indicating the new width.

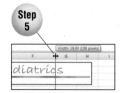

6. Position the mouse pointer on the boundary line in the column indicator row between columns G and H until the pointer changes to a vertical line with a left- and right-pointing arrow and then double-click the left mouse button.

   Double-clicking the boundary line sets the width to fit the length of the longest entry within the column, referred to as *AutoFit*.

⑦ Increase the width of column D to *11 (82 pixels)* using either the Column Width dialog box or by dragging the column boundary.

> After reviewing the worksheet, you decide the four columns with dollar values should be the same width. In the next steps, you will learn how to set the width of multiple columns in one operation.

⑧ Click column indicator letter *D*, hold down the Ctrl key, and click column indicator letters *G*, *H*, and *I*.

⑨ Position the mouse pointer on *any* of the right boundary lines within the selected range of columns until the pointer changes to a vertical line with a left- and right-pointing arrow.

> Any change made to the width of one column boundary will affect all of the selected columns.

⑩ Drag the boundary line right until *Width: 12.00 (89 pixels)* displays in the ScreenTip and then release the mouse button.

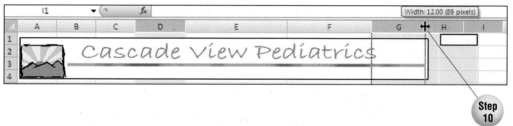

Step 10

⑪ Click in any cell to deselect the columns.

> Do not be concerned that the columns appear too wide—you have many formatting tasks to complete that will improve the layout as you work through the next four activities.

⑫ Position the mouse pointer on the boundary line below row 10 until the pointer changes to a horizontal line with an up-and-down-pointing arrow.

⑬ Drag the boundary line down until *Height: 21.00 (28 pixels)* displays in the ScreenTip and then release the mouse button.

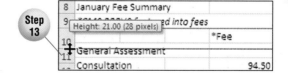

Step 13

⑭ Save **ExcelMedS2-01.xlsx**.

In Brief

Increase or Decrease Column Width
1. Select column(s).
2. Click Format button in Cells group.
3. Click *Column Width*.
4. Type desired width.
5. Click OK.

Increase or Decrease Row Height
1. Select row(s).
2. Click Format button in Cells group.
3. Click *Row Height*.
4. Type desired height.
5. Click OK.

Adjust Width or Height Using Mouse
Drag boundary to right of column or below row, or double-click boundary to AutoFit.

In Addition

Row Height Dialog Box

A sequence of steps similar to the one used for adjusting column width using the Column Width dialog box can be used to increase or decrease the height of a row with the Row Height dialog box, shown at the right. Click any cell within the row, click the Format button in the Cells group in the Home tab, and then click *Row Height* at the drop-down list. Type the desired height and press Enter or click OK.

Changing the Font, Size, Style, and Color of Cells

The *font* is the typeface used to display and print data. The default font in Excel is Calibri, but several other fonts are available. The size of the font is measured in units called *points*. A point is approximately 1/72 of an inch measured vertically. The default font size used by Excel is 11-point. The larger the point size, the larger the type. Each font's style can be enhanced to **bold**, *italic*, or ***bold italic***. Cell entries display in black with a white background. Changing the color of the font and/or the color of the background (called *fill*) adds interest or emphasis to the text.

Project

To add to the visual appeal of Dr. Yarborough's revenue report, you will change the font and font size and apply attributes such as bold and color to titles.

1. With **ExcelMedS2-01.xlsx** open, make A6 the active cell.

2. Click the Font button arrow in the Font group in the Home tab, scroll down the list of fonts, and then point to *Bradley Hand ITC* at the drop-down gallery. Notice that Excel applies the font you are pointing at to the active cell so that you can preview the result. This feature is called ***Live Preview***. Click *Bradley Hand ITC* at the drop-down gallery.

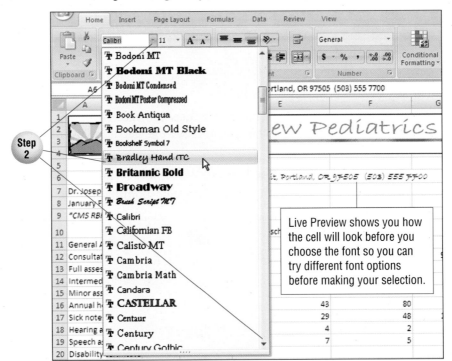

Live Preview shows you how the cell will look before you choose the font so you can try different font options before making your selection.

3. With A6 still the active cell, click the Font Size button arrow in the Font group and then click *14* at the drop-down list.

> The row height is automatically increased to accommodate the larger type size.

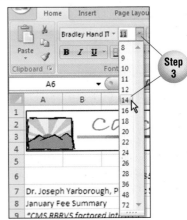

④ With A6 still the active cell, click the Font Color button arrow in the Font group and then click the *Aqua, Accent 5, Darker 50%* color box (second from right in last row) in the *Theme Colors* section of the color gallery.

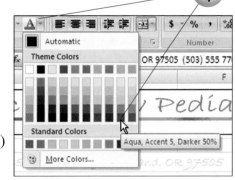

Step 4

⑤ With A6 still selected, click the Fill Color button arrow in the Font group and then click the *Aqua, Accent 5, Lighter 80%* color box (second from right in second row) in the *Theme Colors* section of the color gallery.

> *Fill* is the color of the background in the cell. Changing the fill color is sometimes referred to as *shading* a cell.

⑥ Click the Bold button **B** in the Font group.

⑦ Select A7:I7 and then click the Merge & Center button in the Alignment group.

Step 5

⑧ Change the font size of cell A7 to 12 and change the font color to Dark Red (first button in last row of the color gallery).

⑨ Select A8:I8 and repeat the formatting in Steps 7–8.

> After the first selection of Dark Red as the font color, you can apply the same color in row 8 by clicking the button. (You do not need to display the color palette.)

⑩ Click in any cell to deselect A8. Check your results with the worksheet shown above. If necessary, return to a previous step and redo the font, font size, bold, font color, merge & center, or fill color.

⑪ Save **ExcelMedS2-01.xlsx**.

In Addition

Format Cells Dialog Box

You can use the Format Cells dialog box with the Font tab selected (shown at the right) to change the font, font size, font style, and color of text. Additional Underline style options such as *Single, Double, Single Accounting,* and *Double Accounting* are available, as well as special effects options *Strikethrough, Superscript,* and *Subscript.* Select the cells you want to change and then click the Font group dialog box launcher button 🔲 to open the Format Cells dialog box with the Font tab active.

Change Font
1. Select cells.
2. Click Font button arrow.
3. Click desired font.
4. Deselect cells.

Change Font Size
1. Select cells.
2. Click Font Size button arrow.
3. Click desired size.
4. Deselect cells.

Change Font Attributes
1. Select cells.
2. Click desired attribute button.
3. Deselect cells.

Activity 2.7

Formatting Numeric Cells; Adjusting Decimal Places; Using Undo

In Section 1, in the payroll worksheet for the North Shore Medical Clinic, you learned how to format numeric cells to the Accounting Number Format which adds a dollar symbol ($), comma in the thousands, and two decimal places and displays negative values in brackets. Other numeric formats include Comma, Percent, and Currency. By default, cells are initially set to the General format which has no specific numeric style.

The number of decimal places in a selected range of cells can be increased or decreased using the Increase Decimal and Decrease Decimal buttons in the Number group of the Home tab.

Use the Undo button on the Quick Access toolbar to reverse the last action. Excel stores up to 100 actions that can be undone or redone and you can repeat actions as many times as you need. Some actions (such as Save) cannot be reversed with Undo.

Project

Continue your work on improving the visual appearance of the revenue summary report by applying format options to the numeric cells.

1. With **ExcelMedS2-01.xlsx** open, select D12, hold down the Ctrl key, and then select G12:I12.

2. Click the Accounting Number Format button $ ▾ in the Number group in the Home tab.

3. Click in any cell to deselect the cells.

4. Select G16:I34.

5. Click the Comma Style button in the Number group.

   > Comma style formats cells the same as the Accounting Number format with the exception of the dollar or alternative currency symbol.

6. Click in any cell to deselect the cells and review the numeric values in the worksheet. Notice that only three numeric cells remain that could be improved by applying a format option—columns G38, I38, and I40.

7. Select G38:I40.

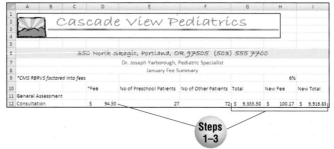

⑧ Click the Increase Decimal button 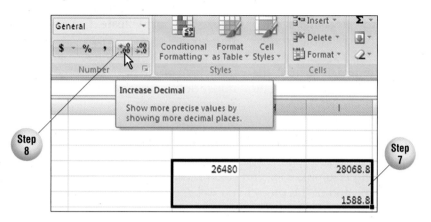 twice in the Number group.

One decimal place is added to or removed from the cells in the selected range each time you click Increase Decimal or Decrease Decimal.

In Brief

Change Numeric Format
1. Select cells.
2. Click desired format style button in Number group.
3. Deselect cells.

Undo Action
Click Undo button on Quick Access toolbar or press Ctrl + Z.

Adjust Decimal Places
1. Select cells.
2. Click Increase Decimal or Decrease Decimal button as needed.
3. Deselect cells.

⑨ With the range G38:I40 still selected, click the Decrease Decimal button once in the Number group.

⑩ Click the Undo button on the Quick Access toolbar.

Excel adds back one decimal place.

⑪ Click the Comman Style button in the Number group and then deselect the cells.

38	Total					26,480.00	28,068.80
39							
40	Increase in January Revenue:						1,588.80

⑫ Save **ExcelMedS2-01.xlsx**.

In Addition

Additional Number Format Options

Click the Number Format button arrow in the Number group to display a drop-down list (shown at the right) with additional numeric format options including date, time, fraction, and scientific options. Click *More Number Formats* at the bottom of the list to open the Format Cells dialog box with the Number tab selected. Using this dialog box, you can access further customization options for a format, such as display negative values in red, or create your own custom format code.

Activity 2.8

Changing the Alignment and Indentation of Cells; Inserting Comments

Data in a cell can be left-aligned, right-aligned, or centered within the column. Cells that have had Merge & Center applied can be formatted to align the text in the merged cell at the left or right. Use the Increase Indent and Decrease Indent buttons to indent text from the left edge of the cell approximately one character width each time the button is clicked. Using buttons along the top row in the Alignment group in the Home tab you can change vertical alignment, rotate text, or wrap text. A *comment* is a yellow pop-up box containing text that displays when the cell pointer is positioned over a cell with an attached comment. A diagonal red triangle in the upper right corner of the cell alerts the reader that a comment exists.

Project

Continue your work on improving the visual appearance of the revenue summary report by editing cells, removing columns, adjusting column widths, aligning cells, and indenting labels. As you near the end of this project you will add two comments in cells to verify values before the report is submitted to Dr. Yarborough.

1. With **ExcelMedS2-01.xlsx** open, edit the following cells:

Cell	*From*	*To*
E10	No of Preschool Patients	Preschool Patients
F10	No of Other Patients	Other Patients

2. Adjust the column widths of columns E and F to AutoFit. Refer to Activity 2.5, Step 6 if you need assistance with this step.

3. Delete columns B and C from the worksheet.

4. Adjust the column width of column A to *35.00 (250 pixels)*.

5. Select B10:G10.

6. Click the Center button ▤ in the Alignment group in the Home tab.

   The Align Left button ▤ aligns entries at the left edge of the cell and the Align Right button ▤ aligns entries at the right edge of the cell.

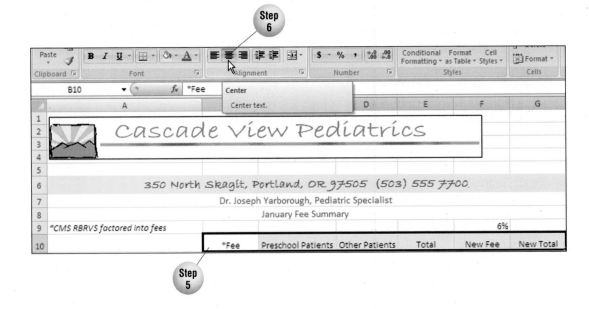

7 Select A12:A24.

8 Click the Increase Indent button in the Alignment group.

> Each time you the click the Increase Indent button, the contents of the selected cells are indented by approximately one character width. If you click the Increase Indent button one too many times, click the Decrease Indent button to return the text to the previous indent position.

Steps 7–8

11	General Assessment
12	Consultation
13	Full assessment
14	Intermediate assessment
15	Minor assessment
16	Annual health exam
17	Sick notes
18	Hearing assessment
19	Speech assessment
20	Disability certificate
21	Travel cancellation illness verification
22	Private insurance form
23	Death certificate
24	Life insurance certificate

9 Select A27:A30 and then click the Increase Indent button.

10 Select A33:A36 and then click the Increase Indent button.

11 Select the range B10:G10. Hold down the Ctrl key and then click A11, A26, A32, A38, and A40.

12 Click the Bold button in the Font group.

> Use the Ctrl key to select multiple ranges or cells to which you want to apply a formatting option.

Steps 11–12

	A	B	C	D	E	F	G
10		*Fee	Preschool Patients	Other Patients	Total	New Fee	New Total
11	**General Assessment**						
12	Consultation	$ 94.50	27	72	$ 9,355.50	$ 100.17	$ 9,916.83
13	Full assessment						
14	Intermediate assessment						
15	Minor assessment						
16	Annual health exam	60.00	43	80	7,380.00	63.60	7,822.80
17	Sick notes	16.50	29	48	1,270.50	17.49	1,346.73
18	Hearing assessment	26.50	4	2	159.00	28.09	168.54
19	Speech assessment	31.50	7	5	378.00	33.39	400.68
20	Disability certificate						
21	Travel cancellation illness verification						
22	Private insurance form	85.00	6	18	2,040.00	90.10	2,162.40
23	Death certificate						
24	Life insurance certificate						
25							
26	**Specific Assessment**						
27	Day care assessment	55.00	34	0	1,870.00	58.30	1,982.20
28	Day care form	30.00	34	0	1,020.00	31.80	1,081.20
29	Camp physical assessment	40.00	10	33	1,720.00	42.40	1,823.20
30	Camp form						
31							
32	**Other Charges**						
33	Replication						
34	Telephone prescription renewal	16.50	24	54	1,287.00	17.49	1,364.22
35	Missed appointments						
36	Missed annual physical						
37							
38	**Total**				26,480.00		28,068.80
39							
40	**Increase in January Revenue:**						1,588.80

continues

13 Click in any cell to deselect the multiple cells.

14 Select B10:G10.

> In Activity 2.5, you increased the height of row 10 to 21.00. The Alignment group contains buttons that also allow you to control the alignment of the text between the top and bottom of the cell boundaries. In the next step, you will center the text vertically within the cells.

15 Click the Middle Align button ≣ in the Alignment group.

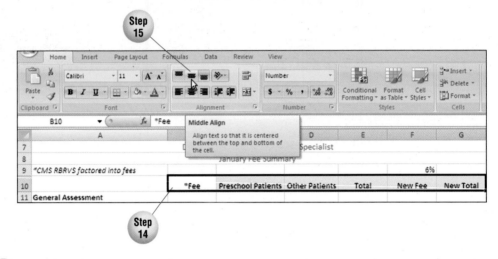

16 Deselect the range.

17 Make C30 the active cell.

> You want to insert a note in a comment to Sydney Larsen to confirm that there were no charges for camp forms in January.

18 Click the Review tab and then click the New Comment button in the Comments group.

> A yellow comment box displays anchored to the active cell with the user's name inserted in bold text at the top of the box and a blinking insertion point. In worksheets accessed by multiple users, the user's name is important to inform the reader of the name of the person who made the comment.

19 Type **Sydney, please confirm no camp forms were issued in January. Thanks.**

Steps 17–19

26	Specific Assessment				
27	Day care assessment	55.00	34	0	1,870.00
28	Day care form	30.00	34	0	1,020.00
29	Camp physical assessment	40.00	10		0.00
30	Camp form				
31					
32	Other Charges				
33	Replication				

Student Name:
Sydney, please confirm
no camp forms were
issued in January.
Thanks.

20 Click in any cell outside the comment box.

> The comment box closes and a diagonal red triangle appears in the upper right corner of C30 indicating a comment exists for the cell.

21 Right-click B28 and then click *Insert Comment* at the shortcut menu.

22 Type **Check fee. This is the same rate as last year.**

23 Click in any cell outside the comment box.

24 Hover the cell pointer over B28.

When you hover the cell pointer over a cell that contains a comment, the comment box appears.

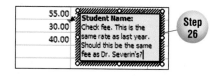

26	Specific Assessment	
27	Day care assessment	55.00
28	Day care form	30.00
29	Camp physical assessment	40.00
30	Camp form	

Student Name:
Check fee. This is the same rate as last year.

25 Right-click B28 and then click *Edit Comment* at the shortcut menu.

26 Add the following sentence to the end of the existing comment text:

Should this be the same fee as Dr. Severin's?

55.00
30.00
40.00

Student Name:
Check fee. This is the same rate as last year. Should this be the same fee as Dr. Severin's?

Step 26

27 Click in any cell outside the comment box.

28 Make A9 the active cell and then click the Next button ▣ in the Comments group in the Review tab.

Excel opens the comment box in B28.

29 Click the Next button in the Comments group.

Excel opens the comment box in C30.

30 Click the Next button and then click Cancel at the message indicating Excel has reached the end of the workbook to instruct Excel not to continue reviewing from the beginning of the workbook.

The Comments group also contains a Previous button ▣ to view the comment box prior to the active comment.

31 Click in any cell to remove the display of the comment in C30.

32 Save **ExcelMedS2-01.xlsx**.

In Brief

Change Horizontal or Vertical Alignment
1. Select cells.
2. Click desired alignment button.
3. Deselect cells.

Indent Text within Cells
1. Select cells.
2. Click Increase Indent button.
3. Deselect cells.

Insert Comment
1. Make active the cell in which to attach a comment.
2. Click Review tab.
3. Click New Comment.
4. Type comment text.
5. Click outside comment box.

In Addition

Printing Comments

By default, comments do not print with the worksheet. To print a worksheet with the comment boxes, you need to specify a *Comments* option at the Page Setup dialog box. Display the worksheet in Print Preview, click the Page Setup button, click the Sheet tab, and then click the down-pointing arrow next to *Comments* in the *Print* section (shown at the right). Choose to print the comment text at the end of the sheet or as displayed on the sheet.

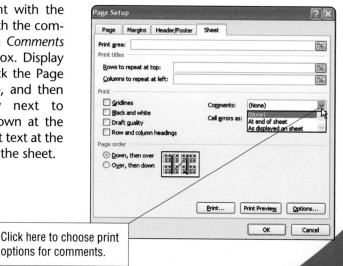

Click here to choose print options for comments.

Activity 2.9

Adding Borders; Copying Formats with Format Painter; Using Cell Styles

Borders in various styles and colors can be applied to display and print in selected cells within the worksheet. Borders can be added to the top, left, bottom, or right edge of a cell. Use borders to underscore headings or totals or to emphasize other cells. Format Painter copies formats from a selected cell to another cell. Use this feature to apply multiple format options from one cell to another cell. Cell Styles contain a group of predefined formatting options stored in a name. Styles are an efficient method to consistently apply formats, creating a professional, consistent worksheet appearance. Excel includes several pre-defined styles which you can apply or modify; you also can choose to create your own cell style.

Project

As you near completion of the report, you will spend time improving the presentation of the worksheet by adding borders and applying cell styles.

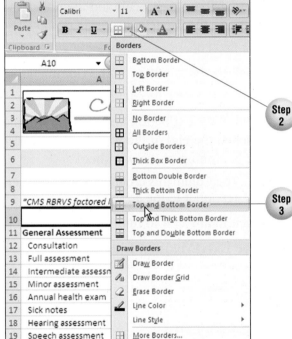

1. With **ExcelMedS2-01.xlsx** open, select A10:G10.

2. Click the Bottom Border button arrow in the Font group in the Home tab.

   A drop-down list of border style options displays. The *More Borders* option at the bottom of the list opens the Format Cells dialog box with the Border tab selected in which you can create a custom border.

3. Click *Top and Bottom Border* at the drop-down list.

4. Click in any cell to deselect the range and view the border.

5. Select A11, click the Top and Bottom Border button arrow, and then click *Outside Borders* at the drop-down list.

6. Select A26 and then click the Outside Borders button. (Do not click the arrow.)

   Since the Borders button updates to the most recently selected border style, you can apply the Outside Borders option to the active cell without displaying the drop-down list.

7. Select A32, click the Outside Borders button, and then deselect the cell.

8. Make E38 the active cell, click the Outside Borders button arrow, and then click *Top and Double Bottom Border* at the drop-down list.

   In the next steps, you will copy the formats from E38 to the other total values.

(9) With E38 still the active cell, double-click the Format Painter button ✐ in the Clipboard group.

> A moving marquee surrounds the source cell and a paintbrush displays attached to the cell pointer. This icon means that the formats are copied from the source cell and can be pasted to multiple cells or ranges. Single-clicking Format Painter allows you to copy formats to the next cell or range that you click. Double-click the Format Painter button to toggle the feature on until you turn it off by clicking Format Painter again.

(10) Click G38 and G40. Click the Format Painter button to turn off the feature.

Moving marquee in E38 indicates cell formats are being copied from this cell.

Step 10

(11) Select A7:A8.

> You decide to change the formatting of the these titles to one of the predefined cell styles that Excel provides.

(12) Click the Cell Styles button in the Styles group in the Home tab.

Step 12

(13) Move the mouse over several of the cell style designs in the drop-down gallery and watch Live Preview show you the style applied to the titles.

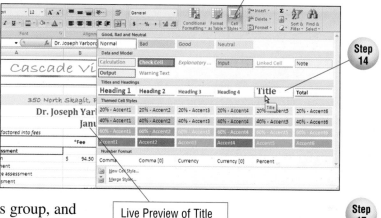

Step 14

(14) Click the *Title* style in the *Titles and Headings* section of the gallery.

(15) Select A10:G10, click the Cell Styles button in the Styles group, and then click the *Accent1* style in the *Themed Cell Styles* section.

Live Preview of Title style applied to A7:A8

(16) Select A11, A26, and A32 and apply the *Accent5* style in the *Themed Cell Styles* section in the Cell Styles drop-down gallery.

(17) Click the Page Layout tab.

Step 17

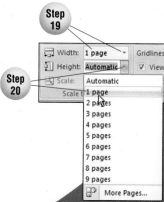

Step 18

(18) Click the Orientation button in the Page Setup group and then click *Landscape* at the drop-down list.

(19) Click the Width button arrow (currently displays *Automatic*) in the Scale to Fit group and then click *1 page* at the drop-down list.

Step 19

(20) Click the Height button arrow (currently displays *Automatic*) in the Scale to Fit group and then click *1 page* at the drop-down list.

Step 20

(21) Click the Quick Print button on the Quick Access toolbar.

(22) Save **ExcelMedS2-01.xlsx**.

In Brief

Add Borders
1. Select cells.
2. Click Borders button arrow in Font group.
3. Click desired border style.
4. Deselect cells.

Copy Formats
1. Make active cell containing source formats.
2. Click Format Painter button in Clipboard group.
3. Click destination cells.

Apply Cell Styles
1. Select cells.
2. Click Cell Styles button.
3. Click desired style in drop-down gallery.
4. Deselect cells.

Activity 2.10

Using Find and Replace

Use the Find command to search for specific labels or values that you want to verify or edit. The Find command will move to each cell containing the text you specify. The Replace command will search for a label, value, or format and automatically will replace it with another label, value, or format. The Find and Replace feature ensures that all occurrences of the specified text are included.

Project

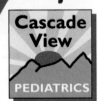

As part of your review before finalizing the fee summary report, you want to search the worksheet to make sure you included all of the forms. Sydney Larsen has also reviewed the report and requested that you change all occurrences of *assessment to evaluation*.

1 With **ExcelMedS2-01.xlsx** open, press Ctrl + Home to make A1 the active cell.

2 Click the Home tab.

3 Click the Find & Select button in the Editing group and then click *Find* at the drop-down list.

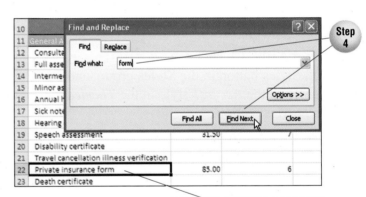

4 Type **form** in the *Find what* text box and then click the Find Next button.

> The first occurrence in A22 becomes active and contains the text *Private insurance form*.

? PROBLEM

Can't see the active cell? Drag the Find and Replace dialog box out of the way if the box is obscuring your view of the worksheet.

5 Click the Find Next button.

> The cell containing *Day care form* (A28) becomes active.

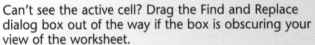

6 Click Find Next.

> The cell containing *Camp form* (A30) becomes active.

Active cell moves to the next occurrence each time you click the Find Next button.

7 Click the Find Next button.

> Excel returns to the first occurrence in A22. Although in this small worksheet you could easily have reviewed the form entries by scanning column A, in a large worksheet with many rows and columns, the Find command is an efficient method of moving to a specific cell. Typing a specific entry into the *Find what* text box could move you to a section title or label very quickly.

8 Click the Close button to close the Find and Replace dialog box.

9 Click the Find & Select button in the Editing group and then click *Replace* at the drop-down list.

10 Drag to select *form* in the *Find what* text box and then type **assessment**.

(11) Press Tab to move the insertion point to the *Replace with* text box and then type **evaluation**.

(12) Click the Replace All button.

Excel searches through the entire worksheet and automatically changes all occurrences of *assessment* to *evaluation*.

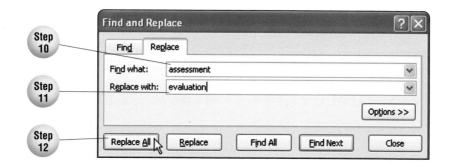

Step 10

Step 11

Step 12

(13) Click OK at the message that Excel has completed the search and has made nine replacements.

(14) Click the Close button to close the Find and Replace dialog box.

(15) Review the labels in the worksheet in column A and note the replacements that were made.

(16) Print the revised worksheet.

(17) Save **ExcelMedS2-01.xlsx**.

Step 15

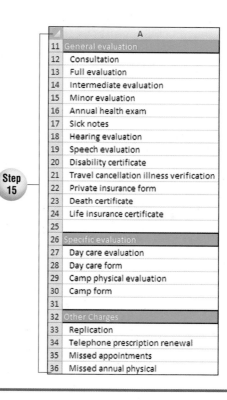

	A
11	General evaluation
12	Consultation
13	Full evaluation
14	Intermediate evaluation
15	Minor evaluation
16	Annual health exam
17	Sick notes
18	Hearing evaluation
19	Speech evaluation
20	Disability certificate
21	Travel cancellation illness verification
22	Private insurance form
23	Death certificate
24	Life insurance certificate
25	
26	Specific evaluation
27	Day care evaluation
28	Day care form
29	Camp physical evaluation
30	Camp form
31	
32	Other Charges
33	Replication
34	Telephone prescription renewal
35	Missed appointments
36	Missed annual physical

In Addition

Replacing Formats

You can use the Replace feature to find formats and replace them with other formats or no formatting. For example, you could use Excel to find all occurrences of bold and blue font color applied to a cell and replace with bold and green font color. At the Find and Replace dialog box with the Replace tab selected, click the Options button to display Format buttons to the right of the *Find what* and *Replace with* text boxes (shown at the right). Use these buttons to specify the required format options. The Preview box (initially displays *No Format Set*) displays the formats Excel will find and replace.

Activity 2.11

Freezing Panes; Changing the Zoom

When you scroll to the right or down to view parts of a worksheet that do not fit in the current window, some column or row headings may scroll off the screen making it difficult to relate text or values. The Freeze Panes option causes rows and columns to remain fixed when scrolling.

Magnify or reduce the worksheet display by dragging the Zoom slider bar button, clicking the Zoom In or Zoom Out buttons, or by specifying a percentage to zoom to at the Zoom dialog box. Changing the magnification does not affect printing since worksheets print at 100% unless scaling options are changed.

Project

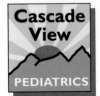

You will freeze row headings in the report to facilitate scrolling and practice with various Zoom settings to view more cells within the current window.

① With **ExcelMedS2-01.xlsx** open, make A11 the active cell.

② Click the View tab.

③ Click the Freeze Panes button in the Window group.

④ Click *Freeze Panes* at the drop-down list.

All rows above the active cell are frozen. A horizontal black line appears indicating which rows remain fixed when scrolling as shown in Figure E2.1.

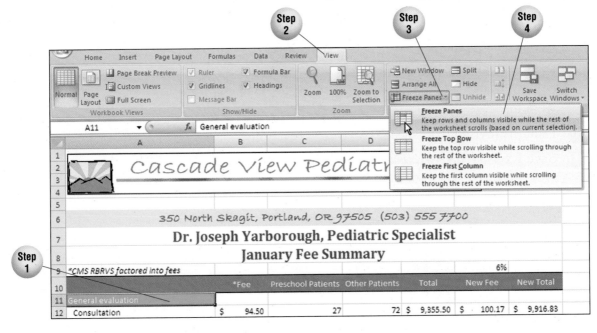

⑤ Press the Page Down key a few times to scroll down the worksheet.

Notice rows 1 through 10 do not scroll off the screen.

⑥ Press Ctrl + Home. Notice that Excel returns to A11 instead of A1 since A1 is frozen.

⑦ Click the Freeze Panes button in the Window group and then click *Unfreeze Panes*.

The Freeze Panes option changes to Unfreeze Panes when rows or columns have been frozen.

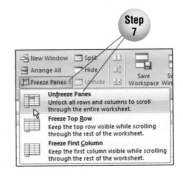

FIGURE E2.1 Worksheet with Panes Frozen

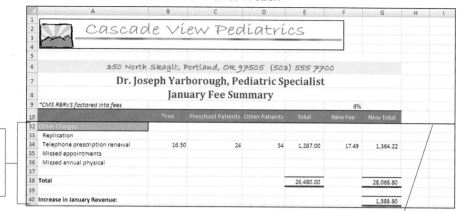

Rows 1 to 10 remain fixed in place as you scroll down.

A horizontal black line indicates the rows above are frozen.

In Brief

Freeze Panes
1. Make cell active below and right of row or column headings you want to freeze.
2. Click View tab.
3. Click Freeze Panes button.
4. Click *Freeze Panes*.

Change Zoom Setting
Drag Zoom slider bar button.
OR
Click Zoom In or Zoom Out buttons.
OR
Click zoom percentage value and choose magnification option at Zoom dialog box.

8 Practice dragging the button on the Zoom slider bar  (located at the right end of the Status bar above the system time) and watch the cells magnify and shrink as you drag right and left.

Step 8

9 Drag the slider bar button to the halfway mark on the slider bar to redisplay the worksheet at 100%.

10 Click over *100%* at the left edge of the slider bar to open the Zoom dialog box.

11 Click *75%* and then click OK.

12 Click the Zoom In button at the right side of the Zoom slider bar (displays as a plus symbol inside a circle).

13 Continue to click the Zoom In button until the zoom percentage returns to 100%.

> When the worksheet is set to 100% magnification, clicking the Zoom In or Zoom Out buttons at either side of the slider bar magnifies or shrinks the display of the worksheet by 10% each time the button is clicked.

Step 11

14 Save and then close **ExcelMedS2-01.xlsx**.

In Addition

Zoom to Selection

The View tab contains a Zoom group with three buttons to change zoom settings. Click the Zoom button in the Zoom group to open the Zoom dialog box. This is the same dialog box that you displayed in Step 10. Click the 100% button to return the view to 100%. Select a range of cells and then click the Zoom to Selection button to cause Excel to scale the zoom setting so that the selected range fills the worksheet area.

Activity 2.12

Adjusting Page Breaks in Page Break Preview

Page Break Preview allows you to view and adjust page breaks in a multipage worksheet. Page breaks are displayed as dashed or solid blue lines. A dashed line indicates the position of page breaks calculated automatically by Excel. If you do not like the position in which the page break has occurred, drag the blue line to a new location. In Normal View, insert your own page break at the Page Layout tab by clicking the Breaks button in the Page Setup group. At the Breaks drop-down list you can insert, remove, or reset all page breaks.

Project North Shore Medical Clinic's Supplies Inventory and Exam Room Standard Cost report needs to be printed in its entirety. You will preview the page breaks in Page Break Preview and adjust the location of page breaks.

1. Open **NSMCSupplies.xlsx** and use Save As to name it **ExcelMedS2-02**.

2. Click the View tab and then click the Page Break Preview button.

3. Click OK if the Welcome to Page Break Preview message box displays.

4. Change the zoom setting to 80%.

5. Review the worksheet in Page Break Preview as shown in Figure E2.2.

6. Position the mouse pointer on the vertical dashed blue line between Page 1 and Page 3 until the pointer changes to a double-headed left- and right-pointing arrow and then drag the page break to the right edge of the worksheet (column N).

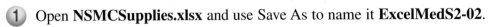

Step 6

Drag the dashed blue line to the right past column N at the right edge of the worksheet.

7. Display the worksheet in Print Preview to view the new layout.

8. Close Print Preview.

9. Click the Page Layout tab.

10. Look at the value in the *Scale* text box in the Scale to Fit group. Excel automatically calculated this number as the percent of 100 that cells had to be reduced when you dragged the page break to fit more columns on a page.

FIGURE E2.2 Supplies Inventory and Exam Room Standard Cost Report in Page Break Preview

	A	B	C	D	E	F	G	H	I	J	K	L	M	N
1	North Shore Medical Clinic								Exam Room Standard Cost					
2	Clinic Supplies Inventory Units and Price								GE- General Room, DT- Dermatology Room, WC - Women and Children's Room					
3	Item	Unit	Price	Standard Stock		GE Room 1	GE Room 2	GE Room 3	WC Room 4	DT Room 5	WC Room 6	WC Room 7	WC Room 8	Total Cost
4	Sterile powder-free synthetic gloves, size S	per 100	35.95	4		71.90	71.90	71.90	71.90	71.90	71.90	71.90	71.90	575.20
5	Sterile powder-free synthetic gloves, size M	per 100	35.95	4		71.90	71.90	71.90	71.90	71.90	71.90	71.90	71.90	575.20
6	Sterile powder-free synthetic gloves, size L	per 100	35.95	4		71.90	71.90	71.90	71.90	71.90	71.90	71.90	71.90	575.20
7	Sterile powder-free latex gloves, size Small	per 100	16.25	4		32.50	32.50	32.50	32.50	32.50	32.50	32.50	32.50	260.00
8	Sterile powder-free latex gloves, size Medium	per 100	16.25	4		32.50	32.50	32.50	32.50	32.50	32.50	32.50	32.50	260.00
9	Sterile powder-free latex gloves, size Large	per 100	16.25	4		32.50	32.50	32.50	32.50	32.50	32.50	32.50	32.50	260.00
10	Sterile powder-free vinyl gloves, size Small	per 100	11.50	4		23.00	23.00	23.00	23.00	23.00	23.00	23.00	23.00	184.00
11	Sterile powder-free vinyl gloves, size Medium	per 100	11.50	4		23.00	23.00	23.00	23.00	23.00	23.00	23.00	23.00	184.00
12	Sterile powder-free vinyl gloves, size Large	per 100	11.50	4		23.00	23.00	23.00	23.00	23.00	23.00	23.00	23.00	184.00
13	Disposable earloop mask	per 50	5.61	8		11.22	11.22	11.22	11.22	11.22	11.22	11.22	11.22	89.76
14	Disposable patient gown	per dozen	7.90	16		15.80	15.80	15.80	15.80	15.80	15.80	15.80	15.80	126.40
15	Disposable patient slippers	per dozen	4.27	16		4.27	4.27	4.27	4.27	4.27	4.27	4.27	4.27	34.16
16	Cotton patient gown	per dozen	133.00	16		0.00	0.00	0.00	133.00	133.00	133.00	133.00	133.00	665.00
17	Cotton patient robe	per dozen	147.00	16		0.00	0.00	0.00	147.00	147.00	147.00	147.00	147.00	735.00
18	Disposable examination table paper	per roll	8.90	8		8.90	8.90	8.90	8.90	8.90	8.90	8.90	8.90	71.20
19	Lab coat, size Small	each	32.95	12		0.00	0.00	0.00	0.00	32.95	0.00	0.00	0.00	32.95
20	Lab coat, size Medium	each	32.95	12		0.00	0.00	0.00	0.00	32.95	0.00	0.00	0.00	32.95
21	Lab coat, size Large	each	32.95	12		0.00	0.00	0.00	0.00	32.95	0.00	0.00	0.00	32.95
22	Disposable shoe cover	per 100	37.75	1		0.00	0.00	0.00	0.00	0.00	0.00	0.00	0.00	7.09
23	Disposable bouffant cap	per 100	7.89	2		0.00	0.00	0.00	0.00	0.00	0.00	0.00	0.00	7.09
24	CPR micromask	each	18.95	4		18.95	18.95	18.95	18.95	0.00	18.95	18.95	18.95	128.45
25	Weight scale	each	410.87	0		410.87	410.87	410.87	410.87	0.00	410.87	410.87	410.87	2876.09
26	Pediatric weight scale	each	192.50	0		0.00	0.00	0.00	192.50	0.00	192.50	192.50	192.50	770.00
27	Syringe	per dozen	16.99	16		33.98	33.98	33.98	33.98	33.98	33.98	33.98	33.98	271.84
28	Sutures	per dozen	32.95	16		65.90	65.90	65.90	65.90	65.90	65.90	65.90	65.90	527.20
29	Needles	per dozen	18.55	16		37.10	37.10	37.10	37.10	37.10	37.10	37.10	37.10	296.80
30	Sharps disposal unit	each	26.77	16		26.77	26.77	26.77	26.77	26.77	26.77	26.77	26.77	214.16
31	Tongue depressor	per 100	2.75	4		2.75	2.75	2.75	2.75	2.75	2.75	2.75	2.75	19.25
32	Laryngoscope	each	125.88	4		125.88	125.88	125.88	125.88	0.00	125.88	125.88	125.88	881.16
33	Cutters	per dozen	35.50	16		35.50	35.50	0.00	0.00	35.50	0.00	0.00	0.00	106.50
34	Knives	per dozen	22.75	16		0.00	0.00	0.00	22.75	0.00	0.00	0.00	0.00	22.75
35	Shears	each	9.33	8		9.33	9.33	9.33	9.33	9.33	9.33	9.33	9.33	74.64
36	Disposable skin stapler	per dozen	87.34	4		0.00	0.00	0.00	0.00	87.34	0.00	0.00	0.00	87.34
37	Disposable skin staple remover	per dozen	92.40	4		0.00	0.00	0.00	0.00	92.40	0.00	0.00	0.00	92.40

Page 1   Page 3

11 Click the Orientation button in the Page Setup group and then click *Landscape* at the drop-down list.

In Brief

View Page Break
1. Click View tab.
2. Click Page Break Preview button.
OR
Click Page Break Preview button in Status bar.

Adjust Page Break
Drag horizontal and/or vertical dashed blue line to desired location in Page Break Preview.

12 Scroll down the worksheet and view the position of the dashed blue line indicating a new page break has been added.

13 Display the worksheet in Print Preview. Notice that Excel does not automatically scale the cells larger to fill up the space created when the page width was increased at Step 11.

14 Close Print Preview.

15 Select the value in the *Scale* text box in the Scale to Fit group, type **75** and then press Enter.

Width: Automatic
Height: Automatic
Scale: 75%
Scale to Fit

Step 15

16 Scroll down the worksheet and notice the location of the dashed blue line has been adjusted when the scaling percentage was increased.

17 Position the mouse pointer on the horizontal dashed blue line until the pointer changes to a double-headed up-and-down-pointing arrow and then drag the page break between rows 40 and 41.

Step 17

36	Disposable skin stapler	per dozen	37.34	4	0.00	0.00	0.00
37	Disposable skin staple remover	per dozen	92.40	4	0.00	0.00	0.00
38	Vaginal specula	each	199.35	4	0.00	0.00	0.00
39	Urine strips	per 100	7.76	12	7.76	7.76	7.76
40	Sterile water	per dozen	18.55	12	18.55	18.55	18.55
41	Gauze	per 100	4.48	16	8.96	8.96	8.96
42	Cotton pads	per 500	3.22	16	3.22	3.22	3.22
43	Cotton rolls	per 500	5.67	16	5.67	5.67	5.67
44	Thermometers	each	9.43	8	9.43	9.43	9.43
45	Disposable thermometer tips	per 100	4.12	48	8.24	8.24	8.24
46	Pediatric ear thermometer	each	88.96	4	0.00	0.00	0.00
47	Blood pressure cuff	each	44.65	8	44.65	44.65	44.65
48	Safety goggles	per dozen	18.43	8	18.43	18.43	18.43
49	Nasal irrigator	per dozen	23.14	20	46.28	46.28	46.28
50	Disinfectant	each	4.12	12	4.12	4.12	4.12
51	Alcohol swabs	per dozen	3.22	48	12.88	12.88	12.88
52	Clipboard	each	0.88	12	1.76	1.76	1.76
53	Patient chart	per 100	4.11		4.11	4.11	4.11
54	Lab requisition	per 100	3.65		3.65	3.65	3.65

18 Click the View tab and then click the Normal button in the Workbook Views group.

19 If necessary, scroll down the worksheet until you can see the dashed black line between rows 40 and 41. This line indicates the page break you created at Step 17.

The row at which the dashed blue line is positioned may vary depending on your printer and print settings.

20 Click the Quick Print button on the Quick Access toolbar.

37	Disposable skin staple remover	per dozen	92.40
38	Vaginal specula	each	199.35
39	Urine strips	per 100	7.76
40	Sterile water	per dozen	18.55
41	Gauze	per 100	4.48
42	Cotton pads	per 500	3.22

Step 19

21 Save and then close **ExcelMedS2-02.xlsx**.

In Addition

Repeating Titles when Printing Large Worksheets

When printing worksheets that span multiple pages, column and row headings can be repeated at the top or left edges of a page to make the print-outs easier to read. To do this, display the Page Setup dialog box with the Sheet tab active. In the *Print titles* section, enter the required cell addresses in the *Rows to repeat at top* and/or *Columns to repeat at left* text boxes as shown below.

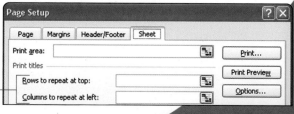

Repeat row or column titles on multiple-page worksheets.

Features Summary

Feature	Ribbon Tab, Group	Button	Quick Access Toolbar	Keyboard Shortcut
Accounting Number format	Home, Number	$		
align text left	Home, Alignment			
align text right	Home, Alignment			
bold	Home, Font	B		Ctrl + B
borders	Home, Font			
cell styles	Home, Styles			
center	Home, Alignment			
clear cell	Home, Editing			
column width	Home, Cells	Format		
Comma style	Home, Number	,		
copy	Home, Clipboard			Ctrl + C
cut	Home, Clipboard			Ctrl + X
decrease decimal	Home, Number			
decrease indent	Home, Alignment			Ctrl + Alt + Shift + Tab
delete cell, column, or row	Home, Cells	Delete		
edit comment	Review, Comments			
fill color	Home, Font			
find	Home, Editing			Ctrl + F
font	Home, Font	Calibri		Ctrl + 1
font color	Home, Font	A		Ctrl + 1
font size	Home, Font	11		Ctrl + 1
Format Painter	Home, Clipboard			
freeze panes	View, Window	Freeze Panes		
increase decimal	Home, Number			
increase indent	Home, Alignment			Ctrl + Alt + Tab
insert cell, column, or row	Home, Cells	Insert		
italic	Home, Font	I		Ctrl + I
insert comment	Review, Comments			Shift + F2
merge and center	Home, Alignment			
middle-align	Home, Alignment			
Page Break Preview	View Workbook Views	Page Break Preview		

continues

Feature	Ribbon Tab, Group	Button	Quick Access Toolbar	Keyboard Shortcut
paste	Home, Clipboard			Ctrl + V
Percent style	Home, Number	%		Ctrl + Shift + %
replace	Home, Editing			Ctrl + H
row height	Home, Cells	Format		
Spelling	Review, Proofing	ABC		F7
Thesaurus	Review, Proofing			Shift + F7
undo an action				Ctrl + Z
zoom	View, Zoom			

Knowledge Check

Completion: In the space provided at the right, write in the correct term, command, or option.

1. Use this feature to remove everything from a cell including text and formats.

2. Make a cell active anywhere in this row to insert a new row between 11 and 12.

3. Make a cell active anywhere in this column to insert a new column between E and F.

4. Use this function key to add dollar symbols in front of row or column numbers to make the addresses absolute references.

5. Perform this action with the mouse on a column boundary to adjust the width to the length of the longest entry.

6. This term refers to the feature where Excel shows the results of a format option while pointing to the option in a drop-down list or gallery.

7. By default, cells are initially set to this format.

8. Click this button in the Alignment group in the Home tab to center cells vertically between the top and bottom cell boundaries.

9. Click this button in the Clipboard group in the Home tab to copy the formats of the active cell.

10. This feature stores predefined format options for a cell.

11. Make this cell active to freeze rows 1 through 9.

12. List three methods for changing the zoom magnification to view more cells in the current window.

Skills Review

Review 1 Editing and Clearing Cells; Deleting Columns and Rows

Columbia
River
General
Hospital

1. Open **CRGHLabReqRpt.xlsx**.
2. Save the workbook with Save As and name it **ExcelMedS2-R1**.
3. Change the fee in E30 from *17.87* to *16.35*.
4. Clear the contents of A3:A4 including formatting.
5. Clear the contents of J40:P40.
6. Change the label in A26 from *Other* to *Immunology*.
7. Make active B6 and then type the label **12 hr fast**.
8. Make active B24 and then type the label **30 min rest**.
9. Delete row 3 and column C.
10. Save **ExcelMedS2-R1.xlsx**.

Review 2 Moving and Copying Cells; Inserting and Deleting Rows; Freezing Panes

Columbia
River
General
Hospital

1. With **ExcelMedS2-R1.xlsx** open, move A2 to A3 and then merge and center A3 within the range A3:F3.
2. Move E44 to A44.
3. Make G5 the active cell and freeze panes.
4. Copy the formula in F44 to I44, K44, M44, and N44.
5. Delete row 2.
6. Delete the row for which no requisitions were ordered in January (*Other swabs*).
7. Insert a new row between *Other tests* and *HDL & LDL* and type **Antiphospholipid antibodies** in column A of the new row.
8. Add the following data for Antiphospholipid antibodies:

Lab Code	29011	Fee	25.57
Reqs	2	Insured Reqs	0
Third Party Bill Reqs	0	Patient Direct Bill Reqs	2

9. Enter the formulas required to finish the total calculations for antiphospholipid antibodies requisitions.
10. Save **ExcelMedS2-R1.xlsx**.

Review 3 Adjusting Column Width; Replacing Data; Formatting Numbers; Indenting Text

Columbia
River
General
Hospital

1. With **ExcelMedS2-R1.xlsx** open, AutoFit columns A, B, and C.
2. Change the width of column G to *1.00 (12 pixels)*.
3. Select columns E, H, J, and L and then adjust the width to *6.00 (47 pixels)*.
4. Use the Replace feature to replace all occurrences of the value *15.45* with *16.23*.
5. Format the values in columns I, K, M, and N to Comma style.
6. Format the values in column F to the Accounting Number format.
7. Format the values in column O to display with two decimal places.

8. Indent once:
> A4:A15
> A18:A22
> A25:A29
> A32:A36
> A39:A41

9. Save **ExcelMedS2-R1.xlsx**.

Review 4 Changing Font, Font Attributes, and Alignment; Applying Cell Styles; Adding Borders and Shading; Using Format Painter

Columbia River General Hospital

1. With **ExcelMedS2-R1.xlsx** open, merge and center the title in A1 across columns A through O.
2. Change the font in A1 to 16-point Bookman Old Style. *Note: If Bookman Old Style is not available on your computer system, substitute another font such as Times New Roman.*
3. Change the fill color to Purple, Accent 4, Lighter 60% in A1.
4. Center the labels in C3:O3 both horizontally and vertically.
5. Select A2:O2, apply bold, and change the fill color to Purple, Accent 4, Lighter 40%.
6. Select C3:O3, and apply the Accent4 cell style.
7. Select cell A3 and apply the Accent2 cell style. Use format painter to copy the formatting from A3 to A17, A24, A31, and A38.
8. Add a top and bottom border to A3:O3.
9. Add a top and double bottom border to F43, I43, K43, M43, and N43.
10. Make cell B3 active and then type **Comments**. Use Format Painter to copy the formats from C3 to B3.
11. Save **ExcelMedS2-R1.xlsx**.

Review 5 Inserting Comments; Modifying Page Breaks in Page Break Preview; Changing the Zoom

Columbia River General Hospital

1. With **ExcelMedS2-R1.xlsx** open, make O6 active and then insert the following comment:
> **Check billings. Two extra requisitions have been added to Insured, Third Party, or Patient Direct.**

2. Make O14 active and then add the same comment text as in Step 1.
3. Display the worksheet in Print Preview. Notice the worksheet will print on two pages.
4. Close the Print Preview window.
5. Display Page Break Preview.
6. Change the Zoom to *85%*.
7. Drag the page break between Page 1 and Page 2 to the right edge of the worksheet.
8. Print the worksheet.
9. Change the orientation to landscape. Adjust the scale percentage until you find the optimum value that fills the page width and height to 1 page.
10. Save, print, and then close **ExcelMedS2-R1xlsx**.

Skills Assessment

Assessment 1 Changing Zoom; Adjusting Column Width; Changing Font Color and Fill Color

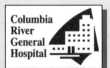

1. Tracy Fitzgerald, manager of support services at Columbia River General Hospital, has asked you to make changes to a worksheet containing recent Canadian healthcare statistical data. Tracy and Michelle Tan, CEO, will be presenting at a medical conference in Vancouver, British Columbia. Their presentation on the differences between patient costs and outcomes between United States and Canada will rely heavily on the data in this worksheet.
2. Open **CRGHCdnHealthStats.xlsx**.
3. Save the workbook with Save As and name it **ExcelMedS2-A1.xlsx**.
4. Make the following changes:
   a. Change the zoom so you can view as much of the worksheet as possible to minimize horizontal scrolling. Make sure the cells are still readable. *Note: Depending on your monitor size and resolution setting, change the custom setting to a value between 70% and 90%.*
   b. Adjust all column widths to the length of the longest entry (AutoFit).
   c. Change the color of the shading behind the title *Total Healthcare Costs in Canada*. You determine the color.
   d. Change the font color and the shading color for *Breakdown of Healthcare Costs by Procedures in Canada* and *Mortality Rates by Age/Sex in Canada by 100,000*. You determine the colors.
   e. Change the font color and the shading color for *Leading Causes of Death in Canada 2008* and *Physical activity by age group and sex in Canada 2008*. You determine the colors.
5. Change the page orientation to landscape.
6. Print page 1 only of the worksheet. To do this, click *Page(s)* in the *Print range* section of the Print dialog box and then type **1** in the *From* and *To* text boxes.
7. Save **ExcelMedS2-A1.xlsx**.

Assessment 2 Editing Cells; Inserting and Deleting Rows; Moving and Copying Cells; Formatting a Worksheet; Page Break Preview and Adjusting Page Breaks

1. There is still work to be done on the Canadian healthcare statistical data worksheet before Tracy and Michelle can prepare the presentation for the conference in Vancouver. Tracy has given you the following changes.
2. With **ExcelMedS2-A1.xlsx** open, edit the worksheet using the following information:
   a. In the *Total Healthcare Costs in Canada* section, for the year 2006, *Hospitals* should be *15,326* instead of *14,175*.
   b. In the *Total Healthcare Costs in Canada* section of the worksheet, insert a new column before *2005* and then enter the data as follows: *Note: Format the column the same as the column to the right when the Insert Options button appears.*

	2004
Hospitals	10299.00
Other institutions	8204.70
Physicians	21978.00
Other professionals	21576.70
Drugs	24660.80
Other	20792.80

c. The formula to sum total healthcare costs for each year is missing. Enter the correct formula for the first year, 2004 (Q10) and then copy the formula to R10, S10, T10, and U10.

d. Format the numeric cells in the *Total Healthcare Costs in Canada* section of the worksheet to comma style with zero decimal places. Adjust column widths after formatting to AutoFit.

e. Type **in millions of dollars** in P2. Apply bold and italics to the label.

f. Change the alignment of any headings throughout the entire worksheet that could be improved in appearance.

g. Merge and center A1, A25, I1, I29, and P1 over the columns in the respective sections.

h. Move P1:U10 (*Total Healthcare Costs in Canada* section) to I58:N67. Adjust column widths after moving the cells as necessary.

i. Apply font, border, and color changes you think enhance the appearance of the worksheet.

3. Display the worksheet in Page Break Preview and then adjust page break(s) to improve the logical flow of the printout.

4. Print the worksheet in landscape orientation.

5. Save **ExcelMedS2-A1.xlsx**.

Assessment 3 Editing and Moving Cells; Entering Formulas; Absolute Referencing; Formatting Numeric Cells

Columbia River General Hospital

1. Tracy has reviewed the latest printout of the Canadian healthcare statistical data worksheet and noted the following changes to be made.

2. With **ExcelMedS2-A1.xlsx** open, display the worksheet in Normal view.

3. Complete the worksheet using the following information:

a. Type the following label in A60:
    Source: Statistics Canada, http://www.statcan.ca

b. In the *Breakdown of Healthcare Costs by Procedures in Canada* section, the data for 2009 was omitted. The costs for 2009 are the same as 2008 with the following exceptions:

Average	12.27
Consultations	78.94
Major assessments	22
Diagnostic	23.55
Hospital care days	19.78

Move the label *Overall Averages* from N3 to O3 and then type the data for 2008 in the blank cells adjacent to 2008 including calculating the total in N20. Autofit column N.

c. Cancer and cardiac disease are the two top leading causes of death in Canada in 2008. In G3 and H3, Tracy would like a total for males and a total for females of these two diseases **only** from the *Leading Causes of Death in Canada* section. In F3, calculate the total of male and female cardiac and cancer cases as a percentage of E18.

   d. Format F3 to percent with 1 decimal place.

   e. Enter the formula in B20 that will calculate the total of deaths by psychoses and suicide as a percentage of E18. Format the result to percent with 1 decimal place.

   f. Enter the formula in B21 that will calculate the increase in death by psychoses and suicide in the next year. Use the percent in D21 as the increase and reference D21 as an absolute reference. Format the result to comma style.

4. Select and then print the following two sections of the worksheet. (Print the selected ranges only. To do this click *Selection* in the *Print range* section of the Print dialog box with the range selected.)

       Breakdown of Healthcare Costs by Procedures in Canada I1:N20
       Leading Causes of Death in Canada 2008 A1:H21

5. Save **ExcelMedS2-A1.xlsx**.

Assessment 4 Performing Spell Check; Adjusting Column Width; Editing and Clearing Cells; Using Replace

1. Further research at the Statistics Canada Web site has revealed that some input errors exist in the Canadian healthcare statistics worksheet. Make the following changes to the worksheet.

2. With **ExcelMedS2-A1.xlsx** open, make the following corrections:

   a. Perform a spelling check and correct any errors that occur.

   b. AutoFit all column widths except column F which should be set to 8.

   c. Correct the following data entry errors in the *Physical activity by age group and sex in Canada 2008* section:

15–19 years, Females, Physically active:	830,212
20–24 years, Males, Physically inactive:	392,789
25–34 years, Males, Physically active:	472,345
35–44 years, Females, Physically inactive:	1,567,954
65–74 years, Males, Physically inactive:	736,854
75 years and over, Females, Physically active:	69,124

   d. Clear the contents of I4:N4.

   e. Make O5 the active cell and enter the formula that will calculate the overall average from 2005 to 2009 for *Major surgery* healthcare costs as =SUM(j5:n5)/5. Copy this formula to the remaining rows in the section. Format the values to one decimal place.

   f. Replace all occurrences of *Disease* with *Illness*. Be careful that other word forms of Disease (such as Diseases) are changed appropriately.

   g. Make cell A62 active, type **Date:**, and then type today's date.

3. Display the Page Setup dialog box. Click the Margins tab and then change the top, bottom, left, and right margins to 0.5-inch. Click the Page tab and then click *Fit to [1] page(s) wide by [1] page(s) tall.* Click OK.

4. Print **ExcelMedS2-A1.xlsx**.

5. Save and then close **ExcelMedS2-A1.xlsx**.

Assessment 5 Finding Information on Dates

HELP

1. Use Excel's Help feature to find more information on how Excel stores dates and how they can be used in a formula.
2. Open **ExcelMedS2-A1.xlsx**.
3. Add the label *Presentation Date:* to A63.
4. Enter the date *February 28, 2011* in B63.
5. Add the label *Final Preparation Date:* in A64.
6. Create a formula in B64 that will subtract 5 days from the presentation date.
7. Save **ExcelMedS2-A1.xlsx**.
8. Print **ExcelMedS2-A1.xlsx**.
9. Change the presentation date to *January 31, 2008*.
10. Print **ExcelMedS2-A1.xlsx**.
11. Save and then close **ExcelMedS2-A1.xlsx**.

Assessment 6 Locating Information on U.S. Healthcare Costs

1. Tracy Fitzgerald has asked you to research healthcare costs in the United States for the presentation at the medical conference in Vancouver. Search the Internet for healthcare cost statistics for the United States.
2. Create a workbook that summarizes the information you found.
3. Include the sources for your data in the workbook.
4. Save the workbook and name it **ExcelMedS2-A6**.
5. Print and then close **ExcelMedS2-A6.xlsx**.

Marquee Challenge

Challenge 1 Preparing a Weekly Staffing Schedule for Neurology

1. Create the worksheet shown in Figure E2.3 including all formatting options. Use your best judgment to determine font, font size, font and fill colors, column widths, and/or row heights.
2. Change the page orientation to landscape.
3. Save the workbook and name it **ExcelMedS2-C1**.
4. Print and then close **ExcelMedS2-C1.xlsx**.

Challenge 2 Preparing a Radiology Requisition Form

1. Open the workbook named **CRGHRadiologyReq.xlsx**.
2. Edit and format the worksheet as shown in Figure E2.4 including performing a spelling check. Use your best judgment to match as closely as possible the colors and fonts shown.
3. Save the workbook and name it **ExcelMedS2-C2**.
4. Print and then close **ExcelMedS2-C2.xlsx**.

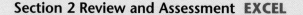

FIGURE E2.3 Challenge 1

Columbia River General Hospital							
Staffing Worksheet							

Dept	Neurology	Shift 1	7 am - 7 pm	*Rotation*			
Beds	6	Shift 2	7 pm - 7 am	2 days followed by 2 nights			
				4 on followed by 5 off			

Bed	Shift	Mon	Tue	Wed	Thu	Fri	Sat	Sun
1	1	McAllister	McAllister	Keller	Keller	Rashmi	Rashmi	Hillman
1	2	Yoshiko	Yoshiko	McAllister	McAllister	Huang	Huang	Baird
2	1	Hillman	Graham	Johan	Johan	McKenna	Petrovic	Zukic
2	2	Baird	Hillman	Hillman	Zukic	Zukic	Graham	Graham
3	1	Graham	Baird	Santos	Santos	Bernis	McKenna	Huang
3	2	Santos	Santos	Bernis	Bernis	Anatolius	Alvarez	Alvarez
4	1	Jorgensen	Jorgensen	Wei	Wei	Vezina	Zukic	Petrovic
4	2	McKenna	Wells	Wells	Jenkins	Johan	Johan	McKenna
5	1	Alvarez	Alvarez	Yoshiko	Yoshiko	Orlowski	Bernis	Jenkins
5	2	Petrovic	Petrovic	Jorgensen	Jorgensen	Jenkins	Anatolius	Lind
6	1	Huang	Biorje	Baird	Wells	Wells	Tomasz	Anatolius
6	2	Keller	Keller	Rashmi	Rashmi	Wei	Wei	Tomasz

FIGURE E2.4 Challenge 2

Columbia River General Hospital				
Radiology Requisition				
Patient LastName		Date		
Patient FirstName		Office Use Only		
Chart No		Dept Charge Code		
Physician		Amount		
Technician			Left	Right
Esophagus		Ribs		
Upper G.I. Series		Sternoclavicular Joints		
Small Bowel		Clavicle		
Barium Enema		Shoulder		
		A.C. Joints		
Acute Abdomen		Scapula		
Chest		Humerus		
Sternum		Elbow		
Facial Bones		Forearm		
Mandible		Write		
Nasal Bones		Hand		
Skull		Finger or Thumb		
Sinuses		Hip		
T.M. Joints		Femur		
Cervical Spine		Knee		
Thoracic Spine		Tibia and Fibula		
Lumbosacral Spine		Ankle		
Pelvis		Heel		
Sacrum and Coccyx		Foot		
		Toe		
*Esophagus, Stomach or Small Bowel		**Mammogram		

Nothing to eat or drink after midnight prior to examination.
**Wear separate blouse with skirt or slacks.*

Excel SECTION 3

Using Functions, Adding Visual Elements, Printing, and Working with Tables

Skills

- Create AVERAGE, COUNT, MAX, and MIN formulas to perform statistical analysis
- Create TODAY, NOW, and DATE formulas
- Create an IF formula to return a result based on a logical test
- Create, edit, and format a column chart
- Create, edit, and format a pie chart
- Insert, size, and move a picture and clip art
- Draw shapes and text boxes
- Change margins
- Center a worksheet horizontally and vertically
- Scale a worksheet to fit within a set number of pages
- Work with a worksheet in Page Layout view
- Insert headers and footers
- Format data as a table
- Sort and filter a table

Projects Overview

Calculate statistics and set print options for the standard exam room supplies report; compare discounts from two medical supply vendors and add graphics to the report; calculate dates in the dermatology patient tracking worksheet; create charts summarizing dermatology diagnosis by age group of patient.

Calculate statistical functions, add dates, calculate expense variance, add a logo, sort, and set print options for a quarterly expense report; create a chart, draw objects, and add clip art to a rent and maintenance cost report.

Finish a weekly adult cardiac bypass surgery report; calculate average standard costs for cardiac surgery patient stays; create charts, add clip art, and change print options for a quarterly expense report; filter and sort the cardiac nurse casual call list; filter and sort the nursing professional development list; create and format a patient cost report and a chart on U.S. cancer statistics.

Activity
3.1

Using Statistical Functions
AVERAGE, COUNT, MAX, and MIN

You learned about functions when you used the Sum button in Section 1. Excel includes numerous other built-in formulas that are grouped into function categories. The Statistical category contains several functions that can be used to perform statistical analysis on data, such as calculating medians, variances, frequencies, and so on. The structure of a function formula begins with the equals sign (=), followed by the name of the function, and then the argument within parentheses. *Argument* is the term given to the values to be included in the calculation. The structure of the argument is dependent on the function being used and can include a single range of cells, multiple ranges, single cell references, or a combination thereof.

Project Lee Elliott, office manager of North Shore Medical Clinic, would like you to compile statistics on the cost of supplies for eight exam rooms.

1. Open **NSMCSupplies.xlsx**.

2. Save the workbook with Save As and name it **ExcelMedS3-01**.

3. Make F4 the active cell and then freeze the panes.

4. Type the following labels in the cells indicated:

A65	**Average exam room standard cost:**
A66	**Maximum exam room standard cost:**
A67	**Minimum exam room standard cost:**
A68	**Count of exam room items:**

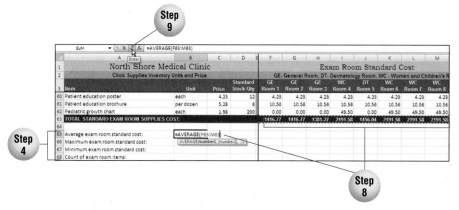

5. Make B65 the active cell.

   In the next steps, you will insert the AVERAGE function to determine the arithmetic mean of the total cells in row 63. If an empty cell or a cell containing text is included in the argument, Excel ignores the cell when determining the result. If, however, the cell contains a zero value, it is included in the average calculation.

6. Click the Sum button arrow in the Editing group in the Home tab.

7. Click *Average* in the drop-down list.

   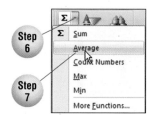

   Excel inserts the formula *=AVERAGE()* in the active cell with an insertion point between the parentheses. Since no values are immediately above or left of the active cell, Excel does not offer a suggested range. In the next step, you will drag to select the correct range and then complete the formula.

(8) Position the cell pointer over F63, hold down the left mouse button, drag right to M63, and then release the left mouse button.

(9) Press Enter or click the Enter button on the Formula bar.

Excel returns the result *1804.64625* in B65.

(10) Make B66 the active cell.

(11) Click the Sum button arrow and then click *Max* at the drop-down list.

The MAX function returns the largest value in the argument.

(12) Type **f63:m63** and then press Enter.

Excel returns the result *2191.58* in B66. Typing the range into the formula is sometimes faster if you are sure of the starting and ending cell references.

Step 12

65	Average exam room standard cost:	1804.64625
66	Maximum exam room standard cost:	=MAX(f63:m63)
67	Minimum exam room standard cost:	MAX(number1, [number2], ...)
68	Count of exam room items:	

(13) With B67 the active cell, type the function **=min(f63:m63)** and then press Enter.

65	Average exam room standard cost:	1804.64625
66	Maximum exam room standard cost:	2191.58
67	Minimum exam room standard cost:	1381.27
68	Count of exam room items:	

Step 13

The MIN function returns the smallest value in the argument. Type the entire function directly into the cell if you know the name of the function you want to use and the structure of the argument.

(14) With B68 the active cell, type the function **=count(d4:d62)** and then press Enter.

COUNT returns the number of cells that contain numbers or numbers that have been formatted as text and

65	Average exam room standard cost:	1804.64625
66	Maximum exam room standard cost:	2191.58
67	Minimum exam room standard cost:	1381.27
68	Count of exam room items:	=count(d4:d62)

Step 14

dates. Empty cells, text labels, or error values in the range are ignored.

(15) Format B65:B68 to the Number format with two decimal places.

To change the Number format, click the Number Format button arrow and then click *Number* at the drop-down list.

(16) Click in any cell to deselect B65:B68.

(17) Save, print, and then close **ExcelMedS3-01.xlsx**.

In Brief

AVERAGE, MAX, MIN, COUNT Functions
1. Make desired cell active.
2. Click Sum button arrow.
3. Click desired function.
4. Type or select argument range.
5. Press Enter or click Enter button.

In Addition

Other Statistical Functions

Click More Functions at the Sum button arrow list to access the Insert Function dialog box from which you can access Excel's complete list of functions. A sampling of other statistical functions and their descriptions includes the following:

Function Name	Description
=COUNTA	counts the number of cells (including those that contain labels); ignores empty cells
=COUNTBLANK	counts the number of empty cells
=MEDIAN	returns the number in the middle of the range

Activity 3.2

Using Date Functions TODAY, NOW, and DATE

Dates are stored as a serial number starting from January 1, 1900, as serial number 1 and increased sequentially. Times are stored as decimal fractions representing portions of a day. Storing these entries as numbers enables calculations to be performed on cells containing a date or a time. The Date & Time category in the Insert Function dialog box contains functions that can be used to write formulas for cells containing dates. Cells containing dates and times can be formatted using the Number Format drop-down list in the Number group in the Home tab or using the Format Cells dialog box. Various combinations of year, month, day, hour, minutes, and seconds are available for displaying dates and times.

Project

You will finish the weekly adult cardiac bypass surgery report for Columbia River General Hospital by entering dates and formulas to track patient movement from surgery to a 30-day follow-up visit at the surgeon's office.

Columbia
River
General
Hospital

① Open **CRGHCardiacSurg-NovWk2.xlsx**.

② Save the workbook with Save As and name it **ExcelMedS3-02**.

③ Make I4 the active cell, type **=now()**, and then press Enter.

> The current date and time are inserted in I4. In the next step, you will try the TODAY function to see the difference between the two.

④ Make I4 the active cell, press Delete to clear the cell, type **=today()**, and then press Enter.

> The current date is inserted in the cell with the time displayed as *0:00*. Normally, the time does not display when TODAY is used; however, since we first entered the NOW function, Excel retained the time format for the cell. In a later step, you will format the cell to display the month, day, and year only.

⑤ Make B4 the active cell, click the Sum button arrow, and then click *More Functions* at the drop-down list.

> The Insert Function dialog box opens. Search for a function by typing a phrase describing the type of formula you want in the *Search for a function* text box and then clicking the Go button or by selecting a category name and then browsing a list of functions.

⑥ At the Insert Function dialog box, click the down-pointing arrow to the right of the *Or select a category* list box and then click *Date & Time* at the drop-down list.

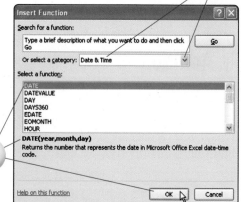

> The *Select a function* list box displays an alphabetical list of date and time functions. Clicking a function name causes the formula with its argument structure and a description to appear below the list box.

⑦ With *DATE* already selected in the *Select a function* list box, read the description of the formula and then click OK.

> The Function Arguments dialog box opens with a text box for each section of the function argument.

8 Type **2011** in the *Year* text box.

Step 8

9 Press Tab to move the insertion point to the *Month* text box and then type **11**.

Step 9

10 Press Tab to move the insertion point to the *Day* text box, type **06**, and then click OK.

Step 10

Function Arguments

DATE

Year	2011		= 2011
Month	11		= 11
Day	06		= 6

= 40853

Returns the number that represents the date in Microsoft Office Excel date-time code.

Day is a number from 1 to 31 representing the day of the month.

Formula result = 40853

Help on this function   OK   Cancel

This is the serial number representing November 6, 2011.

The Function Arguments dialog box displays the serial number for November 6, 2011, as *40853* which is the value Excel stores in the cell. Notice the formula in the Formula bar is *=DATE(2011,11,6)*.

In Brief

Date Functions
1. Make desired cell active.
2. Click Sum button arrow.
3. Click *More Functions*.
4. Change category to *Date & Time*.
5. Click desired function name.
6. Click OK.
7. Enter references in Function Arguments dialog box.
8. Click OK.

11 Make D4 the active cell, type **=b4+6**, and then press Enter.

Since dates are stored as values, formulas can be used to perform calculations on dates. Excel displays the result *11/12/2011* in the cell (6 days from the week start date).

12 Make G6 the active cell, type **=f6+1**, and then press Enter.

Each patient moved through the system at normal speed during this report week, which is 1 day in the CSRU unit.

13 Make H6 the active cell, type **=g6+4**, and then press Enter.

Your date will vary.

Bypass patients each spent four days after CSRU on the cardiac floor.

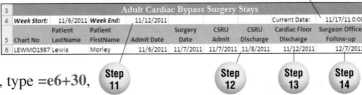

3	Adult Cardiac Bypass Surgery Stays							
4	**Week Start:** 11/6/2011 **Week End:** 11/12/2011						Current Date:	11/17/11 0:00
5	Chart No	Patient LastName	Patient FirstName	Admit Date	Surgery Date	CSRU Admit	CSRU Discharge	Cardiac Floor Discharge	Surgeon Office Follow-up
6	LEWMO1987 Lewis		Morley	11/6/2011	11/7/2011	11/7/2011	11/8/2011	11/12/2011	12/7/2011

Step 11   **Step 12**   **Step 13**   **Step 14**

14 Make I6 the active cell, type **=e6+30**, and then press Enter.

Bypass patients attend a follow-up hospital visit 30 days after their surgery date.

15 Select G6:I6 and then use the fill handle to copy the formulas to the remaining rows (G7:I24).

16 Select I6:I24.

In the next steps, you will format the date entries for the surgeon's follow-up visit to display the day of the week.

17 Click the Number Format button arrow.

18 Click *Long Date* at the drop-down list.

19 AutoFit column I.

You need to change the dates of follow-up visits that calculated to a Saturday or Sunday since the surgeon's office is closed weekends.

ABC 123	General — No specific format
12	Number — 40884.00
	Currency — $40,884.00
	Accounting — $40,884.00
	Short Date — 12/7/2011
	Long Date — Wednesday, December 07, 2011
	Time — 12:00:00 AM
%	Percentage — 4088400.00%
½	Fraction — 40884
10²	Scientific — 4.09E-04
	More Number Formats...

Step 17

Step 18

20 Make I15 the active cell, type **=date(2011,12,12)**, and then press Enter.

21 Copy I15 to each cell that resulted in a Saturday follow-up visit.

22 Make I21 the active cell, type **=date(2011,12,13)**, and then press Enter.

23 Copy I21 to each cell that resulted in a Sunday follow-up visit.

24 Save, print, and then close **ExcelMedS3-02.xlsx**.

Activity 3.3

Using the Logical IF Function

The IF function returns one of two values in a cell based on a true or false answer to a question called a *logical test*. The format of an IF function is =IF(logical_test,value_if_true,value_if_false). For example, assume a medical supplies salesperson earns a 3 percent commission if sales are greater than or equal to $100,000, or a 2 percent commission for sales less than $100,000. Assume the sales value resides in B4. The statement B4>=100000 (*logical_test*) can only return a true or false answer. Depending on the answer, the salesperson's commission will be calculated at either B4*3% (*value_if_true*) or B4*2% (*value_if_false*).

Project

Columbia River General Hospital

Continuing your work for the Division of Cardiology at Columbia River General Hospital, your next project involves calculating standard costs for patient stays for Dr. Novak's patients. Average standard cost is based on a per diem rate and an overhead surcharge. Both the per diem rate and the surcharge are dependent on the duration.

1. Open **CRGHCardiacCosts-Novak.xlsx**.

2. Save the workbook with Save As and name it **ExcelMedS3-03**.

3. Make E6 the active cell, type **=i** and then read the ScreenTip that appears next to *IF* in the Formula AutoComplete list box below the cell.

Step 3

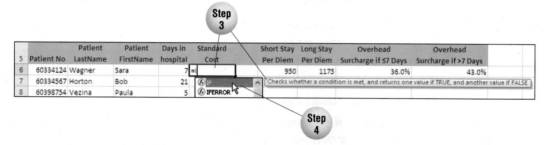

Step 4

4. Double-click *IF* in the Formula AutoComplete list box.

   Excel completes the entry in the cell to the first bracket =IF(and displays in a ScreenTip the required syntax for the argument. The ScreenTip displays the next required entry in the formula in bold (*logical_test*). At any point, you can click the Insert Function button to display the dialog box to assist you.

5. Click the Insert Function button [fx] on the Formula bar.

6. Position the cell pointer on the Function Arguments dialog box Title bar and then drag the dialog box down and right until you can see all of the cells in row 6.

7. With the insertion point positioned in the *Logical_test* text box, type **d6<=7** and then press Tab.

   To begin the IF statement, you want Excel to test whether the value in D6 is less than or equal to 7. This test determines whether Excel calculates the cost using the short stay per diem or the long stay per diem and then adds the overhead surcharge at the short stay or long stay percentage. Longer patient stays cost the hospital more per day than shorter stays.

8. With the insertion point positioned in the *Value_if_true* text box, type **(d6*g6)+(d6*g6*i6)** and then press Tab.

   If the value in D6 is less than or equal to 7, the formula calculates the value times the short stay per diem (7 × 950) and then adds the short stay overhead surcharge (7 × 950 × 36%). The dollar symbol in front of the column and row numbers is needed to make the cells absolute. Since the formula will be copied to rows 7–20, absolute references are required for G6 and I6.

9 With the insertion point positioned in the *Value_if_false* text box, type **(d6*h6)+(d6*h6*j6)**.

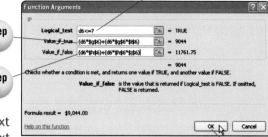

If the value in D6 is greater than 7, the formula calculates using the long stay per diem and the long stay overhead surcharge. Absolute references are used for the long stay per diem (H6) and the long stay overhead surcharge (J6). Notice Excel displays = *TRUE* next to the *Logical_test* text box, *9044* next to *Value_if_true*, and *11761.75* next to *Value_if_false*. Below the text boxes, Excel shows the result that will be placed in the active cell ($9,044.00) since the value in D6 is 7.

10 Click OK.

11 Drag the fill handle in E6 down to row 20 and then click in any cell to deselect the range.

Excel copies the formula in row 6 to rows 7–20. The cell addresses containing the days in hospital are changed relative to each row (D6 is changed to D7, D8, and so on); however, the cell addresses containing the per diem rates (G6 and H6) and overhead surcharges (I6 and J6) do not change. This is an example of a formula that uses *mixed addressing*—with some addresses relative and some addresses absolute.

12 Make E22 the active cell and then use the Sum button to calculate the total.

13 Click each cell individually within the range E7 to E20 and review the formula in the Formula bar.

14 Save **ExcelMedS3-03.xlsx**.

15 Print and then close **ExcelMedS3-03.xlsx**.

	A	B	C	D	E	F	G	H	I	J
1					**Columbia River General Hospital**					
2					**Division of Cardiology**					
3					**Adult Cardiac Surgery Average Cost Statistics (All Surgeries)**					
4	Month:	November		Surgeon:	Novak					
5	Patient No	Patient LastName	Patient FirstName	Days in hospital	Standard Cost		Short Stay Per Diem	Long Stay Per Diem	Overhead Surcharge if ≤7 Days	Overhead Surcharge if >7 Days
6	60334124	Wagner	Sara	7	$9,044.00		950	1175	36.0%	43.0%
7	60334567	Horton	Bob	21	$35,285.25					
8	60398754	Vezina	Paula	5	$6,460.00					
9	60347821	Dowling	Jager	15	$23,203.75					
10	60328192	Ashman	Carl	4	$5,168.00					
11	60321349	Kaiser	Lana	12	$20,163.00					
12	60398545	Van Bomm	Emily	7	$9,044.00					
13	60342548	Youngblood	Frank	6	$7,752.00					
14	60331569	Lorimar	Hannah	8	$13,442.00					
15	60247859	Peterson	Mark	5	$6,460.00					
16	60158642	Harper	Norlon	5	$6,460.00					
17	60458962	Jenkins	Esther	10	$16,802.50					
18	68521245	Norfolk	Marianne	8	$13,442.00					
19	63552158	Adams-Wiley	Susan	6	$7,752.00					
20	68451278	Emerson	Kiley	4	$5,168.00					
21										
22		Total Standard Cost:			$187,646.50					

In Addition

IF Function Syntax

If you prefer to type the IF statement directly into the cell, follow these tips to avoid typing errors:
- Do not use spaces within the formula.
- A comma separates the three sections within the argument.

If you make a typing error, Excel displays a message and highlights the approximate area within the formula where the error occurred.

Activity 3.4

Creating a Column Chart

Numerical values are often more easily understood when presented visually in a chart. Excel includes several chart types such as column, line, pie, bar, area, scatter, and others with which you can graphically portray data. The chart can be placed in the same worksheet as the data or it can be inserted into its own sheet. To create a chart, first select the cells containing the data you want to graph and then choose the chart type. Excel graphs the data in a separate object which can be moved, resized, and formatted.

Project

Hanna Moreland, manager of the Supplies Department at Columbia River General Hospital, has asked you to create a chart to compare operating expenses in each quarter.

1. Open **CRGHSuppliesOpExp.xlsx**.

2. Save the workbook with Save As and name it **ExcelMedS3-04**.

3. Select A3:E9.

   The first step in creating a chart is to select the range of cells containing the data you want to chart. Notice in the range in Step 3 you are including the row labels in column A. Labels are included to provide the frame of reference for each bar, column, or other chart series.

4. Click the Insert tab.

5. Click the Column button in the Charts group.

6. Click *3-D Clustered Column* at the drop-down list (first from left in *3-D Column* section).

   Excel graphs the data in a 3-D column chart and places the chart inside an object box in the center of the worksheet (see Figure E3.1).

FIGURE E3.1 3-D Column Chart in an Object Box

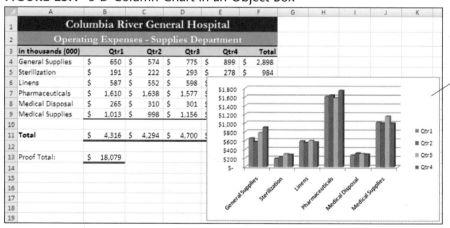

3-D column chart created in Step 6 is placed in an object box which can be moved, resized, and formatted as needed.

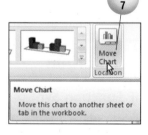

7. Click the Move Chart button in the Location group in the Chart Tools Design tab.

 PROBLEM

Can't see the Chart Tools Design tab? You probably clicked outside the chart to deselect the object and the contextual tab disappeared. Click over the chart to select the object and the contextual Chart Tools Design tab reappears.

⑧ At the Move Chart dialog box, click *New sheet*.

⑨ With *Chart1* selected in the *New sheet* text box, type **ColumnChart** and then click OK.

> The chart object is moved to a new sheet in the workbook with a tab labeled *ColumnChart*. The chart is automatically scaled to fill the entire page in landscape orientation.

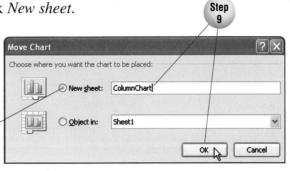

Step 9

Step 8

In Brief
Create Column Chart
1. Select cells.
2. Click Insert tab.
3. Click Column button.
4. Click desired chart type.
5. Move and/or resize as required.
6. Apply design options.

⑩ Click *Layout 3* in the Chart Layouts group.

> This layout adds a title to the top center of the chart and moves the legend to the bottom center.

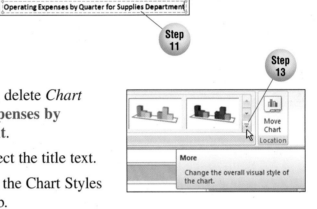

Step 10

⑪ Click once over *Chart Title* to select the title object, click a second time at the beginning of the text to place an insertion point inside the chart title box, delete *Chart Title*, and then type **Operating Expenses by Quarter for Supplies Department**.

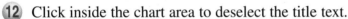

Step 11

Step 13

⑫ Click inside the chart area to deselect the title text.

⑬ Click the More arrow button in the Chart Styles group in the Chart Tools Design tab.

⑭ Click *Style 8* in the drop-down list (last option in the first row).

⑮ Save **ExcelS3-04.xlsx**.

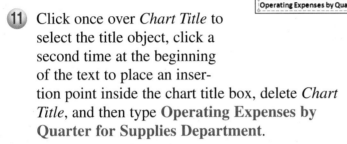

Step 14

In Addition

Changing the Data in a Chart

Click the Select Data button in the Data group in the Chart Tools Design tab to add cells to, or delete cells from, the source range that was selected to generate the chart. At the Select Data Source dialog box shown at the right, you can add, edit, or delete a data series or edit the category axis labels.

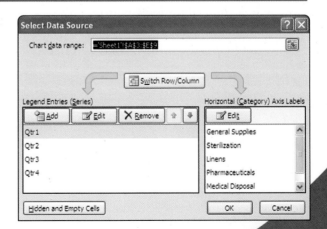

Activity 3.5

Creating a Pie Chart

Pie charts illustrate each data point's size in proportion to the total of all items in the data source range. Each slice in the pie chart is displayed as a percentage of the whole pie. You can choose to display the percent values, the actual values used to generate the chart, or both values as data labels inside or outside the pie slices. Use a pie chart when you have only one data series you want to graph and there are no negative or zero values within the data range.

Project

Columbia River General Hospital

Hanna Moreland is pleased with the column chart you created for the operating expenses by quarter. Hanna would like another chart that will show each expense as a proportion of the total expenses.

① With **ExcelS3-04.xlsx** open, click the tab labeled *Sheet1* near the bottom left corner of the window above the Status bar.

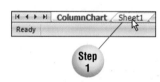

Step 1

② Click in any cell to deselect the range that was used to generate the column chart in the previous activity.

③ Select the range A3:A9, hold down the Ctrl key, and then select the range F3:F9.

④ Click the Insert tab.

⑤ Click the Pie button in the Charts group.

⑥ Click *Pie in 3-D*, the first pie chart in the *3-D Pie* section in the drop-down list.

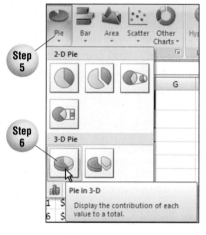

Step 5

Step 6

⑦ Point to the border of the chart object until the pointer displays with the four-headed-arrow move icon, hold down the left mouse button, and then drag the chart below the worksheet. Position the chart centered below columns A–F with the top edge in row 16.

? PROBLEM

You may find it helpful to scroll the worksheet until you see several blank rows below row 16 before moving the chart.

⑧ Click the Chart Tools Layout tab.

⑨ Click the Data Labels button in the Labels group and then click *More Data Label Options* at the drop-down list.

Step 8

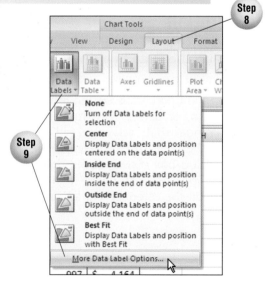

Step 9

10 At the Format Data Labels dialog box with *Label Options* selected in the left pane, click the *Value* check box in the *Label Contains* section to clear the box and then click the *Percentage* check box to add a check mark.

11 Click *Outside End* in the *Label Position* section.

12 Click *Number* in the left pane, click *Percentage* in the *Category* list box, select the number in the *Decimal places* text box, and then type 1.

13 Close the Format Data Labels dialog box.

14 Click the Chart Tools Design tab.

15 Click the More arrow button in the Chart Styles group and then click *Style 10* at the drop-down list (second from left in second row).

16 Change the chart title to **Total Operating Expenses**. Refer to Activity 3.4, Steps 11–12 if you need assistance with this step.

17 Click in the worksheet area outside the chart to deselect the chart.

18 Save **ExcelS3-04.xlsx**.

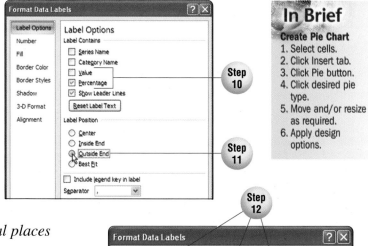

Step 10

Step 11

Step 12

Step 16

In Brief
Create Pie Chart
1. Select cells.
2. Click Insert tab.
3. Click Pie button.
4. Click desired pie type.
5. Move and/or resize as required.
6. Apply design options.

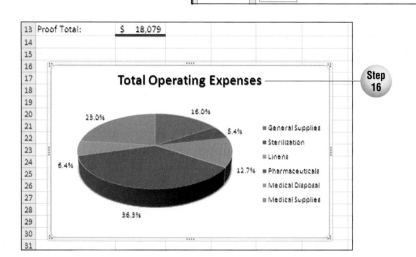

In Addition

Other Chart Types

Deciding the most appropriate chart type for graphing data can be difficult. Following are descriptions of some chart types and the type of data for which each is designed.

Chart Type	Type of Data
area	emphasizes magnitude by summing the plotted values and then graphing the relationship of each range to the whole
bar	displays individual figures at a specific time or shows variations between data ranges using horizontal bars
doughnut	shows the relationship of parts to a whole in a similar manner as a pie chart
line scatter	depicts trends and change over time intervals, also called an *XY* chart; shows relationships among numeric values or plots interception points between x and y values

Activity 3.6

Modifying and Formatting Charts

To make changes to an existing chart, click inside a chart or chart element to display the translucent border around the perimeter of the chart object. Point to the border to move the chart or point to one of the eight sizing handles to resize the chart. When the chart is selected, the Chart Tools Design, Layout, and Format tabs become available. Use these tabs to add, delete, or modify the chart or chart elements.

Project

Columbia
River
General
Hospital

You will modify the charts created for the Operating Expenses worksheet by formatting the legend, applying bold to data labels, changing the font in the chart title, and changing the chart type.

1. With **ExcelMedS3-04.xlsx** open, click anywhere inside the pie chart to select the chart object.

    Once a chart is selected, the three contextual Chart Tools tabs become available—Design, Layout, and Format.

2. Click inside the pie chart legend.

    Eight sizing handles appear around the legend indicating the object is selected. You can drag the legend to another location or resize the legend using one of the handles.

3. Click the Chart Tools Format tab.

4. Click the Shape Outline button in the Shape Styles group and then click the *Light Blue* color box in the color palette (fourth from right in *Standard Colors* section).

    This adds a thin, light blue border around the legend.

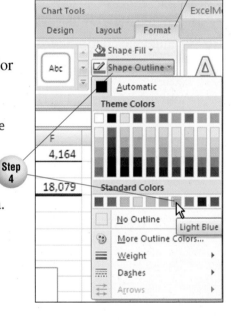

5. Right-click the chart title and then use the Font and Font Size buttons in the Mini toolbar to change the title to 16-point Verdana.

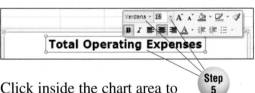

6. Click inside the chart area to deselect the chart title.

7. Click inside any one of the percent values around the edge of the pie.

    This selects all six data labels.

8. Click the Home tab and then click the Bold button in the Font group.

9. Click in the worksheet area outside the pie chart.

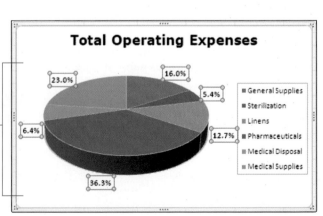

10 Click the ColumnChart tab located near the bottom left corner of the window above the Status bar and then click inside the column chart to select the chart.

11 Click the Chart Tools Design tab and then click the Change Chart Type button in the Type group.

12 At the Change Chart Type dialog box, click *Bar* in the left pane and then click *Clustered Bar in 3-D* in the *Bar* section in the right pane (fourth from left in first row).

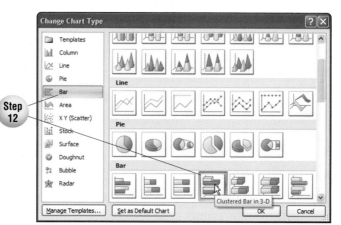

Step 12

13 Click OK.

14 Click *Layout 1* in the Chart Layouts group.

> This layout moves the legend to the right side of the chart where there is more room.

FIGURE E3.2 Layout 1 and Style 2 Applied to Bar Chart in Steps 14–15

15 Click the More arrow button in the Chart Styles group and then click *Style 2* in the drop-down list. Figure E3.2 shows the application of Style 2.

16 Save **ExcelMedS3-04.xlsx**.

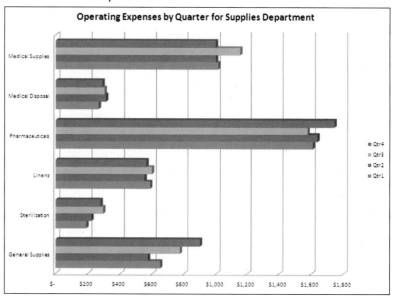

In Addition

Chart Elements

Another method to edit a chart is to right-click a chart element to display a context-sensitive shortcut menu. For example, right-clicking the axis labels in the bar chart displays the shortcut menu shown at the right. The bottom section of the shortcut menu changes dependent on the element you clicked.

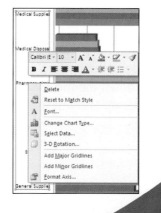

Activity 3.7

Inserting, Moving, and Resizing Pictures and Clip Art

When connected to Office Online, the Microsoft Office suite includes a clip art gallery containing thousands of images. Once a clip art image has been inserted, it can be moved, resized, or deleted. The Clip Art task pane allows you to view images in the gallery and insert them into the worksheet with a single click. By default, Excel searches Office Online if you are connected to the Internet. A company logo or other digital picture can also be inserted into a worksheet using the Picture button in the Illustrations group of the Insert tab.

Project

Hanna asked you to enhance the worksheet's appearance for the report submission. You decide to add two images to the top of the worksheet.

1. With **ExcelMedS3-04.xlsx** open, click the Sheet1 tab.

2. Insert 5 rows above row 1 and then make A1 the active cell.

3. Click the Insert tab and then click the Clip Art button in the Illustrations group.

   The Clip Art task pane opens at the right side of the worksheet area.

4. Click in the *Search for* text box at the top of the Clip Art task pane. Delete existing text if necessary, type **medicine**, and then click Go. Click Yes if a message box appears asking if you want to search Microsoft Office Online.

   Available images associated with the keyword *medicine* display in the *Results* section of the Clip Art task pane. By default, Excel searches all media collections (clip art, photographs, movies, and sounds) in all categories of the Office gallery, in Office Online, and in all favorites, unclassified clips, and downloaded clips that have been added to the computer you are using.

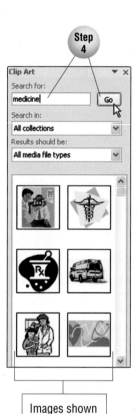

Step 4

Images shown may vary.

5. Scroll the images in the *Results* section until you see the clip art shown at the right. Position the mouse pointer over the picture and then click the mouse once.

   The picture is inserted in the worksheet starting at A1.

Step 5

❓ PROBLEM

Select an alternative image if the clip art shown is not available.

6. Position the pointer on the round white sizing handle at the bottom right corner of the image, hold down the left mouse button, and drag the pointer up and left until the image fits within the first five rows above the worksheet title.

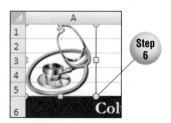

Step 6

7 Move the pointer over the image until the four-headed-arrow move icon appears attached to the pointer, hold down the left mouse button, and then drag the image until the right edge of the picture is aligned at the right edge of the worksheet.

8 Click the Close button in the upper right corner of the Clip Art task pane.

9 Click A1, click the Insert tab, and then click the Picture button in the Illustrations group.

10 At the Insert Picture dialog box, navigate to the ExcelMedS3 folder on your storage medium and then double-click the file named **CRGHLogo.jpg**.

11 Use the sizing handles to resize the picture until the logo image fits above the top left edge of the worksheet.

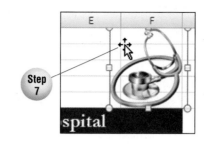

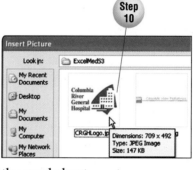

In Brief

Insert Clip Art
1. Click Insert tab.
2. Click Clip Art button.
3. Search for image by keyword.
4. Click desired image in *Results* section.
5. Move and/or resize as required.
6. Close Clip Art task pane.

Insert Picture from File
1. Click Insert tab.
2. Click Picture button.
3. Navigate to drive and/or folder.
4. Double-click file containing picture.
5. Move and/or size as required.

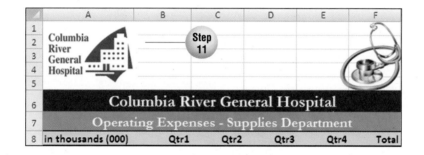

12 Click in any cell to deselect the logo image.

13 Save **ExcelMedS3-04.xlsx**.

In Addition

Picture Tools

When a clip art image or picture inserted from a file is selected, the contextual Picture Tools Format tab becomes available. Customize the image using picture tools or picture styles. Use the crop button to cut an unwanted area or set a specific height or width measurement for the image. Buttons in the Arrange group allow you to control the alignment, rotation, or order of the image within the worksheet.

Inserting Shapes and Text Boxes

The Shapes button in the Insert tab includes buttons with which you can draw lines, rectangles, basic shapes, block arrows, equation shapes, flowchart symbols, stars and banners, and callouts. Enclosed shapes can also contain text. Draw shapes, arrows, or add text boxes to add emphasis or insert explanatory notes in a worksheet.

Project

Columbia River General Hospital

An upcoming increase in price from the hospital's medical waste disposal contractor is higher than normal. Hanna wants you to use drawing tools to add an explanatory note to the operating expenses worksheet.

1. With **ExcelMedS3-04.xlsx** open, click the Insert tab.

2. Click the Shapes button in the Illustrations group and then click the Arrow button in the Lines group.

> When a shape object tool has been selected, the pointer changes to a crosshairs ✛.

Step 2

3. Position the crosshairs near the bottom left boundary of D18, drag the crosshairs up toward the value *310* in C13, and then release the left mouse button. If you are not happy with the arrow, press Delete to delete the arrow and then try again.

8	in thousands (000)		Qtr1		Qtr2		Qtr3
9	General Supplies	$	650	$	574	$	775
10	Sterilization	$	191	$	222	$	293
11	Linens	$	587	$	552	$	598
12	Pharmaceuticals	$	1,610	$	1,638	$	1,577
13	Medical Disposal	$	265	$	310	$	301
14	Medical Supplies	$	1,013	$	998	$	1,156
15							
16	**Total**	$	4,316	$	4,294	$	4,700
17							
18	Proof Total:	$	18,079				
19							

Step 3

4. Click the Text Box button in the Insert Shapes group in the Drawing Tools Format tab.

> When the Text Box tool has been selected, the pointer changes to a downward-pointing arrow ↓.

5. Position the pointer at the top left boundary of D19 and then drag the pointer down and right to draw the text box the approximate size shown in the image below.

> An insertion point appears inside the box when you release the left mouse button, indicating you can begin typing the text.

6. Type **Contractor increase next year will be 8% in Quarter 2!** inside the text box.

13	Medical Disposal	$	265	$	310	$	301	$	288	$	1,164
14	Medical Supplies	$	1,013	$	998	$	1,156	$	997	$	4,164
15											
16	**Total**	$	4,316	$	4,294	$	4,700	$	4,769	$	18,079
17											
18	Proof Total:	$	18,079								
19								Contractor increase next year will			
20								be 8% in Quarter 2!			

Steps 5–6

(7) Click outside the text box to deselect the object. If necessary, resize the text box to view all of the text.

(8) Click the arrow to select the drawn object, hold down the Ctrl key, and then click the text box object. Both drawn shapes are now selected.

(9) Click the Drawing Tools Format tab.

(10) Click the Shape Outline button in the Shape Styles group and then click the *Light Blue* color box in the color palette (fourth from right in *Standard Colors* section).

(11) Click the Shape Outline button a second time, point to *Weight*, and then click *1½ pt* at the weight gallery.

(12) Click in any cell to deselect the drawn shapes.

Figure E3.3 shows the text box and arrow after formatting options have been applied.

Step 9

Step 10

Step 11

In Brief

Draw Shape
1. Click Insert tab.
2. Click Shapes button.
3. Click desired shape.
4. Drag to create shape.
5. Move, resize, or format as required.

Draw Text Box
1. Click Insert tab.
2. Click Text Box button.
3. Drag to create box size.
4. Type text.
5. Click outside text box object.

FIGURE E3.3 Formatted Text Box and Arrow

	Columbia River General Hospital									
6										
7	Operating Expenses - Supplies Department									
8	in thousands (000)		Qtr1		Qtr2		Qtr3		Qtr4	Total
9	General Supplies	$	650	$	574	$	775	$	899	$ 2,898
10	Sterilization	$	191	$	222	$	293	$	278	$ 984
11	Linens	$	587	$	552	$	598	$	564	$ 2,301
12	Pharmaceuticals	$	1,610	$	1,638	$	1,577	$	1,743	$ 6,568
13	Medical Disposal	$	265	$	310	$	301	$	288	$ 1,164
14	Medical Supplies	$	1,013	$	998	$	1,156	$	997	$ 4,164
15										
16	Total	$	4,316	$	4,294	$	4,700	$	4,769	$ 18,079
17										
18	Proof Total:	$	18,079							
19							Contractor increase next year will			
20							be 8% in Quarter 2!			

applied formatting options

(13) Print the worksheet.

(14) Click the ColumnChart tab located near the bottom left corner of the window above the Status bar and then print the bar chart.

(15) Save **ExcelMedS3-04.xlsx**.

Activity 3.9

Changing Margins; Centering a Worksheet on a Page; Scaling a Worksheet

The margin on a worksheet is the blank space at the top, bottom, left, and right edges of the page and the beginning of the printed text. Center a smaller worksheet horizontally and/or vertically to improve the appearance of the worksheet for printing purposes. For larger worksheets, you can choose to shrink the text by scaling the height and/or the width of the worksheet to force the printout to a maximum number of pages.

Project You will adjust print options in the operating expenses and cardiac nurse casual relief call list worksheets to improve the appearance and minimize paper requirements.

① With **ExcelMedS3-04.xlsx** open, click the Sheet1 tab.

② Click the Office button, point to *Print*, and then click *Print Preview*.

Notice the content is unbalanced at the left edge of the page with a larger amount of white space on the right side. One method of correcting this is to change the left margin.

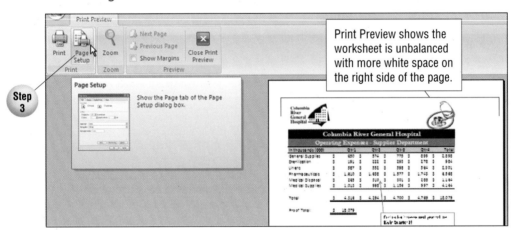

Show the Page tab of the Page Setup dialog box.

Step 3

Print Preview shows the worksheet is unbalanced with more white space on the right side of the page.

③ Click the Page Setup button in the Print group in the Print Preview tab.

④ If necessary, click the Margins tab at the Page Setup dialog box.

⑤ Select the current entry in the *Left* text box, type **1.25**, and then click OK.

The worksheet now appears balanced between the left and right edges of the page.

⑥ Click the Print button in the Print group.

The Print Preview window closes and the Print dialog box appears.

⑦ At the Print dialog box, click OK.

⑧ Save and then close **ExcelMedS3-04.xlsx**.

⑨ Open **CRGHCardiacNurseCasualList.xlsx**.

⑩ Save the workbook with Save As and name it **ExcelMedS3-05**.

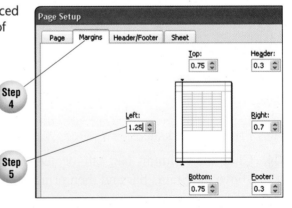

Step 4

Step 5

11 Click the Page Layout tab, click the Orientation button in the Page Setup group, and then click *Landscape*.

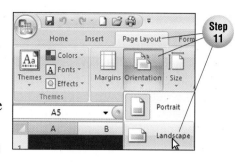

In Brief

Change Margins and/or Center Worksheet
1. Display worksheet in Print Preview.
2. Click Page Setup button.
3. Change required margin setting and/or click *Horizontally* and/or *Vertically* check box.
4. Click OK.

Scale Worksheet
1. Click Page Layout tab.
2. Click Width button arrow.
3. Click desired number of pages to scale width.
4. Click Height button arrow.
5. Click desired number of pages to scale height.

12 Click the Margins button in the Page Setup group and then click *Custom Margins* at the drop-down list.

> The Page Setup dialog box opens with the Margins tab active.

13 Click the *Horizontally* check box in the *Center on page* section and then click OK.

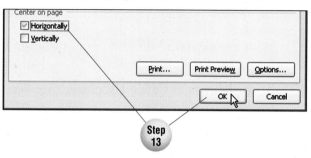

> Centering the worksheet horizontally is another method that can be used to ensure the worksheet prints balanced between the left and right edges of the page. You can choose both the *Horizontally* and *Vertically* check boxes to print a worksheet that is centered between both the left and right edges (horizontally), and the top and bottom edges (vertically) of the page.

14 Display the worksheet in Print Preview. Notice the worksheet requires two pages to print.

15 Click the Close Print Preview button in the Preview group.

16 With the Page Layout tab active, click the Width button arrow (currently displays *Automatic*) in the Scale to Fit group and then click *1 page* at the drop-down list.

17 Click the Height button arrow (currently displays *Automatic*) in the Scale to Fit group and then click *1 page* at the drop-down list.

18 Print the worksheet.

19 Save **ExcelMedS3-05.xlsx**.

In Addition

Manually Inserting and Removing Page Breaks

In Section 2 you learned to adjust page breaks for multipage worksheets in Page Break Preview. You can also insert and remove page breaks in Normal view using the Breaks button in the Page Setup group in the Page Layout tab (shown at the right). Position the active cell in the row below where you want the page break to occur, click the Breaks button, and then click *Insert Page Break* at the drop-down list. To remove a page break, position the active cell just below the page break, click the Breaks button, and then click *Remove Page Break*.

Activity 3.10

Using Page Layout View; Inserting Headers and Footers

Page Layout view allows you to view the worksheet along with the print settings. Page Layout view also displays a horizontal and vertical ruler to assist with measurements. A **header** is text that prints at the top of each worksheet and a **footer** is text that prints at the bottom of each worksheet. Excel includes predefined headers and footers that can be selected from a drop-down list or you can create your own custom header or footer text.

Project

You have reviewed the printout for the cardiac nurse casual relief call list and decide to add identifying information such as the workbook name and the date the report is printed to the printout. You will use Page Layout view to add a header and footer for this information.

Columbia River General Hospital

1. With **ExcelMedS3-05.xlsx** open, click the Page Layout button  located at the right side of the Status bar near the Zoom slider bar.

   Step 1

2. At the Microsoft Office Excel message box indicating that freeze panes is not compatible with Page Layout view, click OK to continue and have the panes unfrozen.

3. If necessary, use the horizontal and vertical scroll bars to adjust the window so that the worksheet including the white space for the top, left, and right margins is entirely visible.

4. Click over the text *Click to add header* near the top center of the page.

   A header and footer are divided into three sections. Click at the left or right side of the header area to open the left or right section text box in which you can type or insert header and footer elements. By default, text in the left section is left-aligned, text in the center section is centered, and text in the right section is right-aligned.

5. Click at the left edge of the Header area to open the left section text box and then type your first and last names.

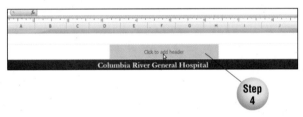

Step 4

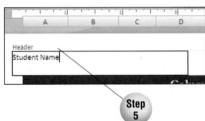

Step 5

6. Click at the right edge of the Header area to open the right section text box, type **Date Printed:**, and then press the spacebar once.

7. Click the Current Date button in the Header & Footer Elements group in the Header & Footer Tools Design tab.

   Excel inserts the code *&[Date]*, which causes the current date to be inserted at the location of the code when the worksheet is printed.

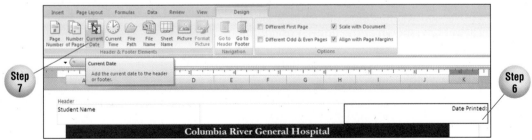

Step 7

Step 6

In Brief

Insert Header or Footer
1. Switch to Page Layout view.
2. Click over *Click to add header* or *Click to add footer*.
3. Insert desired header and footer elements and/or type text in left, center, or right section.
4. Click in worksheet area to end header or footer editing.

8 Click the Go to Footer button in the Navigation group in the Header & Footer Tools Design tab.

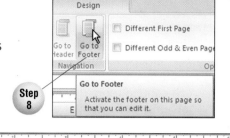

The right footer section at the bottom of the page opens for editing.

9 Click in the center of the Footer area to open the center section for editing.

Step 8

Go to Footer
Activate the footer on this page so that you can edit it.

10 Click the File Name button in the Header & Footer Elements group, press the spacebar once, and then click the Sheet Name button in the same group.

Steps 9–10

	A	B	C	D	E	F	G	H
	Updated:	1-Oct-09						

&[File] &[Tab]

Footer

Excel inserts the codes *&[File]* and *&[Tab]*, which causes the workbook file name followed by the worksheet name to be inserted at the location of the codes when the worksheet is printed.

11 Click anywhere in the worksheet area outside the footer to close the footer section.

12 Scroll to the top of the worksheet to view the header. Notice that Excel now displays the current date in place of the *&[Date]* code.

13 Scroll to the bottom of the worksheet and notice that the *&[File]* and *&[Tab]* codes now display the workbook file name followed by the sheet name.

Step 15

14 If necessary, click the Page Layout tab.

15 Click the Align button in the Arrange group.

16 Click *View Gridlines* at the drop-down list.

Since gridlines do not print by default, removing the display of the gridlines provides a closer representation of how the worksheet will look when printed with the print options that have been applied in Page Layout view.

Step 16

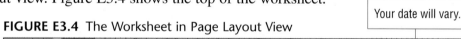

17 Review the appearance of the worksheet with the header and footer in Page Layout view. Figure E3.4 shows the top of the worksheet.

Your date will vary.

FIGURE E3.4 The Worksheet in Page Layout View

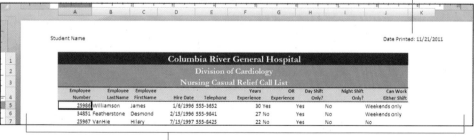

Review the worksheet layout with the gridlines removed and print options displayed while in Page Layout view.

18 Print the worksheet.

19 Click the Normal button ⊞ located at the right side of the Status bar near the Zoom slider bar (immediately left of the Page Layout View button).

20 Save **ExcelMedS3-05.xlsx**.

Activity 3.11

Formatting Data as a Table; Applying Table Design Options

Create a table in Excel to manage data independently from other cells in the worksheet, or to filter and sort a list. A worksheet can contain more than one range formatted as a table. By default, filter arrows appear in the first row of the table and a border surrounds the table range with a sizing arrow at the bottom right corner. In previous versions of Excel, this feature was called a List. Excel includes a variety of predefined table styles to apply attractive formatting features to the range within a table. The contextual Table Tools Design tab becomes available when a range of cells is defined as a table.

Project

Luisa Gomez, cardiac nurse manager, often uses the casual relief call list when a full-time nurse calls in sick. Luisa would like the list to be in a format that she can sort and filter based on shift preference and/or experience. You decide to format the information about each individual in a table to accommodate sorting and filtering.

1. With **ExcelMedS3-05.xlsx** open, select A4:J35.

   The first step to defining a table is to specify the range of cells to be included in the list. Do not include cells in the range that are merged titles or other data that should not be included if you sort and filter the rows.

2. Click the Format as Table button in the Styles group in the Home tab.

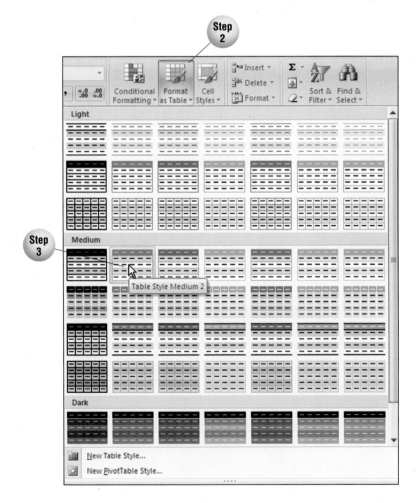

3 Click *Table Style Medium 2* (second from left in first row in *Medium* section) at the drop-down gallery.

> Excel includes 60 predefined table styles grouped into *Light*, *Medium*, and *Dark* categories with which you can add color, borders, and shading formats to cells within the table. In addition, you can create your own custom table style saved with the current workbook.

4 At the Format As Table dialog box, with =$A$4:$J$35 selected in the *Where is the data for your table?* text box, click OK.

> Excel applies the table style formats to the range, displays filter arrows in the first row of the table, and adds a border to the table, including a sizing handle to the bottom right cell.

Step 4

5 Click in any cell to deselect the range.

> In the next step, you will add a new record to the table.

6 Right-click row 36, click *Insert* at the shortcut menu and then type the new record in the columns indicated. Press Enter after typing the last cell.

Employee Number	**99823**
Employee LastName	**Awad**
Employee FirstName	**Rania**
Hire Date	**=date(2009,8,11)**
Telephone	**555-4652**
Years Experience	**7**
OR Experience	**Yes**
Day Shift Only?	**No**
Night Shift Only?	**No**
Can Work Either Shift	**Yes**

> Since you typed data in the row immediately below the table, Excel automatically expands the table to include the new row and applies the table style formats. You can also insert a new row by pressing Tab at the last cell in the table to insert a new blank row below and then type the data.

7 Make J36 the active cell and then press Tab.

> A new row is inserted within the table.

continues

8 Type the following text in the columns indicated in row 37. Press Enter after typing the last cell (do not press Tab as this action will cause another new row to be added to the table.)

Employee Number	**99828**
Employee LastName	**Fernandez**
Employee FirstName	**Natalio**
Hire Date	**=date(2009,8,15)**
Telephone	**555-7643**
Years Experience	**3**
OR Experience	**Yes**
Day Shift Only?	**No**
Night Shift Only?	**Yes**
Can Work Either Shift	**Weekends only**

36	99823	Awad	Rania	8/11/2009	555-4652	7	Yes	No	No	Yes
37	99828	Fernandez	Natalio	8/15/2009	555-7643	3	Yes	No	Yes	Weekends only
38	*Updated:*	1-Oct-09								

Steps 6–8

9 Make active any cell within the table.

The contextual Table Tools Design tab is not active unless the active cell is positioned within the range of cells defined as the table.

10 With the Table Tools Design tab active, click the *Banded Rows* check box in the Table Style Options group to clear the box.

Banding the rows means that every other row is formatted differently. Banding makes it easier to read text across multiple columns in a list. The style of formatting for every other row is dependent on the table style that has been applied. Notice that when the check box is cleared, all rows are now formatted the same.

11 Click the *Banded Columns* check box in the Table Style Options group.

Notice every other column is now formatted with a different fill color.

12 Click the *First Column* check box in the Table Style Options group.

The cells in the first column are now bolded. The type of formatting applied is dependent on the table style.

Step 10

Step 12

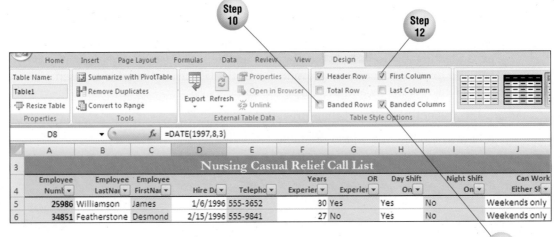

Step 11

In Brief
Format Table
1. Select range.
2. Click Format as Table button.
3. Click desired table style
4. Click OK.

(13) Select A5:A37, click the Home tab and then click the Center button in the Alignment group.

(14) Select E5:J37 and then click the Center button in the Alignment group.

(15) Center the labels in A4:J4 and then click in any cell to deselect the range.

	A	B	C	D	E	F	G	H	I	J
1	Columbia River General Hospital									
2	Division of Cardiology									
3	Nursing Casual Relief Call List									
4	Employee Number	Employee LastName	Employee FirstNar	Hire Date	Telephon	Years Experienc	OR Experienc	Day Shift Only?	Night Shift Only?	Can Work Either Shift
5	25986	Williamson	James	1/6/1996	555-3652	30	Yes	Yes	No	Weekends only
6	34851	Featherstone	Desmond	2/15/1996	555-9841	27	No	Yes	No	Weekends only
7	25967	VanHie	Hilary	7/15/1997	555-8425	22	No	Yes	No	No
8	14586	Kellerman	Rodney	8/3/1997	555-7412	24	Yes	No	No	Yes
9	48652	Casselman	Dana	10/15/1997	555-6325	22	Yes	No	No	Yes
10	78452	Mason	Terry	5/3/1998	555-1279	24	Yes	No	Yes	No

Step 15

Step 14

(16) Save **ExcelMedS3-05.xlsx**.

In Addition

Converting a Table to a Normal Range

A range that has been formatted as a table can be converted back to a normal range using the Convert to Range button in the Tools group of the Table Tools Design tab (shown below). Convert a table to a range if you no longer need to treat the table data as a range independent of data in the rest of the worksheet. For example, you may want to format a range as a table simply to apply the color, shading, and border effects that are available in Table Styles. Converting to a normal range preserves the formatting; however, features unique to a table such as banding, adding a total row, checking for duplicates, and so on are no longer available to the range.

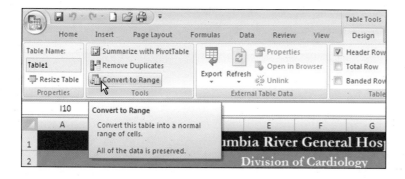

Activity 3.12

Sorting a Table by Single and Multiple Criteria

In Section 1 you learned to sort the payroll worksheet alphabetically by last names. To sort rows in a table by single or multiple criteria involves the same process as the one used in Section 1. To sort by a single column, click in any cell in the column by which you wish to sort and then use the *Sort A to Z* or *Sort Z to A* options at the Sort & Filter drop-down list. To group the rows first by one column and then sort the rows within each group by another column, open the Sort dialog box. You can continue to group and sort by multiple criteria as needed.

Project

Columbia River General Hospital

You decide to print the nursing casual relief call list with the data sorted alphabetically by last name. Next, you want to print the list grouped first in descending order by years of experience, grouped second by OR experience, and grouped third by whether the individual can work either shift.

1. With **ExcelMedS3-05.xlsx** open, click any cell in column B within the table range.

2. Click the Sort & Filter button in the Editing group in the Home tab.

3. Click *Sort A to Z* at the drop-down list.

> The table is rearranged in ascending order by last name. Excel displays an up-pointing black arrow in the filter arrow button to indicate that the table is ordered by the *Employee LastName* column.

4. Print the worksheet.

5. Click the Sort & Filter button and then click *Custom Sort* at the drop-down list.

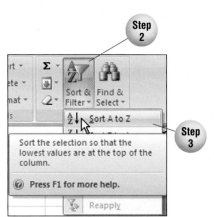

6. At the Sort dialog box, click the down-pointing arrow at the right of *Sort by* in the *Column* section (currently reads *Employee LastName*) and then click *Years Experience* at the drop-down list.

7. Click the down-pointing arrow at the right of the list box in the *Order* section (currently reads *Smallest to Largest*) and then click *Largest to Smallest* at the drop-down list.

8. Click the Add Level button in the Sort dialog box.

9. Click the down-pointing arrow at the right of *Then by* in the *Column* section and then click *OR Experience* at the drop-down list.

10 Click the down-pointing arrow at the right of the list box in the *Order* section (currently reads *A to Z*) and then click *Z to A* at the drop-down list.

> If the employee has OR experience, you want them to be ordered first within the group of employees with the same number of years of experience. Since cells in this column have only a Yes or No in the cell, sorting in descending order will ensure those with OR experience are shown first.

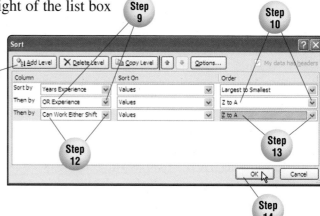

11 Click the Add Level button.

12 Click the down-pointing arrow at the right of the second *Then by* list box in the *Column* section and then click *Can Work Either Shift* at the drop-down list.

13 Click the down-pointing arrow at the right of the list box in the *Order* section (currently reads *A to Z*) and then click *Z to A* at the drop-down list.

> If the employee can work either shift, he or she will have the word *Yes* in the cell. Sorting the last column in descending order will ensure that those who have no shift restrictions will be listed first within those groups of employees who have OR experience and the most experience.

14 Click OK to begin the sort.

15 Examine the sorted worksheet and compare your results with the partial worksheet shown in Figure E3.5.

16 Print the worksheet.

17 Save **ExcelMedS3-05.xlsx**.

FIGURE E3.5 Sorted Partial Worksheet

> Notice in the two highlighted groups the employees with the same years of experience and with OR experience have those with *Yes* in the *Can Work Either Shift* column listed before those who have a restriction on the shift he/she can work.

	Employee Number	Employee LastName	Employee FirstName	Hire Date	Telephone	Years Experience	OR Experience	Day Shift Only?	Night Shift Only?	Can Work Either Shift
	25986	Williamson	James	1/6/1996	555-3652	30	Yes	Yes	No	Weekends only
		smond		2/15/1996	555-9841	27	No	Yes	No	Weekends only
		ginia		6/22/2002	555-6969	25	Yes	Yes	No	Weekends only
		dney		8/3/1997	555-7412	24	Yes	No	No	Yes
		rry		5/3/1998	555-1279	24	Yes	No	Yes	No
		na		10/15/1997	555-6325	22	Yes	No	No	Yes
		ra		3/31/2000	555-6127	22	No	No	Yes	No
		ary		7/15/1997	555-8425	22	No	Yes	No	No
		ila		4/28/2000	555-3485	21	No	No	No	Yes
		nn		10/22/1998	555-2548	20	Yes	Yes	No	Weekends only
		vid		9/9/2001	555-5961	20	No	No	No	Yes
		lly		11/19/1998	555-3684	20	No	Yes	No	Weekends only
		lando		11/10/2001	555-1186	20	No	Yes	No	No
		anda		4/27/1999	555-4896	19	Yes	No	Yes	No
		per		2/10/1999	555-6482	19	No	Yes	No	No
		da		7/7/2009	555-3498	16	Yes	No	No	Yes
		il		9/12/2008	555-2387	15	Yes	No	No	Yes
				4/23/2006	555-7383	15	Yes	Yes	No	No
		a		7/15/2008	555-9012	10	Yes	Yes	No	No
		a		12/10/2002	555-7822	10	Yes	No	Yes	No
25	99576	Diaz	Anna	7/5/2009	555-9378	10	No	No	Yes	No
26	34668	Fontana	Mario	1/31/2004	555-7433	10	No	No	Yes	No
27	69417	LaPierre	Denis	8/23/2003	555-8643	10	No	No	Yes	No

(Worksheet header: **Columbia River General Hospital** / Division of Cardiology / Nursing Casual Relief Call List)

In Addition

More about Sorting

By default, Excel sorts the data in a column by cell values alphanumerically. Alphanumeric sorting arranges rows with entries that begin with symbols first, then numbers, then letters. The *Sort On* drop-down list in the Custom Sort dialog box provides three additional methods with which you can group rows in the sort range: *Cell Color, Font Color,* or *Cell Icon.* In other words, you can arrange records in a table grouped by colors or icons.

Activity 3.13

Filtering a Table

A *filter* is used to display only certain records within the table that meet specified criteria. The records that do not meet the filter criteria are temporarily hidden from view. Using a filter, you can view and/or print a subset of rows within a table. For example, you might want to print a list of employees who have OR experience. Once you have printed the list, removing the filter redisplays all of the rows. Excel displays filter arrows in the first row of the table with which you specify the filter criteria.

Project

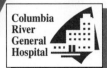

Luisa Gomez has asked you for a list of employees who can only work the night shift and another list of employees with OR experience who can work either shift.

1 With **ExcelMedS3-05.xlsx** open, click the filter arrow button ▼ next to the label *Night Shift Only?*

For each column in the table, a filter arrow button appears. Excel looks in the active column and includes in the filter drop-down list each unique field value that exists within the column. In addition, the entries *Sort A to Z, Sort Z to A,* and *Sort by Color* appear at the top of the list.

2 Click the check box next to *No* in the drop-down list to remove the check mark.

Clearing a check mark for a check box causes rows with the value that matches the entry in the filtered column to be hidden from view. Since the only other entry in the column is *Yes*, the criterion for the filter is to display rows within the table that have the text entry *Yes* in column I.

3 Click OK.

Excel hides any records that have a value other than *Yes* in the column as shown in Figure E3.6. The row numbers of the matching items that were found are displayed in blue and a filter icon appears in the filter arrow button in I4 to indicate the column that was used to filter by. The Status bar also shows the message that 9 of 33 records were found. A filtered worksheet can be edited, formatted, charted, or printed.

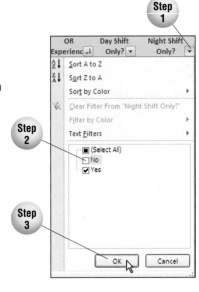

Filter icon indicates the column used to filter the table.

FIGURE E3.6 Filtered Worksheet

Excel hides rows that do not meet the criterion. Matching row numbers are displayed in blue.

	A	B	C	D	E	F	G	H	I	J
1				Columbia River General Hospital						
2				Division of Cardiology						
3				Nursing Casual Relief Call List						
4	Employee Number	Employee LastName	Employee FirstNam	Hire Date	Telephon	Years Experienc	OR Experienc	Day Shift Only?	Night Shift Only?	Can Work Either Shift
9	78452	Mason	Terry	5/3/1998	555-1279	24	Yes	No	Yes	No
11	24861	Orlowski	Kara	3/31/2000	555-6127	22	No	No	Yes	No
18	56983	Silverman	Amanda	4/27/1999	555-4896	19	Yes	No	Yes	No
24	27846	Fairchild	Tina	12/10/2002	555-7822	10	Yes	No	Yes	No
25	99576	Diaz	Anna	7/5/2009	555-9378	10	No	No	Yes	No
26	34668	Fontana	Mario	1/31/2004	555-7433	10	No	No	Yes	No
27	69417	LaPierre	Denis	8/23/2003	555-8643	10	No	No	Yes	No
33	99027	Kumar	Hashil	6/10/2009	555-2398	6	No	No	Yes	No
35	99828	Hernandez	Natalio	8/15/2009	555-7643	3	Yes	No	Yes	Weekends only
38	Updated:	1-Oct-09								

④ Print the filtered worksheet.

⑤ Point to the filter icon in the filter arrow button in I4. Notice the filter criterion displays in the ScreenTip.

⑥ Click the filter arrow button in I4.

⑦ Click *Clear Filter From "Night Shift Only?"* at the filter drop-down list.

> All rows within the table are restored to view.

⑧ Click the filter arrow button in G4.

⑨ Clear the check mark in the *No* check box at the drop-down list and then click OK.

> Only the employees with OR experience are displayed.

⑩ Click the filter arrow button in J4.

⑪ Clear the check marks in the *No* and *Weekends only* check boxes at the drop-down list and then click OK.

> Only those employees with OR experience who can work either shift are now displayed (see Figure E3.7). Notice that a filtered list can continue to be filtered until you reach only those records that meet your criteria.

⑫ Print the filtered worksheet.

⑬ Redisplay all records for both filtered columns.

⑭ Save and then close **ExcelMedS3-05.xlsx**.

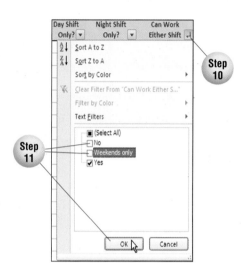

In Brief

Filter Table
1. Click desired filter arrow button.
2. Clear check boxes for items you do not want to view.
3. Click OK.

Remove Filter
1. Click desired filter arrow button.
2. Click *Clear Filter from (column title)*.

FIGURE E3.7 Filtered Worksheet Using Two Criteria

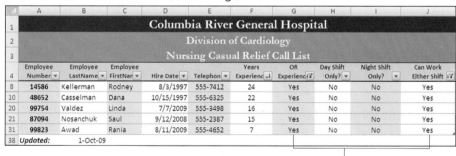

> Only those employees with OR experience AND who can work either shift are shown. You can continue filtering a worksheet to drill down to the records that you need to see.

In Addition

Filtering Data Not Formatted as a Table

Data in a worksheet that has not been formatted as a table can also be filtered using similar techniques as you learned in this activity. Select the range of cells that you wish to filter, click the Sort & Filter button in the Editing group in the Home tab, and then click *Filter* at the drop-down list. Excel adds filter arrows in each column of the first row of the selected range.

Features Summary

Feature	Ribbon Tab, Group	Button
change margins	Page Layout, Margins	
create a column chart	Insert, Charts	
create a pie chart	Insert, Charts	
draw a shape	Insert, Illustrations	
draw a text box	Insert, Text	
filter table	Home, Editing	
format table	Home, Styles	
insert clip art	Insert, Illustrations	
insert function	Formulas, Function Library	f_x
insert header or footer	Insert, Text	
Page Layout view	View, Workbook Views	OR
scale page width and/or height	Page Layout, Scale to Fit	
sort table	Home, Editing	

Knowledge Check

Completion: In the space provided at the right, write in the correct term, command, or option.

1. AVERAGE and COUNT are two of the functions grouped in this function category.
2. This Date and Time function inserts the current date (without the time) in the active cell.
3. The DATE function argument requires dates in this order separated by commas.
4. The IF function returns one of two values based on this criterion.
5. This type of chart is used to illustrate each value as a proportion of the total.
6. When a chart is selected, these three contextual Chart Tools tabs appear.
7. Click this tab and button to search for art on Office Online.
8. The mouse pointer changes to this as you are drawing a shape.
9. To center a worksheet horizontally and vertically, click this tab in the Page Setup dialog box.
10. A header is text that prints here.
11. A worksheet can be scaled to print on a specific number of pages with buttons from this group in the Page Layout tab.

12. Click this button in the Styles group in the Home tab to define an area of a worksheet as an independent range that can be formatted and managed separately from the rest of the worksheet. _____

13. Select this option from the Sort & Filter list to open a dialog box in which to define more than one sort column. _____

14. This term refers to temporarily hiding rows that do not meet a specified criterion. _____

Skills Review

Review 1 Inserting Statistical Functions

1. Open **CVPOpExp.xlsx**.
2. Save the workbook and name it **ExcelMedS3-R1**.
3. Make A15 the active cell.
4. Type **Average Expense** and then press Enter.
5. Type **Maximum Expense** and then press Enter.
6. Type **Minimum Expense** and then press Enter.
7. Make B15 the active cell and then create the formula that will calculate the average of the expense values in the range B4:B9.
8. Make B16 the active cell and then create the formula that will return the maximum expense value within the range B4:B9.
9. Make B17 the active cell and then create the formula that will return the minimum expense value within the range B4:B9.
10. Copy the formulas in B15:B17 to C15:F17.
11. If necessary, format the values in B15:F17 to Comma style with zero decimals.
12. Save **ExcelMedS3-R1.xlsx**.

Review 2 Using Date Functions

1. With **ExcelMedS3-R1.xlsx** open, make A19 the active cell.
2. Type **Date Created:** and then press the Right Arrow key.
3. With B19 the active cell, use the DATE function to insert the current date. *Note: You do not want to use the TODAY function, because the date will update each time you open the file.*
4. Format B19 to display the date in the format *14-Mar-01* (dd-mm-yy).
5. Make A20 the active cell.
6. Type **Next Revision Date:** and then press the Right Arrow key.
7. With B20 the active cell, type the formula **=b19+360** and then press Enter.
8. Save **ExcelMedS3-R1.xlsx**.

Review 3 Using the IF Function

Cascade
View
PEDIATRICS

1. With **ExcelMedS3-R1.xlsx** open, insert two rows above row 19.
2. Make A19 the active cell.
3. Type **Expense Over Target** and then press Enter.
4. Sydney Larsen, office manager of Cascade View Pediatrics, has set a quarterly target of $960 thousand for total expenses. Sydney wants you to create a formula to show the amount by which a quarter's total expenses are over the target when the target has been exceeded. Make B19 the active cell and then type the following IF function:

    =if(b11>960,b11-960,0)
5. Drag the fill handle from B19 to C19:E19.
6. In the space provided, write the values displayed as the results in the cells indicated.

    B19 _____
    C19 _____
    D19 _____
    E19 _____
7. In the space provided, write in your own words a brief explanation of the IF function entered in B19.

    _____

    _____

    _____

8. Assume that Sydney Larsen wants to experiment with various different targets and see the impact on each quarter. Make D21 the active cell and type **Quarterly Target**. Make F21 the active cell and type **960**. Revise the IF function in B19 to reference the value in F21 instead of the static value 960 that is currently used in the formula. ***Note: Be sure to use an absolute reference for F21 since the formula will have to be recopied to C21:E21.***
9. Copy the revised IF formula in B19 to C19:E19.
10. Change the value in F21 from *960* to *955*.
11. Save **ExcelMedS3-R1.xlsx**.

Review 4 Inserting a Picture; Sorting a List; Setting Print Options

Cascade
View
PEDIATRICS

1. With **ExcelMedS3-R1.xlsx** open, change the height of row 1 to 52.50 (70 pixels).
2. Select A1:F1 and change the fill color to white.
3. Make A1 the active cell, click the Insert tab, and then click the Picture button in the Illustrations group.
4. Navigate to the location of your student data files and then double-click *CVPLogo.jpg*.
5. Move the logo until it is centered over columns A through F.
6. Select A4:F9 and sort the range in ascending order. Click in any cell to deselect the range.
7. Change the top margin to 2 inches and the left margin to 1 inch.
8. Create a header that will print your first and last names at the left margin and the current date and time at the right margin separated by one space.
9. Create a footer that will print the word *Page* followed by the page number separated by one space at the left margin and the file name at the right margin.
10. Save, print, and then close **ExcelMedS3-R1.xlsx**.

Review 5 Creating and Modifying a Chart; Drawing an Arrow and Text
Box; Inserting Clip Art

Cascade View
PEDIATRICS

1. Open **CVPRent&MaintCosts.xlsx**.
2. Save the workbook with Save As and name it **ExcelMedS3-R2**.
3. Select the range A3:E10 and create a column chart as follows:
   a. 3-D Clustered Column
   b. Chart layout 3
   c. Chart Title: *Rent and Maintenance Costs*
   d. Move the chart to a new sheet labeled *ColumnChart*
4. With *ColumnChart* the active sheet, draw an arrow pointing to the column in the chart
   representing Clinic Cleaning for the fourth quarter. Draw a text box anchored to the end
   of the arrow and then type the following text inside the box:
   > **Includes price increase from new contractor Universal Cleaning Corporation.**
5. Format the text box to 10-point Candara with a Dark Red Shape Outline.
6. Format the Shape Outline of the arrow to the same color as the text box outline and then
   display Sheet 1.
7. Select A3:F10 and format the range as a table using *Table Style Light 20* (sixth from left
   in last row of *Light* section). Band the columns instead of the rows. Click the Home tab,
   click the Sort & Filter button in the Editing group, and then click *Filter* at the drop-down
   list to remove the filter arrows from the labels in row 3.
8. Save **ExcelMedS3-R2.xlsx**.
9. Print the entire workbook and then close **ExcelMedS3-R2.xlsx**.

Skills Assessment

Assessment 1 Using Statistical and IF Functions

North Shore
Medical Clinic

1. Lee Elliott, office manager of North Shore Medical Clinic, has started a
   worksheet that includes the clinic's top 15 medical supply purchases. Lee
   wants to calculate purchase quantity discounts from the clinic's two preferred
   medical supply vendors. Both vendors charge the same unit price but each
   offers a discount plan that varies the discount percent and quantity levels. Lee has asked
   for your help in writing the correct formulas to calculate the savings from each vendor.
   Specifically, Lee wants to know which supplier provides the better offer.
2. Open **NSMCTop15SuppliesDisc.xlsx**.
3. Save the workbook and name it **ExcelMedS3-A1**.
4. Create a formula to calculate the discount from AllCare Medical Supplies in E4 using the
   following criteria:
   - AllCare offers a 1.75% discount on the product's unit price for a quantity ordered of
     zero to four units.
   - The discount rises to 2.5% when five or more units are ordered.
   - Reference the percentage values in cells B22 and B23 within your IF statement. ***Hint:***
     Keep in mind the formula will be copied to rows 5 through 18 in a later step.
5. Create a formula to calculate the discount from BestCare Health Supply in F4 using the
   following criteria:
   - BestCare offers a 1.8% discount on the product's unit price for a quantity ordered of
     zero to five units.

- The discount rises to 2.25% when six or more units are ordered.
- Reference the percentage values in cells B24 and B25 within your IF statement. *Hint: Keep in mind the formula will be copied to rows 5 through 18 in a later step.*

6. Copy the formulas to the remaining rows in columns E and F.
7. Calculate the total discount value in E20 and F20.
8. Apply formatting options as needed.
9. Enter an appropriate label and create a formula to calculate the average discount below the total row for each vendor.
10. Print the worksheet in landscape orientation, centered horizontally.
11. Save and then close **ExcelMedS3-A1.xlsx**.

Assessment 2 Changing Print Options; Using Date and IF Functions

1. Darrin Lancaster, CMA at North Shore Medical Clinic, has asked you to finish the worksheet he started with Dr. Hydall's dermatology patient tracking records.
2. Open **NSMCDermPatientTrack.xlsx**.
3. Save the workbook and name it **ExcelMedS3-A2**.
4. Medical records are completed on the system 12 days after Dr. Hydall's report has been mailed to the referring physician. Create a formula in H4 that calculates the date the system report should be filed.
5. Copy the formula to the remaining rows in column H.
6. Create a formula for a recall date in column I using the following information:
    - If *Repeat Assessment* contains *Y* for Yes, then calculate the recall date 45 days from the date of the consultation visit.
    - If *Repeat Assessment* does not contain *Y*, instruct Excel to place the words *Not required* in the cell. *Hint: Use quotation symbols before and after a text entry in an IF statement. For example, =IF(G4="Y", ...).*
    - Format the column to display the date consistently with other dates within the worksheet.
    - Expand the column width as necessary.
7. Set the following print options:
    a. Change the orientation to landscape.
    b. Change the top margin to 2 inches and center the worksheet horizontally.
    c. Create a header that will print your name at the left margin and the current date at the right margin.
8. Adjust column widths as necessary to ensure the worksheet requires only one page to print and apply other formatting changes as needed to improve the worksheet's appearance.
9. Save, print, and then close **ExcelMedS3-A2.xlsx**.

Assessment 3 Creating and Formatting Charts; Drawing an Arrow and Text Box

1. Dr. Hydall at North Shore Medical Clinic has asked you to create charts from the dermatology patient analysis report for a presentation to the local members of the American Academy of Dermatology. Dr. Hydall has specifically requested a line chart depicting the numbers for all diagnoses by age group, and a pie chart summarizing the diagnosis by total number of patients.

2. Open **NSMCDermAgeStats.xlsx**.
3. Save the workbook and name it **ExcelMedS3-A3**.
4. Create a line chart in its own sheet labeled *LineChart* that will display the values for 0–12 through 50+ patient ages for each diagnosis. Include an appropriate chart title. You determine any other chart elements to include that will make the chart data easy to interpret.
5. Create a 3-D pie chart that will display the number of patients in each age group as a percentage of 100. ***Hint: Select the ranges B3:G3 and B9:G9 before selecting the 3-D pie option.*** Include an appropriate chart title and display percentages as the data labels. Place the pie chart at the bottom of the worksheet starting in row 12.
6. Resize the chart so that its width extends to the right edge of column H and the height to the bottom boundary of row 30.
7. Draw an arrow pointing to the 13–20 age group slice in the pie chart. Create a text box at the end of the arrow containing the text *Patients in this age group growing greater than 10% per year!*
8. If necessary, resize the arrow and text box.
9. Change the font color of the text inside the text box to red, the line color of the border of the text box to blue, and the fill color to light green.
10. Change the line color of the arrow to blue.
11. Center the worksheet horizontally.
12. Print the entire workbook.
13. Save and then close **ExcelMedS3-A3.xlsx**.

Assessment 4 Working with Tables

1. Laura Latterell, education director at Columbia River General Hospital, has started a worksheet in which she tracks professional development activity completion for full-time nursing staff. Laura assists nurses with selection of professional development activities and plans workshops throughout the year to provide in-service training. Laura would like the worksheet to be used to provide printouts she needs for planning upcoming workshops.
2. Open **CRGHNurseEd.xlsx**.
3. Save the workbook and name it **ExcelMedS3-A4**.
4. Format A4:A32 as a table. You determine the table style.
5. Filter the table to obtain a list of nurses who are RNs and work in the ICU unit.
6. Sort the list in ascending order by last name.
7. Print the filtered list changing print options as necessary to fit the printing on 1 page.
8. Redisplay all records.
9. Filter the list to obtain a list of nurses working in the PreOp unit who are not current with professional development (PD) activities.
10. Sort the list in ascending order by last name.
11. Print the filtered list.
12. Redisplay all records.
13. Sort the entire list first by *PD Current?*, then by *Years Experience*, and then by *Last Name*, all in ascending order.
14. Print the sorted list changing print options as necessary to fit the printing on 1 page.
15. Save and then close **ExcelMedS3-A4.xlsx**.

Assessment 5 Inserting Clip Art

1. Lee Elliott, office manager at North Shore Medical Clinic, has requested that you enhance the vendor discount evaluation worksheet before presentation at the next clinic meeting.
2. Open **ExcelMedS3-A1.xlsx**.
3. Save the workbook and name it **ExcelMedS3-A5**.
4. Insert four blank rows above the title row and then add appropriate clip art images at the top of the worksheet. You determine how many images, size, and location within the new rows.
5. Select A8:F22 and apply all borders to the cells within the range.
6. Format the values in E8:F22 to Accounting Number format.
7. Apply other formatting attributes that would enhance the appearance of the remainder of the worksheet.
8. Save **ExcelMedS3-A5.xlsx**.
9. Print and then close **ExcelMedS3-A5.xlsx**.

Assessment 6 Finding Information on Themes and Saving a Workbook in a Different File Format

1. Use the Help feature to find information on *Themes* in Excel 2007.
2. Open **ExcelMedS3-A1.xlsx**.
3. Save the workbook and name it **ExcelMedS3-A6**.
4. Apply the *Technic* theme to the worksheet.
5. Print **ExcelMedS3-A6.xlsx**.
6. Use the Help feature to find out how to save a workbook in a different file format. Specifically, you want to save the workbook in Excel 2003 file format.

HELP

7. Save the workbook in Excel 2003 file format using the same file name. Click Continue at any compatibility messages that may appear.
8. Close **ExcelMedS3-A6.xls**.

Assessment 7 Finding Information on Renaming and Deleting Worksheets

1. Use the Help feature to find out how to rename and delete worksheets.
2. Open **ExcelMedS3-A3.xlsx**.
3. Save the workbook and name it **ExcelMedS3-A7**.
4. Rename *LineChart* to *AgeStatsChart*.
5. Rename *Sheet1* to *DiagnosisByAge*.
6. Delete the blank Sheet2 and Sheet3 worksheets.
7. Create a footer on each sheet that prints the file name followed by the worksheet

HELP

name in the center section. *Hint: Use the Page Setup dialog to create a footer in a chart sheet.*
8. Print the entire workbook.
9. Save and then close **ExcelMedS3-A7.xlsx**.

Assessment 8 Researching and Calculating Conference Costs

1. Visit the Web site for the American Association of Medical Assistants (AAMA) and find the dates and location for the upcoming annual convention.
2. Assume that the local chapter of the AAMA is willing to sponsor a student to attend the conference. As part of the application for sponsorship, you need to submit a detailed expense estimate.
3. Use the Internet to research airfare, hotel accommodation, conference registration fees, and any other expenses that would be related to attending the conference.
4. Create an Excel workbook to present with your application that summarizes the cost of the conference.
5. Apply formatting enhancements to the worksheet to produce a professional report.
6. Save the workbook and name it **ExcelMedS3-A8**.
7. Print and then close **ExcelMedS3-A8.xlsx**.

Marquee Challenge

Challenge 1 Preparing a Patient Cost Record

1. Create the worksheet shown in Figure E3.8 including all formatting options. Use your best judgment to determine font, font size, column widths, and/or row heights.
   a. For all date entries, use a DATE function.
   b. Use a formula to calculate *Length of Stay*.
   c. Use a formula to calculate *Direct Overhead* at 15% of *Total Direct Charges*.
   d. Use a formula to calculate *Indirect Overhead* at 10% of *Total Direct Charges*.
   e. Use a formula to calculate *TOTAL COST* as the sum of *Total Direct Charges, Direct Overhead,* and *Indirect Overhead*.
2. Center the worksheet horizontally.
3. Create a header to print your name at the left margin and the current date at the right margin.
4. Create a footer to print the workbook name centered between the margins.
5. Save the workbook and name it **ExcelMedS3-C1**.
6. Print and then close **ExcelMedS3-C1.xlsx**.

Columbia River General Hospital
Patient Cost Record

Date of Cost Report	12-Mar-11		TOTAL COST			$	27,143.53

Patient Chart #	70176345		Attending Physician			Dr. Lekha Priyanka
PIN #	2365		Diagnosis/Principal Procedure			Hip Replacement
Patient Last Name	**Nguyen**		Admit Date:		10-Feb-11	
Patient First Name	Mary		Discharge Date:		16-Feb-11	
Date of Birth	22-Oct-76		Length of Stay:		6.0	

Department	Dept Code	Service Code	Description		Charges
Patient Registration	521	13	IP Registration	$	65.15
Health Records	534	17	Clerical		187.50
Food Services	341	67	Patient Meals		375.15
Nursing	122	27	Orthopaedics		4,576.12
Operating Room	431	26	OR		6,548.55
Operating Room	431	31	Respiratory Therapy		235.00
Recovery Room	658	87	Recovery Level 4		678.23
Laboratory Services	377	18	Lab Requisitions		349.00
General Radiology	876	35	HIP LT AP		134.66
General Radiology	876	44	Pelvis & HIP LT		175.33
General Radiology	876	64	Ultrasound		133.28
Pharmacy	912	38	Inpatient Drugs		873.44
Physiotherapy	765	29	Physiotherapy		673.44
Occupational Therapy	844	28	Occupational Therapy		534.22
Physican Service	115	34	OR Surgeon		3,587.75
Inpatient Ward	239	12	General Ward		2,588.00
			Total Direct Charges	$	21,714.82
			Direct Overhead	$	3,257.22
			Indirect Overhead	$	2,171.48

Challenge 2 Charting 10-Year New Cancer Rate Statistics

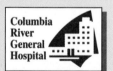

Columbia
River
General
Hospital

1. Open the workbook named **CRGHUSCancerStats.xlsx**.
2. Save the workbook and name it **ExcelMedS3-C2**.
3. Using the data in the worksheet, create the chart shown in Figure E3.9 in its own sheet including all formatting options and drawn objects.
4. Create a header to print your name at the left margin and the current date at the right margin.
5. Create a footer to print the workbook name centered between the margins.
6. Save **ExcelMedS3-C2.xlsx**.
7. Print only the chart and then close **ExcelMedS3-C2.xlsx**.

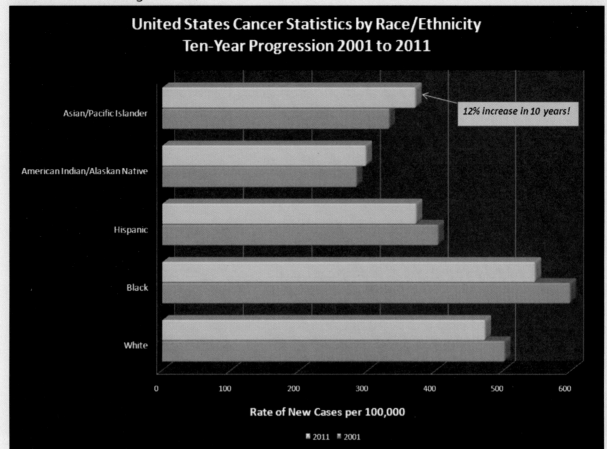

United States Cancer Statistics by Race/Ethnicity
Ten-Year Progression 2001 to 2011

12% increase in 10 years!

Asian/Pacific Islander

American Indian/Alaskan Native

Hispanic

Black

White

0   100   200   300   400   500   600

Rate of New Cases per 100,000

2011   2001

Integrating Programs
Word and Excel

Skills

- Copy and paste Word data into an Excel worksheet
- Link an Excel worksheet with a Word document
- Update linked data
- Link an Excel chart with a Word document
- Embed an Excel worksheet into a Word document
- Edit an embedded worksheet

Student Resources

Before beginning this section:
1. Copy to your storage medium the IntegratingMed1 subfolder from the IntegratingPrograms folder on the Student Resources CD.
2. Make IntegratingMed1 the active folder.

In addition to containing the data files needed to complete section work, the Student Resources CD contains model answers in PDF format for each of the projects in this section; model answers for end-of-section exercises are not provided.

Projects Overview

Copy and paste quarterly statistics on new patients; calculate depreciation values, edit data, and link an equipment worksheet to a Word document; link and update a chart depicting actual and projected expenditures to an Operations report in Word; and embed a flu shot clinic form from Excel into a Word document.

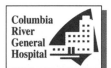

Copy and paste volunteer information from a worksheet to a Word document; link and update tuition fee billing data and a chart from a worksheet to a Word document; and embed a fact sheet into a hospital foundation document.

Activity 1.1

Copying and Pasting Word Data into an Excel Worksheet

Microsoft Office is a suite that allows integration, which is the combining of data from two or more programs into one document. Integration can occur by copying and pasting data between programs. The program containing the data to be copied is called the *source program* and the program where the data is pasted is called the *destination program*. For example, you can copy data from a Word document into an Excel worksheet. Copy and paste data between programs in the same manner as you would copy and paste data within a program.

Project Copy data on new patients for North Shore Medical Clinic from a Word document into Excel and then use Excel to total the patients by month and by specialty.

1. Open Word and then open the document named **NSMCNewPatientRpt.docx**.

2. Open Excel and then open the workbook named **NSMCNewPatients-Qtr1.xlsx**.

3. Save the workbook with Save As and name it **IntMedE1-01**.

4. Click the button on the Taskbar representing the Word document **NSMCNewPatientRpt.docx**.

5. Select the last six rows of the table as shown below.

6. Click the Copy button in the Clipboard group in the Home tab.

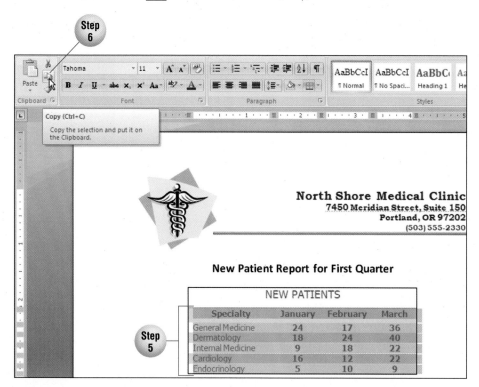

7. Click the button on the Taskbar representing the Excel workbook **IntMedE1-01.xlsx**.

8 With A5 the active cell, click the Paste button in the Clipboard group.

9 Click the Paste Options button and then click *Match Destination Formatting*.

10 Click in any cell to deselect the range.

11 Select B5:D10 and then move the range to D5:F10.

12 Make H5 the active cell and then type the label **Total**.

13 Make H6 the active cell, click the Sum button **Σ ▾** in the Editing group, and then press Enter to add the range D6:G6.

14 Use the fill handle to copy the formula in H6 down to cells H7:H10.

15 Make A12 the active cell and then type the label **Total**.

16 Make D12 the active cell and then use the Sum button **Σ ▾** in the Editing group to add the range D6:D11.

17 Use the fill handle to copy the formula in D12 to E12:H12.

18 Clear the contents of G12 to remove the zero.

19 Apply formatting changes as desired to improve the appearance of the worksheet.

20 Save, print, and then close **IntMedE1-01.xlsx**.

21 Click the button on the Taskbar representing the Word document **NSMCNewPatientRpt.docx**.

22 Close **NSMCNewPatientRpt.docx**. Click No if prompted to save changes to the document.

	A	B	C	D	E	F	G	H
1								
2			North Shore Medical Clinic					
3			New Patient Report					
4			Quarter 1 - January, February, March					
5	Specialty			January	February	March		Total
6	General Medicine			24	17	36		77
7	Dermatology			18	24	40		82
8	Internal Medicine			9	18	22		49
9	Cardiology			16	12	22		50
10	Endocrinology			5	10	9		24
11								
12	Total			72	81	129		282

Steps 11–18

In Addition

Cycling between Open Programs

Cycle through open programs by clicking the button on the Taskbar representing the desired program. You can also cycle through open programs by pressing Alt + Tab. Pressing Alt + Tab causes a menu to display. Continue holding down the Alt key and pressing the Tab key until the desired program icon is selected by a border in the menu and then release the Tab key and the Alt key.

Activity 1.2

Linking an Excel Worksheet with a Word Document

In the previous activity, you copied data from a Word document and pasted it into an Excel worksheet. If you continuously update the data in the Word document, you would need to copy and paste the data each time into the Excel worksheet. If you update data on a regular basis that is copied to other programs, consider copying and linking the data. When data is linked, the data exists in the source program but not as separate data in the destination program.

The destination program contains only a code that identifies the name and location of the source program, the document name, and the location in the document. Since the data resides only in the source program, changes made to the data in the source program are reflected automatically in the destination program. Office updates a link whenever you open the destination program or you edit the linked data in the destination program.

Project

Open a worksheet with equipment purchase information, use a function to calculate straight-line depreciation, and then copy and link the data to a Word document.

1. With Word the active program, open the document named **NSMCEquipGERm3-SLD.docx**.

2. Save the document with Save As and name it **IntMedW1-01**.

3. Make Excel the active program and then open the workbook named **NSMCEquipGERm3.xlsx**.

4. Save the workbook with Save As and name it **IntMedE1-02**.

   In the next steps, you will use Excel's SLN function to calculate the annual depreciation value to be recorded for each equipment item. Straight-line depreciation requires three values: the equipment's original cost, the estimated value of the equipment when taken out of service (salvage), and the expected number of years the clinic will use the item (life).

5. Make I6 the active cell and then click the Insert function button on the Formula bar.

6. Type **straight-line depreciation** in the *Search for a function* text box and then press Enter or click Go.

7. If necessary click to select *SLN* in the *Select a function* list box and then click OK.

8. With the insertion point positioned in the *Cost* text box, type **f6** and then press Tab.

9. Type **g6** in the *Salvage* text box and then press Tab.

10. Type **h6** in the *Life* text box and then press Enter.

    Excel returns the value *$112.50* in I6. In the Formula bar, the function is *=SLN(F6,G6,H6)*.

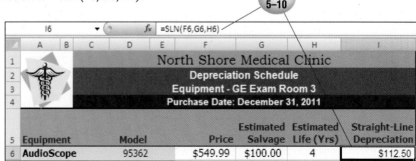

11 Copy the formula in I6 to I7:I10.

12 Make I11 the active cell and then use Sum button to add I6:I10.

Straight-Line Depreciation
$112.50
$1,100.00
$89.98
$112.50
$146.67
$1,561.64

Steps 11–12

13 Select the range A5:I11 and then click the Copy button in the Clipboard group in the Home tab.

14 Click the button on the Taskbar representing the Word document **IntMedW1-01.docx**.

15 Press Ctrl + End to move the insertion point to the end of the document.

16 Click the Paste button arrow and then click *Paste Special* at the drop-down list.

17 Click *Microsoft Office Excel Worksheet Object* in the *As* list box, click *Paste link*, and then click OK.

In Brief

Link Data between Programs
1. Open desired programs and documents.
2. Select data in source program.
3. Click Copy button.
4. Click button on Taskbar representing destination program.
5. Click Paste button arrow, *Paste Special*.
6. Click object in *As* list box.
7. Click *Paste link*.
8. Click OK.

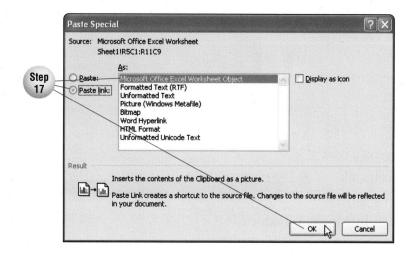

Step 17

18 Save, print, and then close **IntMedW1-01.docx**.

19 Click the button on the Taskbar representing the Excel workbook **IntMedE1-02.xlsx**.

20 Press the Esc key to remove the moving marquee around the range A5:I11 and then click any cell to deselect the range.

21 Save, print, and then close **IntMedE1-02.xlsx**.

In Addition

Linking Data within a Program

Linking does not have to be between two different programs—you can link data between files in the same program. For example, you can create an object in a Word document such as a table or chart and then link the object with another Word document (or several Word documents). If you make a change to the object in the original document, the linked object in the other document (or documents) is automatically updated.

Activity
1.3

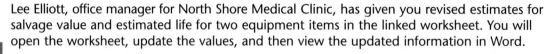

Updating Linked Data

The advantage of linking data over copying data is that editing the data in the source program will automatically update the data in the destination program. To edit linked data, open the document in the source program, make the desired edits, and then save the document. The next time you open the document in the destination program, the data is updated.

Project

Lee Elliott, office manager for North Shore Medical Clinic, has given you revised estimates for salvage value and estimated life for two equipment items in the linked worksheet. You will open the worksheet, update the values, and then view the updated information in Word.

① With Excel the active program, open **IntMedE1-02.xlsx**.

The salvage value and estimated life for the AudioScope has been revised to $75.00 and 3 respectively.

② Make G6 the active cell and then edit the cell to *$75.00*.

③ Make H6 the active cell and then edit the cell to *3*.

④ Save and close **IntMedE1-02.xlsx** and then exit Excel.

⑤ With Word the active program, open **IntMedW1-01.docx**.

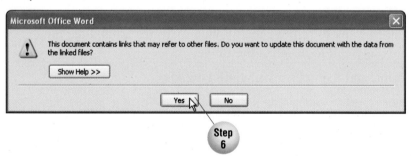

⑥ Click Yes at the message asking if you want to update the document with the data from the linked files.

The document opens and the linked data is updated to reflect the changes made in Steps 2–3.

⑦ Review the Word document and notice the estimated salvage and estimated life values for the AudioScope have been updated.

Another method that can be used to edit linked data is to double-click the linked object in the source program.

⑧ Position the mouse pointer over the linked object and then double-click the left mouse button.

Excel opens with **IntMedE1-02.xlsx** open in the Excel window. The linked range is highlighted. You need to change the salvage value and estimated life for the Wall Transformer to $50.00 and 2 respectively.

9. Make G10 the active cell and then edit the cell to *$50.00*.

10. Make H10 the active cell and then edit the cell to *2*.

11. Click the Save button on the Quick Access toolbar and then exit Excel.

12. Notice the values in the linked object in Word have updated.

In Brief

Update Linked Data
1. Open document in source program.
2. Make desired edits.
3. Save and close document.
4. Open document in destination program.
5. Click Yes to update links.
6. Save and close document.

Equipment Purchase – GE Exam Room 3
Purchase Date: December 31, 2011
Straight-Line Depreciation Schedule

Equipment	Model	Price	Estimated Salvage	Estimated Life (Yrs)	Straight-Line Depreciation
AudioScope	95362	$549.99	$75.00	3	$158.33
ECG Monitor	2350-500	$3,800.00	$500.00	3	$1,100.00
Otoscope	53620	$179.95	$0.00	2	$89.98
ThermoScan	40560	$225.00	$0.00	2	$112.50
Wall Transformer	652-A	$440.00	$50.00	2	$195.00
Total		$5,194.94			$1,655.81

Step 12

13. Save, print, and then close **IntMedW1-01.docx**.

In Addition

Breaking a Link

The link between an object in the destination and source programs can be broken. To break a link, right-click on the object, point to *Linked Worksheet Object*, and then click *Links*. At the Links dialog box, click the Break Link button. At the question asking if you are sure you want to break the link, click the Yes button.

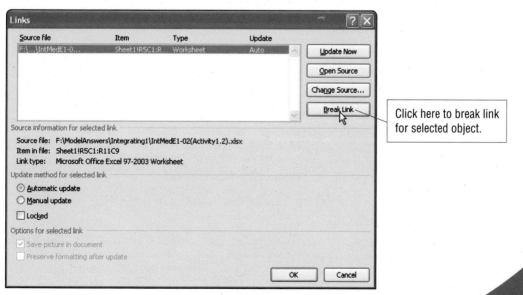

Click here to break link for selected object.

Activity 1.4

Linking an Excel Chart with a Word Document

While a worksheet does an adequate job of representing data, you can present some data more visually with a chart. A *chart* is a visual representation of numeric data and, like a worksheet, can be linked to a document in another program. Link a chart in the same manner as you would link a worksheet.

Project Link a chart depicting North Shore Medical Clinic's actual expenditures to projected expenditures with the Operations Report in Word. After linking the chart, you will update the data used to generate the chart.

1. With Word the active program, open **NSMCOpReport.docx**.

2. Save the document with Save As and name it **IntMedW1-02**.

3. Start Excel and then open the workbook named **NSMCQtrlyExpCht.xlsx**.

4. Save the workbook with Save As and name it **IntMedE1-03**.

5. Click once over the chart to select the chart object. (A translucent border displays around the chart.)

   > Make sure you do not select an individual chart element when you select the chart. If you see a thin border around a chart element (such as the legend) with white sizing handles, click outside the chart and select the chart again. Click in a white area around the inside perimeter to select the chart without selecting an individual chart element.

6. Click the Copy button in the Clipboard group in the Home tab.

7. Click the button on the Taskbar representing the Word document **IntMedW1-02.docx**.

8. Press Ctrl + End to move the insertion point to the end of the document.

9. Click the Center button in the Paragraph group in the Home tab.

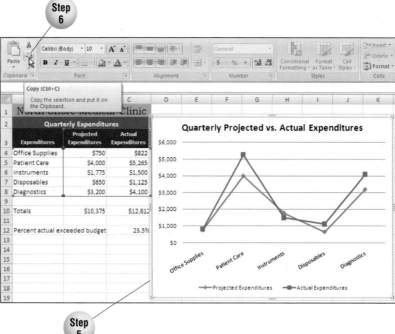

10. Click the Paste button arrow in the Clipboard group and then click *Paste Special*.

11. If necessary, click *Microsoft Office Excel Chart Object* in the *As* list box, click *Paste link*, and then click OK.

12. Save **IntMedW1-02.docx**.

13 Make Excel the active program and then press the Esc key to remove the translucent turquoise border from the chart.

> The actual *Diagnostics* expenditure value is incorrect. You will enter the correct value and examine the change in the chart in both Excel and Word.

14 Make C8 the active cell and then edit the cell to *3400*.

15 Examine the revised chart in Excel.

16 Save and then close **IntMedE1-03.xlsx**.

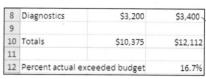

8	Diagnostics	$3,200	$3,400
9			
10	Totals	$10,375	$12,112
11			
12	Percent actual exceeded budget		16.7%

Step 14

17 Make Word the active program.

> To instruct Word to update the open document, open the Links dialog box and use the Update button.

18 Click the Office button, point to *Prepare*, and then click *Edit Links to Files*.

19 At the Links dialog box with the linked object selected in the list box, click the Update Now button.

20 Click OK to close the Links dialog box.

21 Edit the percent value in the second-to-last sentence in the paragraph above the chart to *16.7%* so that the sentence reads *Overall, the clinic spent 16.7% more on operations than projected.*

22 Save, print, and then close **IntMedW1-02.docx**.

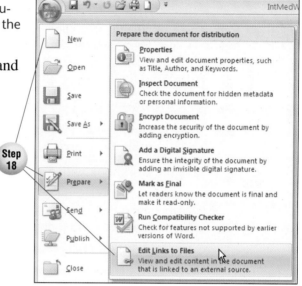

Step 18

Step 21

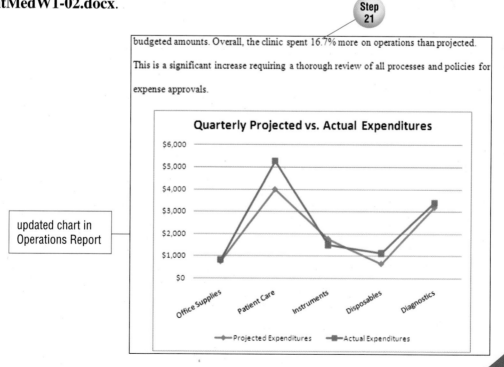

budgeted amounts. Overall, the clinic spent 16.7% more on operations than projected. This is a significant increase requiring a thorough review of all processes and policies for expense approvals.

Quarterly Projected vs. Actual Expenditures

updated chart in Operations Report

→ Projected Expenditures ■ Actual Expenditures

Activity 1.5

Embedding an Excel Worksheet into a Word Document

You can copy an object between documents in a program, link an object, or embed an object. A linked object resides in the source program but not as a separate object in the destination program. An embedded object resides in the document in the source program as well as the destination program. If a change is made to an embedded object at the source program, the change is not made to the object in the destination program. Since an embedded object is not automatically updated as is a linked object, the only advantage to embedding rather than simply copying and pasting is that you can edit an embedded object in the destination program using the tools of the source program.

Project

Copy and embed a flu shot clinic form created by Heather Mitsui, RMA at North Shore Medical Clinic, from an Excel worksheet into a Word document.

1. With Word the active program, open **NSMCFluShotClinics.docx**.

2. Save the document with Save As and name it **IntMedW1-03**.

3. Make Excel the active program and then open the workbook named **NSMCFluShotForm.xlsx**.

4. Save the workbook with Save As and name it **IntMedE1-04**.

   Heather Mitsui used Excel to create a flu shot dispensing record form for the upcoming flu shot clinics. You decide to embed Heather's form into a Word document since the Word document has the clinic's letterhead at the top of the page.

5. Select A9:K29 and then click the Copy button ⧉ in the Clipboard group in the Home tab.

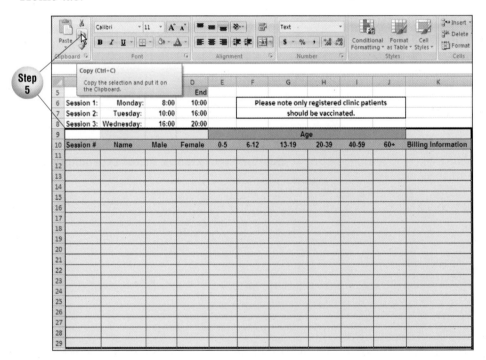

6. Make Word the active program and then press Ctrl + End to move the insertion point to the end of **IntMedW1-03.docx**.

7. Click the Paste button arrow in the Clipboard group and then click *Paste Special*.

(8) If necessary, click *Microsoft Office Excel Worksheet Object* in the *As* list box and then click OK.

? PROBLEM

Make sure you do not click the *Paste link* option.

(9) Display the form in Print Preview to view how the form will look when printed.

(10) Close Print Preview.

(11) Save, print, and then close **IntMedW1-03.docx**.

(12) Make Excel the active program and then press the Esc key to remove the moving marquee from the selected range.

(13) Click in any cell to deselect the range.

(14) Close **IntMedE1-04.xlsx** and then exit Excel.

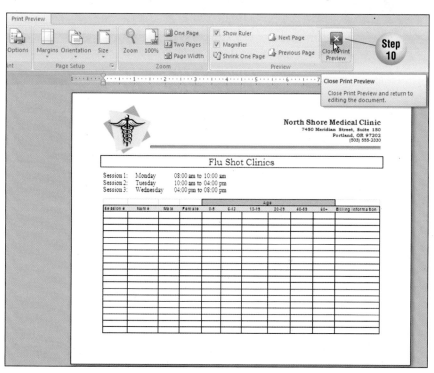

In Addition

Inserting an Embedded Object from an Existing File

You embedded an Excel worksheet in a Word document using the Copy button and options at the Paste Special dialog box. Another method is available for embedding an object from an existing file. In the destination program document, position the insertion point where you want the object embedded and then click the Object button in the Text group in the Insert tab. At the Object dialog box, click the Create from File tab. At the Object dialog box with the Create from File tab selected as shown at the right, type the desired file name in the *File name* text box or click the Browse button and then select the desired file from the appropriate folder. At the Object dialog box, make sure the *Link to file* check box does not contain a check mark and then click OK.

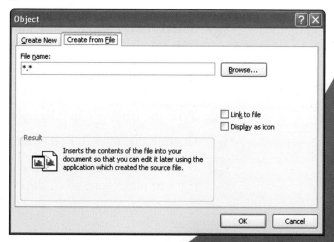

Activity 1.6

Editing an Embedded Worksheet

An embedded object can be edited in the destination program using the tools of the source program. Double-click the embedded object in the destination document and the ribbon from the source program becomes active. For example, if you double-click an Excel worksheet that is embedded in a Word document, the Excel ribbon tabs and groups display at the top of the Word document window.

Project

After embedding the flu shot clinic form into Word, you decide to make some changes to the form's layout.

1. With Word the active program, open **IntMedW1-03.docx**.

2. Save the document with Save As and name it **IntMedW1-04**.

3. Change the start time for the *Session 3* clinic from *04:00 pm* to *06:30 pm*.

Session 1:	Monday	08:00 am to 10:00 am
Session 2:	Tuesday	10:00 am to 04:00 pm
Session 3:	Wednesday	06:30 pm to 08:00 pm

Step 3

4. Double-click anywhere over the embedded worksheet.

    In a few seconds, the worksheet displays surrounded by a gray border; column and row designations; and the Excel ribbon displays at the top of the Word document window.

5. Click in any cell within the embedded worksheet to deselect the range.

6. Select columns E–J and then change the column widths to *6.00 (47 pixels)*.

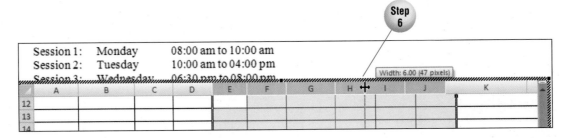

Step 6

7. Click in any cell to deselect the columns.

8. Select A9:D9 and K9 and apply Red, Accent 2, Darker 25% (sixth from left in fifth row in *Theme Colors* section) fill color to the cells.

9. Insert a new column between columns D and E (between *Female* and *0-5*) and then change the column width of the new column to *6.00 (47 pixels)*.

10. Type the label **0-1** in E10 (newly inserted column).

11. Change the label in F10 from *0-5* to *2-5*.

12. If necessary, drag the middle right sizing handle of the embedded worksheet right to make sure all of the columns A–L are visible in the object's border.

13 Merge and Center the label *Age* over columns E–K.

14 Select E9 (merged *Age* label) and apply an outside border.

15 Select A9:L9 and apply an outside border.

16 Make sure the only cells visible within the embedded object border are the range A9:L29. If any other cells from the source worksheet are visible, use the horizontal and vertical scroll arrows to adjust the window.

Figure I1.1 illustrates a portion of the embedded worksheet with the revised formatting applied in Steps 8 to 15. If the same portion of your worksheet does not appear as shown in Figure I1.1, review Steps 8 to 15 to determine if you have missed a step. Also note that you may need to scroll the worksheet to ensure columns A through L and rows 1 through 29 are visible within the object's border.

FIGURE I1.1 Excel Worksheet Embedded in a Word Document

revised formatting, new column (E) inserted, and edits to labels (E10 and F10) in Steps 8–15

	A	B	C	D	E	F	G	H	I	J	K	L
Session 1:	Monday			08:00 am to 10:00 am							
Session 2:	Tuesday			10:00 am to 04:00 pm							
Session 3:	Wednesday			06:30 pm to 08:00 pm							
9							Age					
10	Session #	Name	Male	Female	0-1	2-5	6-12	13-19	20-39	40-59	60+	Billing Information
11												
12												
13												
14												
15												
16												
17												
18												
19												
20												
21												
22												

17 Click outside the worksheet to deselect the embedded object.

18 Save, print, and then close **IntMedW1-04.docx**.

In Addition

Troubleshooting Linking and Embedding Problems

If you double-click a linked or embedded object and a message appears telling you that the source file or source program cannot be opened, consider the following troubleshooting options. Check to make sure that the source program is installed on your computer. If the source program is not installed, convert the object to the file format of a program that is installed. Try closing other programs to free memory and make sure you have enough memory to run the source program. Check to make sure the source program does not have any dialog boxes open and, if it is a linked object, check to make sure someone else is not working in the source file.

Skills Review

Review 1 Copying and Pasting Data

Columbia River General Hospital

1. With Excel the active program, open the workbook named **CRGHInfoDeskVolunteers.xlsx**.
2. Make Word the active program and then open the document named **CRGHVolunteerPost.docx**.
3. Save the document with Save As and name it **IntMedW1-R1**.
4. Make Excel the active program, select C7:F28 and Copy the cells to the Clipboard.
5. Make Word the active program and then press Ctrl + End to move the insertion point to the end of **IntMedW1-R1.docx**.
6. Paste the contents in the Clipboard into the Word document.
7. Select the table, open the Table Properties dialog box, center the table between the left and right margins, and then deselect the table.
8. Display the document in Print Preview.
9. Close Print Preview.
10. Save, print, and then close **IntMedW1-R1.docx**.
11. Make Excel the active program, remove the moving marquee, and then deselect the range.
12. Close **CRGHInfoDeskVolunteers.xlsx**.

Review 2 Linking an Object

Columbia River General Hospital

1. With Word the active program, open the document named **CRGH4thQtrTuitionFees.docx**.
2. Save the document with Save As and name it **IntMedW1-R2**.
3. Make Excel the active program and then open the workbook named **CRGHQtrlyTuitionBillingRpt.xlsx**.
4. Save the workbook with Save As and name it **IntMedE1-R1**.
5. Select A7:G16 and then link the cells to the end of the Word document **IntMedW1-R2.docx**.
6. Save, print, and then close **IntMedW1-R2.docx**.
7. Make Excel the active program, remove the moving marquee, and then deselect the range.
8. Close **IntMedE1-R1.xlsx**.

Review 3 Creating and Linking a Chart

Columbia River General Hospital

1. With Excel the active program, open **IntMedE1-R1.xlsx**.
2. Make Word the active program and then open **IntMedW1-R2.docx**. Click No when prompted to update links.
3. Make Excel the active program and then select the ranges A7:A15 and G7:G15.
4. Create a 3-D pie chart with the following options:
   a. Insert *Fourth Quarter Tuition by Course* as the chart title.
   b. Remove the legend.
   c. Add *Category Name* and *Value* data labels. ***Hint: Use Format Data Labels dialog box***.
   d. Position the chart below the worksheet starting in cell A18 and resize the chart as needed so data labels are readable.

5. With the chart selected, link the chart to the Word document **IntMedW1-R2.docx** a triple space below the linked worksheet. Make changes to the chart or page layout options as needed to fit the document on one page.
6. Save, print, and then close **IntMedW1-R2.docx**.
7. Make Excel the active program and then click any cell to deselect the chart.
8. Save, print, and then close **IntMedE1-R1.xlsx**.

Review 4 Editing Linked Objects

1. With Excel the active program, open **IntMedE1-R1.xlsx**.
2. Make the following changes to the data in the specified cells:

B10	575
D10	1125
E10	850
C14	225
C15	1175

3. Save, print, and then close **IntMedE1-R1.xlsx**.
4. Make Word the active program and then open the document named **IntMedW1-R2.docx**. Click Yes when prompted to update linked data.
5. Save, print, and then close **IntMedW1-R2.docx**.

Review 5 Embedding and Editing an Object

1. With Word the active program, open the document named **CRGHFoundation.docx**.
2. Save the document with Save As and name it **IntMedW1-R3**.
3. Make Excel the active program and then open the workbook named **CRGHFactSheet.xlsx**.
4. Select A6:H23 and then embed the cells to the end of the Word document **IntMedW1-R3.docx**.
5. Make Excel the active program, remove the moving marquee, click any cell to deselect the range, and then close **CRGHFactSheet.xlsx**.
6. Exit Excel.
7. Double-click the embedded object in **IntMedW1-R3.docx**.
8. Select the range A7:H23 and apply Blue, Accent 1, Lighter 60% (fifth from left in third row in *Theme Colors* section) fill color.
9. Change the value for *Volunteer & Auxiliary Members* to *812*.
10. Click outside the embedded object.
11. Save, print, and then close **IntMedW1-R3.docx**.
12. Exit Word.

Using
PowerPoint
in the
Medical Office

Introducing
PowerPoint 2007

Create colorful and powerful presentations using PowerPoint, Microsoft's presentation program that is included in the Office suite. With PowerPoint, you can organize and present information and create visual aids for a presentation. PowerPoint is a full-featured presentation program that provides a wide variety of editing and formatting features as well as sophisticated elements such as clip art, WordArt, drawn objects, and diagrams.

In Section 1, you will choose design templates for presentations; insert slides; choose slide layouts; select, move, and size placeholders; use the Help feature; check spelling and grammar in presentations; run presentations; and add transition and sound to presentations. Section 2 focuses on editing slides and slide elements. In that section, you will rearrange, delete, and hide slides; cut, copy, and paste text within and between slides; apply font and font effects; apply formatting such as alignment, spacing, headers, and footers; change slide design themes; insert and format images, WordArt, and SmartArt diagrams; and apply animation schemes.

In the two PowerPoint sections, you will prepare medical presentations for two clinics and a hospital as described below.

Cascade View Pediatrics is a full-service pediatric clinic that provides comprehensive primary pediatric care to infants, children, and adolescents.

North Shore Medical Clinic is an internal medicine clinic dedicated to providing exceptional care to all patients. The physicians in the clinic specialize in a number of fields including internal medicine, family practice, cardiology, and dermatology.

Columbia River General Hospital is an independent, not-for-profit hospital with the mission of providing high-quality, comprehensive care to patients and improving the health of members of the community.

PowerPoint SECTION 1
Preparing a Presentation

Skills

- Complete the presentation cycle
- Choose a design template
- Add a new slide to a presentation
- Navigate in a presentation
- Insert a slide in a presentation
- Change the presentation view
- Change the slide layout
- Select, move, and size a placeholder
- Use the Help feature
- Check spelling in a presentation
- Use Thesaurus to display synonyms for words
- Run a presentation and use the pen and highlighter during a presentation
- Add transition and sound to a presentation
- Print and preview a presentation

Student Resources

Before beginning this section:
1. Copy to your storage medium the PowerPointMedS1 subfolder from the Unit5PowerPoint folder on the Student Resources CD.
2. Make PowerPointMedS1 the active folder.

In addition to containing the data files needed to complete section work, the Student Resources CD contains model answers in PDF format for each of the projects in this section; model answers for end-of-section exercises are not provided.

Projects Overview

Prepare a presentation introducing PowerPoint 2007; prepare, edit, and format a presentation on diabetes; prepare a presentation on cystic fibrosis; and edit and format a presentation containing information on the clinic.

Prepare, edit, and format a presentation on fibromyalgia; and prepare, edit, and format a presentation containing information on the hospital.

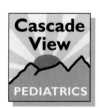

Prepare, edit, and format a presentation containing information on the clinic; and prepare, edit, and format a presentation on chickenpox.

Activity
1.1

Completing the Presentation Cycle

PowerPoint is a presentation graphics program you can use to organize and present information. With PowerPoint, you can create visual aids for a presentation and then print copies of the aids as well as run the presentation. Preparing a presentation in PowerPoint generally follows a presentation cycle. The steps in the cycle vary but generally include opening PowerPoint; creating and editing slides; saving, printing, running, and closing the presentation; and then closing PowerPoint.

Project

You are an employee of North Shore Medical Clinic and Office 2007 has just been installed on your computer. You need to prepare a presentation in the near future so you decide to open a presentation provided by PowerPoint and experiment with running the presentation.

① Open PowerPoint by clicking the Start button ![start] on the Windows Taskbar, pointing to *All Programs*, pointing to *Microsoft Office*, and then clicking *Microsoft Office PowerPoint 2007*.

Depending on your system configuration, the steps you complete to open PowerPoint may vary.

② At the PowerPoint window, click the Office button and then click *New* at the drop-down list.

③ At the New Presentation dialog box, click the *Installed Templates* option that displays in the *Templates* section in the left panel and then double-click the *Introducing PowerPoint 2007* template in the *Installed Templates* panel.

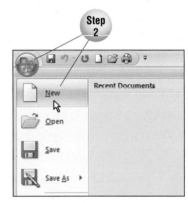

The *Introducing PowerPoint 2007* template opens in the PowerPoint window. What displays in the PowerPoint window will vary depending on what type of presentation you are creating. However, the PowerPoint window contains some consistent elements as identified in Figure P1.1. Refer to Table P1.1 for a description of the window elements.

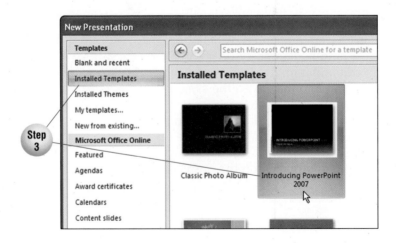

FIGURE P1.1 PowerPoint Window

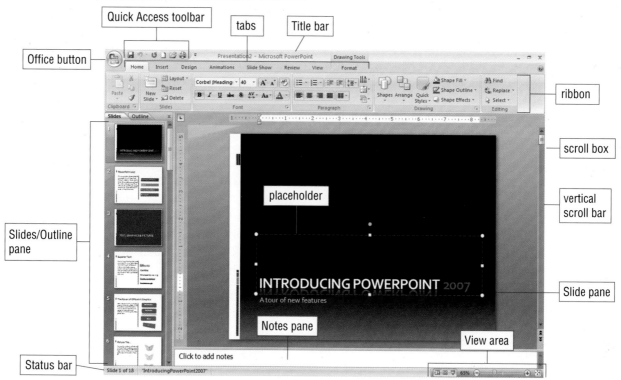

TABLE P1.1 PowerPoint Window Elements

Feature	Description
Office button	Displays as a Microsoft Office logo and, when clicked, displays a list of options and most recently opened presentations.
Quick Access toolbar	Contains buttons for commonly used commands.
Title bar	Displays file name followed by program name.
tabs	Contain commands and features organized into groups.
ribbon	Area containing the tabs and commands divided into groups.
Slides/Outline pane	Displays at the left side of the window with two tabs—Slides and Outline. With the Slides tab selected, slide miniatures display in the pane; with the Outline tab selected, presentation contents display in the pane.
Slide pane	Displays the slide and slide contents.
Notes pane	Add notes to a presentation in this pane.
vertical scroll bar	Display specific slides using this scroll bar.
I-beam pointer	Used to move the insertion point or to select text.
insertion point	Indicates location of next character entered at the keyboard.
View area	Located toward right side of Status bar and contains button for changing presentation view.
Status bar	Displays number of pages and words, View buttons, and Zoom slider bar.

continues

4. Run the presentation by clicking the Slide Show tab and then clicking the From Beginning button in the Start Slide Show group.

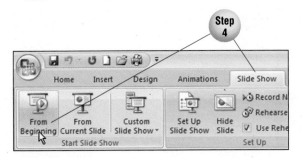

5. When the first slide fills the screen, read the information and then click the left mouse button. Continue reading the information in each slide and clicking the left mouse button to advance to the next slide. When a black screen displays, click the left mouse button to end the slide show.

6. Save the presentation by clicking the Save button on the Quick Access toolbar.

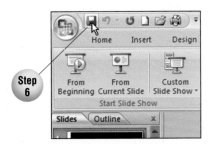

7. At the Save As dialog box, make sure the PowerPointMedS1 folder on your storage medium is the active folder, type **MMPowerPoint2007** in the *File name* text box, and then press Enter.

> The *Save in* option at the Save As dialog box displays the active folder. If you need to make the PowerPointMedS1 folder on your storage medium the active folder, click the down-pointing arrow at the right of the *Save in* option, click your storage medium, and then double-click *PowerPointMedS1* in the list box.

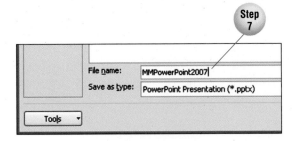

8. At the PowerPoint window, print the presentation information in outline view by clicking the Office button and then clicking *Print* at the drop-down list.

⑨ At the Print dialog box, click the down-pointing arrow at the right of the *Print what* option and then click *Outline View*.

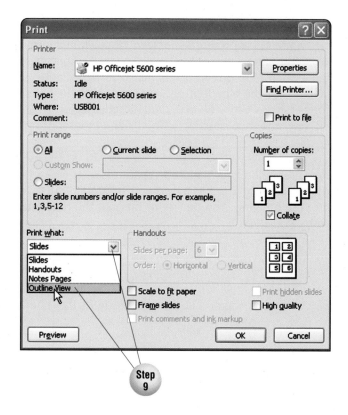

Step 9

⑩ Click OK to close the Print dialog box.

⑪ Close the presentation by clicking the Office button and then clicking *Close* at the drop-down list.

> If a message displays asking if you want to save the presentation, click Yes.

⑫ Close PowerPoint by clicking the Office button and then clicking the Exit PowerPoint button that displays in the lower right corner of the drop-down list.

In Brief

Create Presentation with Installed Template
1. Click Office button, *New*.
2. Click *Installed Templates*.
3. Double-click desired template.

Save a Presentation
1. Click Save button.
2. Type presentation name.
3. Click Save button or press Enter.

Run a Presentation
1. Click Slide Show tab.
2. Click From Beginning button.
3. Click left mouse button to advance slides.

Print a Presentation
1. Click Office button, *Print*.
2. At Print dialog box, specify how you want presentation printed.
3. Click OK.

Close a Presentation
Click Office button, *Close*.

Exit PowerPoint
Click Office button, Exit PowerPoint.

In Addition

Using Tabs

The ribbon area displays below the Quick Access toolbar. The buttons and options in the ribbon area vary depending on the tab selected. PowerPoint commands and features are organized into command tabs that display in the ribbon area. Commands and features are organized into groups within a tab. For example, the Home tab contains the Clipboard, Slides, Font, Paragraph, Drawing, and Editing groups. When you hover the mouse over a button, a ScreenTip displays with the name of the button, a keyboard shortcut (if any), and a description of the purpose of the button.

Activity 1.2

Choosing a Design Theme; Creating Slides; Closing a Presentation

Create a PowerPoint presentation using an installed template as you did in the previous activity or begin with a blank presentation and apply your own formatting or apply formatting with a slide design theme. To display a blank PowerPoint presentation, click the New button on the Quick Access toolbar, press Ctrl + N, or click the Office button, click New, and then double-click the *Blank Presentation* option at the New Presentation dialog box. A PowerPoint presentation screen displays in Normal view with three panes available for entering text—the Slides/Outline pane, Slide pane, and Notes pane. Use either the Slide pane or the Slides/Outline pane with the Outline tab selected to enter text in a slide. Use the Notes pane to insert a note in a slide.

Project

Dr. St. Claire will be presenting information on diabetes at the Greater Portland Healthcare Workers Association meeting. She has asked you to prepare a PowerPoint presentation that she will use during the meeting. You decide to prepare the presentation using a design template offered by PowerPoint.

① Open PowerPoint.

② At the PowerPoint window, click the Design tab.

③ Click the More button located at the right side of the Themes icons.

④ Click *Solstice* at the drop-down gallery (last option in the second row in the *Built-In* section).

When you click the More button, a drop-down gallery displays. This gallery is an example of the ***live preview*** feature. When you hover your mouse pointer over one of the design themes, the slide in the Slide pane displays with the design theme formatting applied. With the live preview feature, you can view a design theme before actually applying it to the presentation.

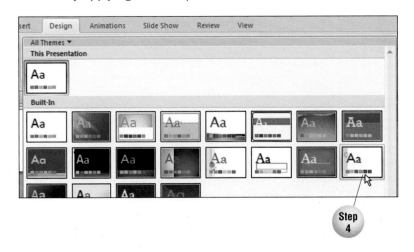

5. Click anywhere in the text *Click to add title* that displays in the slide in the Slide pane and then type **Understanding Diabetes**.

6. Click anywhere in the text *Click to add subtitle* that displays in the slide and then type **Greater Portland Healthcare Workers Association**.

7. Click the Home tab and then click the New Slide button 📄 in the Slides group.

   When you click the New Slide button, a new slide displays in the Slide pane with the Title and Content layout. You will learn more about layouts in Activity 1.4.

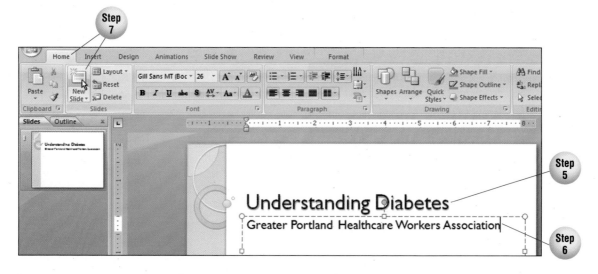

8. Click anywhere in the text *Click to add title* that displays in the slide and then type **Statistics on Diabetes**.

9. Click anywhere in the text *Click to add text* that displays in the slide and then type **Prevalence of diabetes in the United States**.

10. Press the Enter key and then type **Total number of people diagnosed with diabetes**.

11. Press the Enter key and then type **Diabetes by age group**.

    You can use keys on the keyboard to move the insertion point to various locations within a placeholder in a slide. A placeholder is a location on a slide marked with a border that holds text or an object. Refer to Table P1.2 for a list of insertion point movement commands.

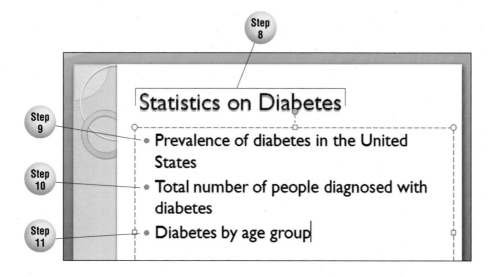

continues

TABLE P1.2 Insertion Point Movement Commands

To move insertion point	Press
One character left	Left Arrow
One character right	Right Arrow
One line up	Up Arrow
One line down	Down Arrow
One word to the left	Ctrl + Left Arrow
One word to the right	Ctrl + Right Arrow
To end of a line of text	End
To beginning of a line of text	Home
To beginning of current paragraph in placeholder	Ctrl + Up Arrow
To beginning of previous paragraph in placeholder	Ctrl + Up Arrow twice
To beginning of next paragraph in placeholder	Ctrl + Down Arrow
To beginning of text in placeholder	Ctrl + Home
To end of text in placeholder	Ctrl + End

⑫ Click the New Slide button the Slides group in the Home tab.

⑬ Click the Outline tab located toward the top of the Slides/Outline pane.

⑭ Click in the Slides/Outline pane immediately right of the slide icon after the number *3*, type **Types of Diabetes**, and then press Enter.

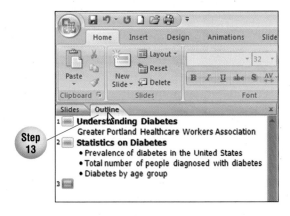

Step 13

⑮ Press the Tab key, type **Type 1 diabetes**, and then press the Enter key.

Pressing the Tab key demotes the insertion point to the next level while pressing Shift + Tab promotes the insertion point to the previous level.

⑯ Type **Type 2 diabetes** and then press Enter.

⑰ Type **Gestational diabetes** and then press Enter.

⑱ Type **Other**.

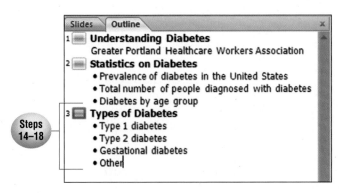

Steps 14–18

19 Click anywhere in the text *Click to add notes* in the Notes pane and then type **Discuss other types of diabetes resulting from surgery, drugs, malnutrition, and infection.**

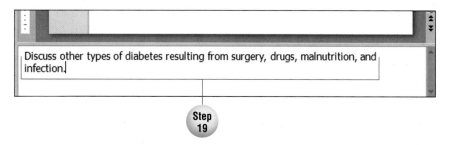

Discuss other types of diabetes resulting from surgery, drugs, malnutrition, and infection.

Step 19

20 Click the Slides tab located toward the top of the Slides/Outline pane.

21 Click the Save button on the Quick Access toolbar.

22 At the Save As dialog box, make sure the PowerPointMedS1 folder on your storage medium is the active folder, type **PPMedS1-01** in the *File name* text box, and then press Enter.

23 Close the presentation by clicking the Office button and then clicking *Close* at the drop-down list.

In Brief

Choose Slide Design
1. Click Design tab.
2. Click More button at right side of Themes icons.
3. Click desired theme at drop-down gallery.

Add Slide
1. Click Home tab.
2. Click New Slide button.

Save Presentation
1. Click Save button on Quick Access toolbar.
2. At Save As dialog box, type presentation file name.
3. Press Enter.

Close PowerPoint
1. Click Office button.
2. Click *Close*.

In Addition

Planning a Presentation

Consider the following basic guidelines when preparing the content for a presentation:

- **Determine the main purpose of the presentation.** Do not try to cover too many topics. Identifying the main point of the presentation will help you stay focused and convey a clear message to the audience.
- **Determine the output.** To help decide the type of output needed, consider the availability of equipment, the size of the room where you will make the presentation, and the number of people who will be attending the presentation.
- **Show one idea per slide.** Each slide in a presentation should convey only one main idea. Too many ideas on a slide may confuse the audience and cause you to stray from the purpose of the slide.

- **Maintain a consistent design.** A consistent design and color scheme for slides in a presentation will create continuity and cohesiveness. Do not use too much color or too many pictures or other graphic elements.
- **Keep slides easy to read and uncluttered.** Keep slides simple and easy for the audience to read. Keep words and other items such as bullets to a minimum.
- **Determine printing needs.** Will you be providing audience members with handouts? If so, will these handouts consist of a printing of each slide? an outline of the presentation? a printing of each slide with space for taking notes?

Opening, Navigating, and Inserting Slides in a Presentation

Open a saved presentation by displaying the Open dialog box and then double-clicking the desired presentation. Display the Open dialog box by clicking the Open button on the Quick Access toolbar or clicking the Office button and then clicking *Open* at the drop-down list. Navigate through slides in a presentation with buttons on the vertical scroll bar by clicking text in the desired slide in the Slides/Outline pane or using keys on the keyboard.

Project

Dr. St. Claire has asked you to add more information to the diabetes presentation. You will insert two new slides in the presentation containing information on statistics and symptoms of diabetes.

1. Click the Open button on the Quick Access toolbar.

   If the Open button does not display on the Quick Access toolbar, click the Customize Quick Access Toolbar button that displays at the right side of the toolbar and then click *Open* at the drop-down list.

2. At the Open dialog box, make sure the PowerPointMedS1 folder on your storage medium is the active folder and then double-click ***PPMedS1-01.pptx*** in the list box.

   ### ? PROBLEM
   If PPMedS1-01.pptx does not display in Open dialog box, you may need to change the folder. Check with your instructor.

3. With **PPMedS1-01.pptx** open, click the Next Slide button located at the bottom of the vertical scroll bar.

   Clicking this button displays the next slide, Slide 2, in the presentation. Notice that *Slide 2 of 3* displays at the left side of the Status bar.

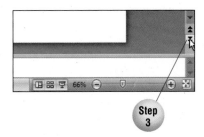

Step 3

4. Click the Previous Slide button located toward the bottom of the vertical scroll bar to display Slide 1.

   When you click the Previous Slide button, *Slide 1 of 3* displays at the left side of the Status bar.

5. Display Slide 3 in the Slide pane by clicking twice the Next Slide button located at the bottom of the vertical scroll bar.

6. Insert a new slide after Slide 3 by clicking the New Slide button in the Slides group in the Home tab.

7 Click anywhere in the text *Click to add title* in the slide in the Slide pane and then type **Symptoms of Diabetes**.

8 Click anywhere in the text *Click to add text* located in the slide and then type the bulleted text as shown in the slide at the right. Press the Enter key after each item *except* the last item.

9 Click the Outline tab located toward the top of the Slides/Outline pane.

10 Click immediately right of the text *Increased fatigue* located toward the middle of the Slides/Outline pane, press the Enter key, and then press Shift + Tab.

> This moves the insertion point back a level and inserts the number *5* followed by a slide icon.

11 Type **Treatment of Diabetes**, press the Enter key, and then press the Tab key. Type the remaining text for Slide 5 as shown at the right. Do not press the Enter key after typing *Self-management education*.

> When you are finished typing the text, the presentation will contain five slides.

12 Click the Save button 💾 on the Quick Access toolbar to save **PPMedS1-01.pptx**.

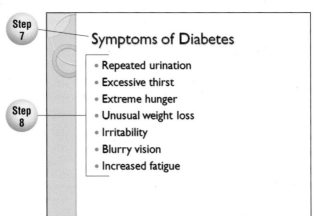

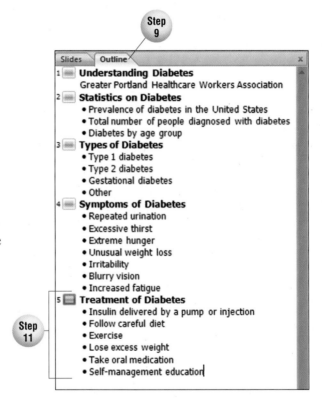

In Brief

Open Presentation
1. Click Open button on Quick Access toolbar.
2. At Open dialog box, double-click desired presentation.

In Addition

Correcting Errors in PowerPoint

PowerPoint's AutoCorrect feature automatically corrects certain words as you type them. For example, type *teh* and press the spacebar and AutoCorrect changes it to *the*. PowerPoint also contains a spelling feature that inserts a wavy red line below words that are not con- tained in the Spelling dictionary or not corrected by AutoCorrect. If the word containing a red wavy line is correct, you can leave it as written. The red wavy line does not print. If the word is incorrect, edit it.

Activity 1.4

Changing Views; Choosing a Slide Layout

PowerPoint provides viewing options for a presentation. Change the presentation view with buttons in the Presentation Views group in the View tab or with buttons in the View area on the Status bar. The Normal view is the default view and displays three panes—Slides/Outline, Slide, and Notes. You can change the view to Slide Sorter view or Notes Page view. Choose the view based on the type of activity you are performing in the presentation. You can also increase the size of the slide in the Slide pane by closing the Slides/Outline pane. Do this by clicking the Close button located in the upper right corner of the pane. Click the New Slide button arrow located in the Slides group in the Home tab and a drop-down list displays with layout choices. Choose the layout that matches the type of text or object you want to insert in the slide.

Project

After reviewing the diabetes presentation, Dr. St. Claire has asked you to edit a slide and add a new slide.

1. With **PPMedS1-01.pptx** open, make sure the Outline tab is selected in the Slides/Outline pane.

2. Click immediately right of *Total number of people diagnosed with diabetes* in the second slide.

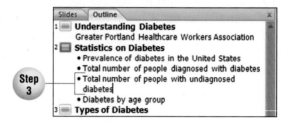

3. Press the Enter key and then type **Total number of people with undiagnosed diabetes**.

4. Display the slides in Notes Page view by clicking the View tab and then clicking the Notes Page button in the Presentation Views group.

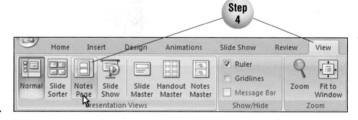

   In Notes Page view, an individual slide displays on a page with any added notes displayed below the slide.

5. Click the Next Slide button on the vertical scroll bar to display Slide 3.

   Notice that the note you created below the slide displays in the page.

6. Increase the zoom by clicking the Zoom button in the Zoom group in the View tab, clicking *100%* at the Zoom dialog box, and then clicking OK.

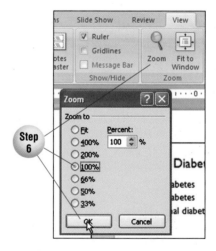

7. You can also change the zoom using the Zoom slider bar. Change the zoom by positioning the mouse pointer on the Zoom slider bar button located at the right side of the Status bar. Hold down the left mouse button, drag to the right until the zoom percentage at the left side of the Zoom slider bar displays as approximately *136%*, and then release the mouse button.

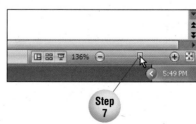

8 Click the minus symbol that displays inside a circle at the left side of the Zoom slider bar until *70%* displays at the left side of the slider bar.

> Click the minus symbol to decrease the zoom display and click the plus symbol to increase the display.

9 View all slides in the presentation in slide miniature by clicking the Slide Sorter button ⊞ in the Presentation Views group.

10 Click the Normal button ▣ in the View area on the Status bar.

11 Click the Slides tab in the Slides/Outline pane.

> With the Slides tab selected, slide miniatures display in the Slides/Outline pane.

12 Click the Slide 1 miniature in the Slides/Outline pane.

> The selected slide in the Slides/Outlines pane displays with an orange background.

13 Click the Home tab, click the New Slide button arrow, and then click the *Title Slide* layout that displays in the drop-down list.

14 Click the text *Click to add title* and then type **What Is Diabetes?**

15 Click the text *Click to add subtitle* and then type the text shown in Figure P1.2.

16 Save **PPMedS1-01.pptx**.

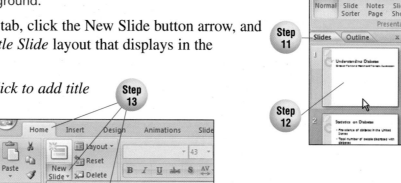

In Brief

Normal View
1. Click View tab.
2. Click Normal button.
OR
Click Normal button in View area on Status bar.

Slide Sorter View
1. Click View tab.
2. Click Slide Sorter button.
OR
Click Slide Sorter button in View area on Status bar.

Notes Page View
1. Click View tab.
2. Click Notes Page button.

FIGURE P1.2 Slide 2

> **What Is Diabetes?**
> Diabetes is a group of diseases characterized by high levels of blood glucose resulting from defects in insulin production, insulin action, or both.

In Addition

Managing Placeholders

When you apply a design theme to a blank presentation, the slide displays with the Title *Slide* layout in the Normal view. This layout contains placeholders for entering the slide title and the slide subtitle. To insert text in a placeholder, click the placeholder text. This moves the insertion point inside the placeholder, removes the default placeholder text, and displays the placeholder with a dashed-line border with sizing handles and a green rotation handle. With the insertion point positioned in a placeholder, type the desired text. If you want to perform an action on the placeholder such as moving or sizing, position the mouse pointer on the dashed-line border until the pointer displays with a four-headed arrow attached, and then click the left mouse button. This changes the dashed-line border to a solid-line border.

Activity 1.5

Changing the Slide Layout; Selecting and Moving a Placeholder

The slides you have created have been based on a slide layout. You can change the slide layout by clicking the Layout button in the Slides group in the Home tab and then clicking the desired layout at the drop-down list. Objects in a slide such as text, a chart, a table, or other graphic element, are generally positioned in a placeholder. Click the text or object to select the placeholder and a border surrounds the placeholder. You can move, size, and/or delete a selected placeholder.

Project

You have decided to make a few changes to the layout of slides in the diabetes presentation.

North Shore Medical Clinic

1. With **PPMedS1-01.pptx** open, make sure Slide 2 displays in the Slide pane.

2. Click the Layout button 📋 Layout ▾ in the Slides group in the Home tab and then click the *Title Only* layout at the drop-down list.

   Position the mouse pointer on a slide layout and the name of the layout displays in a box. When you click the *Title Only* layout, the text is moved down in the slide and a bullet is inserted before the text describing diabetes.

   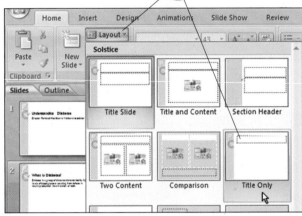

   Step 2

3. Click in the text describing diabetes to display the placeholder borders.

4. Move the placeholder by positioning the mouse pointer on the border of the placeholder until the mouse pointer displays with a four-headed arrow attached. Hold down the left mouse button, drag down until the text is positioned as shown in Figure P1.3, and then release the mouse button.

5. Click in the title *What Is Diabetes?* and then move the title. To do this, position the mouse pointer on the border of the placeholder until the mouse pointer displays with a four-headed arrow attached, hold down the left mouse button, drag down until the title is positioned as shown in Figure P1.3, and then release the mouse button.

FIGURE P1.3 Slide 2

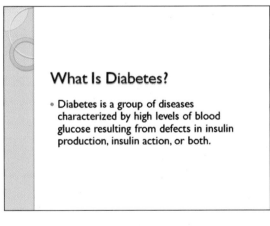

What Is Diabetes?

- Diabetes is a group of diseases characterized by high levels of blood glucose resulting from defects in insulin production, insulin action, or both.

6. Click the Next Slide button ⬇ on the vertical scroll bar until Slide 4 displays.

7. Click anywhere in the bulleted text to display the placeholder borders.

8 Decrease the size of the placeholder by positioning the mouse pointer on the bottom right sizing handle (displays as a white circle) until the arrow pointer turns into a double-headed arrow pointing diagonally.

9 Hold down the left mouse button, drag up and to the left until the placeholder displays as shown at the right, and then release the mouse button.

10 Move the placeholder by positioning the mouse pointer on the border of the placeholder until the mouse pointer displays with a four-headed arrow attached. Hold down the left mouse button, drag down and to the right to the approximate location shown below, and then release the mouse button.

11 Click outside the placeholder to deselect it.

12 Save **PPMedS1-01.pptx**.

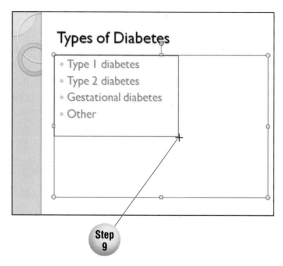

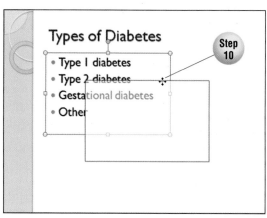

In Brief

Change Slide Layout
1. Make desired slide active.
2. Click Home tab.
3. Click Layout button.
4. Click desired layout at drop-down list.

Move Placeholder
1. Click inside placeholder.
2. Drag with mouse to desired position.

Size Placeholder
1. Click inside placeholder.
2. Drag sizing handles to increase/ decrease size.

In Addition

Using the AutoFit Options Button

If you enter more text than the placeholder is designed to hold, PowerPoint automatically adjusts the text to fit within the placeholder and also displays an AutoFit Options button at the left side of the placeholder. Click this AutoFit Options button and a list of choices displays as shown at the right for positioning objects in the placeholder. The *AutoFit Text to Placeholder* option is selected by default and tells PowerPoint to fit text within the boundaries of the placeholder. Click the middle choice, *Stop Fitting Text to This Placeholder*, and PowerPoint will not automatically fit the text or object within the placeholder. Choose the last option, *Control AutoCorrect Options* to display the AutoCorrect dialog box with the AutoFormat As You Type tab selected. Additional options may display depending upon the placeholder and the type of data inserted in the placeholder.

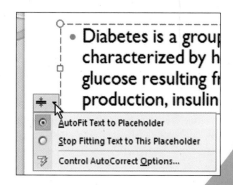

Activity 1.6

Using Help; Checking Spelling; Using the Thesaurus

Use the PowerPoint Help feature to display information on PowerPoint. To use the Help feature, click the Microsoft Office PowerPoint Help button (a circle with a question mark inside) located toward the upper right corner of the screen. At the PowerPoint Help window that displays, type the text for which you want information and then press Enter or click the Search button. A list of topics related to the search text displays in the results window. Click the desired topic and information displays in the PowerPoint Help window. Use PowerPoint's spelling checker to find and correct misspelled words and find dupli-cated words (such as *and and*). The spelling checker compares words in your slide with words in its dictionary. If a match is found, the word is passed over. If no match is found for the word, the spelling checker stops, selects the word, and offers replacements. Use the Thesaurus feature to find synonyms, antonyms, and related words for a particular word. To use the Thesaurus, click the word for which you want to display synonyms and antonyms, click the Review tab, and then click the Thesaurus button in the Proofing group. This displays the Research task pane with information about the word where the insertion point is positioned.

Project

You have decided to create a new slide in the diabetes presentation. Because several changes have been made to the presentation, you know that checking the spelling of all the slide text is important, but you are not sure how to do it. You will use the Help feature to learn how to complete a spelling check and then use the Thesaurus feature to replace a couple of words with synonyms.

1. With **PPMedS1-01.pptx** open, display Slide 6 in the Slide pane and then click the New Slide button in the Slides group in the Home tab.

    This inserts a new slide at the end of the presentation.

2. Click the text *Click to add title* and then type **Complications of Diabetes**.

3. Click the text *Click to add text* and then type the text shown in the slide in Figure P1.4.

    Type the words exactly as shown. You will check the spelling in a later step.

FIGURE P1.4 Slide 7

Complications of Diabetes

- Heart disaese and stroke
- High blood pressure
- Blindness
- Ampitations
- Kidney and nervos system disaese
- Dental disaese
- Complications in pregnancy

4. Learn how to complete a spelling check by clicking the Microsoft Office PowerPoint Help button located toward the upper right corner of the screen.

5. At the PowerPoint Help window, type **spell checking** and then press Enter.

6. Click the *Check spelling and grammar* hyperlink in the PowerPoint Help window.

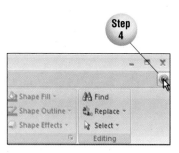

7. Read the information that displays about spell checking in PowerPoint and then click the Close button located in the upper right corner of the PowerPoint Help window.

8. Complete a spelling check by moving the insertion point to the beginning of *Heart*, clicking the Review tab, and then clicking the Spelling button in the Proofing group.

9. When the spelling checker selects *disaese* in Slide 7 and displays *disease* in the *Change to* text box in the Spelling dialog box, click the Change All button.

Refer to Table P1.3 for a description of the Spelling dialog box options.

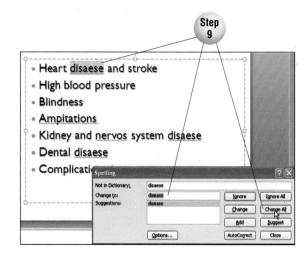

continues

TABLE P1.3 Spelling Dialog Box Options

Button	Function
Ignore	skips that occurrence of the word and leaves currently selected text as written
Ignore All	skips that occurrence of the word and all other occurrences of the word in the presentation
Delete	deletes the currently selected word(s)
Change	replaces selected word in sentence with selected word in the *Suggestions* list box
Change All	replaces selected word with selected word in *Suggestions* list box and all other occurrences of the word in the presentation
Add	adds selected word to the main spelling check dictionary
Suggest	moves the insertion point to the *Suggestions* list box where you can scroll through the list of suggested spellings
AutoCorrect	inserts selected word and correct spelling of word in AutoCorrect dialog box
Options	displays a dialog box with options for customizing a spelling check

10. When the spelling checker selects *Ampitations* in Slide 7 and displays *Amputations* in the *Change to* text box in the Spelling dialog box, click the Change button.

11. When the spelling checker selects *nervos* in Slide 7, click *nervous* in the *Suggestions* list box and then click the Change button.

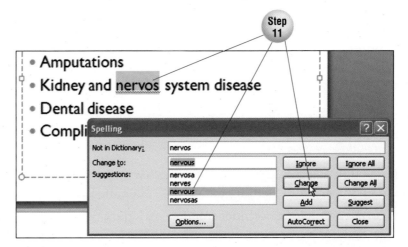

12. At the message telling you that the spelling check is complete, click the OK button.

13. Display Slide 5 in the Slide pane and then click the word *Repeated* located in the first bulleted item (*Repeated urination*).

14. Look up synonyms for *Repeated* by clicking the Thesaurus button 📖 in the Proofing group.

> This displays the Research task pane containing lists of synonyms for *Repeated*. Depending on the word you are looking up, the words in the Research task pane list box may display followed by (n.) for *noun*, (adj.) for *adjective*, or (adv.) for *adverb*. Antonyms may display in the list of related synonyms, generally at the end of the list of related synonyms, and are followed by (Antonym).

15 Position the mouse pointer on the word *frequent* in the Research task pane, click the down-pointing arrow at the right of the word, and then click *Insert* at the drop-down list.

This replaces *Repeated* with *Frequent*.

16 Close the Research task pane by clicking the Close button located in the upper right corner of the task pane.

In Brief

Use Help
1. Click Microsoft Office PowerPoint Help button.
2. Type text for desired information.
3. Click Search button.

Complete Spelling Check
1. Click Review tab.
2. Click Spelling button.
3. Change or ignore highlighted words.
4. When spelling check is completed, click OK.

Use Thesaurus
1. Click desired word.
2. Click Review tab.
3. Click Thesaurus button.
4. Position mouse pointer on desired replacement word in Research task pane, click down-pointing arrow at right of word, and then click *Insert*.

17 Display Slide 7 in the Slide pane, right-click on the word *in* (located in the last bulleted item), point to *Synonyms*, and then click *during*.

The shortcut menu offers another method for displaying synonyms for words.

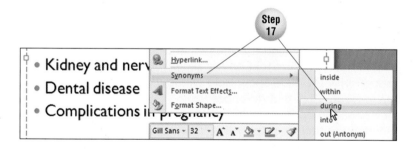

18 Save **PPMedS1-01.pptx**.

In Addition

Changing Spelling Options

Control spelling options at the PowerPoint Options dialog box with the *Proofing* option selected. Display this dialog box by clicking the Office button and then clicking the PowerPoint Options button at the drop-down list. At the PowerPoint Options dialog box, click *Proofing* at the left side of the dialog box. With options in the dialog box, you can tell the spelling checker to ignore certain types of text, create custom dictionaries, and hide spelling errors in the presentation.

Editing While Checking Spelling

When checking a presentation, you can temporarily leave the Spelling dialog box by clicking in the slide. To resume the spelling check, click the Resume button, which was formerly the Ignore button.

Activity 1.7

Running a Presentation

You can run a presentation in PowerPoint manually, advance the slides automatically, or set up a slide show to run continuously for demonstration purposes. To run a slide show manually, click the Slide Show tab and then click the From Beginning button in the Start Slide Show group or click the Slide Show button in the View area on the Status bar. You can also run the presentation beginning with the currently active slide by clicking the From Current Slide button in the Start Slide Show group. Use the mouse or keyboard to advance through the slides. You can also use buttons on the Slide Show toolbar that display when you move the mouse pointer while running a presentation.

Project You are now ready to run the diabetes presentation. You will use the mouse to perform various actions while running the presentation.

1. With **PPMedS1-01.pptx** open, click the Slide Show tab and then click the From Beginning button in the Start Slide Show group.

   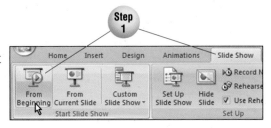

   Clicking this button begins the presentation, and Slide 1 fills the entire screen.

2. After viewing Slide 1, click the left mouse button to advance to the next slide.

3. After viewing Slide 2, click the left mouse button to advance to the next slide.

4. At Slide 3, move the mouse pointer until the Slide Show toolbar displays and then click the left arrow button on the toolbar to display the previous slide (Slide 2).

   With buttons on the Slide Show toolbar you can display the next slide, the previous slide, display a specific slide, and use the pen and highlighter to emphasize text on the slide. You can also display the Slide Show Help window shown in Figure P1.5 that describes all the navigating options when running a presentation. Display this window by clicking the slide icon button on the Slide Show toolbar and then clicking *Help*.

5. Click the right arrow button on the Slide Show toolbar to display the next slide (Slide 3).

6. Display the previous slide (Slide 2) by clicking the right mouse button and then clicking *Previous* at the shortcut menu.

   Clicking the right mouse button causes a shortcut menu to display with a variety of options including options to display the previous or next slide.

FIGURE P1.5 Slide Show Help Window

Slide Show Help	OK
During the slide show:	
'N', left click, space, right or down arrow, enter, or page down	Advance to the next slide
'P', backspace, left or up arrow, or page up	Return to the previous slide
Number followed by Enter	Go to that slide
'B' or '.'	Blacks/Unblacks the screen
'W' or ','	Whites/Unwhites the screen
'A' or '='	Show/Hide the arrow pointer
'S' or '+'	Stop/Restart automatic show
Esc, Ctrl+Break, or '-'	End slide show
'E'	Erase drawing on screen
'H'	Go to next slide if hidden
'T'	Rehearse - Use new time
'O'	Rehearse - Use original time
'M'	Rehearse - Advance on mouse click
Hold both the Right and Left Mouse buttons down for 2 seconds	Return to first slide
Ctrl+P	Change pointer to pen
Ctrl+A	Change pointer to arrow
Ctrl+E	Change pointer to eraser
Ctrl+H	Hide pointer and button
Ctrl+U	Automatically show/hide arrow
Right mouse click	Popup menu/Previous slide
Ctrl+S	All Slides dialog
Ctrl+T	View task bar
Ctrl+M	Show/Hide ink markup

7. Display the next slide by clicking the slide icon button on the Slide Show toolbar and then clicking the *Next* option.

8. Display Slide 5 by typing the number *5* on the keyboard and then pressing Enter.

   Move to any slide in a presentation by typing the slide number and pressing Enter.

Step 7

9. Change to a black screen by typing the letter *B* on the keyboard.

   When you type the letter *B*, the slide is removed from the screen and the screen displays black. This might be useful in a situation where you want to discuss something with your audience unrelated to the slide.

10. Return to Slide 5 by typing the letter *B* on the keyboard.

    Typing the letter *B* switches between the slide and a black screen. Type the letter *W* if you want to switch between the slide and a white screen.

11. Click the left mouse button to display Slide 6. Continue clicking the left mouse button until a black screen displays. At the black screen, click the left mouse button again.

    This returns the presentation to the Normal view.

12. Click Slide 2 in the Slides/Outline pane.

13. Click the From Current Slide button in the Start Slide Show group in the Slide Show tab.

    Clicking this button begins the presentation with the active slide.

14. Click the left mouse button to advance to Slide 3 and then press the Esc key on the keyboard to end the presentation without running the remaining slides.

In Addition

Showing Presenter View

If you want to view your speaker notes and any timings applied to slides while running a presentation, click the *Use Presenter View* check box in the Monitors group in the Slide Show tab. With this option active, you can run your presentation on one monitor while displaying speaker notes and timings on a second monitor. For this feature to work, you must have two monitors attached to your computer or be using a laptop computer that has dual-display capabilities.

Activity
1.8

Using the Pen and
Highlighter during a Presentation

Emphasize major points or draw the attention of the audience to specific items in a slide during a presentation using the pen or highlighter. To use the pen on a slide, run the presentation, and when the desired slide displays, move the mouse to display the Slide Show toolbar. Click the pen button on the toolbar and then click either *Ballpoint Pen* or *Felt Tip Pen*. The felt tip pen draws a thicker line than the ballpoint pen. Use the mouse to draw in the slide to emphasize a point or specific text. If you want to erase the marks you made with the pen, click the mouse pointer button and then click *Eraser*. This causes the mouse pointer to display as an eraser. Drag through an ink mark to remove it. To remove all ink marks at the same time, click the *Erase All Ink on Slide* option. When you are finished with the pen, click the *Arrow* option to return the mouse pointer to an arrow.

Project Dr. St. Claire would like to highlight specific points on the slide by highlighting and drawing on the slide. She wants you to learn these features and then show her how to highlight and draw on slides during a presentation.

1. With **PPMedS1-01.pptx** open, click the From Beginning button in the Start Slide Show group in the Slide Show tab.

2. With the first slide filling the screen, click the left mouse button to advance slides until Slide 3 displays. (This is the slide with the title *Statistics on Diabetes*.)

3. Move the mouse to display the Slide Show toolbar, click the pen button, and then click *Felt Tip Pen*.

   This turns the mouse pointer into a small circle.

4. Using the mouse, draw a circle around the text *Total number of people with undiagnosed diabetes*.

5. Using the mouse, draw a line below *Diabetes by age group*.

6. Erase the pen markings by clicking the pen button on the Slide Show toolbar and then clicking *Erase All Ink on Slide*. If the *Erase All Ink on Slide* option is dim, click in the slide to remove the pop-up list and then click again on the pen button on the Slide Show toolbar.

Statistics on Diabetes

- Prevalence of diabetes in the United States
- Total number of people diagnosed with diabetes
- Total number of people with undiagnosed diabetes
- Diabetes by age group

7 Change the color of the ink by clicking the pen button, pointing to *Ink Color*, and then clicking the Dark Blue color in the Standard Colors section.

8 Draw a dark blue line below the word *United States*.

9 Return the mouse pointer back to an arrow by clicking the pen button and then clicking *Arrow* at the pop-up list.

10 Click the left mouse button to advance to Slide 4.

11 Click the pen button and then click *Highlighter* at the pop-up list.

    This changes the mouse pointer to a light yellow rectangle.

12 Drag through the words *Type 1 diabetes* to highlight them.

13 Drag through the words *Type 2 diabetes* to highlight them.

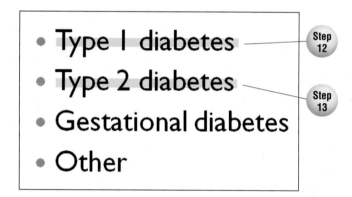

14 Return the mouse pointer back to an arrow by clicking the pen button and then clicking *Arrow*.

15 Press the Esc key on the keyboard to end the presentation without running the remaining slides. At the message asking if you want to keep your ink annotations, click the Discard button.

In Addition

Hiding/Displaying the Mouse Pointer

When running a presentation, the mouse pointer is set, by default, to be hidden automatically after three seconds of inactivity. The mouse pointer will appear again when you move the mouse. You can change this default setting by clicking the pen button on the Slide Show toolbar, pointing to *Arrow Option,* and then clicking *Visible* if you want the mouse pointer always visible or *Hidden* if you do not want the mouse to display at all as you run the presentation. The *Automatic* option is the default setting.

Activity
1.9

Adding Transition and Sound

You can apply interesting transitions and sounds to a presentation. A transition is how one slide is removed from the screen during a presentation and the next slide is displayed. Interesting transitions can be added such as fades, dissolves, push, cover, wipes, stripes, and bar. Add a sound to a presentation and the sound is heard when a slide is displayed on the screen during a presentation. Add transitions and sounds with options in the Animations tab.

Project

Dr. St. Claire has asked you to enhance the presentation by adding transitions and sound to the slides.

1. With **PPMedS1-01.pptx** open, click the Animations tab.

2. Click the More button located at the right side of the transition icons that display in the Transition to This Slide group.

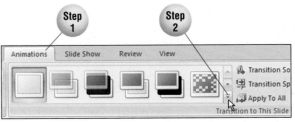

3. At the drop-down gallery, click the *Uncover Up* option (third option in the second row in the *Wipes* section).

> A gallery contains the live preview feature that shows the animation in the slide in the Slide pane as you hover the mouse over an animation option in the drop-down gallery.

4. Click the down-pointing arrow at the right side of the Transition Sound button 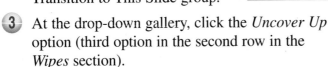 in the Transition to This Slide group.

5. At the drop-down gallery that displays, click the *Click* option.

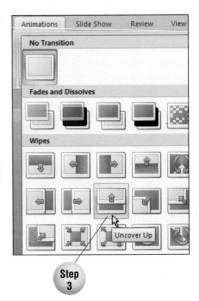

6. Click the down-pointing arrow at the right of the Transition Speed button in the Transition to This Slide group and then click *Medium* at the drop-down list.

7. Click the Apply To All button in the Transition to This Slide group.

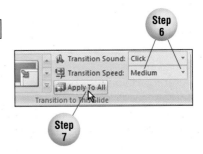

> Notice that a transition icon displays below the slide numbers in the Slides/Outline pane.

8 Click the Slide 1 miniature in the Slides/Outline pane.

9 Run the presentation by clicking the Slide Show button  in the View area on the Status bar.

Step 9

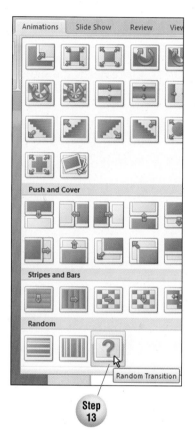

10 Click the left mouse button to advance each slide.

11 At the black screen that displays after the last slide, click the left mouse button again to return the presentation to the Normal view.

12 Click the More button located at the right side of the transition icons that display in the Transition to This Slide group.

13 Scroll down the drop-down gallery and then click the *Random Transition* option (last option in the *Random* section).

14 Click the down-pointing arrow at the right of the Transition Speed button Transition Speed: Medium and then click *Fast* at the drop-down list.

15 Click the Apply To All button Apply To All in the Transition to This Slide group.

16 Run the presentation.

17 Save **PPMedS1-01.pptx**.

Step 13

In Brief

Add Transition to All Slides in Presentation
1. Click Animations tab.
2. Click More button at right side of transition icons.
3. Click desired transition at drop-down gallery.
4. Click Apply To All button.

Add Transition Sound to All Slides in Presentation
1. Click Animations tab.
2. Click Transition Sound button arrow.
3. Click desired option at drop-down gallery.
4. Click Apply To All button.

In Addition

Running a Slide Show Automatically

Slides in a slide show can be advanced automatically after a specific number of seconds by inserting a check mark in the *Automatically After* check box in the Transition to This Slide group. Change the time in the text box by clicking the up- or down-pointing arrow at the right side of the text box or by selecting any text in the text box and then typing the desired time. If you want the transition time to affect all slides in the presentation, click the Apply To All button. In Slide Sorter view, the transition time displays below each affected slide. Click the Slide Show button to run the presentation. The first slide displays for the specified amount of time and then the next slide automatically displays.

Printing and Previewing a Presentation; Changing Page Setup

You can print each slide on a separate piece of paper; print each slide at the top of the page, leaving the bottom of the page for notes; print up to nine slides or a specific number of slides on a single piece of paper; or print the slide titles and topics in outline form. Use the *Print what* option at the Print dialog box to specify what you want printed. Before printing a presentation, consider previewing the presentation. To do this, click the Office button, point to the *Print* option and then click *Print Preview*. Use options in the Print Preview tab to display the next or previous slide, display the Print dialog box, specify how you want the presentation printed, change the zoom (percentage of display), choose an orientation (portrait or landscape), and close Print Preview. You can also change page orientation with the Slide Orientation button in the Page Setup group in the Design tab or with options at the Page Setup dialog box.

Project

Dr. St. Claire needs the slides in the diabetes presentation printed as handouts and as an outline. You will preview and then print the presentation in various formats.

1) With **PPMedS1-01.pptx** open, display Slide 1 in the Slide pane. Click the Office button (📋), point to *Print*, and then click *Print Preview*.

This displays Slide 1 in the Print Preview window as it will appear when printed.

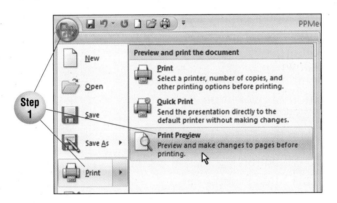

2) Click the Next Page button in the Preview group in the Print Preview tab.

This displays Slide 2 in the Print Preview window.

3) You decide to print all slides on one page and you want to preview how the slides will appear on the page. To do this, click the down-pointing arrow below the *Print What* option box, and then click *Handouts (9 Slides Per Page)* at the drop-down list.

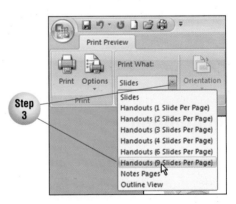

4) Click the Print button in the Print group in the Print Preview tab.

5) At the Print dialog box, click OK.

6) Click the Close Print Preview button.

7) You want to print all slide text on one page and use the printing as a reference. To do this, click the Office button and then click *Print* at the drop-down list.

8 At the Print dialog box, click the down-pointing arrow at the right side of the *Print what* option and then click *Outline View* at the drop-down list.

9 Click the OK button.

With the Outline View option selected, the presentation prints on one page with slide numbers, slide icons, and slide text in outline form.

10 Change the slide orientation from landscape to portrait by clicking the Design tab, clicking the Slide Orientation button in the Page Setup group, and then clicking *Portrait* at the drop-down list.

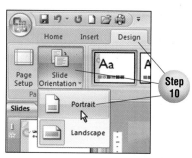

11 You need a printing of Slide 5. To do this, click the Office button and then click *Print* at the drop-down list.

12 At the Print dialog box, click the down-pointing arrow at the right side of the *Print what* option and then click *Slides* at the drop-down list.

13 Click the *Slides* option in the *Print range* section, type **5** in the text box, and then click OK.

14 Return the orientation for slides back to landscape by clicking the Slide Orientation button in the Page Setup group in the Design tab and then clicking *Landscape* at the drop-down list.

15 Save **PPMedS1-01.pptx**.

16 Close the presentation by clicking the Office button and then clicking *Close* at the drop-down list.

In Brief

Print Presentation
1. Click Office button.
2. Click *Print*.
3. At Print dialog box, specify how you want presentation printed.
4. Click OK.

Preview Presentation
1. Click Office button.
2. Point to *Print*.
3. Click *Print Preview*.

Change Slide Orientation
1. Click Design tab.
2. Click Slide Orientation button.
3. Click desired orientation at drop-down list.

In Addition

Using Options at the Page Setup Dialog Box

You can change orientation with the Slide Orientation button or with options at the Page Setup dialog box shown at the right. Display this dialog box by clicking the Design tab and then clicking the Page Setup button. With options at this dialog box you can specify how you want slides sized; page width and height; orientation for slides; and orientation for notes, handouts, and outline.

Features Summary

Feature	Ribbon Tab, Group	Button	Quick Access Toolbar	Office Button Drop-down List	Keyboard Shortcut
apply transitions and sounds to all slides	Animations, Transition to This Slide	Apply To All			
close				Close	
exit PowerPoint		X Exit PowerPoint		Exit PowerPoint	
Help			?		F1
layout	Home, Slides	Layout			
New Presentation dialog box				New	
new slide	Home, Slides	▣			
Normal view	View, Presentation Views	▣			
Notes Page view	View, Presentation Views	▣			
open blank presentation			▢		Ctrl + N
Open dialog box			▣	Open	Ctrl + O
Print dialog box				Print	Ctrl + P
print presentation			▣		
Print Preview				Print, Print Preview	
run presentation from current slide	Slide Show, Start Slide Show	▣			Shift + F5
run presentation from Slide 1	Slide Show, Start Slide Show	▣			F5
save			▣		Ctrl + S
save with a new name				Save As	F12
slide orientation	Design, Page Setup	▣			
Slide Sorter view	View, Presentation Views	▣			
Spelling	Review, Proofing	ABC✓			F7
themes	Design, Themes				
Thesaurus	Review, Proofing	▣			Shift + F7

continues

Feature	Ribbon Tab, Group	Button	Quick Access Toolbar	Office Button Drop-down List	Keyboard Shortcut
transitions	Animations, Transition to This Slide				
transition sound	Animations, Transition to This Slide	Transition Sound [No Sound] ▼			
transition speed	Animations, Transition to This Slide	Transition Speed Fast ▼			
Zoom dialog box	View, Zoom	🔍			

Knowledge Check

Completion: In the space provided at the right, write in the correct term, command, or option.

1. Display the New Presentation dialog box by clicking this button and then clicking *New* at the drop-down list.

2. To run a presentation beginning with Slide 1, click the Slide Show tab and then click this button.

3. The Save button is located on this toolbar.

4. The Normal view contains the Slides/Outline pane, the Slide pane, and this pane.

5. The New Slide button is located in this tab.

6. The Zoom slider bar is located at the right side of this bar.

7. Click the Microsoft Office PowerPoint Help button and this displays.

8. Use this feature to find synonyms, antonyms, and related words for a particular word.

9. The Spelling button is located in the Proofing group in this tab.

10. Move the mouse while running a presentation and this toolbar displays.

11. Press this key on the keyboard to change to a black screen while running a presentation.

12. Press this key on the keyboard to end a presentation without running all of the slides.

13. Add transitions and sounds to a presentation with options in this tab.

14. The Slide Orientation button is located in the Page Setup group in this tab.

Skills Review

Review 1 Choosing a Design and Creating Slides

1. With a blank presentation in PowerPoint open, click the Design tab.
2. Click the More button at the right side of the Themes icons and then click *Urban* in the drop-down gallery.
3. Type the title and subtitle for Slide 1 as shown in Figure P1.6.
4. Click the Home tab and then click the New Slide button in the Slides group.
5. Change the slide layout to Title Slide. (You will arrange the text in the placeholder in the next activity.)
6. Type the text shown for Slide 2 in Figure P1.6.
7. Continue creating the slides for the presentation as shown in Figure P1.6.
8. Save the presentation and name it **PPMedS1-R1**.

FIGURE P1.6 Review 1

Slide 1	Title	Columbia River General Hospital
	Subtitle	Facts about Fibromyalgia
Slide 2	Title	What Is Fibromyalgia?
	Subtitle	Fibromyalgia is an arthritis-related condition characterized by generalized muscular pain and fatigue.
Slide 3	Title	Who Is Affected by Fibromyalgia?
	Bullets	• Approximately 1 in 50 Americans may be affected
		• Mostly women but men and children can also have the disorder
		• People with certain diseases such as rheumatoid arthritis, lupus, and spinal arthritis
		• People with a family member with fibromyalgia may be more likely to be diagnosed with the disorder
Slide 4	Title	Treatments for Fibromyalgia
	Bullets	• Medication to diminish pain and improve sleep
		• Exercise programs that stretch muscles
		• Relaxation techniques
		• Education programs to help understand the disorder

Review 2 Inserting a Slide; Changing Layout; Moving a Placeholder

1. With **PPMedS1-R1.pptx** open, insert a new Slide 3 between the current Slides 2 and 3 with the text shown in Figure P1.7.
2. Display Slide 2 in the Slide pane and then change the slide layout to Title Only.
3. Click in the text containing the description of fibromyalgia and then move the placeholder so it is better centered on the slide.
4. Display Slide 3 in the Slide pane, click in the bulleted text to select the placeholder, and then decrease the right side of the placeholder. (Make sure the placeholder does not cause bulleted text to wrap.)
5. Move the placeholder so the bulleted text is more centered on the slide.
6. Save **PPMedS1-R1.pptx**.

FIGURE P1.7 Review 2

Slide 3	Title	Causes of Fibromyalgia
	Bullets	• Infectious illness
		• Physical and/or emotional trauma
		• Muscle abnormalities
		• Hormonal changes
		• Repetitive injuries

Review 3 Adding Transition and Sound; Running and Printing the Presentation

1. With **PPMedS1-R1.pptx** open, click the Animations tab.
2. Click the More button located at the right side of the transition icons that display in the Transition to This Slide group and then click a transition of your choosing.
3. Click the down-pointing arrow at the right of the Transition Sound button and then click a transition sound of your choosing.
4. Apply the transition and sound to all slides in the presentation.
5. Make Slide 1 the active slide and then run the presentation.
6. Print the presentation in Outline view.
7. Print the presentation with all five slides on one page.
8. Save and then close **PPMedS1-R1.pptx**.

Skills Assessment

Assessment 1 Preparing a Presentation for Columbia River General Hospital

1. Prepare a presentation for Columbia River General Hospital with the information shown in Figure P1.8. (You determine the design template.)
2. Add a transition and sound of your choosing to all slides in the presentation.
3. Run the presentation.
4. Print the presentation with all five slides on one page.
5. Save the presentation and name it **PPMedS1-A1**.
6. Close **PPMedS1-A1.pptx**.

FIGURE P1.8 Assessment 1

Slide 1	Title	Columbia River General Hospital
	Subtitle	Our mission is to provide comprehensive and high-quality care for all of our patients.
Slide 2	Title	Hospital Directives
	Bullets	• Highest-quality patient care
		• Exceptional customer services
		• Fully trained and qualified staff
		• Delivery of first-class health education
Slide 3	Title	Facilities
	Bullets	• 400 licensed beds
		• Level II adult trauma system
		• 14 operating rooms
		• 25-bed adult intensive care unit
		• Level III neonatal intensive care unit
		• 24-hour emergency services
Slide 4	Title	Physicians Clinics
	Bullets	• Division Street
		• Lake Oswego
		• Fremont Center
		• Oak Grove
Slide 5	Title	Health Foundation
	Subtitle	Columbia River General Hospital's Health Foundation is a nonprofit organization that promotes the well-being of adults and families served by the hospital.

Assessment 2 Preparing a Presentation for Cascade View Pediatrics

1. Prepare a presentation for Cascade View Pediatrics with the information shown in Figure P1.9. (You determine the design template.)
2. Add a transition and sound of your choosing to all slides in the presentation.
3. Run the presentation.
4. Print the presentation with all five slides on one page.
5. Save the presentation and name it **PPMedS1-A2**.
6. Close **PPMedS1-A2.pptx**.

FIGURE P1.9 Assessment 2

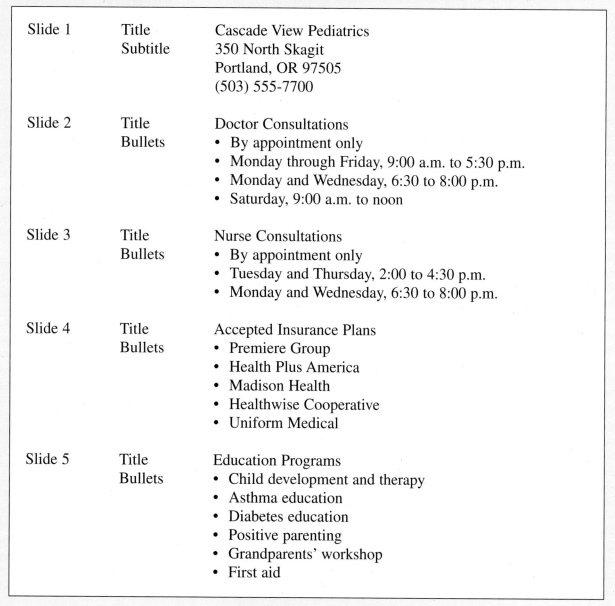

Slide 1	Title Subtitle	Cascade View Pediatrics 350 North Skagit Portland, OR 97505 (503) 555-7700
Slide 2	Title Bullets	Doctor Consultations • By appointment only • Monday through Friday, 9:00 a.m. to 5:30 p.m. • Monday and Wednesday, 6:30 to 8:00 p.m. • Saturday, 9:00 a.m. to noon
Slide 3	Title Bullets	Nurse Consultations • By appointment only • Tuesday and Thursday, 2:00 to 4:30 p.m. • Monday and Wednesday, 6:30 to 8:00 p.m.
Slide 4	Title Bullets	Accepted Insurance Plans • Premiere Group • Health Plus America • Madison Health • Healthwise Cooperative • Uniform Medical
Slide 5	Title Bullets	Education Programs • Child development and therapy • Asthma education • Diabetes education • Positive parenting • Grandparents' workshop • First aid

Assessment 3 Finding Information on the Undo Button

1. Open **PPMedS1-A2.pptx** and then use the Help feature to learn how to undo an action.
2. After learning how to undo an action, make Slide 1 the active slide.
3. In the Slide pane, click immediately right of the telephone number *(503) 555-7700* and then press Enter.
4. Type the e-mail address **CVP@emcp.cvpediatrics.com** and then press Enter. (PowerPoint converts the e-mail address to a hyperlink [changes color and underlines the text].)
5. Undo the action (that converted the text to a hyperlink).
6. Type **Web site: www.emcp.com/cvpediatrics**.
7. Press the Enter key. (This converts the Web site to a hyperlink.)
8. Undo the action (that converted the text to a hyperlink).
9. If neccessary, increase the size of the placeholder to better accommodate the new text.
10. Print only Slide 1.
11. Save and then close **PPMedS1-A2.pptx**.

Assessment 4 Finding Information on Setting Slide Show Timings

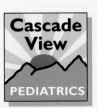

1. Open **PPMedS1-A2.pptx**.
2. Experiment with the options in the Advance Slide section of the Transition to This Slide group in the Animations tab and then set up the presentation so that, when running the presentation, each slide advances after three seconds.
3. Run the presentation.
4. Save and then close **PPMedS1-A2.pptx**.

Assessment 5 Locating Information and Preparing a Presentation on Chickenpox

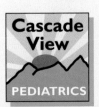

1. You need to prepare a presentation on chickenpox that includes information such as symptoms, treatment, incubation period, and infectious period. Use the information you prepared for **WordMedS3-A7.docx** and research additional information on the Internet.
2. Using PowerPoint, create a presentation about chickenpox that contains a title slide with Cascade View Pediatrics and the name you choose for your presentation and then additional slides that cover a description of chickenpox and symptoms, treatments, and incubation and infectious periods.
3. Run the presentation.
4. Print all of the slides on one page.
5. Save the presentation and name it **PPMedS1-A5**.
6. Close **PPMedS1-A5.pptx**.

Marquee Challenge

Challenge 1 Preparing a Presentation on Cystic Fibrosis

1. Prepare the presentation shown in Figure P1.10. Use the *Flow* design theme and size and position the text as shown in the slides.
2. Save the completed presentation and name it **PPMedS1-C1**.
3. Apply a transition and sound to all slides and then run the presentation.
4. Print the presentation as a handout with all six slides on one page.
5. Save and then close **PPMedS1-C1.pptx**.

FIGURE P1.10 Challenge 1

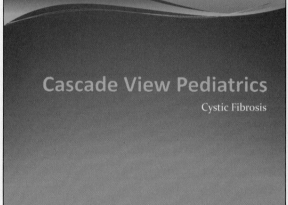

Cascade View Pediatrics
Cystic Fibrosis

What Is Cystic Fibrosis?
Cystic fibrosis is an inherited disease that is passed through the genes from parents to children and involves a genetic mutation that disrupts the cystic fibrosis transmembrane regulator (CFTR) protein.

Cystic Fibrosis Diagnosis

- Usually diagnosed in a child before his/her first birthday
- A sweat test called *pilocarpine iontophoresis* is the standard test for diagnosing cystic fibrosis
- If sweat test is inconclusive, a genetic test for the cystic fibrosis gene is performed

Symptoms of Cystic Fibrosis

- Unusually salty-tasting skin
- Persistent coughing generally with phlegm
- Poor growth/weight gain
- Persistent diarrhea
- Blockage of the intestine
- Abdominal swelling
- Dehydration

Additional Symptoms

- Abdominal pain/discomfort/gassiness
- Frequent respiratory infections
- Difficulty in breathing
- Fever
- Cough
- Fast respirations
- Poor appetite/malnutrition
- Poor growth

Cystic Fibrosis Related Conditions

- Nasal polyps
- Sinusitis
- Pneumothorax
- Enlargement of the right side of the heart
- Liver, pancreatic, and gallbladder problems
- Delayed puberty
- Reproductive abnormalities

Challenge 2 Editing a Presentation on Clinic Services

1. Open the presentation named **NSMCServices.pptx** and then save it with Save As and name it **PPMedS1-C2**.
2. Apply the *Civic* design theme, change the slide layout for the second slide, and then size and move the placeholders as shown in Figure P1.11.
3. Run the presentation.
4. Print the presentation as a handout with six slides per page.
5. Save and then close **PPMedS1-C2.pptx**.

FIGURE P1.11 Challenge 2

PowerPoint SECTION 2
Editing Slides and Slide Elements

Skills

- Open a presentation and save it with a new name
- Rearrange, delete, and hide slides
- Increase and decrease the indent of text
- Select, cut, copy, and paste text
- Apply font and font effects
- Find and replace fonts
- Apply formatting with Format Painter
- Change alignment and line and paragraph spacing
- Draw a text box and shape
- Insert headers and footers
- Change the design theme, theme color, and theme font
- Insert and format images
- Insert and format WordArt
- Insert and format a SmartArt organizational chart and diagram
- Add an animation scheme to a presentation

Student Resources

Before beginning this section:
1. Copy to your storage medium the PowerPointMedS2 subfolder from the Unit5PowerPoint folder on the Student Resources CD.
2. Make PowerPointMedS2 the active folder.

In addition to containing the data files needed to complete section work, the Student Resources CD contains model answers in PDF format for each of the projects in this section; model answers for end-of-section exercises are not provided.

Projects Overview

Open an existing presentation containing information on classes offered by the Education Department and then save, edit, and format the presentation; open an existing presentation containing information on the Community Commitment reorganization plan and then save, edit, and format the presentation.

Open an existing presentation on opening a clinic in Vancouver, save the presentation with a new name, and then edit and format the presentation.

Open an existing presentation containing information on sickle cell anemia and then save, edit, and format the presentation; prepare a presentation on cholesterol.

Activity 2.1

Rearranging, Deleting, and Hiding Slides

If you open an existing presentation and make changes to it, you can then save it with the same name or a different name. Save an existing presentation with a new name at the Save As dialog box. PowerPoint provides various views for creating and managing a presentation. Use the view that most easily accomplishes the task. For example, consider using the Slide Sorter view to delete, rearrange, and hide slides in a presentation.

Project

The doctors at Cascade View Pediatrics are considering expanding by opening a clinic in the Vancouver, Washington, area. Dr. Severin has prepared a presentation with facts about Vancouver and has asked you to edit the presentation.

1. With PowerPoint open, click the Open button on the Quick Access toolbar.

2. At the Open dialog box, make sure PowerPointMedS2 is the active folder and then double-click **CVPVancouver.pptx** in the list box.

3. Click the Office button and then click *Save As*.

4. At the Save As dialog box, type **PPMedS2-01** in the *File name* text box and then press Enter.

5. Click the Slide Sorter button in the View area on the Status bar.

6. Click Slide 3 to select it and then click the Delete button ☒ Delete in the Slides group in the Home tab.

   A slide selected in Slide Sorter view displays surrounded by an orange border. You can also delete a selected slide by pressing the Delete key on the keyboard.

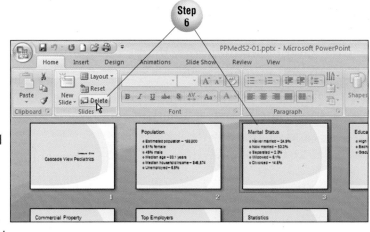

7. Click Slide 7 to make it active.

8. Position the mouse pointer on Slide 7, hold down the left mouse button, drag the arrow pointer (with a rectangle attached) to the left of Slide 3, and then release the mouse button.

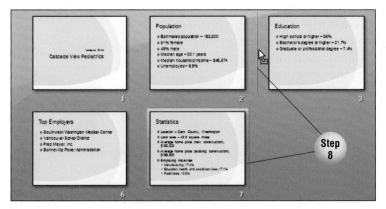

9 Click Slide 5 to make it active and then hide the slide by clicking the Slide Show tab and then clicking the Hide Slide button in the Set Up group.

> When a slide is hidden, a box containing a slash displays around the slide number.

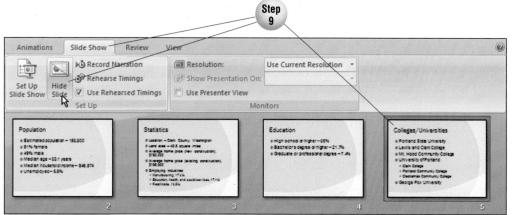

Save Presentation with New Name
1. Click Office button, click *Save As*.
2. Type presentation name.
3. Click Save or press Enter.

Delete Slide
1. Click Slide Sorter button in View area on Status bar.
2. Click desired slide.
3. Press Delete key.

Move Slide
1. Click Slide Sorter button in View area on Status bar.
2. Click desired slide.
3. Drag slide to desired position.

10 Click the Normal button located in the View area on the Status bar.

11 Click the Slides tab in the Slides/Outline pane. (Skip this step if the Slides tab is already selected.)

12 Position the mouse pointer on the Slide 6 miniature, hold down the left mouse button, drag up until a thin, horizontal line displays immediately below the Slide 2 miniature, and then release the mouse button.

13 Make Slide 1 the active slide and then run the presentation.

14 After running the presentation, you decide to redisplay the hidden slide. To do this, click the Slide 6 miniature in the Slides/Outline pane and then click the Hide Slide button in the Set Up group in the Slide Show tab.

15 Save **PPMedS2-01.pptx** by clicking the Save button on the Quick Access toolbar.

In Addition

Copying Slides within a Presentation

Copying a slide within a presentation is similar to moving a slide. To copy a slide, position the arrow pointer on the desired slide in either the Slides/Outline pane with the Slides tab selected or in Slide Sorter view and hold down the Ctrl key and the left mouse button. Drag to the location where you want the slide copied, release the left mouse button, and then release the Ctrl key. When you drag with the mouse, the mouse pointer displays with a rectangle and a plus symbol next to the pointer.

Increasing and Decreasing Text Level

In the Slides/Outline pane with the Outline tab selected, you can organize and develop the content of the presentation by rearranging points within a slide, moving slides, or increasing and decreasing text level indent. Click the Decrease List Level button in the Paragraph group in the Home tab or press Shift + Tab to decrease text to the previous level. Click the Increase List Level button in the Paragraph group or press Tab to increase text to the next level. You can also increase and/or decrease the indent of text in the slide in the Slide pane.

Project

As you continue editing the Vancouver presentation, you will increase and/or decrease the indent of text in slides.

1. With **PPMedS2-01.pptx** open, make sure the presentation displays in Normal view.

2. Make sure Slide 6 displays in the Slide pane and then click the Home tab.

3. Looking at the text in Slide 6, you realize that the school names below *University of Portland* should not be indented and need to be moved to the previous tab stop. To do this, position the mouse pointer immediately left of the *C* in *Clark*, click the left mouse button, and then click the Decrease List Level button 🔽 in the Paragraph group in the Home tab.

   You can also decrease the text level by pressing Shift + Tab.

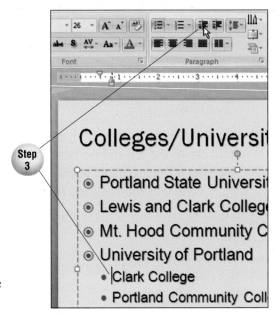

4. In Slide 6, position the insertion point immediately left of the *P* in *Portland Community College* and then move the text to the previous level by pressing Shift + Tab.

5. Use either Step 3 or Step 4 to move *Clackamas Community College* to the previous level.

6. Make Slide 2 active. You decide that the two bulleted items below *Estimated population* should be moved to the next level. To do this, click immediately left of the *5* in *51%* and then click the Increase List Level button 🔽 in the Paragraph group in the Home tab.

   You can also increase the text level by pressing the Tab key.

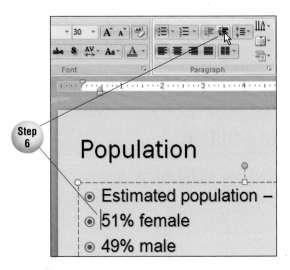

⑦ Position the insertion point immediately left of the *4* in *49%* and then press the Tab key.

⑧ Display Slide 4 in the Slide pane.

⑨ Click the Outline tab in the Slides/Outline pane.

In Brief

Decrease Text Level Indent
Click Decrease List Level button or press Shift + Tab.

Increase Text Level Indent
Click Increase List Level button or press Tab.

⑩ Looking at Slide 4, you notice that the slide contains too much text and decide to make a new slide with some of the text. To do this, click immediately left of the *E* in *Employing* in the text in the Slides/Outline pane and then press Shift + Tab.

> Pressing Shift + Tab moves the text to the previous level and creates a new slide with *Employing industries* as the title of the slide.

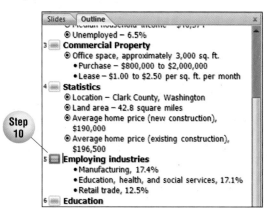

⑪ Change the title of the slide by typing **Employment** and then pressing Enter.

> As you type *Employment*, the text *Employing industries* moves to the right. When you press Enter, *Employing industries* moves to the next line and begins a new slide.

⑫ Move the text *Employing industries* by pressing the Tab key.

> The new slide now contains the title *Employment* with *Employing industries* as a bulleted item with three bulleted items below demoted to the next level.

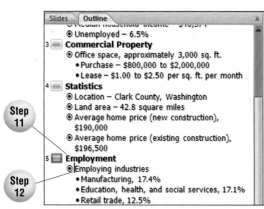

⑬ Click the Slides tab in the Slides/Outline pane.

⑭ Save **PPMedS2-01.pptx**.

In Addition

Rearranging Text in the Slides/Outline Pane

You can use the mouse to move text in the Slides/Outline pane with the Outline tab selected. To do this, position the mouse pointer on the slide icon or bullet at the left side of the text, until the arrow pointer turns into a four-headed arrow. Hold down the left mouse button, drag the arrow pointer (a thin horizontal line displays) to the desired location, and then release the mouse button. If you position the arrow pointer on the bullet and then hold down the left mouse button, all text following that bullet is selected. Dragging selected text with the mouse moves the selected text to a new location in the presentation. You can also copy selected text. To do this, click the slide icon or click the bullet to select the desired text. Position arrow pointer in the selected text, hold down the Ctrl key, and then hold down the left mouse button. Drag the arrow pointer (displays with a light gray box and a plus sign attached) to the desired location, release the mouse button, and then release the Ctrl Key.

Activity 2.3

Selecting, Cutting, Copying, and Pasting Text

Text in a slide can be selected and then the text can be deleted from the slide, cut from one location and pasted into another, or copied and pasted. Select text using the mouse or the keyboard. Cut, copy, and paste text using buttons in the Clipboard group in the Home tab. Select, cut, copy, and/or paste text in slides in the Slide pane or the Slides/Outline pane.

Project

As you review the Vancouver presentation again, you decide to delete, move, and copy specific text items.

1. With **PPMedS2-01.pptx** open, make sure the presentation displays in Normal view and then display Slide 7 in the Slide pane.

2. Click anywhere in the bulleted text.

   Clicking in the bulleted text selects the placeholder containing the text.

3. Position the mouse pointer on the bullet that displays before *University of Portland* until the pointer turns into a four-headed arrow and then click the left mouse button.

   Refer to Table P2.1 for additional information on selecting text.

4. Click the Cut button in the Clipboard group in the Home tab.

5. Position the mouse pointer immediately left of the *L* in *Lewis and Clark College*, click the left mouse button, and then click the Paste button in the Clipboard group.

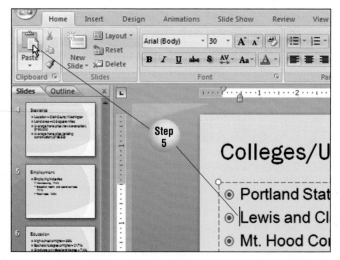

6. Position the mouse pointer on the bullet that displays before *George Fox University* until the pointer turns into a four-headed arrow and then click the left mouse button.

7. Click the Cut button in the Clipboard group.

8. Position the mouse pointer immediately left of the *L* in *Lewis and Clark College*, click the left mouse button, and then click the Paste button in the Clipboard group.

9. Make Slide 6 active, move the insertion point so it is positioned immediately right of *7.4%*, and then press the Enter key.

10. Type **Area Universities** and then press the Enter key.

11 Make Slide 7 active; select *Portland State University, University of Portland,* and *George Fox University*; and then click the Copy button in the Clipboard group.

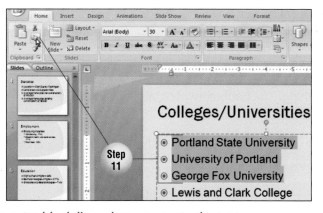

Step 11

In Brief
Cut and Paste Text
1. Select text.
2. Click Cut button.
3. Position insertion point.
4. Click Paste button.

Copy and Paste Text
1. Select text.
2. Click Copy button.
3. Position insertion point.
4. Click Paste button.

When selecting the text, do not include the space after *George Fox University*. If you include the space, which is actually an invisible paragraph symbol, you will get an extra blank line when you paste the text.

12 Make Slide 6 active and then click below the heading *Area Universities.*

This selects the placeholder and positions the insertion point below the *Area Universities* heading.

13 Click the Paste button in the Clipboard group. If a blank line occurs below *George Fox University*, press the Backspace key twice.

If a blank line occurred below *George Fox University*, the invisible paragraph symbol after the text was selected. When selecting text, you may not want to or need to select the space after text.

14 Increase the level of the names by selecting the three universities names (*Portland State University, University of Portland,* and *George Fox University*) and then clicking the Increase List Level button in the Paragraph group in the Home tab.

15 Save **PPMedS2-01.pptx**.

TABLE P2.1 Selecting Text

To select	Perform this action
entire word	Double-click word.
entire paragraph	Triple-click anywhere in paragraph.
entire sentence	Press Ctrl + click anywhere in sentence.
text mouse pointer passes through	Click and drag with mouse.
all text in selected object box	Press Ctrl + A or click Select button in Editing group and then click *Select All*.

In Addition

Copying a Slide between Presentations

You can copy slides within a presentation as well as between presentations. To copy a slide, click the slide you want to copy (either in Slide Sorter view or in Normal view with the Slides tab selected in the Slides/Outline pane) and then click the Copy button in the Clipboard group in the Home tab. Open the presentation into which the slide is to be copied (in either Slide Sorter view or Normal view with the Slides tab selected in the Slides/Outline pane). Click in the location where you want the slide positioned and then click the Paste button. The copied slide will take on the template design of the presentation into which it is copied.

Applying Fonts and Font Effects

The Font group in the Home tab contains two rows of buttons. The top row contains buttons for changing the font and font size and a button for clearing formatting. The bottom row contains buttons for applying font effects such as bold, italic, underline, strikethrough, and shadow as well as a button for changing the case of selected text and font color.

Project

As you continue working to improve the appearance of slides in the Vancouver presentation, you decide to apply font effects to specific text in the presentation.

1. With **PPMedS2-01.pptx** open, display Slide 1 in the Slide pane.

2. Select the clinic name *Cascade View Pediatrics*, click the Bold button **B** in the Font group in the Home tab, and then click the Italic button **I**.

3. With the clinic name still selected, click once on the Decrease Font Size button **A˅** in the Font group.

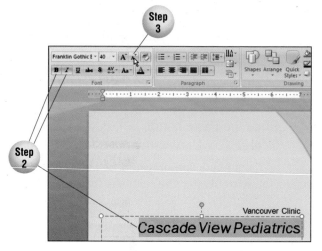

4. Select the subtitle *Vancouver Clinic*, click the Bold button **B**, and then click the Italic button **I** in the Font group.

5. With the subtitle still selected, increase the font size by clicking twice on the Increase Font Size button **A˄** in the Font group.

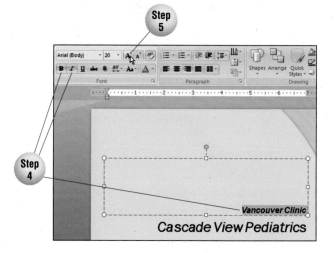

6. Make Slide 2 active, select *158,800*, and then click the Underline button **U** in the Font group.

7. Make Slide 1 active and then select the clinic name *Cascade View Pediatrics*.

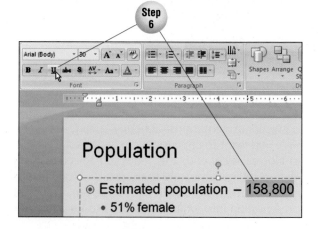

8 Click the Font button arrow in the Font group, scroll down the gallery (fonts display in alphabetic order), and then click *Cambria*.

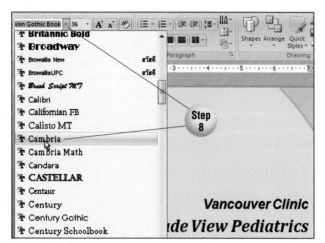

In Brief

Apply Font Effects with Font Group
1. Select text.
2. Click button in Font group.

Change Font Size
1. Click Font Size button.
2. Click desired size at drop-down gallery.

Change Font
1. Click Font button down arrow.
2. Click desired font at drop-down gallery.

9 With the clinic name still selected, click the Font Size button arrow, scroll down the gallery, and then click *44*.

10 Select the subtitle *Vancouver Clinic*, click the Font button arrow, and then click *Cambria* at the drop-down gallery.

> The drop-down gallery displays the most recently used fonts toward the beginning of the gallery.

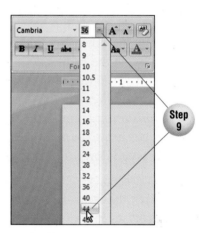

11 With the subtitle still selected, click the Font Color button and then click *Teal, Accent 2* at the drop-down gallery.

12 Print Slide 1.

13 Save **PPMedS2-01.pptx**.

In Addition

Choosing Typefaces

A typeface is a set of characters with a common design and shape. PowerPoint refers to a typeface as a *font*. Typefaces can be decorative or plain and are either monospaced or proportional. A monospaced typeface allots the same amount of horizontal space for each character while a proportional typeface allots a varying amount of space for each character. Proportional typefaces are divided into two main categories: serif and sans serif. A serif is a small line at the end of a character stroke. Consider using a serif typeface for text-intensive slides because the serifs help move the reader's eyes across the text. Use a sans serif typeface for titles, subtitles, headings, and short text lines.

Changing the Font at the Font Dialog Box; Replacing Fonts

In addition to buttons in the Font group in the Home tab, you can apply font formatting with options at the Font dialog box. With options at this dialog box, you can change the font, font style, and size; change the font color; and apply formatting effects such as underline, shadow, emboss, superscript, and subscript. If you decide to change the font for all slides in a presentation, use the Replace Font dialog box to replace all occurrences of a specific font in the presentation.

Project Still not satisfied with the font choices in the Vancouver presentation, you decide to change the font for the title and subtitle and replace the Arial font on the remaining slides.

1. With **PPMedS2-01.pptx** open, make sure Slide 1 is the active slide.

2. Select the clinic name *Cascade View Pediatrics*.

3. Display the Font dialog box by clicking the Font group dialog box launcher in the Home tab.

4. At the Font dialog box, click the down-pointing arrow at the right side of the *Latin text font* option box and then click *Constantia* at the drop-down list. (You will need to scroll down the list box to display *Constantia*.)

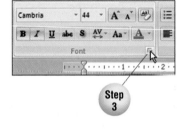

Step 3

5. Click the down-pointing arrow at the right side of the *Font style* option box and then click *Bold* at the drop-down list.

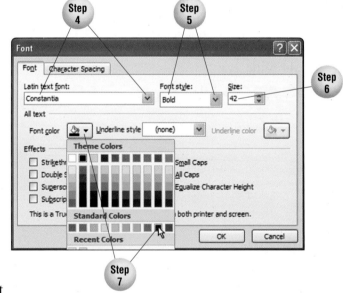

Step 4 Step 5 Step 6

6. Select the current measurement in the *Size* text box and then type **42**.

7. Click the Font color button in the *All text* section and then click *Dark Blue* (second color from the right in the *Standard Colors* row).

Step 7

8. Click OK to close the Font dialog box.

9. Select the subtitle *Vancouver Clinic*.

10. Click the Font group dialog box launcher.

11 At the Font dialog box, click the down-pointing arrow at the right side of the *Latin text font* option box and then click *Constantia* at the drop-down list. (You will need to scroll down the list box to display *Constantia*.)

12 Click the down-pointing arrow at the right side of the *Font style* option box and then click *Bold* at the drop-down list.

13 Select the current measurement in the *Size* text box and then type **32**.

14 Click OK to close the Font dialog box.

15 Make Slide 2 active.

16 You decide to replace all occurrences of the Arial font with the Constantia font. To begin, click the Replace button arrow in the Editing group in the Home tab and then click *Replace Fonts* at the drop-down list.

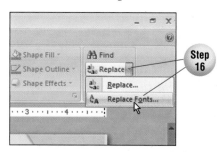

17 At the Replace Font dialog box, make sure *Arial* displays in the *Replace* option box.

18 Click the down-pointing arrow at the right side of the *With* option box and then click *Constantia* at the drop-down list. (You will need to scroll down the list box to display *Constantia*.)

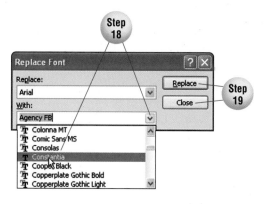

19 Click the Replace button and then click the Close button.

20 Save **PPMedS2-01.pptx**.

In Brief

Change Font at Font Dialog Box
1. Select text.
2. Click Font group dialog box launcher.
3. Click desired options at Font dialog box.
4. Click OK.

Change All Occurrences of Font
1. Click Replace button arrow, then click *Replace Fonts*.
2. At Replace Font dialog box, make sure desired font displays in *Replace* text box.
3. Press Tab.
4. Click down-pointing arrow at right of *With*, click desired font.
5. Click Replace button.
6. Click Close button.

In Addition

Choosing Presentation Typefaces

Choose a typeface for a presentation based on the tone and message you want the presentation to portray. For example, choose a more serious typeface such as Constantia or Times New Roman for a conservative audience and choose a less formal font such as Comic Sans MS, Lucida Handwriting, or Mistral for a more informal or lighthearted audience. For text-intensive slides, choose a serif typeface such as Constantia, Times New Roman, Georgia, or Bookman Old Style. For titles, subtitles, headings, and short text items, consider a sans serif typeface such as Calibri, Arial, Tahoma, or Univers. Use no more than two or three different fonts in each presentation. To ensure text readability in a slide, choose a font color that contrasts with the slide background.

Activity 2.6

Formatting with Format Painter

Use the Format Painter feature to apply the same formatting in more than one location in a slide or slides. To use the Format Painter, apply the desired formatting to text, position the insertion point anywhere in the formatted text, and then double-click the Format Painter button in the Clipboard group in the Home tab. Using the mouse, select the additional text to which you want the formatting applied. After applying the formatting in the desired locations, click the Format Painter button to deactivate it. If you need to apply formatting in only one other location, click the Format Painter button once. The first time you select text, the formatting is applied and the Format Painter is deactivated.

Project Improve the appearance of slides in the Vancouver presentation by applying a font and then using the Format Painter to apply the formatting to other text.

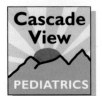

1. With **PPMedS2-01.pptx** open, make sure Slide 2 is the active slide.

2. Select the title *Population*.

3. Click the Font group dialog box launcher.

4. At the Font dialog box, click the down-pointing arrow in the *Latin text font* option box and then click *Cambria* at the drop-down list.

5. Click the down-pointing arrow at the right side of the *Font style* option box and then click *Bold* at the drop-down list.

6. Click the Font color button in the *All text* section and then click *Indigo, Accent 1*.

7. Click the *Small Caps* option in the *Effects* section of the dialog box to insert a check mark in the check box.

8. Click OK to close the Font dialog box.

9. At the slide, deselect the text by clicking in the slide outside the selected text.

10. Click anywhere in the title *Population*.

11. Double-click the Format Painter button in the Clipboard group in the Home tab.

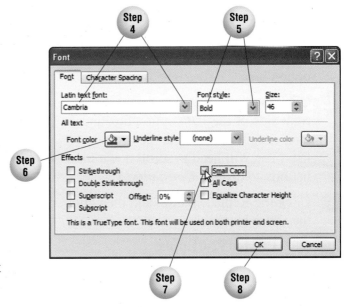

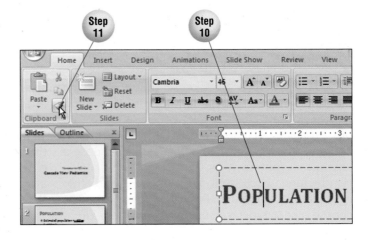

(12) Click the Next Slide button ⬇ to display Slide 3.

(13) Using the mouse, select the words *Commercial Property*.

> The mouse pointer displays with a paintbrush attached. This indicates that the Format Painter feature is active. You can also apply the formatting to a single word by clicking on any character in the word.

(14) Click the Next Slide button ⬇ to display Slide 4.

(15) Click on any character in the title *Statistics*.

(16) Click the Next Slide button ⬇ to display Slide 5.

(17) Click on any character in the title *Employment*.

? PROBLEM

> If the paintbrush is no longer attached to the mouse pointer, Format Painter has been turned off. Turn it back on by clicking in a slide title with the desired formatting and then double-clicking the Format Painter button.

(18) Apply formatting to the titles in the remaining three slides.

(19) When formatting has been applied to all slide titles, click the Format Painter button 🖌 in the Clipboard group in the Home tab.

> Clicking the Format Painter button turns off the feature.

(20) Save **PPMedS2-01.pptx**.

In Brief

Format with Format Painter

1. Position insertion point on text containing desired formatting.
2. Double-click Format Painter button.
3. Select text to which you want to apply formatting.
4. Click Format Painter button.

In Addition

Choosing a Custom Color

Click the Font Color button at the Font dialog box, and a palette of color choices displays. Click the *More Colors* option and the Colors dialog box displays with a honeycomb of color options. Click the Custom tab and the dialog box displays as shown at the right. With options at this dialog box you can mix your own color. Click the desired color in the *Colors* palette or enter the values for the color in the *Red*, *Green*, and *Blue* text boxes. Adjust the luminosity of the current color by dragging the slider located at the right side of the color palette.

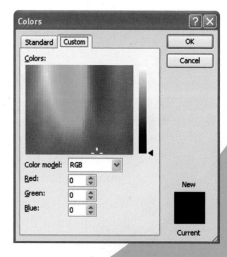

Activity 2.7

Changing Alignment and Line and Paragraph Spacing; Drawing a Text Box and Shape

The slide design template generally determines the horizontal and vertical alignment of text in placeholders. Text may be left-aligned, center-aligned, or right-aligned in a placeholder as well as aligned at the top, middle, or bottom of the placeholder. You can change alignment for specific text with buttons in the Paragraph group in the Home tab or with options from the Align Text drop-down list. Use options at the Line Spacing button drop-down list or the *Line Spacing* option at the Paragraph dialog box to change line spacing. The Paragraph dialog box also contains options for changing text alignment and indentation and spacing before and after text. If you want to add text to a slide and do not want to use the Title and Text layout, consider drawing a text box. Draw a text box in a slide and then type text inside the box. Use the Shapes button in the Home tab or Insert tab to draw shapes in a slide, such as basic shapes, block arrows, callouts, stars, and banners. Use options in the Drawing Tools Format tab to format and customize a text box or a shape.

Project

Change the alignment for specific text in slides and improve the appearance of text in slides by adjusting the vertical alignment and paragraph spacing of text. Dr. Severin has asked you to insert a slide containing a description of Vancouver.

1. With **PPMedS2-01.pptx** open, make Slide 1 active.

2. Click anywhere in the text *Cascade View Pediatrics* and then click the Center button ▤ in the Paragraph group in the Home tab.

   > You can also change text alignment with the keyboard shortcuts shown in Table P2.2.

TABLE P2.2 Alignment Shortcut Keys

Alignment	Keyboard Shortcut
left-align	Ctrl + L
center-align	Ctrl + E
right-align	Ctrl + R
justify-align	Ctrl + J

3. Select the subtitle *Vancouver Clinic* and then click the Center button in the Paragraph group.

4. Click the Align Text button in the Paragraph group and then click *Top* at the drop-down list.

5. Drag the placeholder down so the text *Vancouver Clinic* displays below the title *Cascade View Pediatrics*. Make sure the text is centered below the clinic name.

6. With Slide 1 active, click the New Slide button arrow and then click *Title Only* at the drop-down list.

7. Click the text *Click to add title* and then type **About Vancouver**.

8. Make Slide 3 active, click on any character in the title *Population* and then click the Format Painter button 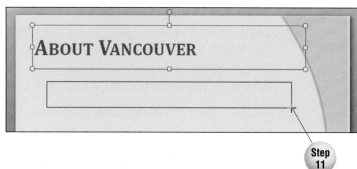 in the Clipboard group.

9. Make Slide 2 active and then select the title *About Vancouver*.

   Clicking the Format Painter button once applies character formatting a single time.

10. Draw a text box in the slide. Begin by clicking the Insert tab and then clicking the Text Box button in the Text group.

    This changes the mouse pointer to a down-pointing arrow.

11. Using the mouse, draw a box that is approximately the size shown at the right.

    To draw a box, hold down the mouse button as you drag in the slide.

12. Type the text shown in Figure P2.1. Do not press the Enter key after typing the web address. If you do, immediately click the Undo button.

FIGURE P2.1 Step 12

Vancouver, Washington, sits on the north bank of the Columbia River directly across from Portland, Oregon. The Pacific Coast is less than 90 miles to the west. The Cascade Mountain Range rises on the east. Mount St. Helens National Volcanic Monument and Mt. Hood are less than two hours away. The spectacular Columbia River Gorge National Scenic Area lies 30 minutes to the east. (www.cityofvancouver.us)

13. Select all of the text in the text box and then change the font to 24-point Constantia.

14. Justify the text by clicking the Justify button in the Paragraph group.

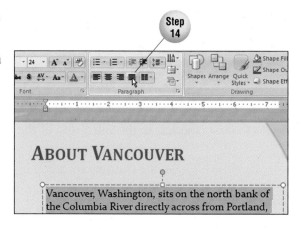

15. Make Slide 3 active, select the bulleted text, click the Line Spacing button, and then click *Line Spacing Options* at the drop-down list.

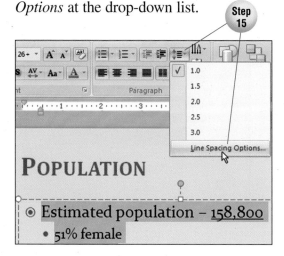

continues

16 At the Paragraph dialog box, click once on the up-pointing arrow at the right side of the *After* option in the *Spacing* section.

> This inserts *6 pt* in the *After* option box.

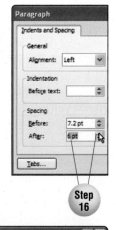

Step 16

17 Click OK to close the dialog box.

18 Make Slide 4 active (contains the title *Commercial Property*) and then select the bulleted text.

19 Click the Line Spacing button and then click *1.5* at the drop-down list.

20 Make Slide 5 active, select text from the second bullet through the fourth bullet, click the Line Spacing button , and then click *Line Spacing Options* at the drop-down list.

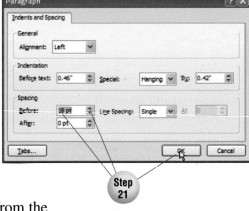

21 At the Paragraph dialog box, click twice on the up-pointing arrow at the right of the *Before* option in the *Spacing* section (this displays *18 pt* in the option box) and then click OK.

22 Make Slide 6 active and then follow steps similar to those in Steps 19 and 20 to change the *Before* spacing to *18 pt*.

Step 21

23 Make Slide 8 active and then select text from the second bullet through the eighth bullet. Display the Paragraph dialog box, change the *Before* spacing to *0*, and then click OK to close the dialog box.

24 Make Slide 9 active and then insert a new blank slide by clicking the New Slide button arrow and then clicking *Blank* at the drop-down list.

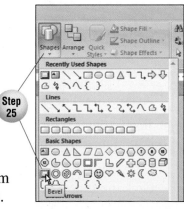

Step 25

25 Draw a shape in the slide. Begin by clicking the Shapes button in the Drawing group, and then clicking *Bevel* at the drop-down list (first option from the left in the third row of the *Basic Shapes* section).

> The Shapes button is also available in the Illustrations group in the Home tab.

26 Position the mouse pointer in the slide, hold down the left mouse button, drag to create the shape as shown right, and then release the mouse button.

> If you are not satisfied with the size and shape of the image, press the Delete key to remove the image and then draw the image again.

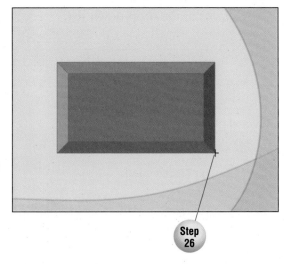

Step 26

(27) With the shape selected, type the text **To schedule a tour of our clinic, please call (503) 555-7700.**

> When the shape is selected, the text will automatically appear in the shape when typed.

(28) With the shape selected, click the Drawing Tools Format tab, click the More button located to the right of the shape style icons in the Shape Styles group, and then click *Subtle Effect, Accent 2* (third option from the left in the fourth row).

(29) Click the Shape Outline button arrow in the Shape Styles group and then click *Dark Blue* in the *Standard Colors* section.

(30) Select the text in the shape, click the Home tab, and then change the font to 36-point Candara Bold and the font color to *Indigo, Accent 1, Darker 50%*.

(31) With the text still selected, click the Drawing Tools Format tab, click the Text Effects button in the WordArt Styles group, point to *Glow*, and then click *Accent color 6, 8 pt glow* (first option from the right in the second row in the *Glow Variations* section).

(32) Print only Slide 2 and Slide 10.

(33) Save **PPMedS2-01.pptx**.

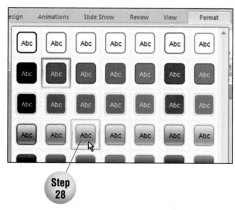

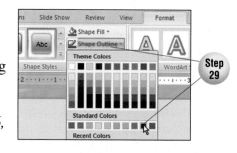

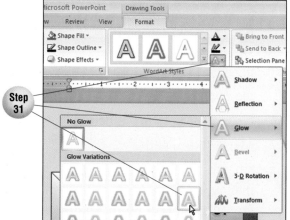

In Brief

Change Horizontal Text Alignment
1. Select text or click in text paragraph.
2. Click desired alignment button in bottom row of Paragraph group.

Change Vertical Text Alignment
1. Click Align Text button.
2. Click desired alignment at drop-down list.

Change Line Spacing
1. Click Line Spacing button.
2. Click desired spacing at drop-down list.
OR
1. Click Line Spacing button.
2. Click *Line Spacing Options* at drop-down list.
3. At Paragraph dialog box, specify desired spacing.
4. Click OK.

Insert Text Box
1. Click Insert tab.
2. Click Text Box button.
3. Click in slide or drag to create text box.

Draw Shape
1. Click Home tab or Insert tab.
2. Click Shapes button.
3. Click desired shape at drop-down list.
4. Drag in slide to draw shape.

In Addition

Inserting a New Line

When creating bulleted text in a slide, pressing the Enter key causes the insertion point to move to the next line, inserting another bullet. Situations may occur where you want to create a blank line between bulleted items without creating another bullet. One method for doing this is to use the New Line command, Shift + Enter. Pressing Shift + Enter inserts a new line that is considered part of the previous paragraph.

Activity 2.8

Inserting Headers and Footers

Insert information you want to appear at the top or bottom of each slide or on note and handout pages with options at the Header and Footer dialog box. If you want the information to appear on all slides, display the Header and Footer dialog box with the Slide tab selected. With options at this dialog box, you can insert the date and time, insert the slide number, and create a footer. To insert header or footer elements in notes or handouts, choose options at the Header and Footer dialog box with the Notes and Handouts tab selected.

Project You decide to insert the current date and slide number in the Vancouver presentation and create a header for notes pages.

1. With **PPMedS2-01.pptx** open, display Slide 1 in the Slide pane.

2. Insert a footer that prints at the bottom of each slide. To begin, click the Insert tab and then click the Header & Footer button in the Text group.

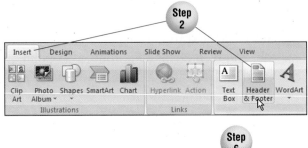

3. At the Header and Footer dialog box with the Slide tab selected, click the *Date and time* check box to insert a check mark. Click the *Update automatically* option to insert a circle in the option button.

4. Click the *Slide number* check box to insert a check mark.

5. Click the *Footer* check box and then type **Vancouver Clinic** in the *Footer* text box.

6. Click the Apply to All button.

7. Make Slide 4 active.

8. Click in the Notes pane and then type **Contact two commercial real estate companies about available office space.**

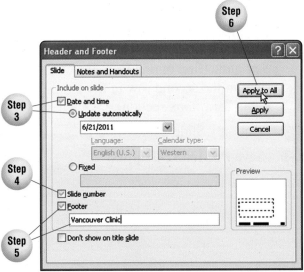

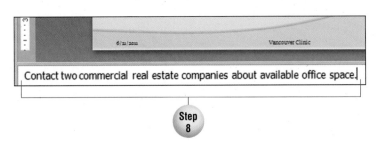

9   Insert a header in notes and handouts by clicking the Header & Footer button in the Text group in the Insert tab.

10 At the Header and Footer dialog box, click the Notes and Handouts tab.

11 Click the *Date and time* check box to insert a check mark and then, if necessary, click the *Update automatically* option to insert a circle in the option button.

12 Click the *Header* check box and then type **Cascade View Pediatrics**.

13 Click the *Footer* check box and then type **Vancouver Clinic**.

14 Click the Apply to All button.

15 Print the presentation as handouts with six slides per page.

16 Print Slide 4 as a notes page. To do this, press Ctrl + P. At the Print dialog box, click the down-pointing arrow at the right side of the *Print what* option and then click *Notes Pages*.

17 Click in the *Slides* option button and then type **4**.

18 Click OK to close the Print dialog box.

19 Remove the footer that displays on each slide. Begin by clicking the Insert tab and then clicking the Header & Footer button in the Text group.

20 With the Slide tab selected, click the *Date and time* check box, click the *Slide number* check box, and click the *Footer* check box to remove the check marks.

21 Click the Apply to All button.

22 Save **PPMedS2-01.pptx**.

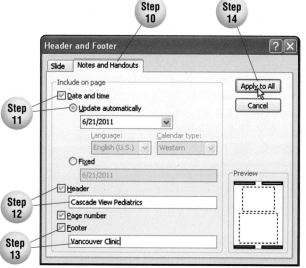

In Brief

Insert Header/Footer on Slide
1. Click Insert tab.
2. Click Header & Footer button.
3. At Header and Footer dialog box with Slide tab selected, choose desired options.
4. Click Apply to All button.

Insert Header/Footer in Notes and Handouts
1. Click Insert tab.
2. Click Header & Footer button.
3. At Header and Footer dialog box, click Notes and Handouts tab.
4. Choose desired options.
5. Click Apply to All button.

In Addition

Using the Package for CD Feature

The safest way to transport a PowerPoint presentation to another computer is to use the Package for CD feature. With this feature you can copy a presentation onto a CD or to a folder or network location and include all of the linked files, fonts, and PowerPoint Viewer program in case the destination computer does not have PowerPoint installed on it. To use the Package for CD feature, click the Office button, point to *Publish*, and then click *Package for CD*. At the Package for CD dialog box, type a name for the CD and then click the Copy to CD button.

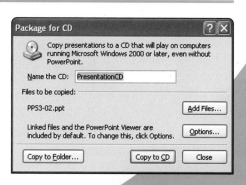

Changing the Design Theme, Theme Color, and Theme Font

You can change the design theme applied to slides in a presentation or change the color, font, or effects of a theme. To change the design theme, click the Design tab and then click the desired theme in the Themes group or click the More button and then click the desired theme. You can customize a theme by changing the colors, fonts, and effects. Click the Colors button in the Themes group and then click the desired color scheme at the drop-down gallery. Click the Fonts button and then click the desired font at the drop-down gallery. Theme effects are sets of lines and fill effects. You can change theme effects with options from the Effects button drop-down gallery.

Project

You are not pleased with the design theme for the Vancouver presentation and decide to apply a different theme and then change the colors and fonts for the theme.

Cascade View PEDIATRICS

1. With **PPMedS2-01.pptx** open, click the Design tab.

2. Click the More button that displays at the right side of the Themes icons.

3. At the Themes drop-down gallery, click the *Oriel* theme.

4. With Slide 1 active, move *Vancouver Clinic* below *Cascade View Pediatrics*.

5. Run the presentation beginning with Slide 1 and notice how the theme change affected the slides.

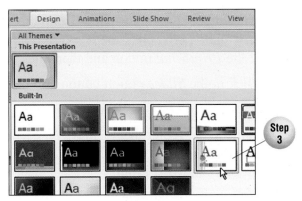

6. Display the presentation in Normal view, make Slide 3 active, and then click the Design tab.

7. Click the Colors button [Colors] in the Themes group and then click *Concourse* at the drop-down gallery.

8. Run the presentation beginning with Slide 1 and notice how the color change affected the slides.

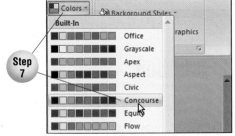

9. Click the Design tab, click the Colors button [Colors], and then click *Technic* at the drop-down gallery.

10. Make Slide 3 active.

11. Click the Fonts button 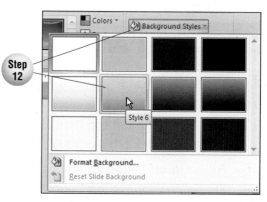 in the Themes group and then click *Opulent* at the drop-down gallery. (You will need to scroll down the gallery to display *Opulent*.)

12. Apply a background style by clicking the Background Styles button in the Background group and then clicking the *Style 6* option (second option from the left in the second row) at the drop-down gallery.

> Background styles display in slides in a presentation but do not print.

13. Run the presentation beginning with Slide 1.

14. After running the presentation, remove the background style by clicking the Design tab, clicking the Background Styles button in the Background group, and then clicking *Style 1* at the drop-down gallery (first option from the left in the top row).

15. Make Slide 1 active.

16. Left-align the text in both placeholders and then move the placeholders so the text displays as shown in Figure P2.2.

17. Save **PPMedS2-01.pptx**.

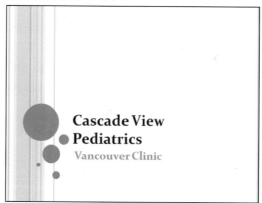

In Brief

Change Design Theme
1. Click Design tab.
2. Click More button at right side of Themes icons.
3. Click desired theme at drop-down gallery.

Change Theme Colors
1. Click Design tab.
2. Click Colors button.
3. Click desired option at drop-down gallery.

Change Theme Fonts
1. Click Design tab.
2. Click Fonts button.
3. Click desired option at drop-down gallery.

FIGURE P2.2 Slide 1

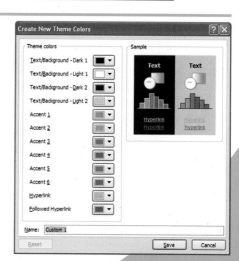

Cascade View Pediatrics
Vancouver Clinic

In Addition

Customizing Theme Colors

Design theme colors consist of four text colors, six accent colors, and two hyperlink colors. You can customize these theme colors with options at the Create New Theme Colors dialog box shown at the right. Display this dialog box by clicking the Colors button in the Themes group in the Design tab and then clicking *Create New Theme Colors* at the drop-down list. Change a color by clicking the desired color option in the *Theme colors* section and then clicking the desired color at the color palette. Changes made to colors display in the *Sample* section of the dialog box. You can name a custom color theme with the *Name* option in the dialog box. Click the Reset button to return the colors to the default theme colors.

Activity 2.10

Inserting and Formatting Images

Add visual appeal to a presentation by inserting a graphic image such as a logo, picture, or clip art in a slide. Insert an image from a drive or folder with the Picture button in the Insert tab or by choosing a slide layout containing a Content placeholder. Click the Picture button in the Insert tab or click the Picture button in a Content placeholder and the Insert Picture dialog box displays. At this dialog box, navigate to the desired drive or folder and then double-click the image. Insert a clip art image with the Clip Art button in the Insert tab or by choosing a slide layout containing a Content placeholder. Click the Clip Art button in the Insert tab or click the Clip Art button in a Content placeholder and the Clip Art task pane displays where you can choose the desired clip art image. Use buttons in the Picture Tools Format tab to recolor an image, apply a picture style, arrange the image in the slide, and size the image. You can also size an image using the sizing handles that display around the selected image and move the image using the mouse.

Project

Dr. Severin has asked you to insert the clinic logo on the first slide and to enhance the visual appeal of some of the slides by inserting clip art images.

1. With **PPMedS2-01.pptx** open, make sure Slide 1 is active.

2. Insert the clinic logo in the slide. To begin, click the Insert tab and then click the Picture button 🖼 in the Illustrations group.

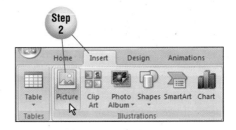

Step 2

3. At the Insert Picture dialog box, navigate to the PowerPointMedS2 folder on your storage medium and then double-click the file named *CVPLogo.jpg*.

   The image is inserted in the slide, selection handles display around the image, and the Picture Tools Format tab is selected.

4. Decrease the size of the logo by clicking in the *Shape Height* measurement box, typing **0.9**, and then pressing Enter.

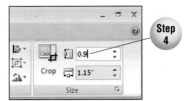

Step 4

   When you change the height of the logo, the width automatically changes to maintain the proportions of the logo. You can also size an image using the sizing handles that display around the selected image. Use the middle sizing handles to increase or decrease the width of an image. Use the top and bottom handles to increase or decrease the height and use the corner sizing handles to increase or decrease both the width and height of the image at the same time.

5. Move the logo so it is positioned in the lower right corner of the slide. To do this, position the mouse pointer on the image until the pointer displays with a four-headed arrow attached, drag the image to the lower right corner, and then release the mouse button.

6. With the image selected, click *Drop Shadow Rectangle* in the Picture Styles group (fourth option from the left).

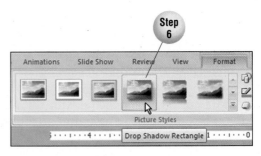

Step 6

7. Add a glow to the image by clicking the Picture Effects button [🖻 Picture Effects ▾], pointing to *Glow*, and then clicking *Accent color 1, 11 pt glow* at the drop-down gallery (first option from the left in the third row).

8. Make Slide 4 active and then insert a clip art image. Begin by clicking the Insert tab and then clicking the Clip Art button [🖾] in the Illustrations group.

9. At the Clip Art task pane, select any text that displays in the *Search for* text box, type **building** in the *Search for* text box, and then press Enter.

10. Scroll down the list of clip art images and then click the image shown in Figure P2.3.

> If the building clip art shown in Figure P2.3 is not available, insert a building clip art image of your choosing.

FIGURE P2.3 Slide 4

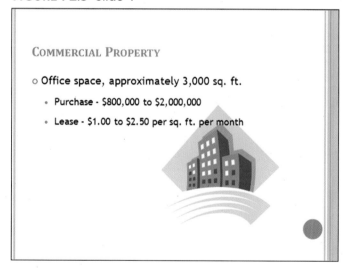

11. Close the Clip Art task pane by clicking the Close button (contains an X) that displays in the upper right corner of the task pane.

12. With the image selected increase the size by clicking in the *Shape Height* measurement box, typing **3.6**, and then pressing Enter.

13. Move the image behind the text by clicking the Send to Back button [🖫 Send to Back ▾] in the Arrange group in the Picture Tools Format tab.

14. Move the clip art image so it is positioned as shown in Figure P2.3.

15. Make Slide 8 active, click the Insert tab, and then click the Clip Art button.

16. At the Clip Art task pane, select any text that displays in the *Search for* text box, type **university**, and then press the Enter key.

continues

(17) Scroll through the list of images and then click the image shown in Figure P2.4.

> If the university clip art shown in Figure P2.4 is not available, insert a university clip art image of your choosing.

(18) Close the Clip Art task pane.

(19) Click in the *Shape Height* measurement box, type **2.4**, and then press Enter.

(20) Recolor the image so it complements the slide design color scheme. To do this, click the Recolor button [Recolor ▾] in the Adjust group and then click the *Accent color 1 Dark* option in the *Dark Variations* section.

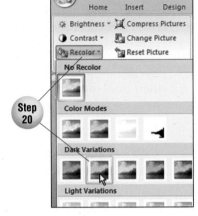

Step 20

(21) Using the mouse, drag the image so it is positioned as shown in Figure P2.4.

FIGURE P2.4 Slide 8

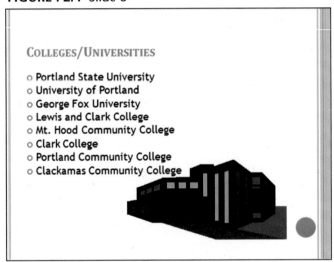

COLLEGES/UNIVERSITIES

- ○ Portland State University
- ○ University of Portland
- ○ George Fox University
- ○ Lewis and Clark College
- ○ Mt. Hood Community College
- ○ Clark College
- ○ Portland Community College
- ○ Clackamas Community College

(22) Make Slide 2 active, click the Insert tab, and then click the Clip Art button.

(23) At the Clip Art task pane, select any text that displays in the *Search for* text box, type **mountain**, and then press the Enter key.

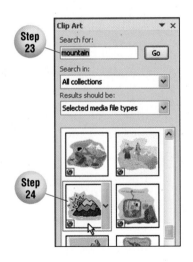

Step 23

Step 24

(24) Scroll through the list of images and then click the image shown at the right (and in Figure P2.5).

> If the mountain clip art shown in Figure P2.5 is not available, insert a mountain clip art image of your choosing.

(25) Close the Clip Art task pane.

(26) Click in the *Shape Height* measurement box, type **6**, and then press Enter.

27 Format the image as a watermark by clicking the Recolor button in the Adjust group in the Picture Tools Format tab and then clicking *Washout* in the *Color Modes* section (third option from the left).

28 Click the Send to Back button [Send to Back ▾] in the Arrange group in the Picture Tools Format tab.

29 Using the mouse, drag the image so it is positioned as shown in Figure P2.5.

30 Save **PPMedS2-01.pptx**.

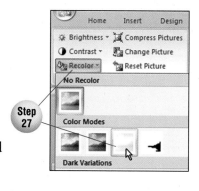

Step 27

FIGURE P2.5 Slide 2

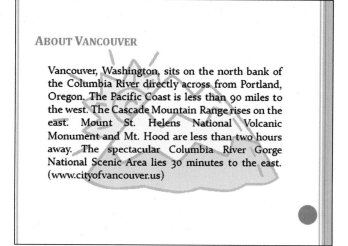

ABOUT VANCOUVER

Vancouver, Washington, sits on the north bank of the Columbia River directly across from Portland, Oregon. The Pacific Coast is less than 90 miles to the west. The Cascade Mountain Range rises on the east. Mount St. Helens National Volcanic Monument and Mt. Hood are less than two hours away. The spectacular Columbia River Gorge National Scenic Area lies 30 minutes to the east. (www.cityofvancouver.us)

In Addition

Formatting with Buttons in the Picture Tools Format Tab

You can format images in a slide with buttons and options in the Picture Tools Format tab shown below. Use buttons in the Picture Tools group to control the brightness and contrast of the image; recolor the image; change to a different image; reset the image to its original size, position, and color; and compress the image. Compress a picture to reduce resolution or discard extra information to save room on the hard drive or to reduce download time. Use buttons in the Picture Styles group to apply a predesigned style, insert a picture border, or apply a picture effect. The Arrange group contains buttons for positioning the image, wrapping text around the image, and aligning and rotating the image. Use options in the Size group to crop the image and specify the height and width of the image.

Downloading Clip Art Images

If you are connected to the Internet, click the *Clip art on Office Online* hyperlink that displays toward the bottom of the task pane. This takes you to the Office Online Clip Art window where you can search for and download a wide variety of images. Type the desired category in the search text box and then press Enter. At the list of clip art images, click the check box below the desired image. This inserts the image in the selection basket. When you have finished making all clip art selections, click the download option in the selection basket section located at the left side of the window.

Activity 2.11

Inserting and Formatting WordArt

Use the WordArt application to distort or modify text and to conform text to a variety of shapes. To insert WordArt, click the Insert tab, click the WordArt button in the Text group, and then click the desired WordArt style at the drop-down gallery. When WordArt is selected, the Drawing Tools Format tab displays. Use options and buttons in this tab to modify and customize WordArt.

Project To complete the presentation, Dr. Severin has asked you to insert a WordArt image containing the proposed opening date of the Vancouver clinic.

1. With **PPMedS2-01.pptx** open, make Slide 9 active.

2. Click the New Slide button in the Slides group in the Home tab.

3. Click the Layout button in the Slides group and then click the *Blank* layout (first option from the left in the third row).

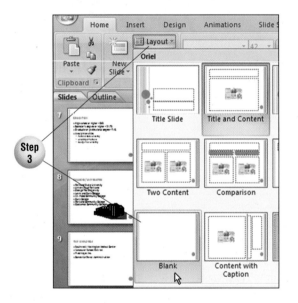

Step 3

4. Insert WordArt by clicking the Insert tab, clicking the WordArt button in the Text group, and then clicking *Fill - Accent 2, Warm Matte Bevel* (third option from the left in the fifth row).

   This inserts a text box with *Your Text Here* inside and also selects the Drawing Tools Format tab.

5. Type **Opening**, press the Enter key, and then type **September 2011**.

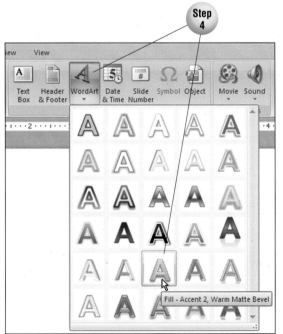

Step 4

Fill - Accent 2, Warm Matte Bevel

6 Select the text *Opening September 2011*, click the Text Effects button in the WordArt Styles group, point to *Transform* at the drop-down list, and then click *Deflate* at the drop-down gallery (second option from the left in the sixth row in the *Warp* section).

7 Click the Text Effects button, point to *Glow* at the drop-down list, and then click *Accent color 1, 8 pt glow* at the drop-down gallery (first option from the left in the second row in the *Glow Variations* section).

8 Click in the *Shape Height* measurement box in the Size group, type **3**, and then press Enter.

9 Click in the *Shape Width* measurement box in the Size group, type **7**, and then press Enter.

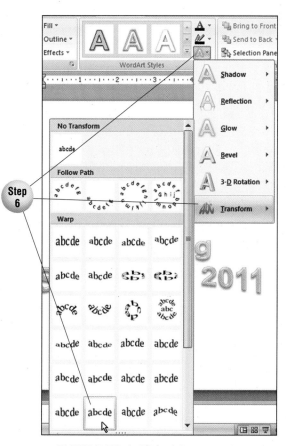

10 Drag the WordArt text so it is centered on the slide as shown in Figure P2.6.

11 Save **PPMedS2-01.pptx**.

In Brief

Insert WordArt
1. Click Insert tab.
2. Click WordArt button.
3. Click desired WordArt option.
4. Type WordArt text.
5. Apply desired formatting.

FIGURE P2.6 Slide 10

In Addition

Using Buttons and Options in the Drawing Tools Format Tab

When WordArt is selected in a slide, the Drawing Tools Format tab displays as shown below. You can draw a shape or text box with buttons in the Insert Shapes group. Apply a style, fill, outline, and effects to the WordArt text box with options in the Shape Styles group. Change the style of the WordArt text with options in the WordArt Styles group, specify the layering of the WordArt text with options in the Arrange group, and identify the height and width of the WordArt text box with options in the Size group.

Activity 2.12

Inserting and Formatting a SmartArt Organizational Chart

If you need to visually illustrate hierarchical data, consider creating an organizational chart with SmartArt. To display a menu of SmartArt choices, click the Insert tab and then click the SmartArt button in the Illustrations group. This displays the Choose a SmartArt Graphic dialog box. At this dialog box, click *Hierarchy* in the left panel and then double-click the desired organizational chart in the middle panel. This inserts the organizational chart in the slide. Some diagrams are designed to include text. You can type text in a diagram by selecting the shape and then typing text in the shape or you can type text in the *Type your text here* window that displays at the left side of the diagram.

Project

As part of the presentation, Dr. Severin has asked you to insert an organizational chart identifying project personnel.

1 With **PPMedS2-01.pptx** open, make Slide 9 active and then click the New Slide button in the Slides group in the Home tab.

2 Create the organizational chart shown in Figure P2.7. To begin, click the Insert tab and then click the SmartArt button in the Illustrations group.

> You can also click the Insert SmartArt Graphic button in the Content placeholder.

3 At the Choose a SmartArt Graphic dialog box, click *Hierarchy* in the left panel of the dialog box and then double-click the first option in the middle panel, *Organization Chart*.

> This displays the organizational chart in the slide with the SmartArt Tools Design tab selected. Use buttons in this tab to add additional boxes, change the order of the boxes, choose a different layout, apply formatting with a SmartArt style, and reset the formatting of the organizational chart.

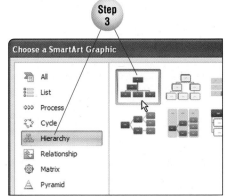

4 If a *Type your text here* window displays at the left side of the organizational chart, close it by clicking the Text Pane button Text Pane in the Create Graphic group.

> You can also close the window by clicking the Close button that displays in the upper right corner of the window.

5 Delete one of the boxes in the organizational chart by clicking the border of the first box from the left in the bottom row to select the border and then pressing the Delete key.

> Make sure that the selection border that surrounds the box is a solid line and not a dashed line. If a dashed line displays, click the box border again. This should change it to a solid line.

6 With the bottom left box selected, click the Add Shape button arrow in the Create Graphic group in the SmartArt Tools Design tab and then click *Add Shape Below* at the drop-down list.

> This inserts a box below the selected box. Your organizational chart should contain the same boxes as shown in Figure P2.7.

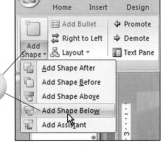

(7) Click *[Text]* in the top box, type **Dr. Severin**, press the Enter key, and then type **Project Leader**. Click in each of the remaining boxes and type the text as shown in Figure P2.7.

(8) Click the Change Colors button in the SmartArt Styles group in the SmartArt Tools Design tab and then click the second color option from the left in the *Colorful* section (*Colorful Range - Accent Colors 2 to 3*).

(9) Click the More button located at the right side of the SmartArt Styles group.

(10) Click the *Inset* option located in the *3-D* section.

(11) Click the SmartArt Tools Format tab.

(12) Click the Size button located at the right side of the tab, click in the *Width* measurement box, type **8.4**, and then press Enter.

(13) Click the text *Click to add title* and then type **Project Personnel**.

(14) Make Slide 9 active and then click the Home tab.

(15) Click on any character in the title *Top Employers* and then click the Format Painter button in the Clipboard group.

(16) Make Slide 10 active and then select the title *Project Personnel*.

> This applies 30-point Cambria bold small caps formatting with *Aqua, Accent 1* text color applied.

(17) Save **PPMedS2-01.pptx**.

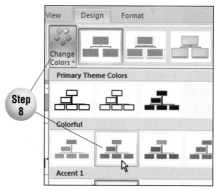

In Brief

Create Organizational Chart
1. Click Insert tab.
2. Click SmartArt button.
3. Click *Hierarchy* at Choose a SmartArt Graphic dialog box.
4. Double-click desired organizational chart.

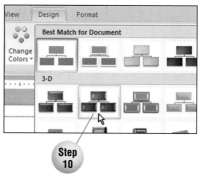

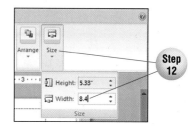

FIGURE P2.7 Organizational Chart

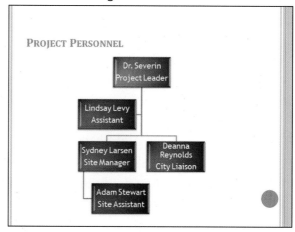

In Addition

Moving a SmartArt Organizational Chart or Diagram

Move an organizational chart by positioning the arrow pointer on the chart border until the pointer displays with a four-headed arrow attached, holding down the left mouse button, and then dragging the diagram to the desired location. You can increase the size of the diagram with the *Height* and *Width* options or by dragging a corner of the diagram border. If you want to maintain the proportions of the diagram, hold down the Shift key while dragging the border to increase or decrease the size.

Activity 2.13

Inserting and Formatting a SmartArt Diagram; Applying Animation to an Object

Use the SmartArt feature to create a variety of diagrams including process, cycle, relationship, matrix, and pyramid diagrams. Click the Insert tab and then click the SmartArt button to display the Choose a SmartArt Graphic dialog box. Click the desired diagram type in the left panel of the dialog box and then use the scroll bar at the right side of the middle panel to scroll down the list of diagram choices. Double-click a diagram in the middle panel of the dialog box and the diagram is inserted in the document. Use buttons in the SmartArt Tools Design tab and the SmartArt Tools Format tab to customize a diagram. You can animate an individual object in a slide with options from the Animate button located in the Animations group in the Animations tab.

Project

Dr. Severin has asked you to include a diagram identifying the major steps in the new clinic project. He also wants you to apply an animation effect to some of the slides.

1. With **PPMedS2-01.pptx** open, make Slide 10 active and then click the New Slide button in the Slides group in the Home tab.

2. Click the Layout button in the Slides group and then click the *Blank* layout at the drop-down list.

3. Create the diagram shown in Figure P2.8. To begin, click the Insert tab and then click the SmartArt button in the Illustrations group.

4. At the Choose a SmartArt Graphic dialog box, click *Relationship* in the left panel of the dialog box and then double-click the third option from the left in the fifth row (*Converging Radial*).

5. If necessary, close the *Type your text here* window by clicking the Close button that displays in the upper right corner of the window.

6. Click the Add Shape button in the Create Graphic group in the SmartArt Tools Design tab.

7. Click in each of the shapes and insert the text shown in Figure P2.8.

8. Click the Change Colors button in the SmartArt Styles group and then click the first color option from the left in the *Colorful* section (*Colorful - Accent Colors*).

9. Click the More button located at the right side of the SmartArt Styles group.

10. Click the *Inset* option located in the *3-D* section (second option from the left in the top row).

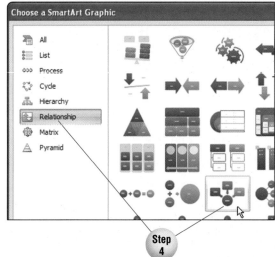

Step 4

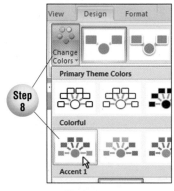

Step 8

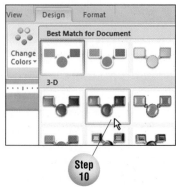

Step 10

11. With the diagram selected, apply an animation. Begin by clicking the Animations tab.

12. Click the down-pointing arrow at the right side of the *Animate* option box in the Animations group and then click *From center one by one* in the *Fly In* section of the drop-down gallery.

13. Make Slide 10 active and then click the organizational chart to select it.

14. Click the down-pointing arrow at the right side of the *Animate* option box and then click *By branch one by one* in the *Wipe* section.

15. Click Slide 3 to make it active and then click in the bulleted text to select the placeholder.

16. Click the down-pointing arrow at the right side of the *Animate* option box and then click *By 1st Level Paragraphs* in the *Fly In* section.

> Applying this animation creates a **build** for the bulleted items. A build displays important points in a slide one point at a time and is useful for keeping the audience's attention focused on the point being presented rather than reading ahead.

17. Apply the same animations to Slides 4 through 8 that you applied to Slide 3 by completing steps similar to those in Steps 15 and 16.

18. Delete Slide 9.

> The presentation should now contain 12 slides.

19. Make Slide 1 active and then run the presentation. Click the mouse button to advance slides and to display the individual organizational chart boxes, bulleted items, and diagram boxes.

20. Print the presentation as handouts with six slides per page. To do this, press Ctrl + P to display the Print dialog box.

21. At the Print dialog box, click the down-pointing arrow at the right side of the *Print what* option box and then click *Handouts* at the drop-down list. Make sure the *Slides per page* option displays as *6* and then click OK.

22. Save and then close **PPMedS2-01.pptx**.

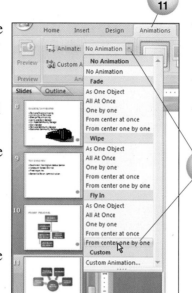

Step 11

Step 12

FIGURE P2.8 SmartArt Diagram

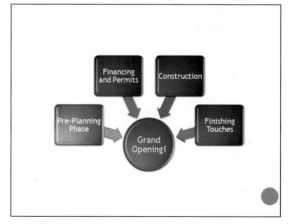

In Addition

Applying a Custom Animation

Apply a custom animation to selected objects in a slide by clicking the Custom Animation button in the Animations group in the Animations tab. This displays the Custom Animation task pane at the right side of the screen. Use options in this task pane to control the order in which objects appear on a slide, specify entrance and exit effects, choose animation direction and speed, and specify how objects will appear in the slide.

Features Summary

Feature	Ribbon Tab, Group	Button	Keyboard Shortcut
align text left	Home, Paragraph		Ctrl + L
align text right	Home, Paragraph		Ctrl + R
align text vertically	Home, Paragraph		
animate object	Animations, Animations	Animate No Animation	
bold	Home, Font	**B**	Ctrl + B
center	Home, Paragraph		Ctrl + E
copy selected text	Home, Clipboard		Ctrl + C
cut selected text	Home, Clipboard		Ctrl + X
decrease font size	Home, Font	A	Ctrl + Shift + <
decrease text level	Home, Paragraph		Shift + Tab
delete slide	Home, Slides	Delete	Delete
design theme	Design, Themes		
draw shape	Insert, Illustrations OR Home, Drawing		
Find	Home, Editing		Ctrl + F
font	Home, Font	Calibri	
font color	Home, Font	A	
Font dialog box	Font group dialog box launcher		Ctrl + Shift + F
font size	Home, Font	11	
Format Painter	Home, Clipboard		
header and footer	Insert, Text		
hide slide	Slide Show, Set Up		
increase font size	Home, Font	A	Ctrl + Shift + >
increase list level	Home, Paragraph		Tab
insert clip art image	Insert, Illustrations		
insert picture	Insert, Illustrations		
insert SmartArt	Insert, Illustrations		
italic	Home, Font	*I*	Ctrl + I
justify	Home, Paragraph		Ctrl + J
line spacing	Home, Paragraph		
paste selected text	Home, Clipboard		Ctrl + V

continues

Feature	Ribbon Tab, Group	Button	Keyboard Shortcut
replace	Home, Editing	Replace	Ctrl + H
text box	Insert, Text	A	
theme colors	Design, Themes	Colors ▾	
theme effects	Design, Themes	Effects ▾	
theme fonts	Design, Themes	A Fonts ▾	
underline	Home, Font	U	Ctrl + U
WordArt	Insert, Text	A	

Knowledge Check

Completion: In the space provided at the right, write in the correct term, command, or option.

1. Delete a slide by selecting the slide and then clicking the Delete button in this group in the Home tab.
2. The Hide Slide button is located in this tab.
3. Increase the text level by clicking the Increase List Level button or by pressing this key on the keyboard.
4. Decrease the text level by clicking the Decrease List Level button or by pressing these keys on the keyboard.
5. The Cut button is located in this group in the Home tab.
6. This group in the Home tab contains two rows of buttons for changing fonts, font size, and font effects.
7. The Replace button is located in this group in the Home tab.
8. Use this feature to apply the same formatting in more than one location in a slide or slides.
9. Click this button in the Paragraph group in the Home tab to change the text alignment to right.
10. This dialog box contains options for changing line spacing and text alignment, indentation, and spacing.
11. Click in a text box in a slide and this tab is active.
12. The Shapes button is available in the Home tab and this tab.
13. Create footer text that displays at the bottom of all slides with options at this dialog box.
14. Click this tab to display the Themes group.
15. Use buttons in this tab to recolor the selected picture, apply a picture style, arrange the picture, and size the picture.
16. Use this feature to distort or modify text and to conform to a variety of shapes.
17. Use this feature to create an organizational chart or a variety of diagrams.
18. The Animate button is located in this tab.

Skills Review

Review 1 Rearranging and Deleting Slides

1. With PowerPoint open, open the presentation named **CRGHCommunityEd.pptx** located in the PowerPointMedS2 folder on your storage medium.
2. Save the presentation with Save As and name it **PPMedS2-R1**.
3. Click the Slide Sorter View button.
4. Select and then delete Slide 8 (contains the title *Pregnancy Exercise*).
5. Move Slide 3 (*Professional Education*) to the right of Slide 8 (*Support Groups*).
6. Move Slide 4 (*Babysitting*) immediately left of Slide 7 (*Support Groups*).
7. Save **PPMedS2-R1.pptx**.

Review 2 Decreasing and Increasing Indents

1. With **PPMedS2-R1.pptx** open, click the Normal View button.
2. Make Slide 4 (*Childbirth Preparation Refresher*) the active slide.
3. Increase the indent of the bulleted text *Breathing and relaxation* to the next level.
4. Increase the indent of the bulleted text *Coach's role* to the next level.
5. Make Slide 6 active and then decrease the indent of the bulleted text *Designed for boys and girls 11 to 13* to the previous level.
6. Save **PPMedS2-R1.pptx**.

Review 3 Copying and Pasting Text

1. With **PPMedS2-R1.pptx** open, make Slide 3 (*Childbirth Preparation*) the active slide.
2. Select the text *Cost:* (including the space after the colon) and then click the Copy button.
3. Make Slide 4 (*Childbirth Preparation Refresher*) the active slide.
4. Move the insertion point immediately left of the dollar sign (located in the last bulleted item) and then click the Paste button.
5. Make Slide 5 (*Bringing up Baby*) the active slide, move the insertion point immediately left of the dollar sign, and then click the Paste button.
6. Make Slide 6 (*Babysitting*) the active slide, move the insertion point immediately left of the dollar sign, and then click the Paste button.
7. Make Slide 7 (*Support Groups*) the active slide, move the insertion point immediately left of the *F* in *Free* (located after the last bullet), and then click the Paste button.
8. Save **PPMedS2-R1.pptx**.

Review 4 Applying Fonts and Using Format Painter

1. With **PPMedS2-R1.pptx** open, make Slide 1 the active slide.
2. Select the text *Columbia River General Hospital*, change the font to *Candara*, and then turn on bold.
3. Make Slide 2 active, select the text *Community Education*, change the font to *Candara*, and then turn on bold.

4. Select the text *Class Offerings*, change the font to *Candara*, the font size to *36*, and then turn on bold.
5. Make Slide 3 active, select the heading *Childbirth Preparation*, change the font to *Candara*, and turn on bold.
6. Using Format Painter, apply the same formatting to the title in Slides 4, 5, 6, 7, 9, and 10. (Skip Slide 8.)
7. Make Slide 2 active, click on any character in the title *Community Education*, and then click once on the Format Painter button. Make Slide 8 active and then select *Professional Education*.
8. Make Slide 2 active, click on any character in the subtitle, and then click once on the Format Painter button. Make Slide 8 active and then select all of the text below the title *Professional Education*.
9. Save **PPMedS2-R1.pptx**.

Review 5 Changing Alignment and Line Spacing

1. With **PPMedS2-R1.pptx** open, make Slide 1 the active slide.
2. Click anywhere in the title and then click the Center button.
3. Make Slide 2 active and then center the title and subtitle
4. Make Slide 3 active, click in the heading, and then click the Align Text Left button.
5. Make Slide 4 active, select the bulleted text, and then change the line spacing to *1.5*.
6. Make Slide 9 active, select the bulleted text, and then change the spacing after paragraphs to *12 pt*.
7. Make Slide 10 active, select the bulleted text, and then change the spacing before paragraphs to *18 pt*.
8. Save **PPMedS2-R1.pptx**.

Review 6 Changing Color Scheme and Editing Colors

1. With **PPMedS2-R1.pptx** open, click the Design tab.
2. Click the Color button and then click the *Flow* option.
3. Click the Fonts button and then click the *Opulent* option.
4. Save **PPMedS2-R1.pptx**.

Review 7 Inserting and Formatting Images

1. With **PPMedS2-R1.pptx** open, delete Slide 1.
2. Insert a new slide at the beginning of the presentation and change the slide layout to *Blank*. **Hint: To insert a new slide at the beginning of the presentation, click immediately above the Slide 1 miniature in the Slides/Outline pane and then click the New Slide button arrow.**
3. Insert the image **CRGHLogo.jpg** using the Picture button in the Insert group and then size and move the image so it displays as shown in Figure P2.9.
4. Make Slide 3 active and then search for clip art images related to *pregnancy*. Insert, size, and move to position the image as shown in Figure P2.10. (If this clip art is not available, choose a similar clip art related to *pregnancy*.)
5. Make Slide 6 active and then search for clip art images related to *babysitting*. Insert, size, and position the clip art image as shown in Figure P2.11. Recolor the image to *Text color 2 Dark*. **Hint: Do this with the Recolor button in the Picture Tools Format tab.** (If this clip art is not available, choose a similar clip art related to *babysitting*.)

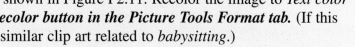

6. Make Slide 9 active and then insert a clip art image related to *nurse*. You determine the clip art as well as the formatting, size, and positioning of the clip art.
7. Save **PPMedS2-R1.pptx**.

FIGURE P2.9 Slide 1

FIGURE P2.10 Slide 3

Childbirth Preparation

- Topics
  - Nutrition
  - Prenatal exercise
  - Breathing and relaxation
  - Labor and delivery
- Number of classes: 10
- Cost: $100 per couple

FIGURE P2.11 Slide 6

Babysitting

- Topics
  - Basic lifesaving techniques
  - Safety precautions
  - Preventing accidents
  - Basic child care
- Designed for boys and girls 11 to 13
- Number of classes: 4
- Cost: $30 per person

Review 8 Creating and Formatting SmartArt Diagrams

1. With **PPMedS2-R1.pptx** open, make Slide 10 active and then insert a new slide with the *Blank* layout.
2. Insert the SmartArt hierachy diagram shown in Figure P2.12 with the following specifications:
   - Click the *Hierarchy* option in the left panel at the Choose a SmartArt Graphic dialog box and then double-click *Hierarchy* in the middle panel.
   - To create the boxes in the order shown in the figure, click the outside border (of the white inside box) of the second box in the second row and then press the Delete key. Press the Delete key a second time and your hierarchy diagram boxes should display in the same order as the boxes in Figure P2.12.
   - With the SmartArt Tools Design tab selected, change the colors to *Colorful - Accent Colors* and change the SmartArt style to *Inset*.
   - Type the text in the boxes as shown in Figure P2.12.
   - Increase the size and then position the hierarchy diagram so it displays as shown in Figure P2.12.

3. With Slide 11 active, insert a new slide with the *Title Only* layout. Click the *Click to add title* text and then type **Health Philosophy**.
4. Insert the SmartArt diagram shown in Figure P2.13 with the following specifications:
   - Click the *Relationship* option in the left panel at the Choose a SmartArt Graphic dialog box and then double-click *Basic Venn* in the middle panel.
   - With the SmartArt Tools Design tab selected, change the colors to *Colorful - Accent Colors* and change the SmartArt style to *Polished*.
   - Type the text in the diagram as shown in Figure P2.13.
   - Increase the size and then position the diagram so it displays as shown in Figure P2.13.
5. Save **PPMedS2-R1.pptx**.

FIGURE P2.12 Slide 11

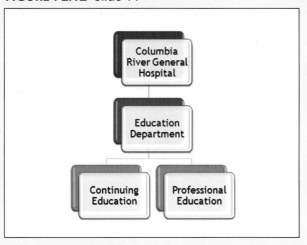

FIGURE P2.13 Slide 12

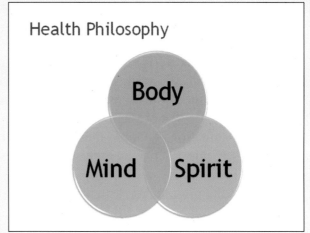

Review 9 Creating and Formatting WordArt

1. With **PPMedS2-R1.pptx** open, make active the last slide in the presentation, and then insert a new slide with the *Blank* layout.
2. Insert the WordArt shown in Figure P2.14 with the following specifications:
   - Click the *Fill - Accent 2, Warm Matte Bevel* option at the WordArt button drop-down list.
   - Type the text shown in Figure P2.14.
   - Click the Text Effects button in the Drawing Tools Format tab, point to *Transform*, and then click *Inflate* (first option from the left in the sixth row in the *Warp* section).
   - Increase the shape height to 3.2" and the shape width to 8".
   - Position the WordArt as shown in Figure P2.14.
3. Save **PPMedS2-R1.pptx**.

FIGURE P2.14 Slide 13

> # Health education
> # is our priority!

Review 10 Applying Animation Schemes

1. With **PPMedS2-R1.pptx** open, make Slide 11 active and then animate the hierarchy diagram using the *Animate* option box in the Animations group in the Animations tab. (You determine the type of animation.)
2. Make Slide 9 active and then animate the bulleted items using the *Animate* option box in the Animations group in the Animations tab. (You determine the type of animation.)
3. Make Slide 1 active and then run the presentation.
4. Delete Slide 5.
5. Print the presentation as a handout with six slides per page.
6. Save and then close **PPMedS2-R1.pptx**.

Skills Assessment

Assessment 1 Formatting a Presentation for Columbia River General Hospital

1. Open the presentation named **CRGHCCPlan.pptx**.
2. Save the presentation with Save As and name it **PPMedS2-A1**.
3. Apply the Equity design theme, change the design theme colors to *Flow*, and change the design theme fonts to *Opulent*.
4. Make Slide 1 active and then insert the file named ***CRGHLogo.jpg. Hint: Do this with the Picture button in the Insert tab.*** Set the background color of the logo to transparent. To do this, click the Recolor button in the Adjust group in the Picture Tools Format tab and then click *Set Transparent Color* at the drop-down list. Move the mouse pointer to any white color in the logo background and then click the left mouse button. (With the white color transparent, the lines in the slide design are visible behind the logo.) Change the shape width to 6" and then center the logo below the slide title.
5. Display the presentation in Slide Sorter View and then move Slide 3 (*Community Commitment*) to the left of Slide 2 (*Reorganization Factors*).
6. Move Slide 7 (*Changing Demographics*) to the left of Slide 3 (*Reorganization Factors*).
7. Make Slide 4 active and then demote (increase indent) the text *Medicare cost-cutting among doctors and hospitals* to the next level.

8. Make Slide 5 active and then promote (decrease indent) the text *Reconfigure lobby and registration areas* to the previous level.

9. Make Slide 3 active, select the bulleted text, and then change the line spacing to *1.5*.

10. Make Slide 4 active, select the bulleted text, and then change the line spacing before paragraphs to *12 pt*.

11. Make Slide 7 active, select the bulleted text, and then change the line spacing to *1.5*.

12. Insert a new slide after Slide 1 (the new slide will be Slide 2) and specify the *Blank* slide layout. Using the Text Box button in the Insert tab, draw a box in the slide and then type the text shown in Figure P2.15. Change the font size to 24 and justify-align the paragraph of text and right-align the name and title as shown in the figure.

13. Insert a new slide at the end of the presentation that contains the Basic Target SmartArt diagram (located in the *Relationship* group) as shown in Figure P2.16. Add a shape to the diagram, change the colors to *Colorful - Accent Colors*, and apply the *Cartoon* SmartArt style. Type the text as shown in Figure P2.15.

14. Insert a new slide at the end of the presentation with WordArt that contains the words *Plan Completion* on one line and *May 2013* on the next line. You determine the style, shape, size, and position of the WordArt.

15. Print the presentation as handouts with six slides per page.

16. Save, run, and then close **PPMedS2-A1.pptx**.

FIGURE P2.15 Slide 2

"Instead of closing facilities and laying off employees, the Community Commitment plan outlines the investment of $25 million over the next three years to establish a community-based healthcare system that reorganizes services among Columbia River General Hospital facilities in a more cost-effective manner."

Michelle Tan, CEO

FIGURE P2.16 Slide 9

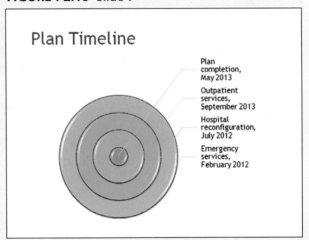

Plan Timeline

Plan completion, May 2013

Outpatient services, September 2013

Hospital reconfiguration, July 2012

Emergency services, February 2012

Assessment 2 Formatting a Presentation for Sickle Cell Anemia

Columbia River General Hospital

1. Open the presentation named **SickleCell.pptx**.

2. Save the presentation with Save As and name it **PPMedS2-A2**.

3. Apply any formatting you feel is necessary to improve the appearance of each slide. Insert at least one clip art image on a slide.

4. Insert a new slide at the end of the presentation that contains the WordArt text *Thank you!* You determine the formatting, size, and positioning of the WordArt.

5. Apply an animation scheme of your choosing to the bulleted text in at least two of the slides in the presentation.

6. Run the presentation.

7. Print the presentation as handouts with six slides per page.

8. Save and then close **PPMedS2-A2.pptx**.

Assessment 3 Drawing a Shape and Changing the Shape

1. Open **PPMedS2-A2.pptx**.
2. Make Slide 9 active and then insert a new slide with the *Blank* layout. Draw a shape of your choosing in the slide and then insert the following information in the shape (use the Symbol button in the Insert tab to insert the *á* symbol) (you determine the formatting, size, and positioning of the text and shape):

   Dr. Maria Cárdenas
   North Shore Medical Clinic
   7450 Meridian Street, Suite 150
   Portland, OR 97202
   (503) 555-2330
3. Save **PPMedS2-A2.pptx** and then print only Slide 10.
4. Use the Help feature to learn how to change a shape into another shape.
5. After learning how to change a shape, change the shape you created in Slide 10.
6. Save **PPMedS2-A2.pptx** and then print only Slide 10.
7. Run and then close **PPMedS2-A2.pptx**.

Assessment 4 Downloading a Design Theme

1. PowerPoint provides a number of design themes you can apply to a presentation. The Microsoft Office Online site contains additional design themes you can download and apply to a presentation. You decide to download a design theme related to healthcare. To do this, click the Office button and then click *New* at the drop-down list. At the New Presentation dialog box, click the *Design slides* option in the *Microsoft Office Online* section in the left panel. Click the *Healthcare* option in the *Design slides* section. Scroll through the list of designs related to healthcare and then double-click the design theme named *Medical design template (surgeon)*. When you download a design theme, the design is available in the Themes group in the Design tab.
2. If the downloaded design theme was applied to a blank presentation, close the presentation without saving it.
3. Open the presentation named **PPMedS2-A1.pptx** and then save it with Save As and name it **PPMedS2-A4**.
4. Apply the *Medical design template (surgeon)* design theme that you downloaded from Microsoft Office Online.
5. Make Slide 1 active and then delete the hospital logo.
6. Check each slide and make any adjustments needed to make the slide look attractive and easy to read.
7. Run the presentation.
8. Save the presentation, print the presentation as handouts with six slides per page, and then close the presentation.

Assessment 5 Locating Information on Support Groups

1. Using the Internet, search for support groups that meet in your town or county for the following diseases or conditions: Alzheimer's, Breast Cancer, Depression, Diabetes, Eating Disorders, Fibromyalgia, Heart Disease, and Multiple Sclerosis.
2. When you have gathered the information, prepare a presentation and include your name and the name of the presentation on the first slide. Prepare a specific slide for each support group that contains the name of the group and any other information you gather such as meeting dates and times, locations, telephone numbers, contacts, and so on.
3. Prepare the final slide in the presentation with the words *Thank you* as WordArt.
4. Apply an animation scheme of your choosing to all slides in the presentation.
5. Save the presentation and name it **PPMedS2-A5**.
6. Run the presentation.
7. Print the slides as handouts with six slides per page.
8. Save and then close **PPMedS2-A5.pptx**.

Assessment 6 Locating Information on Medical Front Office Jobs

1. Using your local newspapers, employment agencies, and/or the Internet, locate information on medical front office jobs such as medical office assistants.
2. Prepare a presentation with the information you find and include at least the following information: job titles, average wages, education requirements, required experience, and required knowledge of or training in specific software (if any).
3. Apply any formatting or enhancements you feel will improve the visual appeal of the presentation.
4. Save the presentation and name it **PPMedS2-A6**.
5. Run the presentation.
6. Print the slides as handouts with six slides per page.
7. Save and then close **PPMedS2-A6.pptx**.

Marquee Challenge

Challenge 1 Preparing a Cholesterol Presentation

1. Prepare the presentation shown in Figure P2.17 with the following specifications:
   - Use the *Concourse* design theme.
   - Change the design theme colors to *Urban*.
   - Change the design theme fonts to *Aspect*.
   - Size and position placeholders as shown in Figure P2.17.

- Insert *NSMCLogo.jpg* in Slide 1 and then size and position the logo as shown in the figure.
- Use the *Blank* layout for Slide 2 and create a text box for the title and another text box for the description. Apply the formatting from one of the titles in Slides 3 through 7 to the title of Slide 2. Increase the size of the font in the description and change the alignment to center.
- Add 18 points of spacing before the bulleted text in Slides 3 through 7.
- Use the *Blank* layout for Slide 8 and create a text box for the title. Apply the formatting from one of the titles in Slides 3 through 7 to the title in Slide 8. Use WordArt to insert the telephone number.

2. Save the completed presentation and name it **PPMedS2-C1**.
3. Print the presentation as handouts with nine slides per page.
4. Close **PPMedS2-C1.pptx**.

FIGURE P2.17 Challenge 1

North Shore
Medical Clinic

North Shore Medical Clinic

Greater Portland Healthcare
Workers Association

What Is Cholesterol?

Cholesterol is a type of fat (lipid) that is made by the body. Cholesterol is essential for good health and is found in every cell in the body. Too much cholesterol in the blood can raise the risk of heart attack or stroke.

Types of Cholesterol

- Low-density lipoproteins (LDL) – Deliver cholesterol to the body. About 70% of cholesterol is transported as LDL. Too much LDL is harmful to the body.
- High-density lipoproteins (HDL) – Removes cholesterol from the bloodstream. About 20% of cholesterol is transported as HDL.

LDL Cholesterol Levels

- Less than 130 is best
- Between 130 to 159 is borderline
- 160 or more means higher risk for heart disease

HDL Cholesterol Levels

- Less than 40 means higher risk for heart disease
- 60 or higher reduces risk of heart disease

Improve Cholesterol Levels

- Do not smoke.
- Eat a healthy, low-fat diet that includes lots of fruits and vegetables.
- Exercise regularly.
- Limit alcohol consumption.
- Take medication.

Cholesterol Medications

- Statins (also called HMG-CoA reductase inhibitors)
- Resins (also called bile acid sequestrants)
- Fibrates (also called fibric acid derivatives)
- Niacin (also called nicotinic acid)
- Ezetimibe

Cholesterol Screening Call for an Appointment

503-555-2330

Challenge 2 Preparing a Hospital Center Presentation

Columbia
River
General
Hospital

1. Prepare the presentation shown in Figure P2.18 with the following specifications:
   - Use the *Solstice* design theme and change design theme colors to *Foundry*.
   - Insert **CRGHLogo.jpg** in Slide 1 and then size and position the logo as shown in the figure.
   - Use the *Title Slide* layout for Slide 2 and then create a text box for the disorder description. Size and position the title and text box as shown in the figure.
   - Insert the *Basic Venn* SmartArt in Slide 3, change the colors to *Colorful Range - Accent Colors 2 to 3*, apply the *Polished* SmartArt style, and then size and position the SmartArt as shown in the figure.
   - In Slide 5, use the word *healthcare* in the Clip Art task pane to locate the clip art. Recolor the picture to *Accent color 4 Dark* and then size and position the clip art as shown in the figure.
   - Insert the *Organization Chart* SmartArt in Slide 6, change the colors to *Colored Fill - Accent 1* (located in the *Accent 1* section), and apply the *Cartoon* SmartArt style.
2. Save the completed presentation and name it **PPMedS2-C2**.
3. Print the presentation as handouts with six slides per page.
4. Close **PPMedS2-C2.pptx**.

FIGURE P2.18 Challenge 2

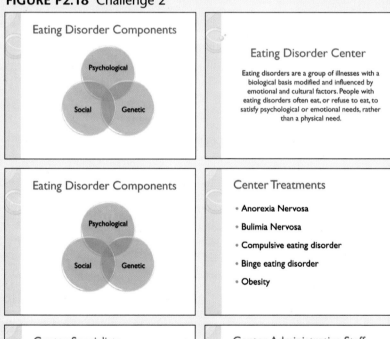

Integrating Programs
Word, Excel, and PowerPoint

Skills

- Export a PowerPoint presentation to a Word document
- Export a Word outline document to a PowerPoint presentation
- Link an Excel chart with a Word document and a PowerPoint presentation
- Edit a linked object
- Embed a Word table in a PowerPoint presentation
- Embed an embedded object

Student Resources

Before beginning this section:
1. Copy to your storage medium the IntegratingMed2 subfolder from the IntegratingPrograms folder on the Student Resources CD.
2. Make IntegratingMed2 the active folder.

In addition to containing the data files needed to complete section work, the Student Resources CD contains model answers in PDF format for each of the projects in this section; model answers for end-of-section exercises are not provided.

Projects Overview

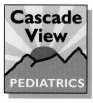

Create and format a Word document containing information on opening a clinic in Vancouver.

Prepare a presentation for the quarterly staff meeting using a Word outline; copy and link an Excel chart to the staff meeting presentation and to a Word document and then edit the linked chart; copy a Word table containing data on new patients, embed it in the staff meeting presentation, and then update the table; and copy a Word table containing information on quarterly equipment purchases and embed it in the staff meeting presentation.

Export a PowerPoint presentation containing information on the Community Commitment plan to a Word document; copy and link an Excel chart containing information on class enrollments to an Education Department presentation and then edit the chart; and embed and edit a table containing information on department contacts into the Education Department presentation.

407

You can send data in one program to another program. For example, you can send Word data to a PowerPoint presentation and data in a PowerPoint presentation to a Word document. To send presentation data to Word, click the Office button, point to *Publish*, and then click *Create Handouts in Microsoft Office Word*. At the Send To Microsoft Office Word dialog box that displays, specify the layout of the data in the Word document, whether you want to paste or paste link the data, and then click OK. One of the advantages to sending presentation data to a Word document is that you can have greater control over the formatting of the data in Word.

Project

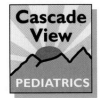

As Dr. Severin prepares his presentation on opening a clinic in Vancouver, he asks you to send the presentation information to Word as a handout.

1. Open PowerPoint.

2. Open the presentation named **CVPVancouver.pptx**.

3. Save the presentation and name it **IntMedP2-01**.

4. Click the Office button, point to *Publish*, and then click *Create Handouts in Microsoft Office Word*.

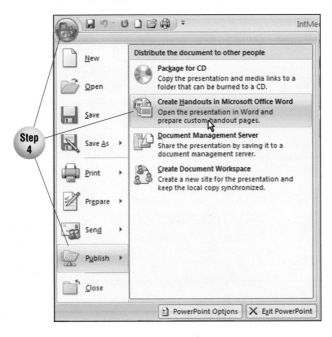

5. At the Send To Microsoft Office Word dialog box, click the *Blank lines next to slides* option.

6. Click the *Paste link* option located toward the bottom of the dialog box and then click OK.

   In a few moments, the slides will display in a Word document.

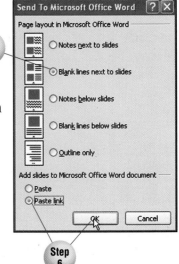

(7) Save the Word document and name it **IntMedW2-01**.

(8) Print and then close **IntMedW2-01.docx**.

(9) Click the button on the Taskbar representing the PowerPoint presentation **IntMedP2-01.pptx**.

(10) Make Slide 2 active and then change *6.5%* to *8.6%*.

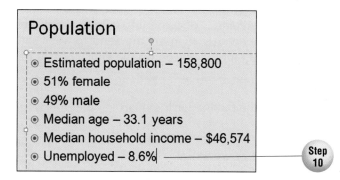
In Brief

Export PowerPoint Presentation to Word
1. Open presentation.
2. Click Office button, *Publish, Create Handouts in Microsoft Office Word.*
3. Choose desired options at Send To Microsoft Office Word dialog box.
4. Click OK.

(11) Make Slide 8 active, change *$190,000* to *$197,000* and change *$196,500* to *$200,800*.

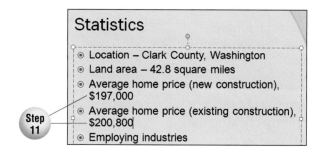

(12) Save and then close **IntMedP2-01.pptx**.

(13) Make Word the active program and then open **IntMedW2-01.docx**. At the message asking if you want to update the document with the data from the linked files, click the Yes button.

(14) Scroll through the document and notice that the percentage in Slide 2 and prices in Slide 8 reflect the changes you made in the PowerPoint presentation.

(15) Save, print, and then close **IntMedW2-01.docx**.

In Addition

Pasting and Linking Data

The *Paste* option at the Send To Microsoft Office Word dialog box is selected by default and is available for all of the page layout options. With this option selected, the data inserted in Word is not connected or linked to the original data in the PowerPoint presentation. If you plan to update the data in the presentation and want the data updated in the Word document, select the *Paste link* option at the Send To Microsoft Office Word dialog box. This option is available for all of the page layout options except the *Outline only* option.

Activity 2.2

Exporting a Word Outline to a PowerPoint Presentation

As you learned in the previous section, you can send data in one program to another program. For example, you can send Word data to a PowerPoint presentation and data in a PowerPoint presentation to a Word document. You can create text for slides in a Word outline and then export that outline to PowerPoint. PowerPoint creates new slides based on the heading styles used in the Word outline. Paragraphs formatted with a Heading 1 style become slide titles. Heading 2 text becomes first-level bulleted text, Heading 3 text becomes second-level bulleted text, and so on. If styles are not applied to outline text in Word, PowerPoint uses tabs or indents to place text on slides. To export a Word document to a PowerPoint presentation, you need to insert the Send to Microsoft Office PowerPoint button on the Quick Access toolbar.

Project Lee Elliott has asked you to take the outline for the quarterly staff meeting and convert it to a PowerPoint presentation.

1. Make sure both Word and PowerPoint are open.

2. With Word the active program, open the document named **NSMCOutline.docx**.

   Text in this document has been formatted with the Heading 1 and Heading 2 styles.

3. Insert a Send to Microsoft Office PowerPoint button on the Quick Access toolbar. Begin by clicking the Customize Quick Access Toolbar button ⋤ that displays at the right side of the Quick Access toolbar.

4. Click *More Commands* at the drop-down list.

5. Click the down-pointing arrow at the right side of the *Choose commands from* list box and then click *All Commands* at the drop-down list.

6. Scroll down the list box that displays below the *Choose commands from* list box and then double-click *Send to Microsoft Office PowerPoint*.

   Items in the list box display in alphabetical order.

7. Click OK to close the Word Options dialog box.

8. Send the outline to PowerPoint by clicking the Send to Microsoft Office PowerPoint button 📄 on the Quick Access toolbar.

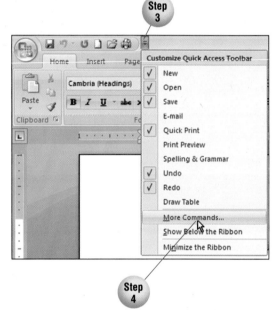

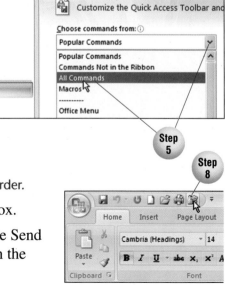

⑨ When the presentation displays on the screen, make sure Slide 1 is the active slide.

> The presentation is created with a blank design template.

⑩ With Slide 1 active, change the layout by clicking the Layout button [🔲 Layout ▾] in the Slides group in the Home tab and then clicking *Title Slide* at the drop-down list.

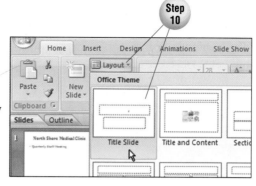

⑪ Make Slide 4 active and then change the layout to *Title Only*. Make Slide 9 active and then change the layout to *Title Only*. Make Slide 10 active and then change the layout to *Title Only*.

⑫ Apply a design theme by clicking the Design tab, clicking the More button at the right side of the Themes icons, and then clicking *Solstice*.

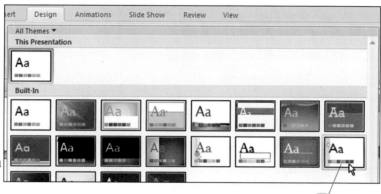

⑬ Save the presentation and name it **IntMedP2-02**.

⑭ Close **IntMedP2-02.pptx**.

⑮ Click the button on the Taskbar representing the Word document **NSMCOutline.docx**.

⑯ Right-click the Send to Microsoft Office PowerPoint button on the Quick Access toolbar and then click the *Remove from Quick Access Toolbar* option at the shortcut menu.

⑰ Close **NSMCOutline.docx**.

In Brief

Insert Send to Microsoft Office PowerPoint Button on Quick Access Toolbar
1. Click Customize Quick Access Toolbar button at the right side of Quick Access toolbar.
2. Click *More Commands*.
3. Click the down-pointing arrow at right side of *Choose commands from* list box.
4. Click *All Commands*.
5. Scroll down *Choose commands from* list box, double-click *Send to Microsoft Office PowerPoint*.
6. Click OK.

Send Word Outline to PowerPoint Presentation
1. Open Word document.
2. Click Send to Microsoft Office PowerPoint button on Quick Access toolbar.

In Addition

Applying a Style in Word

Heading styles were already applied to the text in the **NSMCOutline.docx** Word document. If you create an outline in Word that you want to export to PowerPoint, apply styles using options in the Styles group in the Home tab. A Word document contains a number of predesigned formats grouped into style sets called Quick Styles. Display the available Quick Styles sets by clicking the Change Styles button in the Styles group in the Home tab and then pointing to Style Set. Choose a Quick Styles set and the four styles visible in the Styles group change to reflect the set. To display additional available styles, click the More button (contains a horizontal line and a down-pointing triangle) that displays at the right side of the styles. To apply a heading style, position the insertion point in the desired text, click the More button at the right side of the styles in the Styles group, and then click the desired style at the drop-down gallery.

Activity 2.3

Linking an Excel Chart with a Word Document and a PowerPoint Presentation

You can copy and link an object such as a table or chart to documents in other programs. For example, you can copy an Excel chart and link it to a Word document and/or a PowerPoint presentation. The advantage to copying and linking over just copying and pasting is that you can edit the object in the originating program, called the *source* program, and the object is updated in the linked documents in the *destination* programs. When an object is linked, the object exists in the source program but not as a separate object in the destination program. Since the object is located only in the source program, changes made to the object in the source program are reflected in the destination program.

Project

To improve the readability of data, you will link an Excel chart to the Quarterly Staff meeting presentation and to a Word document.

1. Open Word, Excel, and PowerPoint.

2. Make Word the active program and then open the document named **NSMCQtrlyEx.docx**. Save the document with Save As and name it **IntMedW2-02**.

3. Make PowerPoint the active program, open the presentation named **IntMedP2-02.pptx**, and then make Slide 10 the active slide.

4. Make Excel the active program and then open the workbook named **NSMCChart.xlsx**. Save the workbook with Save As and name it **IntMedE2-01**.

5. Copy and link the chart to the Word document and the PowerPoint presentation. Begin by clicking once in the chart to select it.

    Make sure you select the chart and not a specific chart element. Try selecting the chart by clicking just inside the chart border.

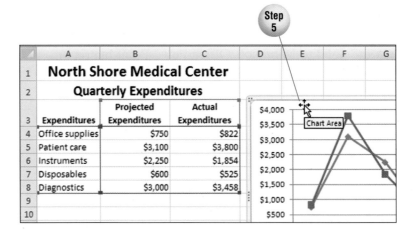

6. With the chart selected, click the Copy button in the Clipboard group in the Home tab.

7. Click the button on the Taskbar representing the Word document **IntMedW2-02.docx**.

8. Press Ctrl + End to move the insertion point to the end of the document.

9. Click the Paste button arrow and then click *Paste Special* at the drop-down list.

10 At the Paste Special dialog box, click the *Paste link* option, click the *Microsoft Office Excel Chart Object* option in the *As* list box, and then click OK.

11 Save, print, and then close **IntMedW2-02.docx**.

12 Click the button on the Taskbar representing the PowerPoint presentation **IntMedP2-02.pptx**.

13 With Slide 10 the active slide, make sure the Home tab is selected, click the Paste button arrow, and then click *Paste Special*.

14 At the Paste Special dialog box, click the *Paste link* option, make sure *Microsoft Office Excel Chart Object* is selected in the *As* list box, and then click OK.

15 Increase the size of the chart so it better fills the slide and then move the chart so it is centered on the slide.

16 Click outside the chart to deselect it.

17 Save the presentation with the same name (**IntMedP2-02**), print only Slide 10, and then close **IntMedP2-02.pptx**.

18 Click the button on the Taskbar representing the Excel worksheet **IntMedE2-01.xlsx**. Click outside the chart to deselect it.

19 Save, print, and then close **IntMedE2-01.xlsx**.

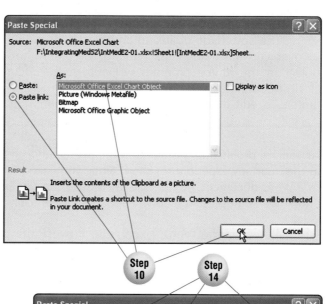

Step 10

Step 14

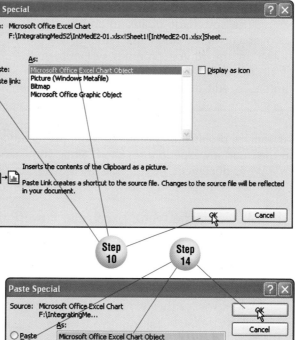

Step 15

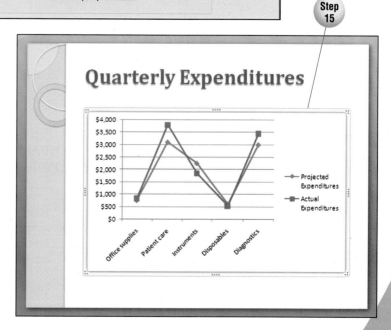

In Brief

Link Object between Programs
1. Open source program, open file containing object.
2. Select object, click Copy button.
3. Open destination program, open file into which object will be linked.
4. Click Paste button arrow, *Paste Special*.
5. At Paste Special dialog box, click *Paste link*, click OK.

In Addition

Linking Data or an Object within a Program

In this section, you learned to link an object between programs using the Paste Special dialog box. You can also link an object in Word using options at the Object dialog box. To do this, click the Insert tab and then click the Object button. At the Object dialog box, click the Create from File tab. At the dialog box, type the desired file name in the *File name* text box or click the Browse button and then select the desired file from the appropriate folder. Click the *Link to file* check box to insert a check mark and then click OK.

Activity 2.4

Editing a Linked Object

The advantage of linking an object over copying data is that editing the object in the source program will automatically update the object in the destination program(s). To edit a linked object, open the document containing the object in the source program, make the desired edits, and then save the document. The next time you open the document, worksheet, or presentation in the destination program, the object is updated.

Project

North Shore Medical Clinic

As you are proofreading the text in the presentation, you realize that you left out a category in the quarterly expenditures chart. Since you linked the Excel chart to the presentation and to a Word document, you decide to edit the chart in Excel. The chart in the Word document and PowerPoint presentation will update automatically.

1. Make sure the Word, Excel, and PowerPoint programs are open.

2. Make Excel the active program and then open the workbook named **IntMedE2-01.xlsx**.

3. You discover that one category was left out of the quarterly ependitures chart. Add a row to the worksheet by clicking once in cell A6 to make it the active cell. Click the Insert button arrow in the Cells group in the Home tab and then click *Insert Sheet Rows*.

4. Insert the following data in the specified cells:

   A6   **Respiratory**
   B6   **925**
   C6   **1200**

5. Click in cell A3.

6. Save, print, and then close **IntMedE2-01.xlsx**.

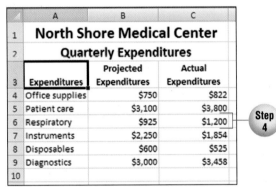

7. Make Word the active program and then open **IntMedW2-02.docx**. At the message asking if you want to update the linked file, click the Yes button.

8. Notice how the linked chart is automatically updated to reflect the changes you made to the chart in Excel.

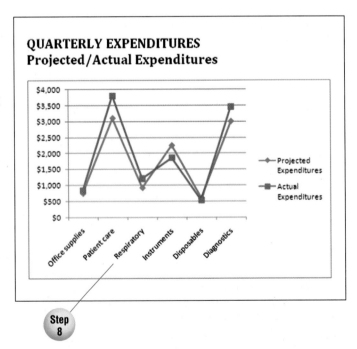

9. Save, print, and then close **IntMedW2-02.docx**.

10. Make PowerPoint the active program and then open **IntMedP2-02.pptx**.

11. At the message telling you that the presentation contains links, click the Update Links button.

12. Make Slide 10 the active slide and then notice how the linked chart is automatically updated to reflect the changes you made to the chart in Excel.

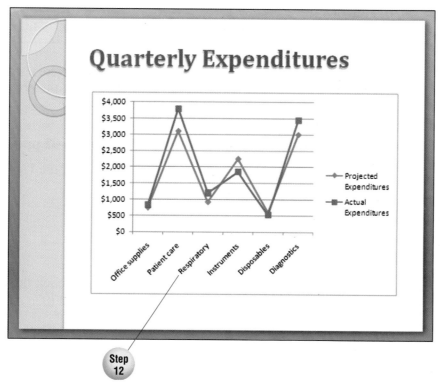

13. Save **IntMedP2-02.pptx**.

14. Print only Slide 10.

15. Close **IntMedP2-02.pptx**.

In Addition

Updating a Link Manually

You can choose to update a link manually in the destination program. To do this, open a Word document containing a linked object. Right-click the object, point to *Linked (type of object) Object*, and then click *Links*. At the Links dialog box, click the *Manual update* option and then click OK. With *Manual update* selected, a link is only updated when you right-click a linked object and then click *Update Link*; or display the Links dialog box, click the link in the list box, and then click the Update Now button.

Embedding and Editing a
Word Table in a PowerPoint Presentation

You can copy an object from one file and paste it into a file in another application or you can copy and link an object or copy and embed an object. A linked object resides in the source program but not as a separate object in the destination program. An embedded object resides in the file in the source program as well as the destination program. If you make a change to an embedded object at the source program, the change is not made to the object in the destination program. Since an embedded object is not automatically updated as is a linked object, the only advantage to embedding rather than simply copying and pasting is that you can edit an embedded object in the destination program using the tools of the source program.

Project

To present information on new patients seen at the clinic, you decide to create a table in Word containing the data and then embed it in a slide in the staff meeting presentation.

1. Open Word and PowerPoint.

2. Make PowerPoint the active program and then open **IntMedP2-02.pptx**.

3. At the message telling you the presentation contains links, click the Update Links button.

4. Make Slide 4 the active slide.

5. Make Word the active program and then open the document named **NSMCTable01.docx**.

6. Click in a cell in the table and then select the table. To do this, click the Table Tools Layout tab, click the Select button in the Table group, and then click *Select Table* at the drop-down list.

7. With the table selected, click the Home tab and then click the Copy button 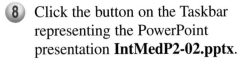 in the Clipboard group.

8. Click the button on the Taskbar representing the PowerPoint presentation **IntMedP2-02.pptx**.

9. With Slide 4 the active slide, click the Paste button arrow and then click *Paste Special* at the drop-down list.

10. At the Paste Special dialog box, click *Microsoft Office Word Document Object* in the *As* list box and then click OK.

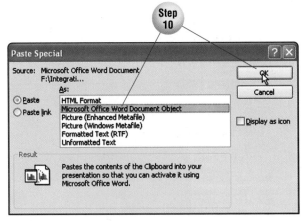

11 With the table selected in the slide, use the sizing handles to increase the size and change the position of the table as shown below.

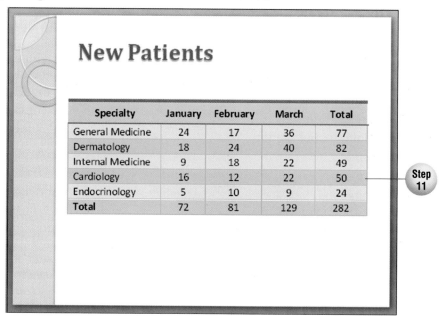

New Patients

Specialty	January	February	March	Total
General Medicine	24	17	36	77
Dermatology	18	24	40	82
Internal Medicine	9	18	22	49
Cardiology	16	12	22	50
Endocrinology	5	10	9	24
Total	72	81	129	282

Step 11

In Brief

Embed Object
1. Open source program, open file containing object.
2. Select object, click Copy button.
3. Open destination program, open file into which object will be embedded.
4. Click Paste button arrow, *Paste Special*.
5. At Paste Special dialog box, click object in *As* list box.
6. Click OK.

Edit Embedded Object
1. Open file containing embedded object.
2. Double-click object.
3. Make edits, click outside object.

12 Click outside the table to deselect it.

13 Save **IntMedP2-02.pptx** and then print Slide 4 of the presentation.

14 Click the button on the Taskbar representing the Word document **NSMCTable01.docx** and then close the document.

15 Click the button on the Taskbar representing the PowerPoint presentation **IntMedP2-02.pptx** and then make Slide 9 the active slide.

16 Make Word the active program and then open the document named **NSMCTable02.docx**.

17 Click in a cell in the table and then select the table. To do this, click the Table Tools Layout tab, click the Select button in the Table group, and then click *Select Table* at the drop-down list.

18 Click the Home tab and then click the Copy button [icon] in the Clipboard group.

19 Click the button on the Taskbar representing the PowerPoint presentation **IntMedP2-02.pptx**.

20 With Slide 9 the active slide, click the Paste button arrow and then click *Paste Special* at the drop-down list.

21 At the Paste Special dialog box, click *Microsoft Office Word Document Object* in the *As* list box and then click OK.

Step 21

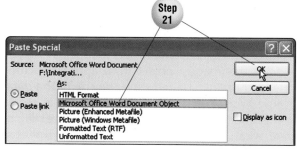

continues

Activity 2.5 **417**

22 Increase the size and position of the table in the slide so it displays as shown at the right.

Step 22

23 As you look over the slide, you realize that the Otoscope price is incorrect. Edit the amount by double-clicking the table in the slide.

> Double-clicking the table displays the Word tabs and ribbon at the top of the screen. A horizontal and vertical ruler also display around the table.

Equipment Purchases

Equipment	Model	Price
AudioScope	95362	$549.99
ECG Monitor	2350-500	$3,800.00
Otoscope	53620	$179.95
ThermoScan	040560	$225.00
Wall Transformer	652-A	$440.00
Total		$5,194.94

24 Using the mouse, select *$179.95* and then type **$299.99**.

25 Recalculate the total by selecting *$5,194.94* and then pressing F9.

> F9 is the update field keyboard shortcut. You could also update the formula by selecting the amount, clicking the Table Tools Layout tab, clicking the Formula button in the Data group, and then clicking OK at the Formula dialog box.

Equipment Purchases

Equipment	Model	Price
AudioScope	95362	$549.99
ECG Monitor	2350-500	$3,800.00
Otoscope	53620	$299.99
ThermoScan	040560	$225.00
Wall Transformer	652-A	$440.00
Total		$5,314.98

Step 24

Step 25

26 Click outside the table to deselect it.

> Clicking outside the table deselects it and also removes the Word tabs.

27 Print Slide 9 of the presentation.

28 Apply a transition and sound of your choosing to all slides in the presentation and then run the presentation.

29 Save and then close **IntMedP2-02.pptx**.

30 Click the button on the Taskbar representing the Word document **NSMCTable02.docx** and then close **NSMCTable02.docx**.

In Addition

Working with a Cropped Object

Some embedded or linked objects may appear cropped on the right or bottom side of the object even if enough room is available to fit the image on the page or slide. A large embedded or linked object may appear cropped because Word converts the object into a Windows metafile (.wmf), which has a maximum height and width. If the embedded or linked object exceeds this maximum size, it appears cropped. To prevent an object from appearing cropped, consider reducing the size of the data by changing formatting such as reducing the font size, column size, line spacing, and so on.

Skills Review

Review 1 Exporting a PowerPoint Presentation to Word

1. Open PowerPoint.
2. With PowerPoint the active program, open the presentation named **CRGHCCPlan.pptx** and then save it with Save As and name it **IntMedP2-R1**.
3. Send the PowerPoint data to Word as slides with blank lines next to the slides. Click the *Blank lines next to slides* option and the *Paste link* option at the Send To Microsoft Office Word dialog box.
4. Save the Word document and name it **IntMedW2-R1**.
5. Print and then close **IntMedW2-R1.docx**.
6. Click the button on the Taskbar representing the PowerPoint presentation **IntMedP2-R1.pptx**.
7. Make Slide 5 active and then delete the second bulleted item.
8. Make Slide 6 active and then insert a new bullet after the *Expand fitness center* bulleted text at the same level that reads *Implement community health education plan.*
9. Save the presentation, print the presentation as handouts with six slides per page, and then close the presentation.
10. Make Word the active program, open **IntMedW2-R1.docx**, and then click Yes at the question asking if you want to update the link.
11. Save, print, and then close the document.

Review 2 Linking and Editing an Excel Chart in a PowerPoint Slide

1. Open Excel and PowerPoint.
2. With PowerPoint the active program, open **CRGHEdDept.pptx**.
3. Save the presentation with Save As and name it **IntMedP2-R2**.
4. Make Slide 6 active.
5. Make Excel the active program and then open the workbook named **CRGHChart01.xlsx**. Save the workbook with Save As and name it **IntMedE2-R2**.
6. Click the chart once to select it (make sure you select the entire chart and not a chart element) and then copy and link the chart to Slide 6 in the **IntMed2-R2.pptx** PowerPoint presentation. (Be sure to use the Paste Special dialog box to link the chart.)
7. Increase the size of the chart to better fill the slide and then center the chart on the slide.
8. Click outside the chart to deselect it.
9. Save the presentation with the same name (**IntMedP2-R2.pptx**).
10. Print only Slide 6 of the presentation and then close **IntMedP2-R2.pptx**.
11. Click the button on the Taskbar representing the Excel workbook **IntMedE2-R2.xlsx**.
12. Click outside the chart to deselect it.
13. Save and then print **IntMedE2-R2.xlsx**.

14. Insert another department in the worksheet (and chart) by making cell A6 active, clicking the Insert button arrow in the Cells group in the Home tab, and then clicking *Insert Sheet Rows* at the drop-down list. (This creates a new row 6.) Type the following text in the specified cells:

    A6   **CPR**
    B6   **85**
    C7   **105**
    D7   **134**

15. Click in cell A3.
16. Save, print, and then close **IntMedE2-R2.xlsx**.
17. Click the button on the Taskbar representing PowerPoint and then open **IntMedP2-R2.pptx**. At the message telling you that the presentation contains links, click the Update Links button. Display Slide 6 and then notice the change to the chart.
18. Save **IntMedP2-R2.pptx** and then print only Slide 6.

Review 3   Embedding and Editing a Word Table in a PowerPoint Slide

Columbia
River
General
Hospital

1. Open Word and PowerPoint.
2. Make PowerPoint the active program, open **IntMedP2-R2.pptx**, and then make Slide 7 the active slide. (At the message asking if you want to update links, click the Cancel button.)
3. Make Word the active program and then open the document named **CRGHContacts.docx**.
4. Select the table and then copy and embed it in Slide 7 in the **IntMedP2-R2.pptx** presentation. (Make sure you use the Paste Special dialog box.)
5. With the table selected in the slide, use the sizing handles to increase the size and change the position of the table so it better fills the slide.
6. Click outside the table to deselect it and then save **IntMedP2-R2.pptx**.
7. Double-click the table and then click in the text *Christina Fuentes*.
8. Insert a row below by clicking the Table Tools Layout tab and then clicking the Insert Below button.
9. In the new row, type **John Shapiro** in the *Contact* column, type **Sterling Health Services** in the *Agency* column, and type **(503) 555-4220** in the *Telephone* column.
10. Click outside the table to deselect it.
11. Print Slide 7 of the presentation.
12. Apply a transition and sound of your choosing to all slides in the presentation.
13. Run the presentation.
14. Save and then close **IntMedP2-R2.pptx** and then exit PowerPoint.
15. Close the Word document **CRGHContacts.docx** and then exit Word.

Index   421